GERMAN ARTILLERY OF WORLD WAR TWO

GERMAN ARTILLERY OF WORLD WAR TWO

Ian V. Hogg

London: Arms and Armour Press
New York: Hippocrene Books Inc.

Published in 1975 by
Arms and Armour Press
Lionel Leventhal Limited
2-6 Hampstead High Street
London NW3 1PR

SBN 85368 249 6

Published in the United States 1975
by HIPPOCRENE BOOKS, INC.
171 Madison Avenue
New York, N.Y. 10016

Library of Congress Catalog Card
Number 74-16695
ISBN 0-88254-311-3

Ammunition line-drawings
by M. Streetly

Printed by T. & A. Constable
Limited, Edinburgh, Scotland.

CONTENTS

NOTES ON PRESENTATION OF DATA

The sections dealing with each individual gun have been laid out in a uniform manner, and the following notes (concerning a hypothetical gun) may be found useful in explaining the various entries.

14.7cm schwere Feldkanone 42

14.7cm s F K 42

The full official nomenclature is shown first, after which comes the officially-accepted abbreviation. The third entry – where applicable – is a codename, designed to simplify stock-control and to facilitate ordering guns for the front.

Then follows a brief summary of the weapon's history and career, and after that the extensive data and performance tables.

Data

Calibre: The actual measured calibre, as opposed to the nominal value. Length of gun: the length measured from the rear face of the breech ring to the front face of the muzzle. It includes the length of muzzle brake (if one is fitted) or, in the case of recoilless guns, the length of the jet nozzle. Length of bore: the actual useful length of the gun, from the chamber mouth to the muzzle. Rifling: the number of grooves, the direction of twist, whether of uniform or of increasing pitch and the degree of twist expressed as one complete turn in so many calibres—*eg* 1/32 is one turn in 32 calibres. The normal German practice expressed this in angular measure, but the British convention of 'turns/calibre' is more easily visualised. The smaller the final figure, the steeper the rifling. For increasing twist weapons the figures quoted are those for the twist at the commencement and at the muzzle. In all cases the rate of increase is constant throughout the bore. Breech mechanism: a type classification, including firing system. Traverse: the amount available on the carriage, from one extreme to the other. One gun is shown as having 720°; this was an anti-aircraft gun which, owing to its electrical connexions, could only make two complete revolutions in either direction. Elevation: from minimum to maximum. Weight in action: this was the weight of the gun in the firing position. The travelling weight was always slightly greater.

Performance

A brief resumé of the maximum performance. Where more than one projectile was in significant use, figures for all are given. In the cases of less common projectiles, deviations from the standard pattern are included in the entry concerning the projectile. Penetration figures are given against homogeneous armour plate for two angles of strike in the case of anti-tank guns; 0° indicates a broadside attack where the shot strikes at exactly right-angles to the plate, while 30° indicates an impact angle 30° away from a right angle. These two were the standard criteria in all countries, but Continental practice measured the angle from the plane of the armour: thus the latter figure of 30° impact is quoted in German documents as *60°*.

Ammunition

For fixed rounds, the lengths of the cartridge cases are given, since otherwise similar guns often used very different cases.

Projectiles

14.7cm FH Sprgr 42: fuzed AZ23/28, weight 15.0 kg(33.1lb).

The official nomenclature of the shell, followed by the standard fuze or fuzes and the weight as fired. If the performance is significantly different from standard, details are given.

Propelling Charge

For fixed rounds, this information is included with the projectile data. For separate-loading rounds it is listed separately after the projectiles. Details of the charge, the primer and the case are given. The weight of propellant given is in every case taken from actual specimens; it must be appreciated that this figure varied from batch to batch of propellants in order to adjust the charge to give the desired ballistic regularity.

Note: in one or two cases the data tables contain blank spaces, indicating that the particular item of information is either unavailable or that conflicting figures cannot be satisfactorily resolved.

INTRODUCTION

From the days of Krupp's first experiments with steel guns and breech-loading, the German gunmakers have rarely been reluctant to try something new, and the years from 1933 to 1945 saw their vast inventive resources at their peak. Even the standard service weapons often incorporated refinements not found in the designs of other nations, and when anything extraordinary was requested the results were invariably brilliant and often awe-inspiring.

For all the inventors' brilliance, the strategic direction of the higher command (which gave the gunmakers their specifications) was less certain of its aim: thus weapon development, which promised much, frequently got side-tracked or spent too much effort travelling in the wrong direction. It was this as much as anything, aided by a certain amount of ill-advised pursuit of better designs, that was responsible for the vast range of weapons deployed by the Wehrmacht. An example of this changeable attitude was the controversy over the standard support weapon of the division—should it have been a 7.5cm gun or a 10.5cm howitzer? During World War I the army had started with a 7.7cm gun and later augmented it with a 10.5cm howitzer, so long postwar discussions took place to try and discover which of the two was the more useful weapon. Towards the end of the 1920s the argument had been resolved in favour of the 10.5cm howitzer and this duly became the standard field support weapon—but by 1943 the argument was raging once more. This time the gun triumphed at the howitzer's expense, leading to designs of a new model that never saw fruition owing to the end of the war. Yet, at the same time as this decision was reached, development was still proceeding on improved versions of the 10.5cm howitzer. This particular line of research can be cited as one of the superfluous efforts. The original 10.5cm howitzer was massively built, but it has since been reliably estimated that over 80% of its ammunition was fired with the various less powerful charges: a gun of half the original's weight would still have been strong enough. An improved weapon was demanded to meet an exacting specification, but it achieved little better results and consumed 20% more propellant into the bargain.

The principal lines of development in prewar guns were much the same as those followed by any other nation—intended to provide an output of reliable and proven weapons in a rational range of guns from light anti-aircraft to heavy siege types, all conventional in concept and also simple and robust. While this aim was reached in most cases, there was still sufficient design capacity to allow development of more advanced weapons to be slowly pursued; much of this effort showed results during the war, when unorthodox solutions stood a better chance of being accepted.

At the end of World War I the Versailles treaty thoroughly disrupted the German armament industry. The two principals, Friedrich Krupp AG and Rheinische Metallwaaren- und Maschinenfabrik (later Rheinmetall-Borsig AG), were limited in the designs they could produce: Krupp were restricted to weapons above 17cm calibre, and RM&M to weapons below 17cm. Moreover, only a very small number of guns of the permitted calibres were allowed to be made. In order to evade these regulations Krupp came to an arrangement with Svenska Aktiebolagst Bofors of Sweden, whereby Bofors acquired the foreign rights of Krupp guns while Krupp sent a number of designers to work in the Bofors factory and thus keep their skills alive. RM&M set up a company in Switzerland called Waffenfabrik Solothurn AG, and designs originating in the German drawing office were marketed as Solothurn weapons. Through this company too, a link with Osterreichische Waffenfabrik-Gesellschaft of Steyr was maintained.

Once the National Socialists came to power most of this subterfuge was abandoned overnight, though it was not until 1945 that the details became plain —which accounts for some amusing Allied wartime intelligence reports in which Rheinmetall-Borsig designed and built guns are described as copies of Solothurn weapons. Rheinmetall also received a boost when they became part of the Reichswerke Hermann Göring 'paper corporation', which accounts for a number of cases where their design was taken into service in preference to a Krupp model.

When the war began the German high command made a serious planning error in assuming that the war would be of short duration. With this opinion firmly fixed, they then ruled that long-term development should not begin if the result could not be brought into service within one year. This had the most serious repercussions in the electronic and radar fields, but it also stifled a good deal of development in artillery. A number of promising projects were abandoned by their developers and when, later in the war, the error was appreciated and the ban removed, it required vast efforts to make up for the time that had been lost.

Once wartime development began, however, it was usually along lines laid down by the Oberkommando der Wehrmacht (OKW—forces' high command) in an attempt either to solve some particular problem or to produce an equipment to fill a specific need. In this respect artillery development was more tightly controlled than in other weapon fields; there appears to have been few cases of individual designers pushing pet theories, resorting to political string-pulling, and scheming to obtain raw materials and production capacity so well seen—for example—in the guided missile field in 1944–5.

At the outbreak of war the artillery equipment of the Wehrmacht was standardised on a few calibres, and the weapons were in general of sound and well-tested design. The army's field weapons were of 10.5cm, 15cm and 21cm calibres, and the design philosophy ensured that a gun of given calibre and a howitzer of the next larger calibre were interchangeable on the same carriage, thus simplifying production, supply and maintenance. Anti-aircraft defence was built around the 2cm and 3.7cm light guns, the 8.8cm medium gun and the 10.5cm heavy gun; anti-tank weapons were the 3.7cm gun and a 7.92mm anti-tank rifle for infantry use. One or two improved designs were undergoing routine development with the intention of bringing them into service as and when the need arose.

The demands of war soon spoiled this arrangement. When it came to forecasting the future, the OKW was no more visionary than any other comparable body and the appearance of new weapons in the hands of the enemy frequently led to sudden demands on designers to develop powerful antidotes. An example of this was the sudden flurry of activity in the anti-tank field consequent upon the appearance of the virtually unstoppable Soviet T34 tank. The users' demands on the gunmakers were always the same: improve the performance of the gun, increase its range, increase its velocity, but please do not increase its weight. How these demands were translated into reality will be seen on subsequent pages but, as a general rule, the paths open to the designers were well-defined. The only way to improve the performance of a conventional gun is by increasing the muzzle velocity, and this can be done in a variety of ways.

The first and most simple technique is to increase the size of the propelling charge or to develop a more efficient propellant, while still operating the gun at the same pressure. This, in round figures, demands a four-fold increase in propellant quantity to obtain a 60% increase in muzzle velocity, and contains several disadvantages in the shape of erosive wear, redesign of the chamber and cartridge case, and economic production of the propellant.

The second simple method is to increase the length of the barrel, thus keeping the projectile exposed to the accelerating effect of the exploding propellant for a longer time. To obtain the 60% increase in velocity would demand a 300% increase in barrel length—scarcely a practical measure.

An increase in chamber pressure combined with a moderate increase in barrel length will also increase velocity. The standard 60% increase could thus be achieved by a 50% increase in pressure coupled to a 50% increase in barrel length, but again this is scarcely a practical answer. One solution, increasingly adopted by many nations towards the end of the war, was a 50% reduction of projectile weight which increased the velocity by 40%—but the ballistic coefficient (the 'carrying power' of the projectile) was proportionately reduced. Deceleration in flight was hence more rapid, leading to less range than a full-weight projectile would have achieved at the same velocity.

Owing to these conventional design limitations, the war initiated the examination of more and more unconventional solutions. One of the first, which had been developed well before the war, was the production of high-velocity guns in which the rifling consisted of a few deep grooves into which fitted curved ribs on the outer surface of the shell, imparting positive rotation. This was developed because the conventional copper driving band was incapable of transmitting the enormous torque of high-velocity projectiles' excessive radial acceleration without shearing. The ribbed or 'splined' shell solved the problem of transmitting spin, but a copper band still had to be fitted to provide the gas-seal necessary at the rear of the shell. This was an expensive and complicated solution, suited only to large weapons produced in limited numbers, and much research was begun to try and overcome the torque defect of the copper driving band, with the additional incentive of trying to find a material in less critical supply.

The first development was the Krupp Sparführung (KpS) band—a bimetallic band of copper and soft iron, although zinc was sometimes added to dilute the copper and to assist in effecting the iron/copper joint. There was little or no performance advantage, merely an economy of copper. Next came the Weicheisen (FeW) soft iron band, the use of which was restricted to large calibre high-velocity guns. It could withstand torque very well, but the process of putting the band on the shell (by a powerful radial press) work-hardened the metal to the point where it became difficult to 'engrave'—or force into the gun's rifling. It was this defect that restricted Weicheisen bands' use to high-pressure large-calibre weapons.

The final development was the Sintereisen (FeS) sintered iron band, formed from small iron particles bonded together under intense pressure to form a malleable band. This engraved well, resisted shear stresses, and was economical of material in short supply, but in its first application was found to wear out the gun barrels faster than a conventional copper band. Further development evolved a new form of barrel rifling with wider lands and grooves, and this—together with the reintroduction of increasing twist—improved matters to a degree where the German technicians opined that even if they had sufficient copper available they would still prefer to use sintered iron, particularly at higher velocities. One interesting result was the discovery that, while copper bands resulted in the gun barrel wearing out first at the chamber end of the rifling, FeS bands promoted wear at the muzzle since the coefficient of friction was directly proportional to the velocity.

When the increases in performance made available by increasing the barrel length and the size of the charge, and the provision of improved rifling and banding, had been taken to their extremes, it became necessary to explore less well-trodden paths. The first unorthodox solution offered was the 'coned bore' gun, the theory of which predicated that if the barrel was made with a gradually-decreasing calibre (and if the projectile was designed to adapt to the diminution) then, since the base area of the shot is reducing while the propelling gas pressure either remains—depending on the cartridge design—constant or increases then the unit pressure on the shot base will increase and the shot will be given greater velocity. The original idea was patented in 1903 by Carl Puff and the drawings accompanying the specification (British Patent 8601 of 27th August 1904) show a projectile almost identical to those later developed in Germany. Puff, however, does not appear to have pursued his ideas as far as a working gun, and the idea lay dormant until taken up by a German engineer named Gerlich in the 1920s. In co-operation with Halbe, a gunmaker, he developed a number of high-velocity sporting rifles with tapered bores and flanged projectiles, marketed in limited numbers during the 1930s under the name *Halger,* while at the same time attempting to interest various governments in the possible use of these weapons as high-velocity military rifles. He also worked for both the United States' government and the British Army on taper-bore rifles, but neither felt that there was much virtue in the idea; Gerlich returned to Germany c. 1935, and his subsequent activities have escaped record.

By this time others were exploring the idea: Rheinmetall-Borsig, Krupp, Bochumer Verein and Polte-Werke all had experimental programmes varying in degree of involvement. Rheinmetall-Borsig eventually became the most involved; the firm's Dr Werner Banck, who took charge of development in late 1939, continued to work on it throughout the war and ultimately became one of the most knowledgeable men in the world on the subject of taper-bore guns.

Two classes of weapon were eventually categorised: the *taper bore,* in which the barrel tapered evenly from breech to muzzle, and the *squeeze bore,* in which the barrel was parallel for some distance and then tapered sharply to effect the 'squeezing' of the projectile, finishing as a parallel bore of smaller dimension. An alternative design of squeeze bore was one in which a tapered extension was placed on the muzzle of an otherwise conventional gun. The projectiles used with these two classes were much the same in design, though experience showed that the taper bore shot had to be somewhat stronger in construction than the squeeze bore models owing to the different times throughout which the shells underwent stress in compression.

Towards the end of the war the taper bore concept was gradually discarded in favour of the squeeze bore designs, since these were a good deal easier to manufacture. Making a tapered and rifled gun barrel was no easy task, even with sophisticated machine tools, whereas production of a smoothbore 'squeeze' extension to fit the muzzle of an otherwise standard gun was much less exacting and less wasteful of time and material. Weapons as large as 24cm calibre were fitted with such extensions (in this case reducing to 21cm) and were fired quite successfully.

The only active-service use of the taper or squeeze systems was in the anti-tank class, where three weapons (2.8cm/2.1cm, 4.2cm/2.8cm and 7.5/5.0cm) entered service. In the anti-aircraft field, while the velocity increases gave promise of considerably improved performance and where many experimental weapons were built and fired, no guns were ready for service before the war ended. There was a rule of thumb that said a squeeze bore adaptor could be expected to increase velocity and maximum range by about a third. Velocities of as much as 1400mps (4595fps) had been achieved but it was felt that, bearing in mind wear-rates and dispersion at extreme ranges, service velocities of 1150–1200mps(3775–3935fps) might be consistently reached. The design of projectiles was an involved business and will be discussed elsewhere. (See page 264.)

While the taper and squeeze bore experiments were progressing, another system of improving performance began to attract attention. The French ordnance engineer Brandt had been experimenting for some years with discarding sabot projectiles, a system in which the gun fired a projectile of less than its own calibre—a 10.5cm gun, for example, might well fire an 8.8cm projectile. In order to make the smaller shot fit the larger bore it was first fitted into a *sabot* (a French term for 'shoe' or 'tub') of full calibre, so engineered that upon leaving the muzzle the sabot was discarded and fell clear to leave the sub-calibre projectile free to proceed to the target. The advantages of this system were manifold; the gun did not require any special adaptors or methods of construction (although subsequent experience has shown that the twist of rifling can be fairly critical), the composite projectile and sabot was lighter than a standard projectile for the gun and thus accelerated faster in the bore to develop a high muzzle velocity, and the full-calibre base area enabled the charge to develop its full potential. Yet the sub-projectile in flight had a favourable sectional density and thus retained its velocity, giving longer ranges, higher terminal velocities and consistent accuracy. As with almost all ordnance ideas, the discarding sabot was far from new; it had been patented as far back as 1862 (British Patent 2064 of 19th July 1862. granted to W. E. Newton as agent for A. A. Emery) but, as with Puff's taper bore, the idea was well in advance of contemporary ballistic knowledge and engineering technique—and had lain unused for a long time.

When the German Army occupied France in 1940 many of Brandt's experimental projectiles were discovered: these and the idea were taken back to Germany for development, which was done to good effect. Krupp were particularly interested and active in this field, and a wide variety of discarding sabot projectiles were produced on an experimental basis together with small numbers that were issued to service more or less in the nature of user trials.

Another weapon discovered in France, and which was considered to hold promise, was the Bassett gun. The brainchild of a French engineer of the same name it was a hyper-velocity 3.7cm gun whose principal feature was the burning of propellant at hitherto unconsidered pressures. Instead of the usual order of 20 to 25ton/in², Bassett proposed operating his gun at 95 to 100ton/in². Since normal rifling and driving bands could not hope to cope at such levels, the barrel was shaped internally into a twisted octagon that, as it approached the muzzle, blended into polygonal (perhaps 16- or 32-sided) shape. The shot was provided with multiple sealing bands of soft iron and Buna rubber, and was of octagonal section to match the barrel; thus it attained spin, a reversion to the Whitworth system of rifling which was briefly touted in the 1850s and 1860s. In order to utilise the expansion of the propellant gas, and thus develop the utmost efficiency, the barrel was 175 calibres long (21ft 3in/6.48m). Bassett signed a development contract with the German Army but progress was slow, since much basic research had to be done before manufacture of the weapon could begin; nobody, for example, was quite sure what would happen to a conventional smokeless propelling powder when it was burned at such high pressures, and special pressure chambers had to be designed in which samples could be ignited and their performance studied. All this took time: and in 1944, before the work was completed, the Allied armies invaded France. When Paris was abandoned by the Germans Bassett moved to Switzerland, but the gun and experimental apparatus were removed to Germany in order to continue development. It soon became apparent that the weapon would never become a viable mechanism in time to influence the war's course and work on it stopped entirely early in 1945. While undoubtedly an interesting concept in ballistics and physics, there seems little useful purpose in the weapon and it has never been revived.

The next project to be examined in the search for longer range was the possibility of providing in-flight assistance to the projectile by means of a rocket boost. The idea was again as old as ammunition, one typical proposition being Taylor's British Patent 1460 of 20th May 1870. Considerable work had already been done in Germany on rocket propulsion and, on the face of it, a rocket-assisted shell sounded most attractive. Numerous designs were tried and two or three were actually issued for service, but the drawbacks were well-nigh insuperable. The rocket propulsion firstly demanded an excessive amount of the limited space available in the shell, leading to a small explosive payload which was hardly worth the expense and effort of getting it to the target. Secondly, the gun shell was rarely—if at all—perfectly aligned with its theoretical trajectory; it was invariably 'yawing' about the perfect line in one direction or another. At the instant the rocket motor ignited and began to deliver thrust, any off-line yaw of the shell resulted in the rocket trajectory being a continuation of the yaw axis and not necessarily the axis of the ballistic trajectory. As a result, the projectile could land anywhere in a large probability area around the intended target. This, coupled with the small payload, rendered the long-range rocket shell an uneconomic proposition, though it undoubtedly had its advantages as a propaganda weapon.

A further disadvantage of the rocket-assisted shell, as seen by some scientists, was the necessity to carry both the fuel and an oxidant required to promote burning. Had it been possible to carry only the fuel and tap the ambient air as the oxidant, then the propulsion unit could have been made smaller by the amount saved in oxidant storage space and the explosive payload correspondingly increased. Dr Tromsdorf spent much time and effort developing his 'pulsating athodyd' shell, which was really a ram-jet running along the axis of a projectile. A quantity of liquid fuel (usually carbon disulphide) was carried and as the incoming air mixed with the fuel in a combustion hamber it was ignited, and the resultant thrust oosted the shell. This development was being xplored with a view to improving anti-aircraft un performance, but the work was still in the xperimental stage when the war ended. It is elieved that both the Americans and the Soviets nowed some interest in the idea during the im- nediate postwar years, but the inaccuracy problem ill existed and the promised increase in payload 'as largely illusory owing to the space needed for ne induction, combustion and exhaust systems. 'he athodyd shell, while theoretically sound nough, is no longer considered to be a practical roposition.

The last field of endeavour, and one which eld considerable promise, was the development of n-stabilised projectiles. Gun shells are customarily pun by the rifling to achieve gyroscopic stability ut this system has some inherent limitations. As as already been seen, high-velocity guns made onsiderable demands on the system of rifling and anding, owing to the high rotational stresses thus eveloped. Furthermore, the pressures needed to ngrave a driving band were on occasion quite arge and led to undesirable peak pressures in the un chamber. The projectile was restricted in ength, since shells much more than six calibres ong could not be satisfactorily stabilised except at ery high spin rates, which in turn demanded pecial rifling and multiple banding to spread the oad on the shell and driving bands. The fin-stabil- sation solution promised freedom from most of hese troubles and in some cases offered a simpler un into the bargain, since the weapon could there- fter be a smooth-bore. The reasons for adopting in-stabilisation varied from attempts to obtain igh velocity—by removing the frictional resistance f rifling and banding—to stabilising projectiles oo long for conventionally rifled guns, in the case f some special designs of anti-concrete shell. Fin- tabilised projectiles could also be fired from a ifled gun and yet avoid much rotation, in order o improve their tactical effect.

Much of the theoretical development in this field ook place at the Raketen-Versuchsstation Peene- nünde (Peenemünde rocket research establishment) vhere wind tunnels were available and where here was considerable knowledge of the aerody- namics of finned missiles. The principal outcome f their work was the *Peenemünder Pfeilgeschoss* Peenemünde arrow shell) which was developed oth as a long range terrestrial-fire projectile and s a high velocity projectile for anti-aircraft work. Little of this work bore fruit in time to be used luring the war, but it formed a considerable base or postwar development by many other nations.

All these developments illustrate the point that he easiest way to improve a gun is to leave it lone and work on the ammunition. As far as the uns themselves were concerned, development was usually aimed at improving efficiency and produc- ng weapons that were lighter to manoeuvre; guns with greater flexibility in terms of elevation and traverse, those which were simpler to operate and those easier to mass-produce were all demanded of the designers. When producing a design incor- porating as many of these desirable characteristics as possible, attempts were made to increase the range (if it could be done) but in many cases the improvement in performance was less apparent than the improvement in other criteria. In certain fields—anti-tank guns, for example—performance was so vital that the guns inevitably grew bigger and bigger: questions of handiness in action and ease of manufacture were subordinated to the over- riding demand that a specific target had to be engaged and destroyed at a specific range until, towards the end of the war, it was obvious that a halt had to be called before the guns became too large for their tactical role. Fresh ballistic solutions had to be devised instead.

There had already been a demand for light- weight weapons for a special application and this had been answered by the development of recoilless guns for use by airborne troops. A number of lightweight shoulder-fired weapons had also appeared during the war, capable by virtue of the ammunition they fired of defeating most of the contemporary tanks. These weapons were the rocket launchers such as the American Bazooka and the German *Ofenrohr,* ('stovepipe'), and the recoilless *Panzerfaust* ('armoured fist'). Using hol- low charge bombs, these weapons could deliver a fatal attack on a tank without need of heavy or high-velocity ordnance, and so the army then asked the manufacturers to contemplate producing some sort of gun that could deliver a hollow charge shell with accuracy, which would be light to move and easy to use, but which (in view of the econo- mic position) would use less propellant than the rocket or the recoilless guns in the process. The response to this demand was Rheinmetall-Borsig's development of the *Hoch-Niederdruck-System* ('high-low pressure system'), one of the few com- pletely new ballistic developments to come out of the war.

The high-low pressure gun confined the cartridge in a robust breech in which the explosion of the charge reached a relatively high pressure of about 8ton/in^2. Between the charge and the projectile was a heavy steel plate pierced with a number of carefully designed holes through which the high pressure was bled into the lightweight barrel. In the barrel the pressure dropped to 2–3ton/in^2 and it was this that moved the fin-stabilised projectile up the smooth-bore barrel, the pressure dropping to as little as 1ton/in^2 at the muzzle. The system was highly successful and at least one weapon embodying it entered service; a number of others were planned but the end of the war stopped their development. In postwar years the high-low pres- sure system was the focus of considerable interest from ballisticians throughout the world but it has, surprisingly, seen little application since 1945.

This brief introduction serves to show that the subject of German artillery during World War 2 is one that is full of interest. Confronted as the war continued with heavier tanks, faster aircraft and more fluid warfare, the German designers were never for long at a loss for the next idea. Admittedly they sometimes produced a disaster, but more often they produced a winner and it noteworthy that the designs that were being take from the drawing board and into service in 194 were examples of gunmaking which have rarel been bettered; many postwar designs owe some o their better features to ideas pioneered by German during the war years.

ORGANISATION

n the Reichswehr all artillery, apart from those eapons organic to the division, belonged to the eneral headquarters pool, from which units were llotted according to tactical requirements—to erform some specific operation or to be 'on loan' a division or corps.

In the normal course of events the divisional rtillery was commanded by an *Artillerieführer* Arfu), who was the divisional commander's adviser n artillery matters. When GHQ pool units were ttached, a complete artillery staff section came ith them; the senior officer of this section became e *Artillerie Kommandeur* (Arko) and took command of the divisional artillery in addition to that f his own specialised units. Since these 'Arkos' ad a permanent staff, they were considered as eparate units and were given (like all other erman Army units) an identifying formation umber that depended on the grade of the Arko.

At GHQ the Arko was a general and acted as n adviser on the employment of the pool units. Ie was rarely called 'Arko' and was instead normally referred to as *General der Artillerie*: his taff formed part of GHQ and was not necessarily iven a distinct identifying number.

At army group or army headquarters level the rtillery commander was known as the *Höherer Artillerie Kommandeur* (HohArko) and was usually Generalleutnant (lieutenant general). These formations were numbered from 301 onwards.

The corps and division Arkos were numbered ither in the block 1–44 or from 101 onwards, lthough towards the end of the war the numbering ystem went awry and the block 401–500 was also sed for corps Arkos.

The non-divisional artillery units were as ollows:

. *Abteilungen und Batterien.* These were the ctual gun units, and could be equipped with eapons of any calibre: mechanical or horse-drawn, self-propelled, railway or fixed-mounting weapons.

. *Artillerie Regimentsstab.* These were the staff nits held under GHQ control and were allotted o sub-units to command the GHQ artillery on oan.

3. *Sturmgeschütz Artillerie.* These were special assault gun regiments which were allotted by GHQ as required.

4. *Heeresflakabteilungen.* Most German anti-aircraft weapons were controlled by the Luftwaffe, but a proportion were manned by the army and were generally attached to motorised or armoured divisions—to act in both anti-aircraft and anti-tank roles.

5. *Beobachtungs Abteilungen.* These observation units dealt with flash-spotting, sound-ranging and general artillery intelligence tasks.

6. *Vermessung und Karten Abteilungen.* These were survey and mapping units, allotted as required, whose duties are self-explanatory.

7. *Velocitäts Mess-Zug.* Such units were small sections whose task in life was to travel round to units to measure the gun velocities and calibrate the guns. They were numbered 701 onwards.

8. *Astronomische Mess-Zug.* These astronomical survey units, were ancillary to the Vermessung und Karten Abteilungen and were numbered 720 onwards.

9. *Wetter Peilzug.* These meteorological sections provided data to firing units and were numbered in the 501–600 block.

10. *Armee Kartenstelle.* The map depots, also numbered in the 501–600 block.

11. *Artillerie-Park.* These were equipment stores units; one was allotted to each army group.

12. *Artillerie Lehr-Regiment.* Three of these instructional and demonstration units existed at the Artillerie Lehrschüle at Juterbög, in Wehrkreis III. The first regiment was horse-drawn, the second was motorised (with one battery of assault guns), and the third dealt with such matters as survey, observation and meteorology.

13. *Heeresküsten Artillerie* (army coast artillery). This was organised in coastal defence sectors and was under the command of either army or navy headquarters—though where a service division was given responsibility for the defence of a coastal zone, the coast artillery located there came under the divisional command. The army units serving in this role were relatively few, for coast defence was primarily the navy's responsibility.

The Divisional Artillery

Infantry division

The peacetime establishment of divisional artillery consisted of one field regiment of three batteries and one medium regiment of two batteries, one of which might be horse-drawn and the other mechanised. On mobilisation the mechanised battery was supposed to be withdrawn to the GHQ pool and the horsed battery incorporated into the field regiment, but this did not always happen.

The field regiment consisted of a regimental headquarters, a signals section, three field batteries and one medium battery. The field batteries had a battery headquarters, a signals section, a survey section, and three troops with an ammunition column. The troops each had a troop headquarters, a signals section, transport and ammunition sections, and two gun sections each with two 10.5cm howitzers. In many cases a section of two 2cm anti-aircraft guns was attached for local air defence. The medium battery contained a battery headquarters, a signals section, a survey section, and three troops—two of four 15cm howitzers and one of four 10cm guns; two 2cm anti-aircraft guns were also sometimes attached. The total establishment strength was 89 officers, 2156 men and 1785 horses plus a variety of motor vehicles; there were also 48 guns and howitzers plus 24 small-calibre anti-aircraft guns. The motorised infantry division possessed the same allocation of guns but the units were entirely mechanised.

Armoured division

The division originally contained one regiment of two fully mechanised batteries, a total of 47 officers, 1065 men and 24 guns. This establishment, however, was later augmented by a third battery of 15cm howitzers.

Mountain division

The regiment consisted of a headquarters, a signals section, and two batteries each of three troops. The troops were each armed with four 7.5cm mountain guns. Transportation was largely achieved by pack mules. As the war progressed the armament altered from time to time, and in some cases *Leichtgeschütze* (recoilless guns) were issued.

Anti-Aircraft Artillery

It is generally accepted that all anti-aircraft artillery in the German forces was manned by the Luftwaffe, whereas most other nations made it an army responsibility; this is not entirely true and warrants a detailed examination.

German Flak artillery (Flak—*Flugzeug Abwehr Flieger-Kanone,* or anti-aircraft gun) originated before World War 1 and formed part of the army. At the same time the use of aircraft was increasing, and on 8th October 1916 a special order authorised the creation of a 'commanding general of air combat forces' (*Kommandierend General der Luftstreitkrafte).* This was the birth of the German airforce as a distinct and separate service, and i the text of this order came the phrase 'the increasing importance of the air war demands that a army defensive and offensive weapons in the fiel and homeland should be united in one service Thus Flak artillery became part of this nev organisation.

Under the provisions of the Treaty of Versailles the German forces were forbidden to own anti aircraft weapons, with the exception of guns aboar naval vessels and some static weapons in the fortress of Königsberg. In view of this restriction th existing Flak guns were converted to field gun by modifying the elevating gear and removing th anti-aircraft sights. They were then used to equi seven motorised batteries, one of which wa attached to each of the Reichswehr's seven permitted army artillery regiments, and in 1925 th officers of these batteries were attached to the nav for duty with Flak guns. In 1928 the seve batteries were equipped with 7.5cm FlAK guns an fire control instruments, and began clandestin training in the anti-aircraft role. Flak-Abteilunge were assembled from 1932 onwards, under th cover designation of 'Transport-Abteilungen', an shortly afterwards Flak machine-gun companie were formed under the cover of the *Deutscher Luftsportsverband* (DLV).

By this time exhaustive studies had been mad of the question of to which branch of the servic anti-aircraft artillery should belong, and in 193 the Reich's defence minister — General vo Blomberg — laid down the following rules:

1. That protection against aircraft in the field wa the responsibility of the army.
2. That protection at sea and on the coast wa the responsibility of the navy.
3. That the aerial protection of the Reich was th responsibility of the Luftwaffe.

In 1934 the existing Transport-Abteilungen wer separated from the army and placed under th Reichsministerium der Luftfahrt, whereupon th units were strengthened with men to make u their full establishment.

Having thus lost all its anti-aircraft weapon overnight, the army demanded the formation o its own Flak units (envisaged by the minister' statement of the previous year), and the navy als demanded that their aerial defences be strengthened in order to discharge their responsibility fo coastal areas. This caused the argument to brea out afresh and, as a result, Generaloberst Rude and General Pohl made a particular study of th whole concept of anti-aircraft defence. On 1st Apri 1935, when the existence of the Luftwaffe wa made public, the air defence troops were officiall transferred to the Luftwaffe and that was the fina word. With the exception of the naval weapons all Flak—whether in the Reich or in the field— was a Luftwaffe responsibility: the army was t have no say in the matter. From then, growth wa steady; from 7 Abteilungen in 1933 the strength f the Luftwaffe's anti-aircraft defences rose to 18 1 1935 and to 115 in 1939. By 1941 it had reached 41 Abteilungen.

The solution never satisfied the army and it never topped agitating for its own Flak. It was not suffici-nt to have Luftwaffe anti-aircraft units attached to rmy formations; too often the Flak staffs with-rew their units to fill demands arising elsewhere, aving the army unprotected. Although the 8.8cm nd other weapons were admirable anti-tank guns, nd could even have been used as fieldguns when ne need arose, the Luftwaffe commanders resisted uch use because of the excessive wear on the un barrels—and because the guns were often ripped of fire control instruments, being thus endered useless for their primary task of shooting t aircraft. Eventually (in 1941) the army were ermitted to form their own Flak troops and two ormations were developed: the Heeresflakbatail-onen, wearing white Waffenfarbe and belonging the infantry, and the Heeresflakabteilungen, earing red Waffenfarbe and belonging to the artil-ry. Such things as the supply of weapons, ammuni-ion and equipment to army units were still the uftwaffe's responsibility, while inspection, training nd replacement of personnel was done by the rmy. The Luftwaffe's authorities were never very appy about the whole thing and considered it duplication of effort, especially when the army et up its own Flak school and practice camp, nd many closely-argued papers on the subject ontinued to be produced throughout the war.

The Luftwaffe Flak was organised into various nits—in diminishing order, Korps, Divisionen, rigaden, Regimenten, Abteilungen and Batterien. he main series of units bore numbers from 1 to 99, though the same number could sometimes be sed by two units of different types.

Numbers 1–70 were generally regiments, each onsisting of a headquarters, two Abteilungen each vith three heavy and two light batteries, one earchlight Abteilung of three or four batteries, nd an Ersatzabteilung responsible for repairs and eplacements.

Numbers 71–99 were light Abteilungen, each of iree or four light batteries. There were also inde-endent regimental staff groups with numbers in iis series. The significance of the numbering lay the final digit—or in the first digit where the umber ended in O—which was a code figure indi-ating the *Luftgau* (a Luftwaffe administrative istrict comparable to the army's Wehrkreis), the rea in which the unit had its origin. The Luftgaue ere represented as follows:

: Luftgau I (generally known as LG I). 2: LG III. : LG IV. 4: LG VI. 5: LG VII. 6: LG XI. : LG VIII. 8: LG XVII. 9: LG XII and XIII. hus 35. Regiment originated in Luftgau VII while 7. Abteilung originated in Luftgau VIII. Appendix 4 lists the distribution of the Luftgaue.)

The sequence 100–999 was allotted to units ormed after mobilisation in 1939. They could be found in size between regiment and battery, not necessarily complete to their paper establishment. Thus a regiment might only possess a single Ab-teilung. The numbers were originally supposed to bear some relationship to either the Luftgau or the parent unit which, by throwing off some trained staff, had formed the mobilisation unit. Thus 35. Regiment might have formed 352. Abteilung, the key figure being retained as the second digit except where it was O (in which case the first digit was the significant one). But, with the best will in the world, these schemes invariably fall to pieces owing to the mobilisation of more units than was origin-ally envisaged; as the war progressed so numbers were allotted arbitrarily.

The *Heeresflakabteilungen* (army anti-aircraft units), while belonging to the army, were numbered by the Luftwaffe in the same series as their own units, the numbers commencing at 271. The Ab-teilung was normally a part of the divisional artillery and consisted of two heavy batteries of 8.8cm guns and two light batteries of 3.7cm or 2cm guns. The Flak battalions comprised six com-panies armed with 3.7cm or 2cm guns, and were originally numbered from 22 to 66. This was later changed to 501 and 601–620, but—later still—many units lost their numbers and their independ-ence, being merged into infantry divisions.

Coast Defence and Fortress Artillery

Coast defence of the Reich was generally the responsibility of the navy, analogous to the anti-aircraft responsibility of the Luftwaffe. Six Ab-teilungen formed the normal establishment, their headquarters being located as follows:

Marine Artillerie-Abteilung I: Kiel.
Marine Artillerie-Abteilung II: Wilhelmshaven.
Marine Artillerie-Abteilung III: Swinemünde.
Marine Artillerie-Abteilung IV: Cuxhaven.
Marine Artillerie-Abteilung V: Pillau.
Marine Artillerie-Abteilung VI: Emden.

Each Abteilung basically mustered one heavy gun company and two Flak companies, but this was capable of variation depending on the area to be covered. In addition, eight Marine Flak-Artillerie-Abteilungen existed to provide further anti-aircraft cover at dockyards and similar installations. Their strength also varied between two and five com-panies, according to their allotted task.

Fortress artillery formed a very small portion of the peacetime army since, under the terms of the Versailles Treaty, the only fortress left armed was that of Königsberg—which had about 25 guns of 17cm calibre or less. Some works on the French and Belgian borders, which formed part of the Siegfried Line defensive system, were armed and manned by fortress artillery troops at the outbreak of war in 1939, but as the war progressed most of the fixed defences in *Festung Europa* ('Fortress Europe') became the responsibility of the normal army field artillery.

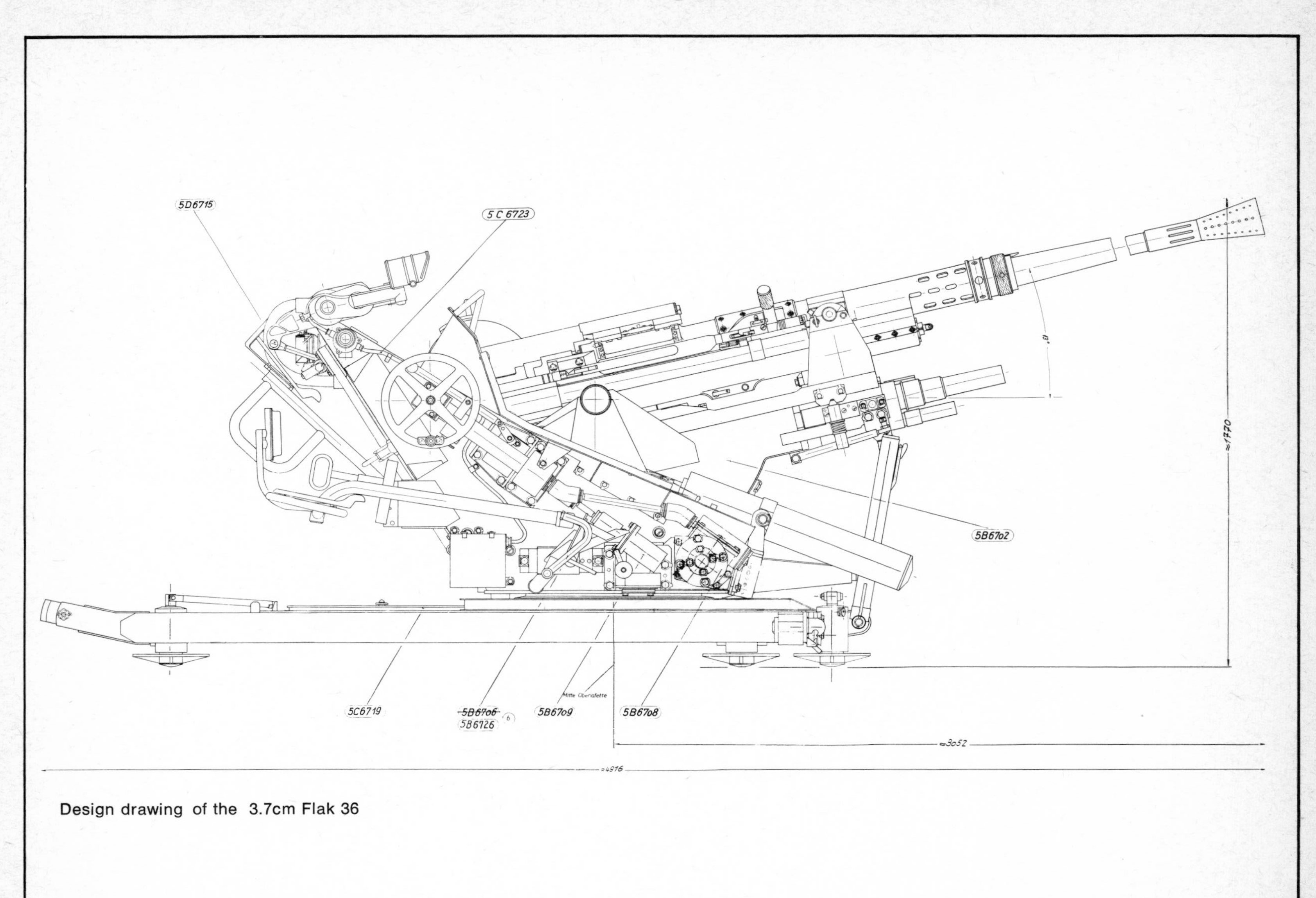

Design drawing of the 3.7cm Flak 36

INFANTRY ARTILLERY

The idea of providing infantry with their own private artillery was born during World War 1 with the introduction by the French of the 37mm trench gun. The idea was taken up during the 1920s by several armies, though it gained little acceptance outside the continent of Europe, but the improvement of the muzzle-loading mortar eventually tended to drive infantry guns out: the mortars were usually easier to transport, simpler to operate, had sufficient range for the infantry's needs, and usually had a higher rate of fire owing to the simple loading system. In addition it was soon realised that mortar projectiles usually caused more damage than their gun equivalents owing to the mortar bomb's steep angle of descent and its higher explosive capacity, factors that combined to give particularly good fragmentation and fragment distribution.

In spite of having numerous highly efficient mortars, the German Army retained its infantry guns throughout the war and—provided that the manpower to operate them was available (one of the reasons why the only British infantry gun, the 95mm Howitzer, never entered service)—there is no doubt that they formed a useful source of instant fire support.

7·5cm leichtes Infanteriegeschütz 18

7·5cm le IG 18 (Ferelle)

The IG 18 was one of the first post-World War 1 weapons issued to the German army; developed by Rheinmetall during the immediate postwar years, it was first issued in 1927 and remained in service until 1945. Light and handy, it was mechanically unique in employing a 'shotgun' breech action. The barrel was carried in a square-section casing within another that carried the fixed breechblock and firing mechanism. When the breech lever was operated, the rear end of the barrel lifted clear of the fixed block owing to the barrel pivot at the muzzle. Once open, the barrel was held by the extractors. On loading the cartridge, the case rim forced the extractors forward to release the barrel, allowing it to drop into place by virtue

IGr 18 AZ 23nA

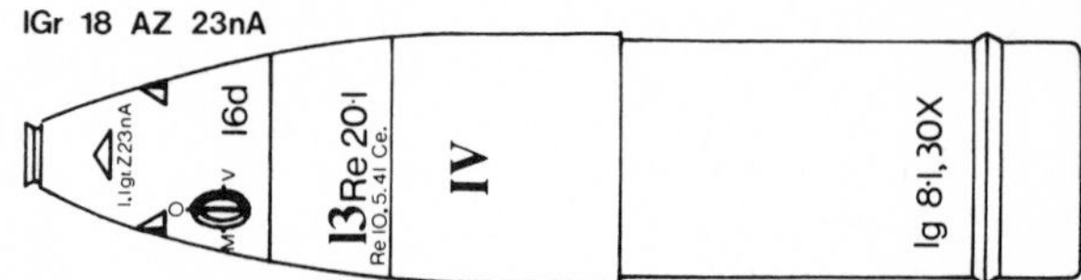

7.5cm le IG 18 being demonstrated to foreign military attachés before the war.

of its own weight—thus effectively closing the breech.

The carriage was a simple box trail with a spade, traversing across the axle; this was a slow system and was only suited to a very light weapon, since owing to the pivoting action about the spade the traversing movement tended to move the wheels. With a heavy gun placed in soft ground the effort became prohibitive. A shield was fitted and the wheels were either of wood-spoked type or steel discs with pneumatic tyres, depending upon whether the gun was to be horse- or vehicle-drawn. A hydro-pneumatic recoil system was carried in the cradle below the barrel.

In 1937 a lighter version, known as the 7.5cm le Gebirg IG 18 (Obermühl), was introduced for use by mountain troops. The ordnance was identical to the earlier model but the carriage had a light tubular split trail, no shield, and lightweight spoked wheels; it could be rapidly dismantled into six mule-pack or ten man-pack loads. Owing to its lightness the le Geb IG 18 was ballistically restricted insofar as the fifth propelling charge could only be fired at ranges greater than 2000m—otherwise the recoil was excessive. Above this range the gun's elevation was such that the downward components of the recoil force exceeded the backward thrust, and thus the gun remained stable.

When steps were being taken in 1939 to equip German Army airborne and parachute forces, an airborne gun—the 7.5cm le IG 18F (F for *Fallschirmjäger* or parachute troops)—was designed. This could be dismantled and packed into four containers each weighing about 140kg(309lb), and was virtually the mountain weapon with smaller disc wheels. Six equipments were made by Rheinmetall for trials but the design was not accepted, since the light recoilless guns were then nearing production and promised equal or better firepower for much less weight.

The IG 18 in use, giving close support to an infantry advance during the battle for the Donets Basin.

Data (7.5cm le IG 18).
Calibre: 7.5cm/2.95in.
Length of gun: 884mm/34.80in.
Length of bore: 783mm/30.83in.
Rifling: 24 grooves, right-hand uniform twist, 1/25.
Breech mechanism: shotgun pattern, percussion fired.
Traverse: 12°.
Elevation: —10° to +75°.
Weight in action: 400kg/882lb.

Performance
Firing standard high explosive shell weighing 6.00kg(13.23lb).
Charge 1: velocity 92mps/302fps, maximum range 800m/875yd.
Charge 2: velocity 110mps/361fps, maximum range 1098m/1200yd.
Charge 3: velocity 131mps/430fps, maximum range 1500m/1640yd.
Charge 4: velocity 167mps/548fps, maximum range 2340m/2560yd.
Charge 5: velocity 210mps/689fps, maximum range 3375m/3690yd.
Firing hollow charge shell weighing 3.00kg(6.62lb)
Charge 5 only: velocity 260mps/853fps, maximum range 3795m/4150yd.

Ammunition
Separate-loading, cased, except for the hollow charge round H1/A.

Projectiles
7.5cm I Gr 18: fuzed AZ 23 or Dopp Z S/60 weight 6.00kg(13.23lb).
The standard high explosive shell, this was filled with 570gm(20.10oz/1.26lb) of amatol 40/60 and with a smoke-box for observation.
7.5cm I Gr 18: fuzed I Gr Z 23 nA v(0.15), weight 5.50kg(12.13lb).
This was similar to the I Gr 18 but was slightly lighter owing to the thinner walls. This improved the performance to give a maximum range of 3550m(3880yd).
7.5cm I Gr 18 Al: fuzed I Gr Z 23 nA v(0.15) weight 5.50kg(12.13lb).
This was similar to the above but carried a bursting charge of 670gm(23.63oz/1.48lb) of TNT/aluminium (90/10) mixture and no smoke-box.
7.5cm I Gr 38 Hl: fuzed AZ 38, weight 3.00kg (6.62lb).
This, an early pattern of hollow charge shell, had a filling of cyclonite/TNT. It was to be fired with charge 5 only and gave a penetration of 45mm (1.77in) at 30° impact.

Left: Rear view of the 7.5cm le IG 18 showing the 'shotgun' breech open.

Right: The 7.5cm le Geb IK 18 mountain version of the standard infantry gun. It was also used to a limited extent by airborne units.

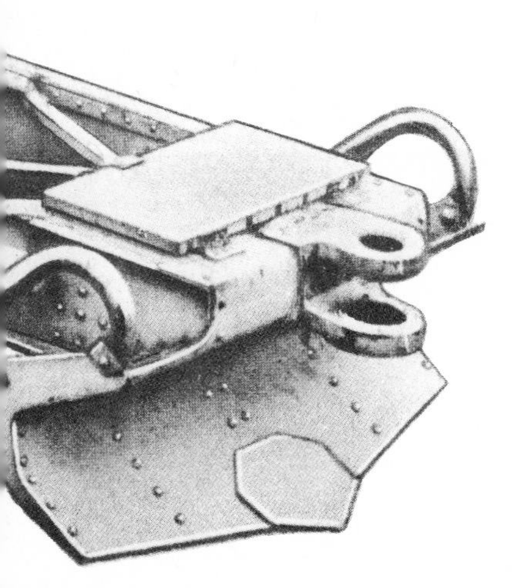

7.5cm I Gr 38 Hl/A FES: fuzed AZ 38 St, weight 3.05kg(6.73lb).
An improved pattern of hollow charge shell. The performance was similar to the I Gr 38 Hl but the chance of hitting was improved by providing the Hl/A as a fixed round, complete with a special propelling charge designed to give a velocity of 345mps(1132fps).
7·5cm I Gr Deut: fuzed Kl AZ 23 Nb, weight 5.98kg(13.19lb).
This was a bursting pattern of smoke shell that gave a cloud of blue smoke for target indication. Performance was similar to that of the I Gr 18, of comparable weight.

Propelling Charge
A five-part charge was provided, consisting of five bundles of perforated discs of propellant each held together with thread and labelled with the portion number. To assemble a charge, the portions up to and including the desired number were retained in the case—the remainder being discarded. The composition of the units was as follows:
Charge 1 portion: 15.8gm/0.56oz Nigl Pl P.
Charge 2 portion: 6.2gm/0.22oz Nigl Pl P.
Charge 3 portion: 9.0gm/0.32oz Nigl Pl P.
Charge 4 portion: 15.8gm/0.56oz Nigl Pl P.
Charge 5 portion: 24.0gm/0.85oz Nigl Pl P.
The fixed hollow charge round Hl/A was provided with a non-adjustable charge of 100gm/3.53oz of Nigl Pl P.

Primer: The percussion primer C/12nA was standard.

Case Identification Number: 6341.

7·5cm Infanteriegeschütz L/13

7·5cm IG L/13

This equipment was developed in the middle 1930s by Rheinmetall as a possible replacement for the IG 18, but only a small number were made. The nomenclature L/13 was derived from the length of the barrel: 13 times the calibre. The design of gun reverted to the more usual type of horizontal sliding-block breech mechanism. The carriage was a tubular split-trail pattern with a shield, and had a hydro-spring recoil system in a cradle beneath the barrel. Disc wheels with solid rubber tyres were fitted. The prototypes were tested by the army but the gun was not accepted for service.

Data

Calibre: 75mm/2.95in.
Length of gun: 975mm/38.37in.
Breech mechanism: horizontal sliding block, percussion fired.
Traverse (top carriage pivot): 50°.
Elevation: —5° to +43°.
Weight in action: 375kg/827lb.

Performance

Firing a 6.50kg(14.33lb) high explosive shell.
Charge 4: velocity 225mps/738fps, maximum range 3800m/4155yd.
Firing a 4.50kg(9.92lb) high explosive shell.
Charge 5: velocity 305mps/1000fps, maximum range 5100m/5575.

Propelling Charge

The 7.5cm IG 18's five-charge cartridge was used, although the fifth charge was not used with the 6.50kg(14.33lb) shell.

7.5cm le IG L/13, showing the conventional horizontal sliding-block breech and tubular trail legs.

7·5cm Infanteriegeschütz 37

7·5cm IG 37

Despite the '37' nomenclature this weapon was not introduced until 1944, the number stemming from the use of redundant 3.7cm PAK 36 carriages. The new design was, in fact, first called the 7.5cm PAK 37 but this caused too much confusion (since it was not primarily an anti-tank gun) and so it was changed to IG 37.

Although the carriage was outdated in its original application, this had been caused principally by the supersession of the 3.7cm calibre as an anti-tank weapon; there was nothing wrong with the basic PAK 36 carriage. The gun mounted on top was an entirely new weapon based on a 1942 Krupp design that had been shelved at the time but which later emerged as the IG 42. It had a much larger barrel than earlier weapons, a four-baffle muzzle brake of about 28% efficiency, and a vertical sliding-block breech—an unusual feature on Krupp designs. The breech mechanism was fitted with semi-automatic gear so that after recoil stopped, and the gun was running out, the breechblock was automatically opened and the case ejected. The block was then held open against a spring by the locking action of the extractors. Loading forced the extractors forward and released the breechblock, which thereafter closed under the pressure of the spring.

The tubular split-trail carriage had disc wheels with solid rubber tyres and an enveloping shield. Spring suspension was used, achieved by cranked stubaxles bearing on coil springs: a legacy of the original anti-tank design.

One of the interesting features of this weapon was the Allies' discovery on the first captured specimens of the Soviet star, impressed into the shield. This caused a certain amount of speculation in technical intelligence circles before it was discovered that the carriages had originally been sold to Russia in prewar days, complete with the 3.7cm gun; they had then been used by the Russians, captured by the Germans on the Eastern front and then cannibalised to provide carriages for the new gun.

Data
Calibre: 75mm/2.95in.
Length of gun: 1798mm/70.77in.
Rifling: 24 grooves, right-hand uniform twist, 1/25.59.
Breech mechanism: vertical semi-automatic sliding block, percussion fired.
Traverse: 58°.
Elevation: −10° to +40°.
Weight in action: 510kg/1125lb.

Performance
Firing standard high explosive shell weighing 5.50kg(12.13lb).
Charge 6: velocity 280mps/918fps, maximum range 5150m/5632yd.

Ammunition
Separate-loading, cased, except the hollow charge shell H1/A which formed part of a fixed round with special non-adjustable charge.

Projectiles
See IG 18.

Propelling Charge
The basic five-part propelling charge was the same as that used with the IG 18 but, in addition, a super charge—Sonderhülsenkart 6—was provided. This, when used, replaced units 1 to 5 in the case. This sixth charge consisted of 100gm(3.53oz) of Nigl Pl P. The propelling charge for the hollow charge fixed round was also the same as that for the IG 18.

Primer
The percussion primers C/12nA and C/12nA St were used.

7·5cm Infanteriegeschütz 42

7·5cm IG 42 (Grauwolf)

After the 1940 campaigns the infantry felt that the IG 38 was outdated, and so they requested a weapon with greater range and a much better anti-tank capability; the hollow charge shell had not then been introduced and they were using the normal high explosive shell as an anti-tank projectile.

In response to this demand, Krupp designed the 7.5cm IG 42, an efficient-looking weapon with tubular split trail, pneumatic tyres, a shield and a cage-type muzzle brake. Although the result was a serviceable weapon, production capacity was not readily available—and since the introduction of the hollow charge shell had by then given the IG 18 a reasonable anti-tank performance, the IG 42 project was dropped.

Later experience in the Russian campaigns, however, convinced the infantry that a new weapon was definitely needed and in 1944 the project was revived. The original design was thereafter called IG 42 aA (alterer Art, or 'old pattern') in order to avoid confusion, and the slightly modified gun was mounted on a lightweight split-trail carriage that had been designed a short time previously by Rheinmetall-Borsig for the 8cm PAW 600 anti-tank gun; the carriage, being a simple design, could be put into production quickly and easily.

The gun was exactly the same as that described for the IG 37, and the carriage was the only difference between the equipments. A severely-angled shield was fitted and the wheels were of disc pattern, with either solid or pneumatic tyres. The spring suspension was achieved by stub-axles and torsion bars were incorporated.

The Krupp prototype of the IG 42, later distinguished as the IG 42 aA.

The 7.5cm IG 42.

Front view of the IG 42 showing the enveloping shield.

Data
Calibre: 75mm/2.95in.
Length of gun: 1798mm/70.77in.
Length of bore: 1424mm/56.04in.
Rifling: 24 grooves, right-hand uniform twist, 1/25.59.
Traverse: 60°.
Elevation: −6° to +32°.
Breech mechanism: vertical sliding block, semi-automatic, percussion firing.
Weight in action: 590kg/1301lb.

Performance
As the IG 37, except that owing to the lower maximum elevation the maximum range was lower—4600m(5030yd)—though, with the trail spades buried, it was possible to reach 5150m(5632yd).

Ammunition
As the IG 37.

Towards the end of the war much development work was done on fin-stabilised hollow charge and high-capacity high explosive (*Minen*) shells, outlined in the sections on development. The 7.5cm IG 42 was selected as a potential vehicle for this type of ammunition, and a smoothbore version with an improved muzzle brake was built at the Hillersleben test range in order to undertake trials with various projectile designs. Had the war continued, the gun might have been further developed into a service weapon.

15cm schweres Infanteriegeschütz 33

15cm s IG 33

Although the nomenclature is '33' this weapon was developed by Rheinmetall at the same time as the 7.5cm IG 18, and was first issued in 1927.

The gun was conventional, with a horizontal sliding-block breech mechanism, and the carriage was a two-wheel box-trail type with a hydropneumatic recoil system in a cradle below the barrel. The gun and cradle were trunnioned well to the rear, to allow high elevation, and two spring balancing-presses were fitted to the outside of the trail to counteract the muzzle weight. Pressed-metal wheels with solid rubber tyres were fitted.

While the s IG 33 was a reliable and robust weapon, it was somewhat on the heavy side for an infantry gun (bearing in mind that it was the largest-calibre weapon ever classed by any nation as an infantry gun). In the late 1930s it was redesigned to incorporate light alloys wherever possible; this effected a reduction in weight of about 150kg (331lb), but only small numbers of this lightened model were built since it was introduced in 1939. The outbreak of war, shortly afterwards, revised priorities and gave the Luftwaffe first call on light alloys to facilitate aircraft production. Production of the s IG 33 thereupon reverted to the original pattern of carriage.

The gun remained in service until 1945, and in postwar years many were kept in use by some of the smaller European nations.

Data

Calibre: 150mm/5.91in.
Length of gun: 1748mm/68.82in.
Length of bore: 1650mm/64.96in.
Rifling: 44 grooves, right-hand uniform twist, 1/21
Breech mechanism: horizontal sliding block, percussion fired.
Traverse: 11.5°.
Elevation: 0 to +73° (some sources give +4° to +75°).

s IG 33 in action.

The s IG 33 in action: notice the unusual tyre-less wheels.

Weight in action: 1700kg/3749lb (standard type) 1550kg/3418lb (lightweight type).

Performance
Firing standard high explosive shell weighing 38.00kg(83.79lb).
Charge 1: velocity 122mps/400fps, maximum range 1475m/1615yd.
Charge 2: velocity 152mps/500fps, maximum range 2125m/2325yd.
Charge 3: velocity 186mps/610fps, maximum range 3000m/3280yd.
Charge 4: velocity 210mps/690fps, maximum range 3750m/4100yd.
Charge 5: velocity 230mps/755fps, maximum range 4375m/4785yd.
Charge 6: velocity 240mps/787fps, maximum range 4700m/5140yd.

Ammunition
Separate-loading, cased charge.

Projectiles
15cm I Gr 33: fuzed s I Gr Z 23, weight 38.00kg(83.79lb).
The standard high explosive shell, of elderly design with a blunt nose and a non-streamlined base. A single sintered-iron driving band replaced the copper band during the war. The filling was 8.30kg (18.31lb) of amatol 50/50.
15cm I Gr 38 Nb: fuzed K1 AZ 1, weight 40.00kg(88.20lb).
Of similar appearance to the high explosive shell, but slightly longer, this shell was filled with the usual oleum/pumice mixture with a high explosive burster charge.
15cm I Gr 39 H1/A: fuzed K1 AZ 40 Nb, weight 25.25kg(55.68lb).
This was the usual type of hollow charge shell, somewhat angular in appearance and with two sintered-iron driving bands. The filling was pre-pressed blocks of cyclonite/TNT/wax and a tracer pellet was fitted in the shell base.
15cm Steilgranate 42: fuzed W Gr Z 36mV, weight as fired 90.00kg(198.5lb).
This unusual projectile was intended to be loaded into the muzzle of the gun so that the driving rod entered the barrel, the fins lay outside and the warhead was in front of the muzzle. A special propelling charge was then loaded and fired to launch the stick bomb. About 150m(165yd) from the muzzle the retardation of the driving rod caused it to separate from the rest of the projectile, which then continued to a maximum range of about 1000m(1095yd). The head was filled with 27.00kg(59.54lb) of amatol and was an effective method of demolishing strongpoints, clearing barbed-wire obstacles and breaching minefields by blast effect. Contrary to the other 'Steilgranaten' projectiles in use, the 15cm type was not intended as an anti-tank weapon. The fuze was a modified mortar pattern with delay or instantaneous settings.

The s IG 33 at maximum elevation.

Propelling Charge

The charge was in six portions, all contained in silk cloth bags carried in the cartridge case. Portions were discarded as required.

Charge 1: 130gm/4.58oz Nigl Bl P, plus 42gm/1.48oz Digl Bl P.
Charge 2: 101gm/3.56oz Nigl Bl P, plus 42gm/1.48oz Digl Bl P.
Charge 3: 117gm/4.13oz Nigl Bl P, plus 42gm/1.48oz Digl Bl P.
Charge 4: 103gm/3.63oz Nigl Bl P, plus 42gm/1.48oz Digl Bl P.
Charge 5: 85gm/3.00oz Nigl Bl P, plus 42gm/1.48oz Digl Bl P.
Charge 6: 40gm/1.41oz Nigl Bl P, plus 42gm/1.48oz Digl Bl P.

A charge made up of Gudol propellant was also available.

Primer

The percussion primer C/12nA was standard

Case Identification Number: 6303.

A Russian soldier examining the breech of a captured s IG 33. The firing mechanism has been removed from the breech block, a hasty and futile attempt at making the gun useless to its captors.

German gunners manhandling a 15 cm s IG 33 into position.

MOUNTAIN ARTILLERY

A specially lightened version of the standard IG 18 (the le Geb IG 18) was issued to mountain artillery units, but this was only in the nature of an interim measure pending the production of purpose-built weapons more suited to such a special employment. The principal requirements of a successful mountain equipment were that it should be as light as possible yet still stable, that it should break down easily and quickly into loads which could be mule-packed, and that it could be sledged or even manhandled over any sort of countryside. The ideal gun was required to have a multiple-charge system giving ample overlaps that, together with a carriage design giving maximum elevation, ensured continuous fire-coverage to maximum range—irrespective of the intervening terrain. It was also advantageous if a large depression angle could be reached, since mountain troops frequently found themselves well above their targets and had to fire downhill at them.

These features have never been easy to reconcile in one equipment and some peculiar mountain guns have as a result been seen in various armies over the years, but the German designers, on the whole, responded well to the problems and produced some excellent weapons.

7·5cm Gebirgskanone 15

7·5cm Geb K 15

This was an elderly Skoda design purchased by the German Army in the days of the Weimar republic, small numbers of which remained in service after 1939. Skoda-Werke later produced an improved version of this weapon, the M28, with a longer barrel and better performance. This was not purchased by the Germans, but Skoda supplied a number to Jugoslavia and, after the German occupation, a number were used by the German forces there under the Fremdengerät title of Geb K 258(j)

The Geb K 15 had the barrel mounted in a 'slipper', a form of heavy jacket which simplified removal and also added weight to the recoiling parts to aid stability. The carriage was a simple 'humped' box trail with two wood-spoked wheels, and a large shield with lowering flaps was fitted. The entire weapon broke into seven pack loads, the heaviest weighing some 156kg(344lb).

Data
Calibre: 75mm/2.95in.
Length of gun: 1155mm/45.47in.
Length of bore: 802mm/31.50in.
Rifling: 28 grooves, uniform right-hand twist, 1/28
Breech mechanism: horizontal sliding block, percussion fired.
Traverse: 7°.
Elevation: −9° to +50°.
Weight in action: 630kg/1389lb.

Performance
Firing the high explosive Geb Gr 15, weight 5.47kg(12.06lb).
Charge 1: velocity 235mps/771fps, maximum range 3900m/4265yd.
Charge 2: velocity 263mps/863fps, maximum range 4600m/5031yd.
Charge 3: velocity 304mps/997fps, maximum

The Geb K 15 in action in a mountain meadow. The shield has been left off during assembly.

The 7.5cm Geb K 15 mountain gun, showing heavy 'slipper' around the barrel, characteristic of mountain guns.

Geb Gr 15 AI.

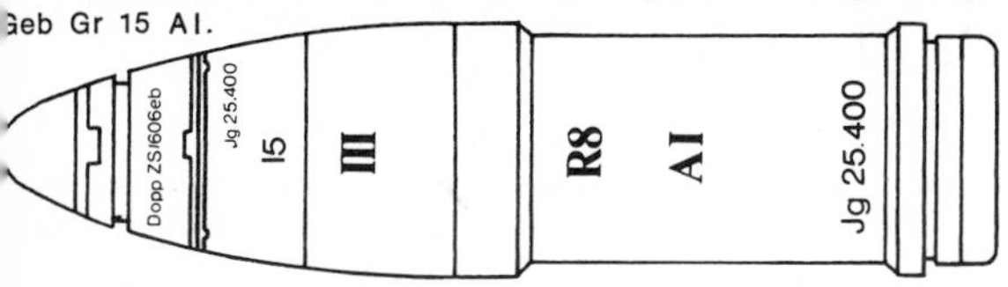

range 5400m/5905yd.
Charge 4: velocity 386mps/1266fps, maximum range 6625m/7245yd.

Ammunition
Separate-loading, cased charge.

Projectiles
Geb Gr 15: Fuzed AZ 23 Geb or Dopp Z S/60, weight.
The standard high explosive shell containing a bursting charge of 500g(17.63oz/1.10lb) of TNT; a smoke-box was included in the internal arrangements to assist observation. The shell was almost identical to the IG 18 shell except that the driving band was narrower.
Geb Gr 15 Al: fuzed AZ 23 Geb or Dopp Z S/60, weight not known.
Similar to the Geb Gr 15, this shell had aluminium powder mixed with the TNT filling in order to produce a flash to aid observation and also to give a more powerful blast effect.
Geb Gr 39: base fuzed, weight 4.50kg(9.92lb).
This was a hollow charge anti-tank shell almost identical to the I Gr 38.
Geb Gr 15 Rot:
Similar to the Geb Gr 15 and of the same weight, this differed in the design of driving band.

Propelling Charge
This consisted of four portions; charge 1 to 3 were the normal charges and charge 4 was the super charge. The normal units were contained in three bags in the cartridge case, the fourth being supplied separately.
Charge 1: 147gm/5.18oz Ngl Bl P.
Charge 2: 35gm/1.23oz Ngl Bl P.
Charge 3: 50gm/1.76oz Nigl Bl P.
Charge 4: 10gm/0.35oz Ngl Pl P plus 320gm/11.29oz Ngl R P.
A flash reducer, a silk bag containing 20gm(0.70oz) of potassium sulphate, was also provided. This was placed on top of the charge bags in the cartridge case when firing at night; the combustion of the potassium salt provided an excess of nitrogen in the propellant gases that effectively blanketed the emerging gases at the muzzle and prevented their combination with the atmospheric oxygen to produce a flash.

Primer
The percussion primer C/12nA was used.

Case Identification Number: 6335.

7·5cm Gebirgsgeschütz 36

7·5cm Geb G 36 (Grünewald)

Designed by Rheinmetall-Borsig AG, this weapon entered service in 1938. The split trail and rear trunnions allowed high elevation, and the recoil system was of the 'variable' type—automatically shortening the recoil as the elevation increased. Lightweight disc wheels with solid rubber tyres were usually fitted, though wood-spoked wheels were to be seen on some examples, and (to save weight) no shield was used. The gun had a perforated muzzlebrake and the breech-ring was unusually massive, since it incorporated a joint that allowed the ring to be separated from the gun barrel for transport. A spring balancing-press was fitted to the carriage to counter the muzzle preponderance owing to the rear trunnions. The whole equipment could be broken down into eight loads.

Although a sound design, the Geb G 36 suffered from lack of stability at low angles of elevation—the price of lightness in any gun. Charge 5 could only be fired when the angle of elevation exceeded 15°, for the gun otherwise jumped dangerously. At high elevation angles the recoil force was directed down but at low angles the force was more rearward, developing a turning moment about the trail spade that tended to lift the wheels from the ground. In spite of this defect the Geb G 36 appears to have been well-liked by its users and it remained in service throughout the war.

An unusual photograph showing a Geb G 36 without muzzle-brake.

Another view of the Geb G 36 in the Caucasian snows.

Data

Calibre: 75mm/2.95in.
Length of gun: 1450mm/57.09in.
Length of bore: 972mm/38.27in.
Rifling: 28 grooves, uniform right-hand twist, 1/24
Breech mechanism: horizontal sliding block, percussion fired.
Traverse: 40°.
Elevation: −2° to +70°.
Weight in action: 750kg/1654lb.

Performance

Firing high explosive shell 7.5cm Gr 34 A1, weight 5.75kg(12.68lb).
Charge 5: velocity 475mps/1558fps, maximum range 9150m/10006yd.

Ammunition

Separate-loading, cased charge.

Projectiles

7.5cm Gr 34 A1: fuzed Kl AZ 23, weight 5.75kg(12.68lb).
This was the standard high-explosive shell, filled with a 90/10 mixture of TNT and aluminium powder.
7.5cm Gr Rot A1: fuzed Dopp Z S/60, weight 5.83kg (12.86lb).
This shell, filled with a mixture of TNT and aluminium powder, was originally designed for the 7.5cm le FK 18, and so the driving band differed from the standard Gr 34 pattern. The shell was also slightly shorter than the standard type in order

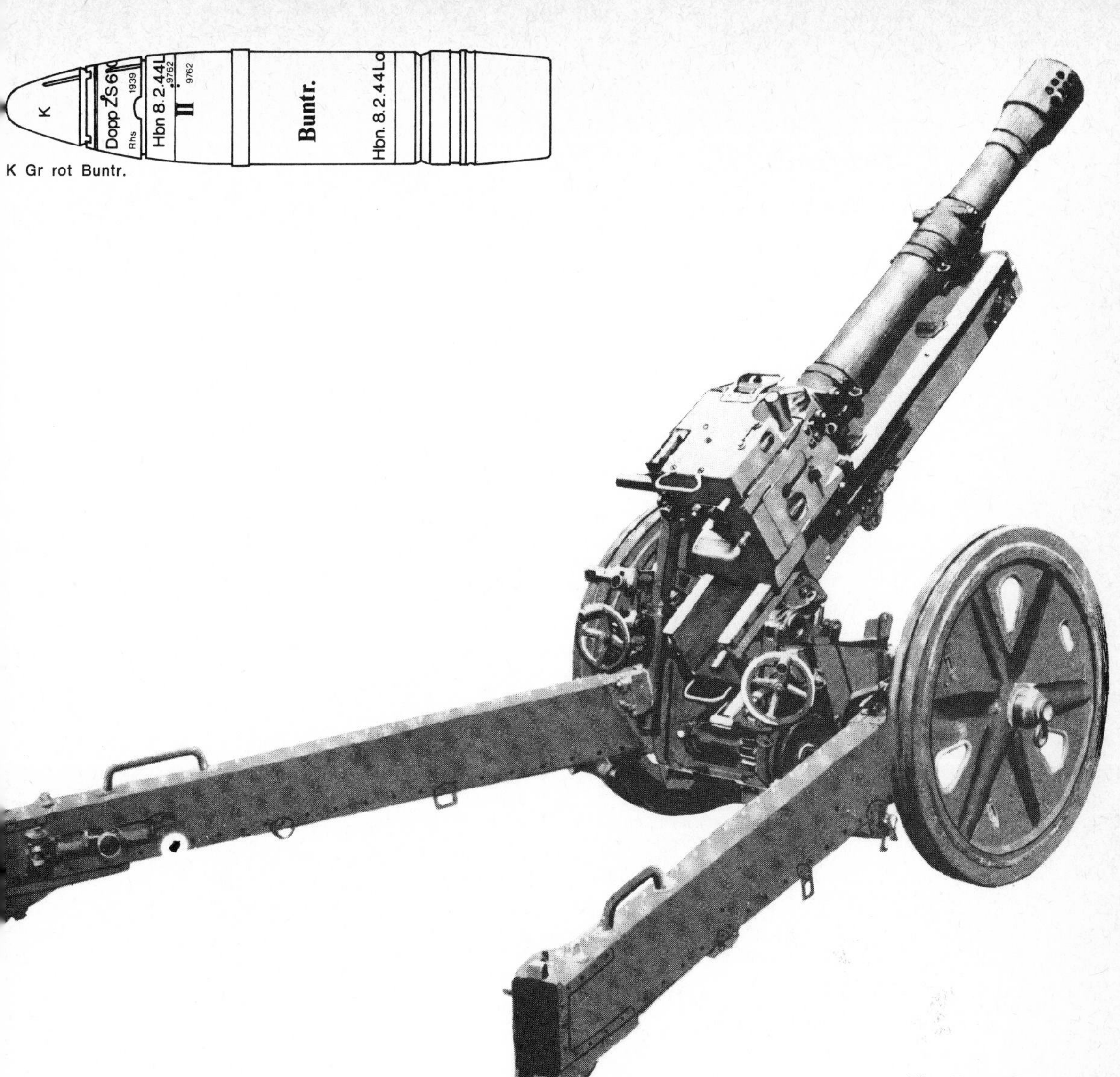

K Gr rot Buntr.

The 7.5cm Geb G 36.

to accommodate the time and percussion fuze within a given length.

7.5cm K Gr Buntrauch: fuzed Dopp Z S/60s, weight 5.83kg(12.86lb).

This was similar to the previous shell differing only in the addition of a dye mixture to the filling, which on detonation gave a coloured smoke cloud

7.5cm Gr 38: fuzed AZ 38, weight 4.40kg(9.70lb)

This, a hollow charge anti-tank shell, was issued as standard and fired only with charge 4—which gave to the projectile a muzzle velocity of 390mps(1280 fps) and an effective range of 1000m(1094yd). Note that this range was not the maximum distance to which the shell would travel but instead the maximum engagement range allowed by the graduations on the gunsight of the Geb G 36.

Propelling Charge

There were five charges, of which 1–4 were issued in the cartridge case; charge 5 was issued separately. On the occasions that charge 5 was used, the charge bag was inserted in the case in place of the discarded 1–4.

Charge 1: 123gm/4.34oz Digl R P.
Charge 2: 158gm/5.57oz Digl R P.
Charge 3: 200gm/7.05oz Digl R P.
Charge 4: 275gm/9.70oz Digl R P.
Charge 5: 530gm/18.69oz Digl R P plus 10gm/0.35oz NZ Man P.

Primer

The percussion primer C/22 was fitted to the case

Case Identification Number: 6359.

7·5cm Gebirgsgeschütz 43

7·5cm Geb G 43(Halensee)

In October 1940 the army requested a redesign of the Geb G 36 in order to improve the stability and do away with the firing restriction on Charge 5. The new equipment was also to be provided with spring suspension and to have a better system of dismantling for transportation; under the title Gebirgs Gerät 99, Rheinmetall-Borsig and the Austrian Böhler company were given development contracts. By 1942 the prototypes had been tested, the Rheinmetall design turned down and the Böhler type accepted. Four weapons were manufactured for field trials, but in 1943 the army decided that the demand for such a weapon no longer existed and that other weapons were in need of a higher production priority. Thus development of the Geb G 43 was stopped and no more weapons were ever made.

The design was a considerable improvement on the Geb G 36. The weight was considerably reduced, a firing pedestal was incorporated to give greater stability, and a muzzle brake (claimed to be 85% efficient) reduced the stresses on the carriage. The wheels were sprung by torsion bars and the legs of the split trail, perforated for lightness, were hinged in the middle to allow the gun to be towed with them either extended or folded. The towing agency could be either a truck or the NSU *Kettenrad* three-quarter-tracked motor cycle; horse-traction was also used on occasions. The whole equipment could alternatively be dismantled into seven loads for pack transport, the heaviest of which weighed 117.5kg(259lb). The weapon was stable in action at all elevations with all charges.

Data
Calibre: 75mm/2.95in.
Length of gun: 1630mm/64.17in.
Length of bore: 973mm/38.31in.
Rifling: 28 grooves, uniform right-hand twist, 1/30
Breech mechanism: horizontal sliding block, percussion fired.
Traverse: 40°.
Elevation: −5° to +70°.
Weight in action: 582kg/1283lb.

Performance
Firing high explosive shell.
Charge 5: velocity 480mps/1575fps, maximum range 9500m/10390yd.
Firing hollow charge shell.
Charge 5: velocity 500mps/1641fps, maximum range 1000m/1094yd owing to the gunsight graduations.

Ammunition
As Geb G 36.

10·5cm Gebirgshaubitze 40

10·5cm Geb H 40(Eberesche)

This remarkable equipment was the heaviest weapon ever developed for mountain use. It was produced by the Austrian firm of Böhler in response to an army development contract issued to both them and Rheinmetall. In the subsequent acceptance trials the latter's entry was turned down. The Böhler weapon was thereafter issued to troops from 1942.

Its appearance gives the impression of too much gun for too little carriage, but the ingenious design ensured stability and safety during firing. It could be towed as a complete equipment, broken into four loads on single-axle trailers to be towed by four NSU Kettenrad tracked motor-cycles, or completely broken into five pack-loads for transport on mule-back. The wheels were attached to the split-trail legs by spring suspension which, together with the independent wheel brakes, was built into each leg. As a result the wheels moved with the trail legs, and when the legs were opened adopted a characteristic 'toed-in' attitude. In common with the Böhler-designed Geb G 43, a firing pedestal was incorporated beneath the carriage to give stable three-point support when firing and to accommodate the weapon to any terrain. The wheels were of light alloy with solid tyres, and large detachable spades were fitted to ends of the trail legs.

Among the best mountain guns ever built, numbers of these weapons survived the war and were to be found in service with a number of European countries until the middle 1960s.

Data
Calibre: 105mm/4.13in.
Length of gun: 3439mm/135.40in/11.28ft.
Length of bore: 2870mm/113.00in/9.42ft.
Rifling: 32 grooves, increasing right-hand twist, 1/31.5 to 1/21.9.
Breech mechanism: horizontal sliding block, percussion fired.
Traverse: 51°.
Elevation: −5.5° to + 71°.
Weight in action: 1660kg/3660lb.

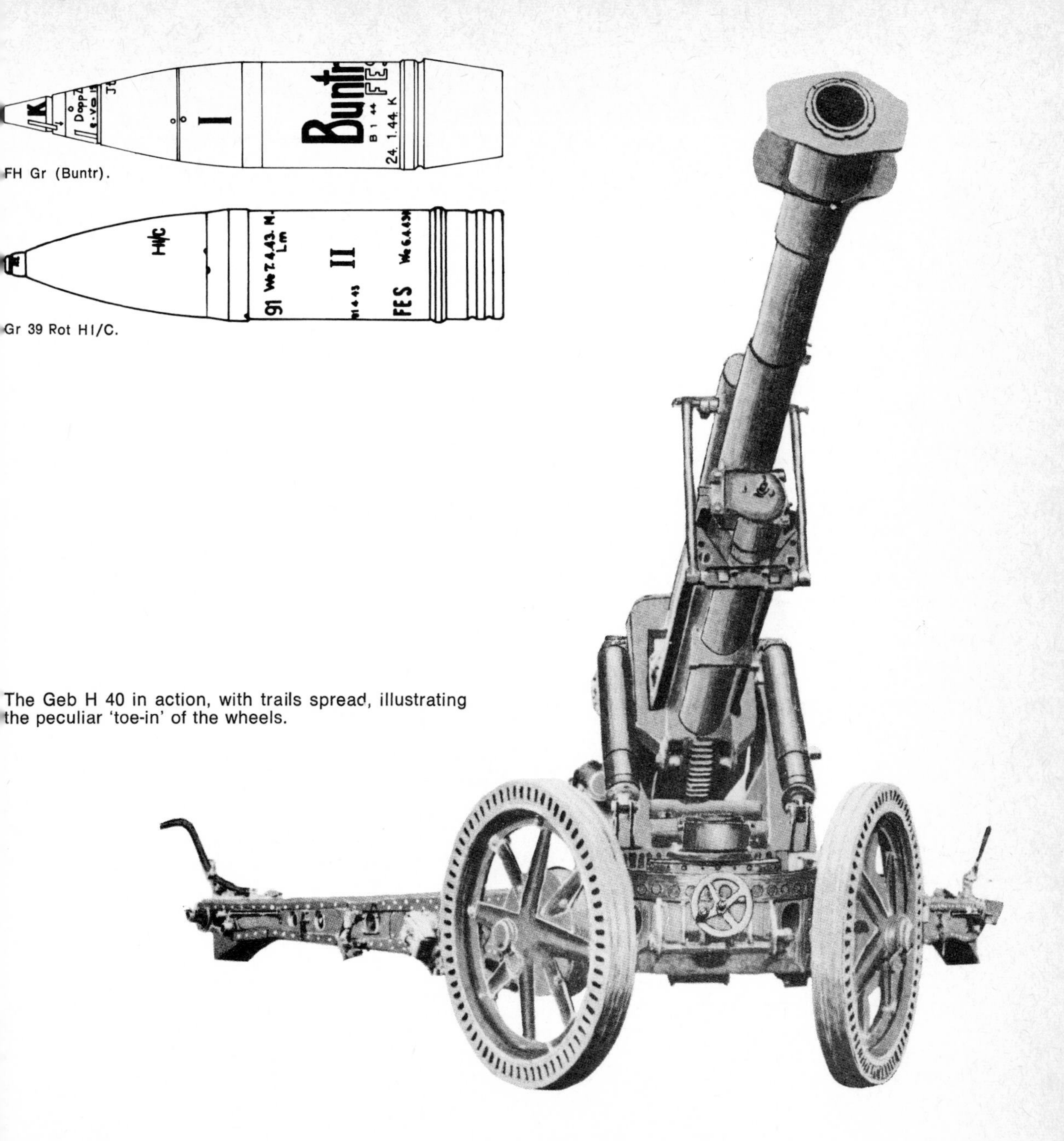

FH Gr (Buntr).

Gr 39 Rot HI/C.

The Geb H 40 in action, with trails spread, illustrating the peculiar 'toe-in' of the wheels.

Performance
Firing high explosive shell FH Gr A1, weight 14.50kg(31.97lb).
Charge 1: velocity 210mps/689fps, maximum range 3845m/4205yd.
Charge 2: velocity 225mps/738fps, maximum range 4470m/4888yd.
Charge 3: velocity 255mps/837fps, maximum range 5300m/5796yd.
Charge 4: velocity 285mps/935fps, maximum range 6540m/7152yd.
Charge 5: velocity 340mps/1116fps, maximum range 8000m/8749yd.
Charge 6: velocity 425mps/1394fps, maximum range 9670m/10575yd.
Charge 7: velocity 565mps/1854fps, maximum range 16740m/18302yd.
Firing hollow charge shell 10cm Gr 39
Charge 6: velocity 460mps/1509fps, maximum range 8000m/8749yd.
Firing star shell 10.5cm Leucht Geschoss
Charge 6: velocity 480mps/1575fps, maximum range 6900m/7546yd.
This gave an ejection height of 500m/1640ft for optimum illumination.

Ammunition
Separate-loading, cased charge.

Projectiles
FH Gr A1: fuzed AZ 23/45(umg 0.15), AZ 1(umg 0.15) or Dopp Z S/60, weight 14.52kg (32.02lb).
This was the standard high explosive shell.
FH Gr Buntrauch: fuzed Dopp Z S/60s, weight 14.80kg(32.63lb).
A coloured-indicating smoke shell.
10cm Gr 39 Rot Hl/A: fuzed AZ 38 or AZ 38 St, weight 12.25kg(27.01lb).
A hollow charge shell.
10cm Gr 39 Rot Hl/B: fuzed AZ 38 or AZ 38 St, weight 9.35kg(20.62lb).
A lightened pattern of hollow-charge shell differing from H1/A in its internal construction
10cm Gr 39 Rot Hl/C: fuzed AZ 38 or AZ 38 St, weight 12.30kg(27.12lb).
Another hollow charge shell in which alterations were made to its internal construction.
10.5cm Lt Ges: fuzed Dopp Z S/60s, weight 14.00kg(30.87lb).
This was a star shell; the Lt Ges in the designation represented Leucht Geschoss (literally 'light or flare shell').

Propelling Charge
The six basic charges were contained in silk-cloth bags contained in the cartridge case. The make-up of the ingredients was unusually complex, using an amalgam of two or three different propellants together with some flash-reducing salts. The seventh charge was a separate unit that replaced the other six when the need arose.
Charge 1: 20gm/0.71oz NZ Man P, 230gm/8.11oz. Digl Bl P, 10gm/0.35oz flash reducer.
Charge 2: 20gm/0.71oz NZ Man P, 267gm/9.42oz. Digl Bl P, 10gm/0.35oz flash reducer.
Charge 3: 20gm/0.71oz NZ Man P, 267gm/9.42oz. Digl Bl P, 55gm/1.94oz Gudol Bl P, 2 15gm/0.53oz flash reducer.
Charge 4: 20gm/0.71oz NZ Man P, 267gm/9.42oz. Digl Bl P, 155gm/5.47oz Gudol Bl P, 20gm/0.71oz flash reducer.
Charge 5: 20gm/0.71oz NZ Man P, 267gm/9.42oz. Digl Bl P, 310gm/10.93oz Gudol Bl P, 20gm/0.71oz flash reducer.
Charge 6: 20gm/0.71oz NZ Man P, 267gm/9.42oz. Digl Bl P, 610gm/21.51oz Gudol Bl P, 25gm/0.88oz flash reducer.
Charge 7: 20gm/0.71oz NZ Man P, 2060gm/72.65oz/4.54lb Digl Bl P, no flash reducer.

Primer
The percussion primer C/12nA or C/12nA St was used.

Case Identification Number: 6327: the case was usually of brass.

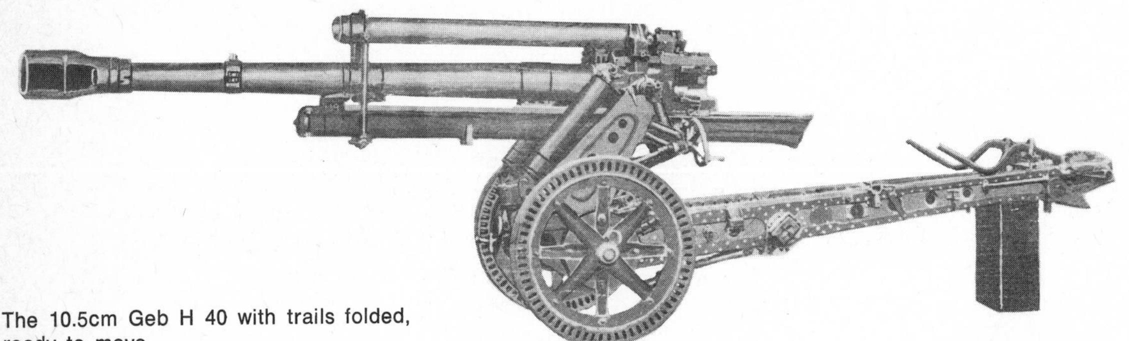
The 10.5cm Geb H 40 with trails folded, ready to move.

15cm Gebirgshaubitze

15cm Geb H

This equipment was never allotted a model number since it never entered service. It was being developed by Böhler at the war's end, having arisen out of a 1944 specification. In an attempt to extract the utmost performance consistent with low weight the gun was designed to make use of the high–low pressure system, the ballistics of which had been developed by Rheinmetall-Borsig for the 8cm PAW 600 anti-tank gun. This system is more fully explained elsewhere, but it can be summarised as containing the propelling charge in a strong chamber and then bleeding the gases into the barrel at a lower pressure. The 15cm Geb H was to fire seven charges in the normal way, but the eighth was to utilise the high-low system to give a velocity of 480mps(1575fps). The high pressure chamber was designed to operate at 2500kg/cm^2(35565lb/in^2, or approximately 16ton/in^2) bleeding to the low-pressure chamber to give a propulsion pressure of about 1800kg/cm^2 (25605lb/in^2, or 11.4ton/in^2).

No illustrations of this interesting weapon are now known to exist.

FIELD ARTILLERY

The German field artillery formed the organic support of the Division: it was the basic foundation of artillery support for the combat troops. The armament ranged from 7.5cm guns to 10.5cm guns and howitzers though, as already discussed, the chosen field calibre had swung from 7.7cm in 1914–18 to 10.5cm in the 1930s and in the 1940s was in the process of swinging back to 7.5cm. It was felt that the advantages in lightness and manöeuverability were of paramount importance, and that deficiencies in shell power could be largely overcome by more modern designs of ammunition than had been available for the old 7.7cm weapons. In spite of this opinion, work was continued on the development of a 10.5cm howitzer that would probably have been the best all-round field weapon of the war had it reached production. There were also a few 10.5cm guns in the field artillery, intended to provide long-range support for the 10.5cm howitzer, but their importance declined with improvements in the howitzer and there was a move away from guns of this calibre shortly after the war began—on the grounds that the size of weapon was not commensurate with the shell power and range attained. It was thought that better results could be obtained in larger calibres for the same weight of weapon.

During World War 2 the British Army coined the phrase *the Golf-Bag system* in relation to artillery, by which was meant the possession of a selection of weapons (varying in range, shell power and mobility) that could be used by the artillery commander to perform particular tasks—in the same way that a golfer selects a particular club from his bag to deal with a particular set of circumstances and replaces it when the stroke has been played. Although neither this phrase nor a statement of the philosophy has ever appeared in German documents, it appears likely that the principle was lurking in the minds of many German artillerymen and that—for such a reason—they were reluctant to commit themselves to one standard design.

Apart from this trend, the development of field artillery during the war years was systematic and uneventful: a simple progression of demands by the army followed by products from the gunmakers to the instructions of the OKH. The army started the war with a good field howitzer and had the sense to stick to it, gradually improving the weapon but without moving too far from the basic design. It was not until the events in Russia changed the basic requirements and priorities that a major redesign was even considered.

A useful addition to the arsenal of standard weapons was the provision of a number of French and Polish 10.5cm howitzers seized when the countries were overrun. The 10cm le FH 14/19(p) was the Polish wz/1933, a Skoda design of the late 1920s that had been improved in 1933 by lengthening the barrel and fitting a muzzle brake. The entire Polish stock was taken, a number of which were then given to the Italian army where they were known as the modello 100/22. Those in German hands remained in extensive use until the end of the war. The French 10.5cm gun-howitzer went into German service as the 10.5cm le FH 325(f) and large numbers were employed for the defence of the French coast: a deployment that not only put them to good use but also simplified the ammunition supply problem by concentrating them in one area. Smaller numbers of other captured weapons were also employed from time to time.

7·5cm Feldkanone 16 neuer Art

7·5cm FK 16 nA

This weapon dated back to World War 1, having originally seen the light of battle as the 7.7cm FK 16. Over 3000 of these Rheinische Metallwaren- und Maschinenfabrik (Rheinmetall)-designed guns were made during the years 1916–18 and they remained to form the basic divisional gun of the postwar Reichsheer. In the early 1930s the barrel was redesigned to the newly adopted standard calibre of 7.5cm, but the remainder of the equipment was unchanged. To indicate this modification the suffix 'nA' for *neuer Art* (or 'new pattern') was added to the nomenclature.

It was originally intended as a horse-drawn cavalry-accompanying gun, but this plan was watered-down and the weapon eventually found itself with any type of formation needing a light gun. It was frequently used with motorised traction.

From a design standpoint the weapon was a distinct relic of World War 1, and absolutely conventional. The straight box trail carried two wood-spoked metal-tyred wheels, and a further legacy of the FK 16nA's horse artillery origin was the provision of two gunners' seats alongside the barrel on the front of the shield—probably the only western gun in service during World War 2 to carry this anachronism. The large shield is a useful recognition feature, the upper section of which was bent sharply back.

One of these guns was used in 1941 at Hillersleben test range to perform the first firing trials with the Peenemünder Pfeilgeschoss. These early projectiles gave a maximum range of over 15000m (16405yd), an increase of some 30% compared with the normal maximum for the gun. It was this encouraging result that led to further development of the fin-stabilised Peenemünde design.

Gr 38 HI/B

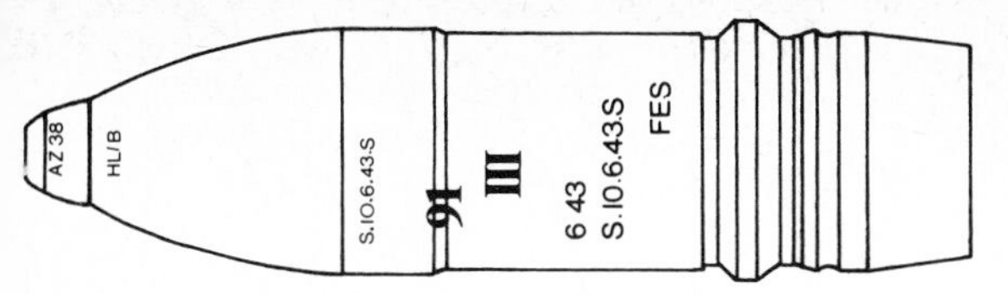

Data
Calibre: 75mm/2.95in.
Length of gun: 2700mm/106.30in.
Lentgh of bore: 2036mm/80.16in.
Rifling: right-hand increasing twist, 1/36 to 1/25.
Breech mechanism: horizontal sliding block, percussion fired.
Traverse: 4°.
Elevation: −9° to +44°.
Weight in action: 1524kg/3360lb.

Performance
Firing standard high explosive shell weighing 5.83kg(12.86lb).
Charge 1: velocity 290mps/950fps, maximum range 5975m/6535yd.
Charge 2: velocity 452mps/1483fps, maximum range 9350m/10225yd.
Charge 3: velocity 580mps/1903fps, maximum range 11300m/12360yd.
Charge 4: velocity 662mps/2172fps, maximum range 12300m/13450yd.
Firing hollow charge shell weighing 4.57kg(10.08lb).
Special charge: velocity 450mps/1476fps, maximum engagement range 1500m/1640yd.
Firing armour-piercing shell weighing 6.80kg/14.99 lb.
Special charge: velocity 630mps/2065fps, maximum engagement range 1500m/1640yd.

The 7.5cm FK 16nA, the re-vamped World War One field piece.

Below: The FK 16nA at firing practice.

Ammunition
Separate-loading, cased charge (except hollow charge and armour piercing shells which formed part of special fixed rounds with non-adjustable charges calculated to give optimum velocity).

Projectiles
7.5cm K Gr: fuzed AZ 23v(0.15) or Dupp Z S/60, weight 5.83kg(12.86lb).
This was the standard high explosive shell filled with 0.52kg(1.14lb) of TNT or amatol.
7.5cm K Gr rot: fuzed AZ 23v(0.15) or Dopp Z S/60, weight 6.62kg(14.60lb).
Similar to the previous shell, but a thicker-walled model designed for use with brass instead of light alloy fuzes and containing less high explosive—0.37kg(0.82lb). The thick walls and heavier fuzes led to increased weight, and this in turn altered the maximum ranges owing to the change in the shells' ballistic coefficient.
Charge 1: maximum range 5650m/6180yd.
Charge 2: maximum range 9225m/10090yd.
Charge 3: maximum range 11500m/12575yd.
Charge 4: maximum range 12875m/14080yd.
7.5cm K Gr rot FPS: fuzed AZ 23v(0.15) or Dopp Z S/60, weight 6.62kg(14.60lb).
This was exactly the same as the foregoing shell but was fitted with a bimetallic driving band instead of a copper one; the weight and the ballistics were the same.
7.5cm K Gr rot Pz: fuzed Bd Z f 7.5cm Pzgr, weight 6.80kg(14.99lb).
An armour piercing high explosive shell of conventional pattern.
7.5cm Gr 38 Hl/B: fuzed AZ 38 or AZ 38 St, weight 4.57kg(10.08lb).
A hollow charge anti-tank shell of the normal 'B' pattern.
7.5cm Gr 38 Hl/C: fuzed AZ 38 St, weight 5.00kg(11.03lb).
A later model of hollow charge shell incorporating minor improvements; for a description of the differences between the models A, B and C hollow charge shells, see *10.5cm le FH 18/40 ammunition*

Propelling Charges
The standard charge was made up of four sections, charges 1 to 4, in silk bags contained in the cartridge case. Charge 1 was slightly unusual in having a number of thin discs of propellant powder stitched to the base of the bag. When placed in the cartridge case these discs were above the primer and acted as an igniter.

Primer
The percussion primer C/12nA St was fitted.

Case Identification Number: 6343.

7·5cm leichte Feldkanone 18

7·5cm le FK 18

It was quickly appreciated that the FK 16 nA was not representative of contemporary design, and in 1930 both Krupp and Rheinische Metallwaren- und Maschinenfabrik (Rheinmetall) were approached with requests to develop a 7.5cm fieldgun of an improved pattern. Development was slow, since other weapons had higher priority, but the Krupp design was eventually accepted as the le FK 18 and issues began in 1938.

It was of lighter construction than the FK 16 nA (as might have been expected) and used a split trail, with the rear section and the spades capable of being folded for travelling. The spring suspension automatically locked out of action when the trail legs were opened, thus giving a stable carriage in action. The trunnions were well to the rear and two spring-operated balancing-presses were fitted. The recoil system was divided, the hydraulic buffer being contained in the cradle beneath the barrel and the hydropneumatic recuperator placed in a cylinder above it. This was an early application of a design that later became almost a German characteristic; the designers claimed this type of construction was a simpler engineering job, lowered the centre of gravity of the recoiling parts, and allowed the heat generated in the recuperator to be more easily dissipated.

All things considered, the FK 18 was a good and sound design in keeping with Krupp's usual standards. But it failed to improve on the FK 16 nA so far as range and velocity were concerned and, although it remained in service throughout the war, the FK 18 was only made in relatively small numbers. Another drawback was its unusual susceptibility to bore damage from cartridge débris, and standing orders for the weapon stressed the importance of inspecting the bore after every round to ensure that it was clear.

Data
Calibre: 75mm/2.95in.
Length of gun: 1940mm/76.38in.
Length of bore: 1660mm/65.35in.
Rifling: 28 grooves, right-hand increasing twist, 1/36 to 1/25.
Breech mechanism: horizontal sliding block, percussion fired.
Traverse: 30°.
Elevation: −5° to +45°.
Weight in action: 1120kg/2470lb.

Performance
Firing standard high explosive shell weighing 5.83kg(12.86lb).

The 7.5cm le FK 18, with the spades and rear end of the trail folded for travelling.

Kleine ladung: velocity 180mps/591fps, maximum range 2725m/2980yd.
Mittelere ladung: velocity 360mps/1181fps, maximum range 7375m/8065yd.
Grosse ladung: velocity 485mps/1591fps, maximum range 9425m/10307yd.

Ammunition
Separate-loading, cased-charge.

Projectiles
7.5cm K Gr rot KPS: fuzed AZ 23v(0.15) or Dopp Z S/60, weight 5.83kg(12.86lb).
The standard high explosive shell, with bimetallic driving band, containing 0.52kg(1.14lb) of TNT.
7.5cm K Gr rot Pz: fuzed Bd Z f 7.5cm Pzgr, weight 6.80kg(14.99lb).
An armour-piercing high explosive shell fitted with penetrating and ballistic caps and tracer; it was only fired with the Grosse Ladung to give 444mps(1457fps) velocity.
7.5cm Gr 39 H1: fuzed AZ 38, weight 4.83kg (10.65lb).
A hollow charge shell of the early 'A' pattern
7.5cm K Gr rot Nb: fuzed AZ 23 Nb, weight 6.20kg(13.67lb).
A screening smoke shell filled with the usual oleum/pumice mixture and a small explosive bursting charge.

Propelling Charge
This consisted of three bags contained in the cartridge case:
Bag 1: 84gm/2.96oz of Digl Pl P plus 10gm/0.35oz NZ Man P.
Bag 2: 270gm/9.52oz of Digl R P.
Bag 3: 225gm/7.93oz Digl R P.
The first bag was used by itself to give the Kleine Ladung, bags 1 and 2 were used for the Mittelere Ladung and all three constituted the Grosse Ladung.

Primer
The percussion primer C/12nA or C/12nA St was used.
Case Identification Number: 6316.

7·5cm Feldkanone 38

7·5cm FK 38

This, although more or less a logical refinement and improvement of the FK 18, was a private venture developed by Krupp to fill an order for the Brazilian Army. About 64 weapons had already been delivered when the war intervened and the balance of the contract, some 80 more, was completed and handed over to the German Army early in 1942.

The FK 38 was based on the same general design as the FK 18, but there were numerous improvements in detail. The barrel was longer and (as originally produced) had an unusual cylindrical muzzle brake with five rows of six slots. Later issues were fitted with a simpler four-port model of standard German type, probably no less efficient. Early examples of the FK 38 had wood-spoked wheels but these were later replaced by pressed-steel disc wheels with solid rubber tyres. Suspension was achieved by leaf springs. The breech mechanism was a semi-automatic modification of the original manual pattern and the ammunition was in the form of fixed rounds instead of the previous separate-loading type. The Brazilian field gun was a considerable improvement over the FK 18 and one is inclined to wonder why the German Army ever accepted the FK 18 in the first place if Krupp was capable of producing such an improved weapon for export.

The 7.5cm FK 38.

Data
Calibre: 75mm/2.95in.
Length of gun: 2550mm/100.39in.
Length of bore: 1914mm/75.35in.
Rifling: 28 grooves, right-hand increasing twist, 1/42 to 1/30.
Breech mechanism: horizontal semi-automatic sliding block, percussion fired.
Traverse: 50°.
Elevation: −5° to +45°.
Weight in action: 1366kg/3012lb.

Performance
Firing standard high explosive shell weighing 5.85kg(12.89lb).
1.06kg charge: velocity 605mps/1985fps, maximum range 11,500m/12.576yd.

Ammunition
Fixed rounds, cartridge case length 398mm (15.67in).

Projectiles
7.5cm K Gr Patr rot FK 38: fuzed AZ 23v(0.15) or Dopp Z S/60, projectile weight 5.85kg(12.90lb), complete round weight 8.30kg(18.30lb).
This was the standard high explosive shell, filled with block TNT: the propelling charge was 1.06kg (2.34lb) of Digl RP.
7.5cm Patr Sprgr L/4.8: fuzed AZ 23v(0.15), projectile weight 6.30kg(13.89lb), complete round weight 8.80kg(19.40lb).
This was an alternative design of high explosive shell; being slightly heavier it gave a muzzle velocity of 580mps(1903fps) and a maximum range of 11290m(12,347yd) using the same propelling charge as the previous round.
7.5cm Gr Patr Hl/B: fuzed AZ 38, projectile weight 4.55kg(10.03lb), complete round weight 6.60kg(14.55lb).
A hollow charge shell of the usual 'B' pattern, giving a muzzle velocity of 440mps(1444fps) and a maximum range of 7695m(8415yd); the shell was filled with a cyclonite/wax mixture and fired by a charge of 400gm(14.11oz) of Gudol B1 P.

Primer
The percussion primer C/12nA St was standard for all the rounds.
Case Identification Number: 6385.

7·5cm Feldkanone 7M85

7·5cm FK 7M85 (Wannsee)

This weapon was intended to be a light dual-purpose field/anti-tank gun and consisted of the gun, cradle and recoil system of the 7.5cm PAK 40 fitted into the carriage of the 10cm le FH 18/40. Some slight modifications had to be made to the carriage to allow all the pieces to fit together. This performance was something of a backward step, since the 10cm le FH 18/40 carriage had, in fact, started life as the 7.5cm PAK 40 carriage, and hence it was being modified to suit it once again to the original gun.

The object behind all this manoeuvering was a 1944 requirement to reinforce the field artillery with a number of dual-purpose weapons to improve their anti-tank capability, bearing in mind the contemporary difficulties of producing an entirely new design. The result of all the hammering and sawing was a weapon that amounted to an overweight 7.5cm anti-tank gun furnished with a greater range of ammunition and an additional 20° elevation.

The nomenclature '7M85' was the first example of a new system authorised in September 1944 and intended to be applied to all equipment thereafter entering service. The initial number (7) indicated the calibre group. The letter (M) signified the ammunition group ballistically suited to the weapon and to others of the same calibre that would also be similarly labelled. This letter was stamped on the gun breech-ring and into the base of all cartridges suited to the chamber dimensions. The final digits (85) were the last two digits of the weapon drawing number.

The projectiles for the weapon were all also labelled 'M' together with a four-digit number, the first three of which were the drawing number; the fourth digit indicated the type of projectile, according to the following code.

1: high explosive
2: hollow charge
3: armour piercing
4: high explosive high capacity
5: smoke
6: gas
7: incendiary
8: propaganda leaflet
9: practice
0: proof projectile

Owing to the late announcement of the system few guns were so classified, and no ammunition was ever discovered marked under it.

Data

Calibre: 75mm/2.95in.
Length of gun: 3700mm/145.67in/12.14ft.
Length of bore: 2471mm/97.28in.
Rifling: 32 grooves, right-hand increasing twist, 1/24 to 1/18.
Breech mechanism: horizontal sliding block, semi-automatic, percussion fired.
Traverse: 30°30′.
Elevation: −5° to +42°.
Weight in action: 1778kg/3920lb.

Performance

Firing standard high explosive shell weighing 5.40kg(11.91lb).
785gm charge: velocity 550mps/1805fps, maximum range 10275m/11237yd.

The 7.5cm FK 7M85, a hastily arranged marriage which turned out to be too heavy.

The 7M85 prepared for towing.

Ammunition
Fixed rounds, cartridge case length 690mm (27.17in).

Projectiles
7.5cm Spr gr Patr 34 Pak 40: fuzed KI AZ 23 or KI AZ 23 Nb Pr, projectile weight 5.40kg(11.91lb), complete round weight 9.20kg(20.29lb).
The standard high explosive shell, filled with amatol or TNT and with a smoke-box to indicate the strike of the shell; the propelling charge was 785gm(27.68oz/1.73lb) of Gudol B1 P.
7.5cm Pzgr Patr 39: fuzed Bd Z 5103, projectile weight 6.80kg(14.99lb), complete round weight 12.20kg(26.90lb).
An armour-piercing high explosive shell with a filling of 15gm(0.53oz) of RDX/Wax; the propelling charge was 2.75kg(606lb) of Digl RP.
7.5cm Patr 38 Hl/B: fuzed AZ 38, projectile weight 4.60kg(10.14lb), complete round weight 7.90kg(17.42lb).
This was a hollow charge shell of the usual 'B' pattern; the propelling charge was 490g(17.28oz/1.08lb) of Gudol B1 P.
7.5cm Patr 38 Hl/C: fuzed AZ 38, projectile weight 4.60kg(10.14lb), complete round weight 8.00kg(17.64lb).
This was an improved hollow charge shell; the propelling charge was 500gm(17.63oz/1.10lb) Gudol B1 P.
7.5cm Nbgr Patr: fuzed K1 AZ 23 Nb, projectile weight 6.45kg(14.22lb), complete round weight not known.
This, the standard type of bursting smoke shell, was filled with an oleum/pumice mixture.

Primer
The percussion primer C/12nA was used.

Case Identification Number: 6340.

7·5cm Feldkanone 7M59

7·5cm FK 7M59

This weapon was a further step on the road trodden by the 7M85, the production of a dual-purpose field/anti-tank weapon. The work involved in the production of this design was of the utmost simplicity, and the 7M59 field gun was no more than the 7.5cm PAK 40 anti-tank gun with the carriage modified to allow a maximum elevation of 35° (compared to 22° on the original gun). This increased the maximum range to 13300m (14545yd). The remainder of the weapon data—dimensions, performance, velocity and ammunition—are exactly the same as those of the original 7.5cm PAK 40, to which reference should be made. (See page 197.)

10·5cm leichte Feldhaubitze 16

10·5cm le FH 16

This was the army's original standard field howitzer. It was designed by Krupp during World War I to provide a 'partner piece' for the original 7.7cm FK 16, and the two weapons used the same carriage in accordance with the declared policy of the time.

While serviceable enough in its day, that day had passed by 1939 and the FH 16 was obsolescent at the outbreak of war—though numbers remained in reserve and training units.

Data
Calibre: 105mm/4.13in.
Length of gun: 2310mm/90.94in.
Length of bore: 1878mm/73.94in.
Rifling: 32 grooves, right-hand increasing twist, 1/45 to 1/18.
Breech mechanism: horizontal sliding block, percussion fired.
Traverse: 4°.
Elevation: −10° to +40°.
Weight in action: 1450kg/3197lb.

Performance
Firing standard high explosive shell weighing 14.81kg(32.66lb).
Charge 1: velocity 199mps/653fps, maximum range 3450m/3773yd.
Charge 2: velocity 233mps/764fps, maximum range 4550m/4976yd.
Charge 3: velocity 265mps/869fps, maximum range 5700m/6233yd.
Charge 4: velocity 320mps/1050fps, maximum range 7425m/8120yd.
Charge 5: velocity 395mps/1296fps, maximum range 9225m/10088yd.
Firing hollow charge shell weighing 12.30kg (27.78lb).
Charge 6: velocity 405mps/1329fps, engagement range 1500m/1640yd.
Actual maximum range attainable with this shell was 7600m(8311yd).

Ammunition
Separate-loading, cased charge.

Projectiles and Propelling Charges
The details for the le FH 16 were the same as those of the le FH 18, except that charge 6 was not used; reference should be made to the le FH 18 section for further details.

10·5cm leichte Feldhaubitze 18

10·5cm le FH 18 (Opladen)

This weapon was designed by Rheinische Metallwaren- und Maschinenfabrik (Rheinmetall) in 1929/30 and was brought into service in 1935 to replace the le FH 16: it soon became the standard field howitzer. Although improved models were developed from time to time, numbers of le FH 18 remained in service throughout the war and in postwar years could be found (together with the improved patterns) in the armies of such countries as Albania, Bulgaria and Hungary.

Of orthodox design, the le FH 18 had a good reputation as a reliable and stable weapon that was easy to handle. The carriage was of the split-trail pattern with folding spades, and had either wood-spoked or pressed-metal wheels. The recoil system followed the pattern of the 7.5cm FK 18 in which the buffer was contained in the cradle and the hydropneumatic recuperator was placed above the barrel. A single hydropneumatic balancing-press was fitted beneath the cradle to counterbalance the muzzle preponderance and thus lighten the gunlayers' task.

Data
Calibre: 105mm/4.13in.
Length of gun: 2941mm/115.78in.
Length of bore: 2612mm/102.83in.
Rifling: 32 grooves, right-hand increasing twist, 1/30 to 1/15.
Breech mechanism: horizontal sliding block, percussion fired.
Traverse: 56°.
Elevation: −6°30′ to +40°30′.
Weight in action: 1985kg/4377lb.

Performance
Firing standard high explosive shell weighing 14.81kg(32.66lb).
Charge 1: velocity 200mps/656fps, maximum range 3575m/3910yd.
Charge 2: velocity 232mps/761fps, maximum range 4625m/5058yd.
Charge 3: velocity 264mps/866fps, maximum range 5760m/6300yd.
Charge 4: velocity 317mps/1040fps, maximum range 7600m/8311yd.
Charge 5: velocity 391mps/1283fps, maximum range 9150m/10006yd.
Charge 6: velocity 470mps/1542fps, maximum range 10675m/11675yd.

Firing smoke shell weighing 14.00kg(30.87lb)
Charge 6: velocity 460mps/1509fps, maximum range 10600m/11592yd.
Firing coloured-smoke shell weighing 14.75kg (32.52lbs).
Charge 6: velocity 470mps/1542fps, maximum range 10400m/11373yd.
Firing hollow charge shells, models A, B or C
Charge 6: velocity 496mps/1627fps, engagement range 1500m/1640yd.

Ammunition
Separate-loading cased charge.

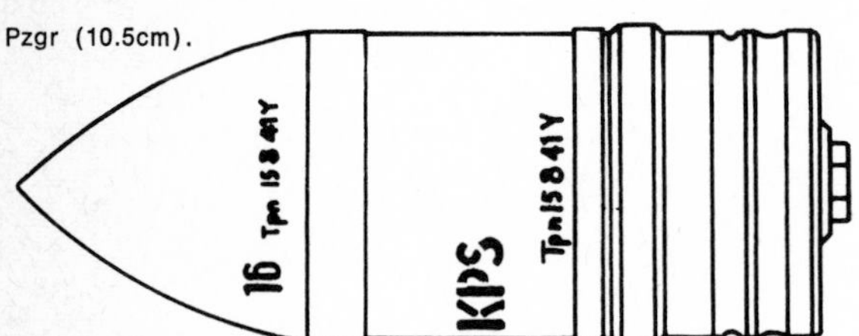

The 10.5cm le FH 18, the standard divisional artillery piece, in its original form.

Projectiles
FH Gr 38: fuzed AZ23v(0.25) or Dopp Z S/60, weight 14.81kg(32.66lb).
This, the standard high explosive shell, was filled with 1.38kg(3.04lb) of TNT. Four shells were covered by this designation, but they did not differ significantly from each other and had approximately the same dimensions, weight and ballistic qualities. They were designated FH Gr, FH Gr 38, FH Gr 38 St, and FH Gr 38 FES; the FH Gr 38 St was of cast-steel (the remainder being forged) and the FH Gr 38 FES had a sintered-iron driving band.
10cm Pzgr: fuzed Bd Z f 10cm Pzgr, weight 14.25kg(31.42lb).
This was the original anti-tank projectile. It had a relatively large filling of 650gm(22.92oz/1.43lb) of TNT and was fired with charge 5 to give a velocity of 395mps(1296fps); it was used to engage tanks at ranges not exceeding 1500m(1640yd)
10cm Pzgr rot: fuzed Bd Z f 10cm Pzgr, weight 15.71kg(34.64lb).
This was provided with penetrating and ballistic caps in order to improve its performance, and replaced the 10cm Pzgr in service. The filling was reduced to 400gm(14.11oz) of TNT. Like the previous shell it could only be fired with charge 5, giving a velocity of 390mps(1280fps). The penetration figures for this shell against homogeneous plates were as follows:
500m range: 0° impact 67mm/2.64in, 30° impact 56mm/2.20in.
1000m range: 0° impact 62mm/2.44in, 30° impact 52mm/2.05in.
1500m range: 0° impact 59mm/2.32in, 30° impact 49mm/1.93in.
10.5cm Gr 39 Hl: fuzed AZ 38, weight 11.75kg (25.91lb).
This was the original hollow charge shell; few were used since it was soon replaced by the improved model H1/A. It was filled with 1.78kg (3.92lb) of cyclonite/TNT/wax, and was restricted to being fired only with charge 5.
10.5cm Gr 39 rot Hl/A: fuzed AZ 38, weight 12.30kg(27.12lb).

An improved model of hollow charge shell, filled with 2.12kg(4.67lb) of cyclonite/TNT/wax; it, like the subsequent models, could be fired with either charge 5 or charge 6. It was a considerable improvement over the early model and was capable of penetrating 100m(3.94in) of plate at normal or 70mm(2.76in) at 30° striking angle.

10.5cm Gr 39 rot Hl/B: fuzed AZ 38, weight 12.25kg(27.01lb).

A further improvement in design, filled with 1.70kg(3.75lb) of cyclonite/TNT/wax. The driving band was either bimetallic or wrought iron. The B-type shell had a similar performance to the A model but achieved it with less explosive.

10.5cm Gr 39 rot Hl/C: fuzed AZ 38, weight 12.35kg(27.23lb).

The final model, which resembled the B, had small internal changes (see below) and the filling altered to cyclonite/wax. The driving band was of sintered-iron. In spite of the improvements the penetration was about the same.

Note on Hollow Charge Shells

All German hollow charge shells were constructed to standard patterns and the differences, introduced at various times for different weapons, were categorised by the suffix A, B or C (although not all weapons were provided with examples of each model). The differences between models were as follows:

The hollow charge shell types used with the le FH 18:

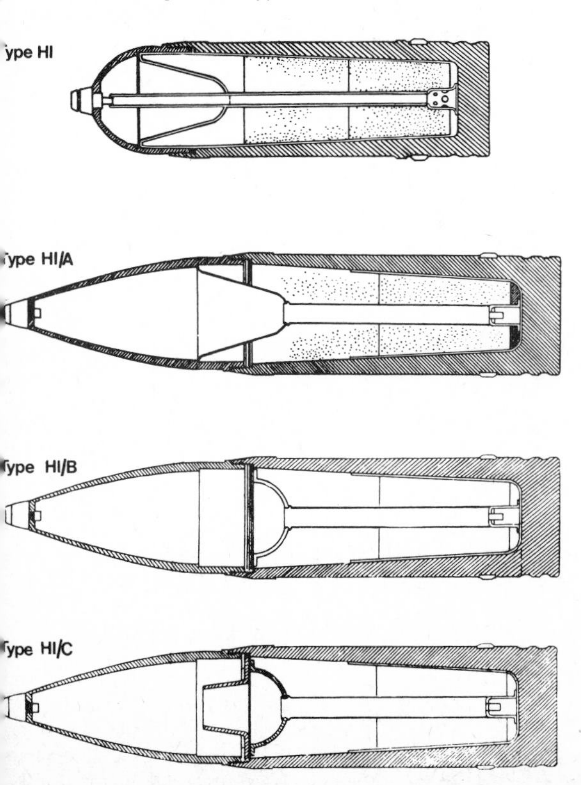

Model Hl. This had a deep conical cavity, a short ogive and a flash tube extending from the base of the fuze through the shaped charge liner to an exploder unit in the base of the filling. The filling was generally in three pre-pressed blocks.

Model Hl/A. This had the same shape of liner cavity but had a wider flash tube, crimped to the liner, that did not extend beyond the liner apex. The shell had a long ogive and was developed in an attempt to give greater stand-off to the charge —and also to prevent interference with the formation of the hollow charge jet by the front portion of the flash tube. The filling was in two pre-pressed blocks and did not extend completely to the rim of the shaped charge liner.

Model Hl/B. This was externally the same as H1/A but the liner was a shallow hemisphere, and the two-block filling extended to the rim of the liner. This was introduced in an attempt to provide a thicker jet that would be more resistant to spin effect. The rear portion of the shell body was lined with a form of glass wool or ceramic material in an endeavour to reflect the explosive force forward into the jet, rather than to allow it to simply fragment the shell body.

Model Hl/C. Again outwardly identical, the only change was the addition of an inverted funnel-shaped washer in front of the liner: a further attempt to counter the effects on the jet of centrifugal force.

10cm FH Gr Nb: fuzed K1 AZ 23 Nb, weight 14.00kg(30.87lb).

The original issue smoke shell, filled with 1.87kg (4.12lb) of the standard oluem/pumice mixture to give a smoke cloud some 25-30ft(82-98ft) in diameter on bursting.

10cm FH Gr 38 Nb: fuzed K1 AZ 23 Nb, weight 14.70kg(32.41lb).

This replaced the foregoing shell; owing to a larger filling it gave a somewhat improved smoke cloud.

10cm FH Gr 40 Nb: fuzed Dopp Z S/60, weight 14.75kg(32.52lb).

A base ejection smoke shell containing a single canister; this type was less common than the bursting variety.

10.5cm Gr 40 Deut: fuzed Dopp Z S/60, weight 14.75kg(32.52lb).

This was on similar lines to the above shell, the only difference being that the smoke composition in the canister was a sugar and dye mixture that, when ignited, emitted a coloured smoke plume for some two minutes. The Gr 40 Deut was used as an indicator shell to mark targets for air strikes, to delineate boundaries in attacks and similar tasks; the smoke cloud was coloured blue.

10cm Spr gr Br: fuzed AZ 23v(0.15), weight 15.90kg(35.06lb).

An explosive/incendiary shell, the TNT filling was mixed with an incendiary composition; the velocity with charge 6 was 462mps(1516fps) and the maximum range was 10700m(11700yd).

10cm Weiss-Rot Geschoss: fuzed Dopp Z S/60fl or Czech M23(t), weight 12.90kg(28.44lb).
A propaganda shell, taking its name from its colouring—a red body and a white ogive. The ogive was filled with a shaped wooden block carrying a gunpowder ejection charge, thus leaving a cylindrical space in the body of the shell. Into this was fitted two semi-circular plates forming a split hollow tube that acted as a strut between the underside of the wooden block and the top surface of the shell's baseplate. The payload of propaganda leaflets was rolled and inserted in the split tube, whereafter the baseplate was fitted in place and pinned. When the fuze ignited the gunpowder charge the wooden block was driven down, pushing on the split tube (and hence on the baseplate) but without exerting any pressure on the leaflets. The baseplate retaining pins sheared and the baseplate, tube and leaflets were then ejected. The baseplate, the split tube halves and the wooden block fell away, allowing the leaflets to disperse in the air and float to the ground. Fired with charges 4 and 6 only, the maximum muzzle velocity was 495mps(1624fps) and the maximum range was 9000m(9842yd). The optimum height of burst to obtain best leaflet distribution was 200m(656ft), which spread the leaflets evenly across a 150m(492ft) square.

The German Army was the only one to develop and manufacture a special leaflet shell; the British and US armies converted their base ejection smoke shells in the field by removing the canisters and replacing them with leaflets. Since there was no equivalent of the German split tube in these conversions, the ejection force was transmitted to the shell baseplate by the roll of leaflets: thus they were usually crumpled, they often jammed and failed to eject, and they were usually scorched or burned by the ejection charge into the bargain.

10.5cm FH Gr 39 Grünring 3 ZB: fuzed K1 AZ 23Nb, weight 15.00kg(33.08lb).
This, a gas shell, was never used in action though extensive stocks were held. The shell was of the double-diaphragm type, in which the head and body (two separate units) were screwed together with their endplates forming a double metal diaphragm between them. The head section contained the explosive bursting charge of 264gr(9.31oz) of cyclonite/TNT, while the body section contained the gas filling—1.60kg(3.53lb) of the nerve gas Tabun. The shells were marked with a green ring to match their name ('Grünring'), the standard indication for an anti-respiratory lethal gas, using a colour code system developed during World War 1. There was also a band of yellow detector paint on the outside of the shell across the joint between the two sections. This method of shell construction allowed the chemical filling to be inserted in the body in a special filling plant under extreme precautions, while the head was loaded with explosive in a normal ammunition filling factory. The units were then brought together and assembled at any convenient location. This method, originally developed in Britain for gas shell manufacture during World War 1, avoided the double hazard of having both explosives and poison-gas filling operations in the same factory.

10.5cm FH Gr 40 Blauring 3: fuzed Dopp Z S/60, weight 15.20kg(31.52lb).
This was an alternative gas shell of the base ejection type, very similar in design to the coloured smoke shell FH Gr 40 Deut, but having the canister filled as a toxic smoke generator which produced DM gas when ignited. The shell was marked with a broken blue ring and the word BLAURING was stencilled on the body.

10.5cm FH Gr 40 Weissring: fuzed AZ 23v(0.25), weight 14.50kg(31.97lb).
The third gas shell provided for the 10.5cm weapons, this was a simple bursting type based on the high explosive shell. The filling was a cardboard container loaded with a mixture of high explosive and CN gas composition. When the explosive was detonated it shattered the shell and dispersed the CN as a fine powder that acted as a nose and throat irritant and as a lachrymator. The shell marking was a white ring.

10.5cm Leuchtgeschoss: fuzed Dopp Z S/60, weight 14.00kg(30.87lb).
An illuminating shell, fired with charge 6 only to give a velocity of 480mps(1575fps) and a maximum range of 7800m(8530yd), at which range optimum length of illumination was obtained at a burst height of 500m(1640ft), the star burning for 25–30 sec while descending under a parachute.

FH Gr 35(f): various fuzes, weight 15.70kg(34.62lb).
This was a French high explosive shell, large stocks of which were captured in 1940. It was found suitable for use with the le FH 18 except with charge 6, and so it was issued as long as stocks lasted. The fuzes were a variety of French percussion types of different models and marks, which accounted for the weight approximation. Fired with charge 5 the FH Gr 35(f) attained an average velocity of 372mps(1221fps) and a maximum range of 9000m(9842yd).

Propelling Charge
The charge for the le FH 18 was of the separate-loading type and was in six parts; charges 1 to 5 were contained in silk-cloth bags in the short cartridge case, while charge 6 was supplied separately and replaced portions 1–5 when necessary (the others were emptied out of the case and the charge 6 unit placed inside). The composition of the charges was as follows:
Charge 1: 180gm/6.35oz Ngl Bl P, or 241gm/8.50oz Digl Bl P.
Charge 2: 55gm/1.94oz Ngl Bl P, or 59gm/2.08oz Digl Bl P.
Charge 3: 60gm/2.12oz Ngl Bl P, or 70gm/2.47oz Digl Bl P.
Charge 4: 115gm/4.06oz Ngl Bl P, or 118gm/4.16oz Digl Bl P.

Charge 5: 185gm/6.52oz Ngl Bl P, or 192gm/6.77oz Digl Bl P.
Charge 6: 784gm/27.65oz/1.73lb Ngl Bl P, plus 200gm/7.05oz Digl Bl P as an igniter.

Primer
The percussion primer C/12nA was standard, although C/12nA St was used as an alternative.

Case Identification Number: 6342.
The cartridge case, which was 155mm(6.10in) long, exhibited more variations and changes than that of any other German weapon—reflecting the vast numbers that must have been made and fired. Originally made of drawn brass, later variations were legion: brass-coated drawn-steel, varnished drawn-steel; galvanised drawn-steel, a tubular steel body welded to a steel base, a seamed steel body connected to a steel base by a washer and nut, a spirally-wrapped steel body attached to a steel base by a nut, and a seamed body and fabricated base held together by nuts and bolts or by screws. All could be identified by the code number 6342 stamped into the base, the variations having suffixes added to the basic number. Appendix 2 gives full details.

The FH 18 cartridge case, being readily available from production, was often used in experimental weapons and also formed the service case for one or two weapons that entered service late in the war.

10·5cm leichte Feldhaubitze 18 (Mündungsbremse)

10·5cm le FH 18M (Opladen)

While the le FH 18 was a satisfactory weapon in most respects, even its most enthusiastic supporter would have admitted that it fell short of the opposition in the matter of maximum range. The standard British fieldgun, the 25-pounder, ranged to 12253m(13400yd) and the standard Soviet divisional gun, the 76.2mm M1939, ranged to 13259m(14500 yd). Admittedly neither fired so heavy a shell, but this was not sufficient argument to offset the le FH 18's maximum range of 10675m(11675yd) In 1940, it was accordingly decided to improve the gun's performance by fitting a muzzlebrake and adjusting the recoil system, to allow the use of a more powerful charge and a new long-range shell. The recoil buffer valves were changed and the air pressure in the recuperator was increased. The original muzzlebrake was a single-baffle pattern of relatively low efficiency; it was later improved by welding two protruding ears to the rear of the port, but in due course this type of brake was found to give trouble when early designs of fin-stabilised and discarding-sabot ammunition were tried. The fins and sabot discards tended to foul the ports, so a more complex cage-type brake was fitted.

The 10.5cm le FH 18M at anti-tank practice on a range in Tunisia, 1942.

Data
Length of gun: 3308mm/130.24in/10.85ft.
(remainder of data the same as the le FH 18).

Performance
As the le FH 18, plus firing long-range projectile with special charge.
Special charge: velocity 540mps/1772fps, maximum range 12325m/13479yd.

Ammunition
As the le FH 18 but with the following additions.

Projectiles
FH Gr Fern: fuzed AZ 23v(0.25) or Dopp Z S/60, weight 14.25kg(31.42lb).
This was the special long-range shell, about 25mm(1in) longer than the standard FH Gr and with a shorter streamlined section behind the driving band; it was filled with 2.10kg(4.63lb) amatol or TNT.

Propelling Charges
The special charge was a bag containing 1.77kg(3.90lb) of Digl R P. It fitted into the standard cartridge case, after the normal charges 1 to 5 had been emptied out, and extended about 50mm(2in) beyond the mouth (it was this extra charge-length that accounted for the shell having a shorter portion behind the driving band).

Primer
The standard percussion primer C/12nA was fitted.

Case Identification Number: 6342.
Since there was a somewhat larger pressure generated by the special charge—2490kg/cm²(35400 lb/in² or 15.8ton/in²) compared with 2360kg/cm² 33600lb/in² or 15.0ton/in²)—seamed or wrapped cases were never used. Hence the drawn-steel case 6342 St was normally supplied with the charge in case only fabricated cases were available at the gun.

10·5cm leichte Feldhaubitze 18/40

10·5cm le FH 18/40 (Drachenfels)

The next demand made in connexion with the standard field piece was for the weight to be reduced without impairing the performance: a familiar cry. The demand was raised in March 1942, together with the other familiar requests that it should be ready as soon as possible and that it must be capable of rapid production. The requirement was met simply enough by taking the carriage of the 7.5cm PAK 40 anti-tank gun (which was in volume production), making a few modifications, and assembling the barrel and recoil system of the le FH 18M on top of it.

The modifications incorporated in the 'new' design included the use of torsion bars running the full width of the carriage to suspend the wheels. This springing was highly satisfactory when travelling and, of course, was automatically locked out of action when the trial legs were opened. The elevating and traversing handwheels, both of which were on the same side of the carriage in as was customary with anti-tank guns, meant a slight change in the sighting and gunlaying arrangements, and finally the muzzle brake had its efficiency improved by welding projecting flanges to the original single-port 18M design (thus deflecting a greater amount of gas). As with the 18M these brakes were later replaced by a cage pattern to permit the firing of sub-calibre ammunition.

The wheels originally used, when the carriage bore the PAK 40, were too small for use in the field howitzer role since they positioned the breech too close to the ground to allow full recoil at high elevations; larger diameter pressed-steel wheels with solid rubber tyres were thus fitted.

The ordnance was slightly changed from that of the le FH 18M, but the performance was the same.

Data
Calibre: 105mm/4.13in.
Length of gun: 2940mm/115.75in.
Length of bore: 2710mm/106.69in.
Rifling: 32 grooves, right-hand increasing twist, 1/18 to 1/12.
Breech mechanism: horizontal sliding block, percussion fired.
Traverse: 56°.
Elevation: −6° to +40°.
Weight in action: 1955kg/4311lb.

Performance
As the le FH 18M.

Ammunition
As the le FH 18M, including the long-range shell, plus a number of projectiles later developed for the 18 range but principally used by the 18/40 and subsequent models.

Projectiles
10.5cm Sprgr 43 Pg: fuzed AZ 23 or Dopp Z S/60, weight 13.48kg(29.72lb).
Introduced in 1944, this was a new type of cast-steel shell filled with high explosive. The steel was cast in the 'pearlitic' condition (Pg or Perlitgussstahl) which, it was hoped, would give an optimum balance between weight, economy and lethality. The war ended too soon for any valid conclusions to be reached about the effectiveness of this material.

The 10.5cm le FH 18/40: this specimen is in a museum collection and has had the muzzle-brake removed.

0.5cm FH Gr Kh: fuzed AZ 23, weight 4.64kg(32.28lb).
'his was the body of the FH Gr 38 Nb smoke hell filled with high explosive. It retained the entral tube of the smoke shell, but contained no moke composition for assisting observation. It vas an extemporary measure to use up an excess f smoke shell body production, and relatively few aw service.
0.5cm Sprgr 42 TS: weight on loading 11.00kg 24.26lb), weight on shot ejection 9.40kg(20.73lb)
'his was a discarding sabot high explosive shell, ith support rings at the base and shoulder. The asic sub-projectile was a reworked 8.8cm high xplosive shell. Unfortunately no performance gures are available.
0.5cm Pzgr 39 TS: weight on shot ejection 7.75kg(17.09lb).
This was the 8.8cm Pzgr 39 armour-piercing shell carried in a 10.5cm sabot device consisting of centering rings at the base and at the shoulder. It was claimed that at a muzzle velocity of 765mps(2510fps) it could penetrate 91mm(3.58in) of plate at 500m(547yd) range and 80mm(3.15in) at 1000m(1094yd).
10.5cm Mi Gr: weight 28.00kg(61.74lb).
This Minengranate projectile had not completed its trials by the end of the war. It was an extra-long shell with a freely-spinning sealing band and four jack-knife fins that sprang out in flight to stabilise the shell. It was estimated that with a special propelling charge the muzzle velocity would have been 270mps(886fps) and the maximum range 5200m(5687yd).

0·5cm leichte Feldhaubitze 18/39

)·5cm le FH 18/39

ıst before the war Friedrich Krupp AG had ıpplied a number of 10.5cm howitzers to the utch Army. Their general dimensions were close those of the le FH 18 but the ammunition was ıt interchangeable. After the occupation of Holnd, about 80 of these weapons were taken by the German Army and stripped of their ordnance in favour of surplus le FH 18M barrels. They were then taken into service as the le FH 18/39, and were ballistically identical to the le FH 18M. The carriage had 60° traverse, elevated from −5° to +45°, and the gun weighed 1950kg(4300lb) in action.

10·5cm leichte Feldhaubitze 18/42

10·5cm le FH 18/42

This appears to have been Krupp's design in answer to the demand that led to the FH 18/40. The barrel was lengthened, a cage muzzlebrake was fitted, and the carriage was a lightened version of the le FH 18 design. Although the gun's performance was a slight improvement on that of the 18M, the equipment was too heavy and the carriage design was not so simple a manufacturing proposition as the one selected for the FH 18/40. In view of these disadvantages the le FH 18/42 was turned down for service.

Data
Calibre: 105mm/4.13in.
Length of gun: 3255mm/128.15in/10.68ft.
Length of bore: not known.
Rifling: 32 grooves, right-hand increased twist, 1/30 to 1/20.
Breech mechanism: horizontal sliding block, percussion fired.
Traverse: 60°.
Elevation: −5° to +45°.
Weight in action: 2035kg/4487lb.

Performance
Firing the same projectile and charges as the le FH 18M.
Charge 6: velocity 585mps/1919fps, maximum range 12700m/13889yd.

Ammunition, Projectiles, Propelling Charges
As the le FH 18 and le FH 18M.

10·5cm leichte Feldhaubitze 42

10·5cm le FH 42

This was intended as a further step along the road of improvement and was to replace the 18, 18M and 18/40 field howitzers. The ordnance was the same as the le FH 18/40 and the carriage was a robust split-trail design with tubular trail legs and folding spades. The track was wider and the silhouette was made lower to aid concealment. The recoil system was redesigned to place both the buffer and the recuperator in the cradle, and torsion bar suspension was used.

In spite of being a sound design the le FH 42 was not accepted for service because events had overtaken its specification. The war in Russia had shown that certain features were vital to all new designs, since field artillery frequently found themselves called on to fight tanks at close range, and —in the forests of Russia—the ability to fire at high angles of elevation (over 45°) was needed. Because of this and other factors, the army had already issued a revised specification that became

The 10.5cm le FH 42, one of the handful made

the le FH 43 and work on the le FH 42 was cancelled in the expectation that the le FH 43 would fulfil its promise: a classical example of the best being the enemy of the good.

Data
Calibre: 105mm/4.13in.
Length of gun: 2940mm/115.74in.
Length of bore: not known.
Rifling: not known.
Breech mechanism: horizontal sliding block, electrically fired.
Traverse: 70°.
Elevation: −5° to +45°.
Weight in action: 1630kg/3594lb.

Performance
Firing the standard shell weighing 14.81kg(32.66lb)
Charge 6: velocity 595mps/1952fps, maximum range 13000m/14217yd.

Ammunition, Projectiles, Propelling Charges
As for the le FH 18M and 18/40, but note that the firing system of the le FH 42 was electric—which meant that the cartridges would have had to be special to the gun and that they would only be interchangeable with the other models if they were reprimed.

10·5cm leichte Feldhaubitze 43

10·5cm le FH 43

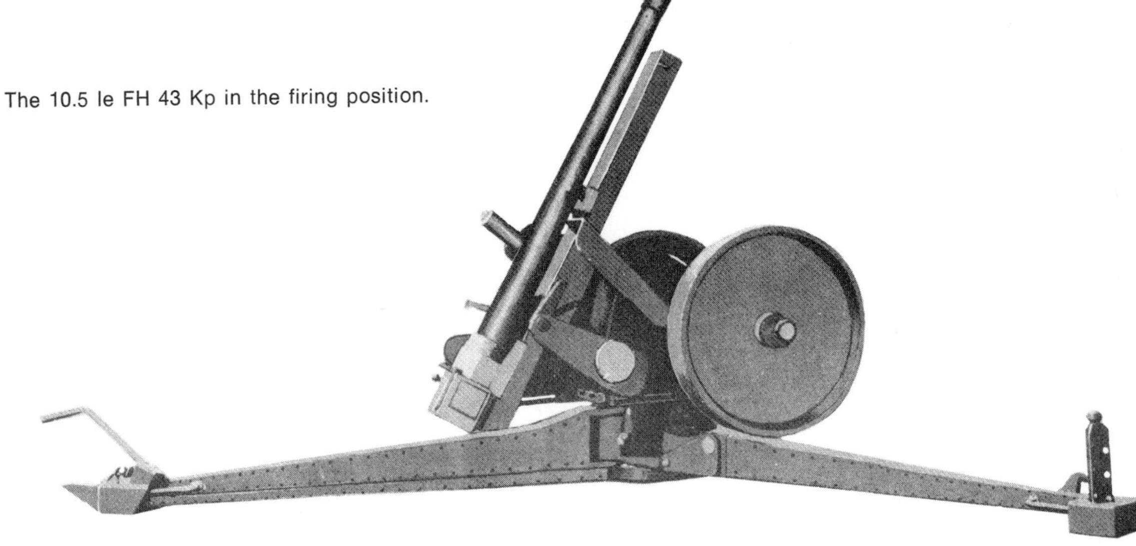

The 10.5 le FH 43 Kp in the firing position.

The Russian campaign led the army to reconsider their field artillery and to devise a fresh set of priorities for future specifications. Inevitably they demanded an improvement in performance, but then made life more difficult by specifying that the weapons had to be capable of covering their fighting ranges at high angles of elevation. In other words, the zone of fire covered by elevating the gun from 0° to 45° had also to be covered by continuing elevation past 45°. As this was done the range shortened once more, so that any given range had two elevations that would reach it—one in the low angle sector and one in the high angle sector. This requirement arose from the necessity to conceal weapons and to deploy them in forests, where they were required to fire up through the trees.

The next requirement was for a range of at least 13000m(14217yd) without resorting to special ammunition. The weapon also had to have all-round traverse—a feature greatly appreciated in positions where artillery was defending a pocket against attack from any and all directions. Finally it had to weigh no more than the standard le FH 18/40 and to be equally manoeuvrable.

This was a formidable specification, and one can hardly blame Rheinmetall-Borsig for declining to compete. However, Krupp and Skoda both produced weapon designs to suit, all of which were known as le FH 43. Their solutions, based on a common ballistic specification, were ingenious and would have doubtless reached production had time allowed, but the work began too late and the war ended before any of the designs progressed from the development stage.

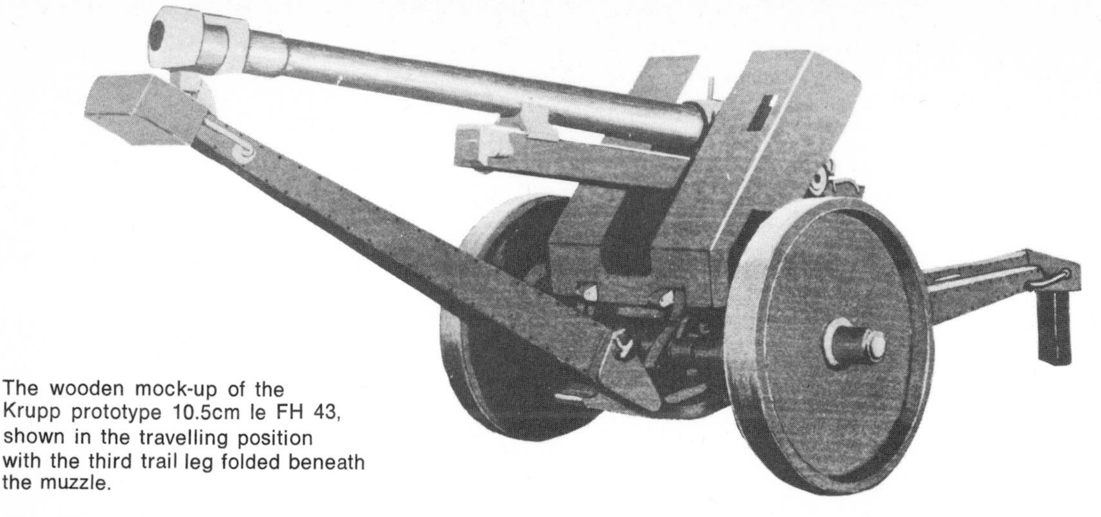

The wooden mock-up of the Krupp prototype 10.5cm le FH 43, shown in the travelling position with the third trail leg folded beneath the muzzle.

The Skoda Design

This was a complete departure from any previous service design, although it bore some resemblance to one or two prewar designs that had been put forward in various places (notably one for the British 25pdr); none, however, had been accepted. It is doubtful if the Skoda designers knew of these previous attempts and the fact that their work so resembled them can be attributed to the simple truism that good designers, given a set of specifications, frequently arrive at similar conclusions independently of one another.

The ordnance itself was little changed from the le FH 18/40 except that the barrel was slightly longer and that the chamber capacity was increased to enable a more powerful cartridge to be used. A muzzle brake of similar pattern to that used on the 18/40 was also fitted.

The carriage was the revolutionary part of the design. Basically it consisted of a normal split-trail two-wheel carriage to which a firing pedestal and two more trail legs—all forward of the axle—were added. The extra legs were beneath the gun barrel, to which they were clamped while travelling. When the gun went into action, the firing pedestal was dropped from its folded position between the two front trail legs and locked in place. The four trail legs were unlocked and swung out to form four equi-spaced outriggers for the pedestal, and the wheels were then swung clear of the ground. Earth pickets were driven through holes in the trail ends to anchor the mounting firmly in the ground, and the result was an exceptionally stable platform on which the gun could traverse through 360°.

On the face of things the design had a built-in drawback: it seemed to demand a large flat and even surface to accommodate the trail legs and pedestal. Four or five-point support is usually avoided in gun-carriage design for this very reason, often being converted to three-point support by pivoting the axle of a split-trail equipment in some way or providing independent wheel suspension so that each of the support points can find its own level. In the Skoda design, with no less than five points of support to be equalised, difficulties were avoided by fitting the two forward legs with a hydraulic locking system. This was valved so that slow movements of the legs (folding and unfolding them) were unimpeded, and hence the legs were easily lowered to the ground and left lying at whatever attitude the terrain allowed. Sudden movements such as the firing shock, however, were resisted by the valves, and the legs were effectively locked in whatever position they had taken up.

This was a very sophisticated system that has never since, to the author's knowledge, been attempted on a field gun mounting. The only cloud on the horizon is the question of the Skoda system's reliability over a long period of field use—hydraulic systems have a habit of developing leaks—but since the weapon never achieved service status the question remains unanswered.

The remainder of the carriage can be briefly described: two spring balancing-presses were fitted to counter the muzzle weight and the shield was in two parts, one attached to the carriage and one attached to the cradle and elevating with the gun. The gun used disc wheels to which pneumatic tyres were fitted, and the hydropneumatic recoil system varied its stroke in three steps to shorten the recoil as the gun was elevated; this was also rather unusual, since variable recoil systems usually varied the stroke proportionately throughout the elevation range and did not simply divide the range into three finite recoil lengths.

The le FH 43 Skoda was undoubtedly one of the best field gun designs ever devised, and it is still held up as a model for designers. It is interesting to see that recent Soviet designs, notably the 122mm gun-howitzer M1963, have adopted a similar if simpler style of mounting.

Data

Calibre: 105mm/4.13in.

The 10.5cm le FH 43 Skoda model in firing position.

The Skoda gun ready for travelling.

Length of gun: 3456mm/136.06in/11.34ft.
Length of bore: 2470mm/97.24in.
Rifling: 32 grooves, uniform right-hand twist, 1/20.
Breech mechanism: horizontal sliding block, percussion fired.
Traverse: 360°.
Elevation: −5° to +75°.
Weight in action: 2200kg/4851lb.

Performance
Based on limited trial firings using the standard high explosive shell weighing 14.80kg(32.63lb).
Experimental charge: velocity 610mps/2001fps, maximum range 15000m/16405yd.

Ammunition, Projectiles, Propelling Charges
Precise details of ammunition were never finalised, but it is assumed that the full range of 105cm le FH projectiles would have been fired and that the propelling charge would have been a six-part charge of improved ballistic performance in a new and larger cartridge case.

The Krupp designs
Krupp managed to produce two designs to meet the specification, though neither of them got past the wooden mock-up stage.

The first used a carriage of rather similar design to Skoda's model, though whether Krupp's designers arrived at this independently or whether the two firms pooled information is not known. This version used a single forward leg without a firing pedestal, giving three-point support when locked down. A light enveloping shield, similar to that on the 8.8cm PAK 43 anti-tank gun, was fitted, together with disc wheels.

Data Krupp Entwurf 1
Calibre: 105mm/4.13in.
Length of gun: 2941mm/115.79in.

Length of bore: not known.
Rifling: 32 grooves, right-hand uniform twist, 1/20
Breech mechanism: horizontal sliding block, electrically fired.
Traverse: 360°.
Elevation: −4° to +70°.
Weight in action: 2400kg/5292lb.

Performance
Figures estimated by Krupp ballisticians, firing standard high explosive shell weighing 14.80kg (32.63lb).
Velocity 595mps/1952fps, maximum range 13000m/14217yd.
The second Krupp model was based on the cruciform platform of the successful 8.8cm PAK 43 anti-tank gun, and was really little more than the PAK 43 carriage with a new barrel and various small modifications. While not so startling in concept as the other two designs it is reasonable to suspect that, had the specification ever reached the production planning stage, the Krupp Entwurf 2 would have been a very strong contender simply by virtue of its readily-available carriage.

Data Krupp Entwurf 2
Calibre: 105mm/4.13in.
Length of gun: 3675mm/144.69in/12.06ft.
Length of bore: not known.
Rifling: 32 grooves, right-hand uniform twist, 1/20
Breech mechanism: horizontal sliding block, electrically fired.
Traverse: 360°.
Elevation: −10° to +70°.
Weight in action: 2450kg/5402lb (estimated).

Performance
Figures estimated by Krupp ballisticians, firing standard high explosive shell weighing 14.80kg (32.63lb).
Velocity 655mps/2149fps, maximum range 14200m/15530yd.

Ammunition, Projectiles, Propelling Charges
As with the Skoda design details of ammunition had not been finalised, though it is known that a seven-charge cartridge was intended for both Krupp weapons. It can be assumed that the standard range of le FH 18 projectiles would have been fully compatible with both designs.

Muzzle view of the Skoda equipment ready for travelling.

Breech end of the Skoda design.

Muzzle view of the Skoda equipment in the firing position.

10cm Kanone 17

10cm K 17

This was another veteran of World War 1, having been introduced in 1917 in order to improve on a predecessor, the 10cm K 14. A longer barrel was introduced and the original hydrospring recoil system was both improved and made more reliable, but as many parts as possible of the K 14 carriage were retained.

The result was a conventional weapon that showed its age by the time of World War 2. The carriage was a robust split-trail pattern with wooden wheels and a small shield. The barrel was detached from the recoil system and pulled back on to the closed trail legs for travelling.

This weapon introduces for the first time a common anomaly in German artillery nomenclature; although the calibre was 10.5cm, the title was *10cm Kanone*. It will be found in many cases that the calibre designation is only an approximation to the correct calibre, and it should never be accepted as an exact measurement.

Data

Calibre: 105mm/4.13in.
Length of gun: 4725mm/186in.
Length of bore: not known.
Rifling: 32 grooves, right-hand increasing twist.
Breech mechanism: horizontal sliding block, percussion fired.
Traverse: 6°.
Elevation: −2° to +45°.
Weight in action: 3300kg/7277lb.

The 10cm K 17 at maximum elevation.

Performance

Firing standard high explosive shell weighing 18.50kg(40.79lb).
Maximum charge: velocity 650mps/2133fps, maximum range 16500m/18045yd.

Ammunition

Separate-loading, cased charge.

Projectiles

10cm Gr 15m H: percussion fuze, weight 18.50kg(40.79lb).
This was the standard high explosive shell when the weapon was first developed; it was unusual in many respects. It was a long and graceful shell, not streamlined behind the driving band but with a long nose ending in a small brass plug. The nose was, in fact, a ballistic cap, and the percussion fuze was assembled beneath the cap with a long wooden actuating rod running from the striker of the fuze to lodge in the base of the brass plug. The fuze itself was an elderly ex-World-War-1 design of unknown name. The maximum range attained with this shell was 14100m(15420yd).
10cm Gr 18 m H: fuze and shell weight unknown
No details are known of this shell, which replaced the previous design as the standard projectile towards the end of World War 1. It appears to have been an improved and streamlined version of the Gr 15. The maximum range of 16500m(18045yd) was attained with this shell.
10cm Gr rot: fuzed AZ 23v(0.25) or Dopp Z S/60, weight 15.00kg(33.08lb).
This was a modern design of nose-fuzed shell, much the same as that designed for the le FH 18 series of howitzers but slightly longer. Its existence is verified by shells recovered and recorded by Allied intelligence agencies, but no German confirmation has ever been found. The reduced weight leads one to expect a greater range, but no ballistic data is available.

Propelling Charges
It is known that the cartridge identification numbers for this weapon were 6302 and 6349. Since this latter was the number associated with the 10cm s K 18, it can be assumed that the same propelling charge was used, no other information is available.

Primer
The percussion primer C/12nA was probably used.

Case Identification Number: 6302 (also associated with 6349).

10·5cm leichte Kanone 41

10·5cm le K 41

This was developed by both Krupp and Rheinmetall-Borsig in answer to an OKH request for a light fieldgun having a longer range than the le FH 18 howitzer but without any sacrifice in mobility or increase in weight.

The Krupp solution was to take the top carriage of the le FH 18 and insert a long barrelled gun into it, a design of weapon derived from the K17; the remainder of the carriage was basically K 17 also.

The Rheinmetall solution was a much more efficient and modern weapon, having distinct affinities with some others among the firm's contemporary designs. It had a split trail, no shield, and spoked cast-steel wheels with solid tyres. Springing was achieved by torsion bars. The whole equipment was remarkable in being much lighter than had previously been considered normal for a weapon of its class.

Although the specification had been met, particularly by the Rheinmetall-Borsig design, work on them ceased in 1941 and the weapons were never accepted for service. This was largely because they were considered to be too much gun for too little shell power.

Left rear view of the K 41 in firing position.

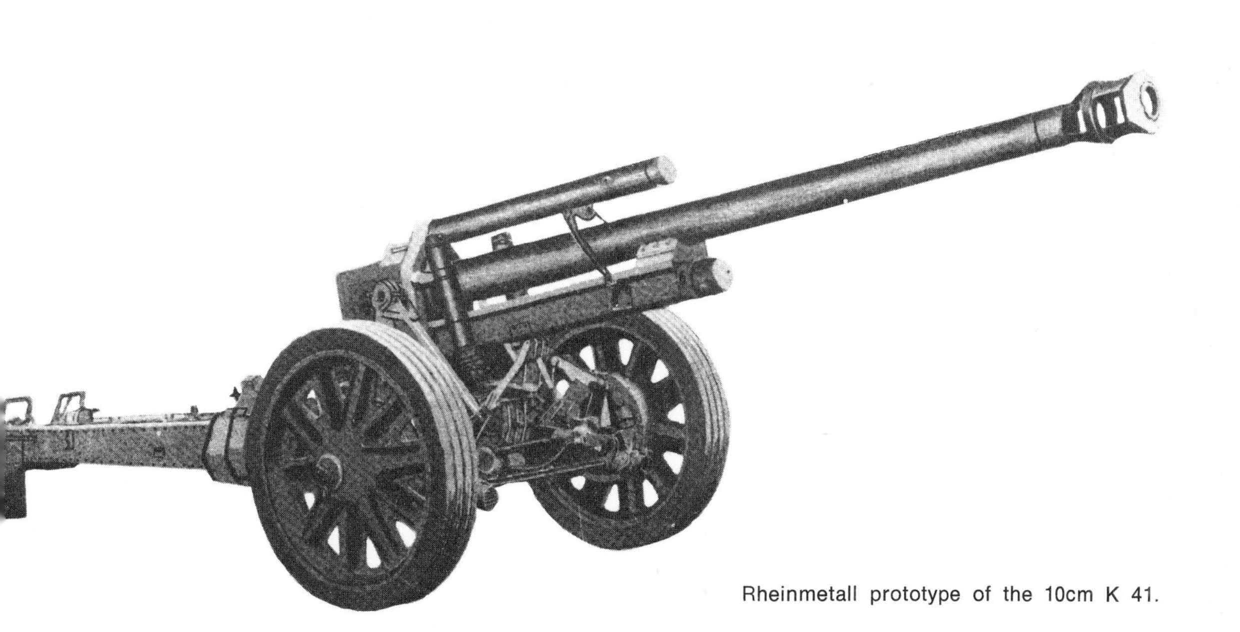

Rheinmetall prototype of the 10cm K 41.

Krupp prototype of the 10cm Kanone 41

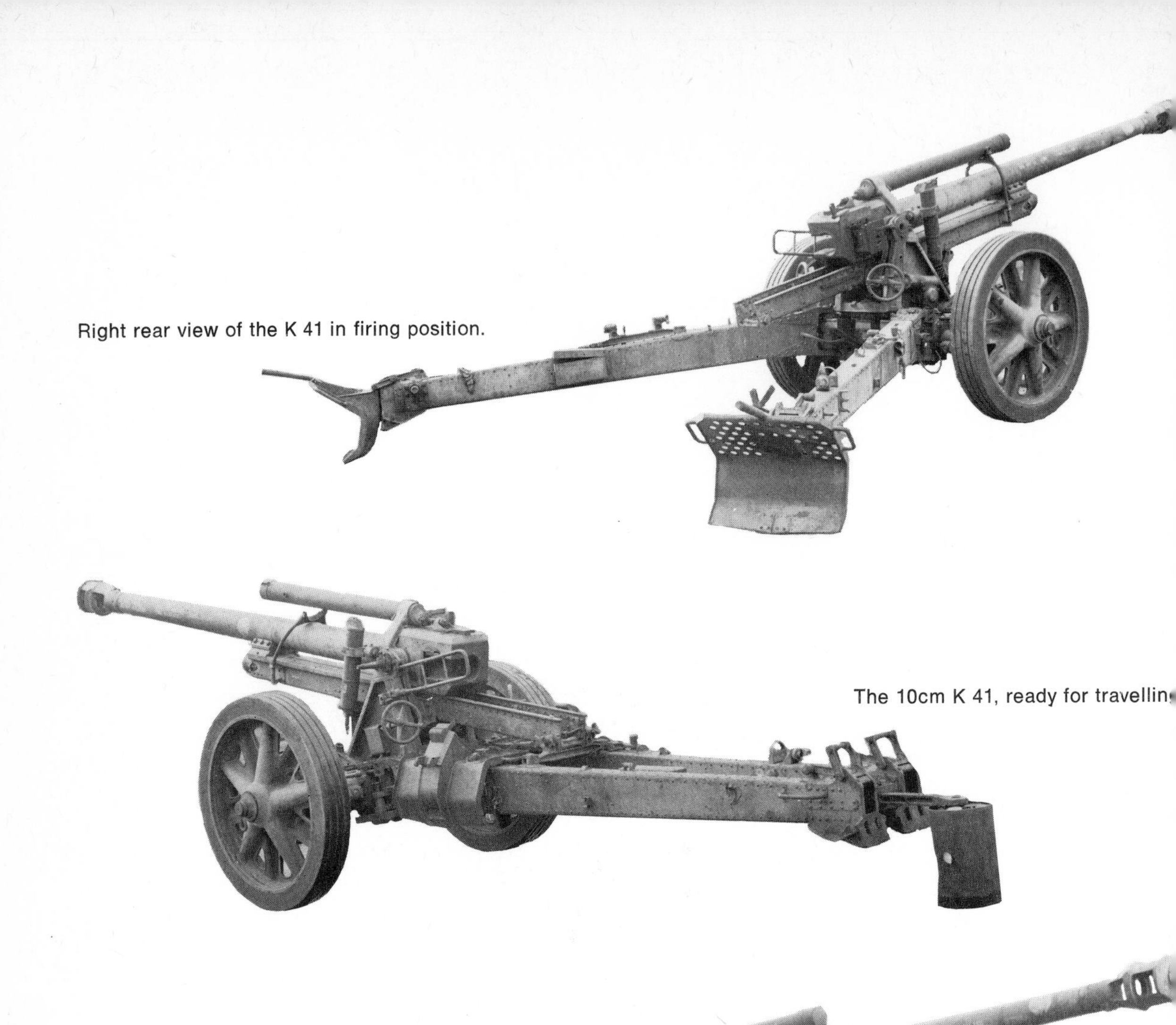

Right rear view of the K 41 in firing position.

The 10cm K 41, ready for travellin

Front view of the 10cm K 41.

Data Rheinmetall Entwurf (no data is available for the Krupp version).
Calibre: 105mm/4.13in.
Length of gun: 4200mm/165.35in/13.78ft.
Length of bore: not known.
Rifling: right-hand twist.
Breech mechanism: horizontal sliding block, percussion fired.
Traverse: 60°.
Elevation: −5° to +45°.
Weight in action: 2640kg/5821lb.

Performance
Firing standard high explosive shell weighir 15.00kg(33.08lb).
Maximum charge: velocity 665mps/2182fps, ma mum range 15000m/16405yd.

Ammunition
Separate-loading, cased charge.

Projectiles, Propelling charges
No details are available.

HEAVY FIELD ARTILLERY

This category of weapons equates to the British term *medium artillery*, the heavier weapons available to the division but which are still relatively manoeuverable and literally capable of being pushed about by their crews.

Almost by tradition, this class of weapon in the German Army was composed of 10cm guns and 15cm howitzers, but by the later stages of the war the army was questioning the value of weapons that weighed 5000–6000kg(4.92–5.91ton) but only threw a 14–15kg(31–33lb) shell, and had instigated a 12.8cm design that promised a heavier projectile without unduly increasing equipment weight. It might be pointed out here that the equivalent British gun in this class was the 5.5in gun-howitzer weighing 6095kg(6.00ton) and firing a 43.35kg (100.00lb) shell, while the equivalent American weapon was the 155mm howitzer weighing 5790kg(5.70ton) and firing a 43.08kg(95.00lb) shell. Admittedly neither had the range of the German 10cm guns, but the increase in shell power was considerable.

schwere 10cm Kanone 18

s 10cm K 18 (Bleiglanz)

Like all the '18' class of weapons, the s 10cm K 18 was developed in the period 1926–30 and brought into service in 1933–4. The specification was given to both Krupp and Rheinmetall and the final result was an amalgam of both designs; the carriage was designed by Krupp and the gun by Rheinmetall.

The ordnance was a simple one-piece barrel inside a jacket, with the usual horizontal sliding-block breech and a cage-type muzzle brake. The carriage was a robust split-trail type with pressed-steel disc wheels with solid tyres, transverse leaf-spring suspension and two spring balancing-presses. It was designed for horse or vehicle traction. For vehicle draught the barrel was disconnected from the recoil system and hauled back to the end of the cradle, where it was clamped. The gun was moved by a wire rope and a hand-winch attached to the carriage. For animal draught the barrel was completely withdrawn from the cradle on to a four-wheeled transport wagon, the carriage forming a second load. In both systems of draught the trail ends were supported on a low two-wheeled limber. In spite of this disassembly the K 18 was generally considered too heavy for animal draught, especially in rough country.

In addition to the field artillery role the weapon could be deployed as an emergency coast artillery gun, and a special ranging projectile was provided for this role.

In postwar years a number of these weapons were to be found in the Albanian and Bulgarian armies.

British troops in Tunisia examine a captured 10.5cm s K 18. The considerable size in relation to calibre is well brought out in this photograph.

The s 10.5cm K 18 prepared for travelling, with the barrel in its cradle and the trail supported by a limber.

Data
:alibre: 105mm/4.13in.
.ength of gun: 5460mm/214.96in/17.91ft.
.ength of bore: 5173mm/203.66in/16.97ft.
Rifling: 36 grooves, right-hand increasing twist, 1/40 to 1/30.
3reech mechanism: horizontal sliding block, per-:ussion fired.
Traverse: 64°.
Elevation: 0 to +48°.
Veight in action: 5642kg/12441lb/5.55ton.

'erformance
'iring standard high explosive shell weighing 5.14kg(33.41lb).
Kleine Ladung: velocity 550mps/1805fps, maxinum range 12725m/13916yd.
Aittelere Ladung: velocity 690mps/2264fps, maxinum range 15750m/17234yd.
3rosse Ladung: velocity 835mps/2740fps, maxinum range 19075m/20860yd.
'iring armour piercing shell weighing 15.56kg 34.31lb).
Kleine Ladung: not used with this projectile.
Aittelere Ladung: velocity 682mps/2238fps, maxinum range 13850m/15146yd.
3rosse Ladung: velocity 827mps/2713fps, maxinum range 16000m/17498yd.
'iring smoke shell weighing 14.71kg(32.44kg).
3rosse Ladung: velocity 827mps/2713fps, maxinum range 18300m/20013yd.

Ammunition
eparate-loading, cased charge.

'rojectiles
0cm Gr 19: fuzed AZ 23v(0.25) or Dopp Z S/60, veight 15.14kg(33.38lb).
'his was the standard high explosive shell; streamned, it had two driving bands of copper, the rear f which had a raised central rib to act as an nproved gas-seal. The filling was an unusual one: 'NT in pre-pressed blocks, packed in cardboard, nd then packed into a metal container and nchored in place by montan wax.

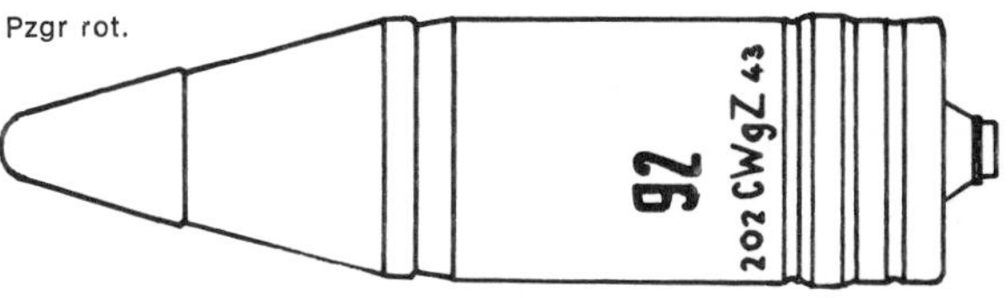

10cm Gr 19 FES: fuzed AZ 23v(0.25) or Dopp Z S/60, weight about 15.50kg(34.18lb).
Similar to the above shell but with sintered-iron driving bands and a simpler filling of poured amatol or TNT.
10cm Pzgr rot: fuzed Bd Z f 10cm Pzgr, weight 15.56kg(34.31lb).
An armour piercing high explosive shell fitted with penetrating and ballistic caps and carrying a tracer unit.
10cm Pzgr rot: fuzed Bd Z f 10cm Pzgr, weight 15.56kg(34.31lb).
An alternative design of piercing shell without caps or tracer.
10cm Gr 38 Nb: fuzed K1 AZ 23 Nb Pr, weight 14.71kg(32.44lb).
A screening smoke shell of the normal bursting pattern filled with the standard oleum/pumice mixture.

Propelling Charges
The Kleine and Mittlere Ladungen (sections 1 and 2) were supplied in the cartridge case, each contained in an artificial silk bag. The Grosse Ladung, Sonderkartusche 3, was packed separately in a container and was used to replace sections 1 and 2 in the cartridge case when required. The make-up of the charges was as follows:
Ladung 1: 2.38kg/5.25lb Digl R P.
Ladung 2: 0.91kg/2.01lb Digl R P.
Sonderkart 3: 5.80kg/12.79lb Digl R P.
The Kleine Ladung was made up of Ladung 1, the Mittelere Ladung of Ladungen 1 and 2, and the Grosse Ladung of Sonderkart 3 alone.

Primer
The percussion primer C/12nA was fitted.
Case Identification Number: 6349.

15cm schwere Feldhaubitze 18

15cm s FH 18 (Immergrün)

This was the partner to the s 10cm K 18, using the same carriage. Beyond that there is not much to be said since, except for barrel dimensions, it was practically identical to the K 18. The only remarkable feature of the s FH 18 is that it became the first weapon to be issued with a rocket-assisted shell, the object of which was to increase the range to equal that of the K 18 which would then have been rendered superfluous, whereupon production could have been terminated and the capacity so released employed on some more important weapons. The shell was issued in 1941; contemporary reports speak with awe of the voluminous and involved firing instructions that accompanied it—instructions which confirmed the users' opinion that the shells were scarcely out of the experimental stage and which did nothing to inspire them with confidence in the new weapon. The rocket-assisted shell was not entirely successful and was withdrawn from service after a short time.

Although the s FH 18 was provided with eight charges it was found that the two largest charges induced considerable strain; neither was normally used, firing being restricted to charges 1 to 6. Firing of charges 7 and 8 was allowed in special cases but had to be authorised by a higher formation and the reasons certified by the troop commander. Not more than ten rounds could be fired consecutively at the high charges, and these had to be entered into the gun history documents so that a record of all such rounds existed.

The use of these charges eventually led to erosion of the chamber so that it became difficult to seal the breech with the cartridge case, and early in 1942 a system of repair (by reaming out the chamber metal and inserting a liner) was introduced. At the same time a muzzle brake was designed and issued to reduce the stress on the carriage, but the special rules regarding the firing of charges 7 and 8 remained in force. Weapons fitted with muzzle brakes were known as the 15cm s FH 18M, the 'M' in which represented Mündungsbremse or muzzle brake.

In postwar years the howitzer saw service with the Albanian, Bulgarian and Czechoslovakian armies. In Czech service it was bored-out to 15.2cm calibre so that it would accept Soviet ammunition, and a muzzle brake of improved pattern was fitted; in this guise it was known as the vz 18/46. It was also used during the war by the Italian army under the title Obice 149/28.

A collection of 15cm s FH 18 guns on display in Moscow, after being captured.

A rear view which shows the abnormally long barrel (for a howitzer) of the s FH 18.

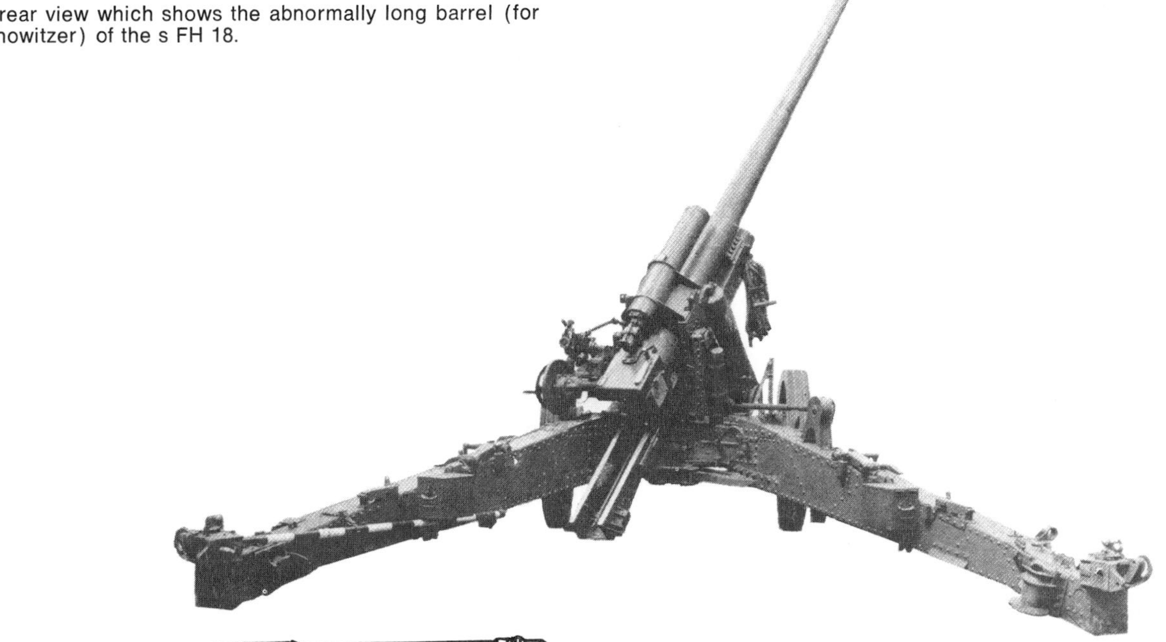

G 39 HI/A.

Data (the s FH 18 and the s FH 18M were similar)
Calibre: 150mm/5.91in.
Length of gun: 4495mm/176.97in/14.75ft.
Length of bore: 4125mm/162.40in/13.53ft.
Rifling: 40 grooves, right-hand increasing twist, 1/36 to 1/18.
Breech mechanism: horizontal sliding block, percussion fired.
Traverse: 64°.
Elevation: −3° to +45°.
Weight in action: 5512kg/12154lb/5.43ton.

Performance
Firing standard high explosive shell weighing 43.50kg(95.92kg).
Charge 1: velocity 210mps/689fps, maximum range 4000m/4374yd.
Charge 2: velocity 230mps/755fps, maximum range 4700m/5140yd.
Charge 3: velocity 250mps/820fps, maximum range 5525m/6042yd.
Charge 4: velocity 278mps/912fps, maximum range 6625m/7245yd.
Charge 5: velocity 320mps/1050fps, maximum range 8200m/8968yd.
Charge 6: velocity 375mps/1230fps, maximum range 9725m/10635yd.
Charge 7: velocity 440mps/1444fps, maximum range 11400m/12467yd.
Charge 8: velocity 495mps/1624fps, maximum range 13250m/14490yd.

Ammunition
Separate-loading, cased charge.

Projectiles
15cm Gr 19: fuzed AZ 23v(0.8) or Dopp Z S/60, weight 43.50kg(95.92lb).
This was the standard high explosive shell filled with TNT. A number of minor variations existed, representing various manufacturing expedients, all of which had similar ballistic performance. Two of the more important were:
15cm Gr 19 Stg made from cast-steel and with two bimetallic driving bands.
15cm Gr 19 Stg FES also of cast-steel but with a single sintered-iron driving band
15cm Gr 36 FES: fuzed AZ 23 or Dopp Z S/60, weight 38.50kg(84.89lb).
An improved high explosive shell, this was 150mm(5.92in) longer than the Gr 19 but had thinner walls and hence weighed less. It was fitted with a single sintered-iron driving band
15cm Gr 19 Be: fuzed Bd Z f 15cm Gr Be, weight 43.50kg(95.92lb).
This an anti-concrete shell, was fitted with a rounded light alloy ballistic cap over a sharp conical point. The body cavity was lined with a sulphur compound and was filled with 4.75kg (10.47lb) of TNT in pre-pressed blocks. The base fuze had three alternative settings: long, short or zero delay.
15cm Gr 19 Be rot: fuzed Bd Z f 15cm Gr Be, weight 43.45kg(95.81lb).
An improved version of the previous shell with the body cavity reduced in order to give greater strength to the shell. The cavity was lined with waxed cardboard and filled with 3.25kg(7.17lb) of TNT.

The 15cm s FH 18, backbone of the German medium artillery.

15cm Gr 39 FES Hl: fuzed K1 AZ 40 Nb, weight 24.55kg(54.13lb).
The first hollow charge shell to be issued, it could also be fired from the 15cm howitzer s FH 13. A tracer pellet was fitted in the base.
15cm Gr 39 Hl/A: fuzed K1 AZ 40 Nb Pr, weight 24.57kg(54.18lb).
The second model of the hollow charge shell, with a longer ogive and internal rearrangements as the 10.5cm le FH 18 patterns. It was fired with charge 6 to give a muzzle velocity of 460mps(1509fps).
15cm Gr 19 Nb: fuzed AZ 23 Nb, weight 39.00kg(86.00lb).
A bursting smoke shell filled with oleum/pumice.
15cm Gr 38 Nb: fuzed K1 AZ 40 Nb, weight 43.47kg(95.85lb).
An improved pattern of bursting smoke shell with a larger bursting charge to give better distribution to the smoke mixture and thus improve the obscuring power.
15cm R Gr 19 FES: fuzed E1 AZ and Bd Z R, or Dopp S/90, weight 45.50kg(100.33lb).
This was the rocket-assisted shell and it was fired by a special charge, slightly larger than the normal charge 8; it could only be fired from weapons fitted with muzzlebrakes, owing to the excessive strain on the recoil system. The shell was fuzed normally with an electric nose fuze and an electric base fuze, or with the Dopp Z S/90 long-running time and percussion fuze. The maximum range achieved by the shell was 19000m(20778yd). The rocket motor was in the rear section of the shell and the efflux passed through ten venturis set around the shell base. It is not entirely clear how the rocket motor was ignited, but it was probably by some form of pyrotechnic delay system initiated by the propellant flash.
15cm Sprgr 42 TS: fuzed AZ 23, weight 29.60kg(65.27lb).
This was a discarding sabot shell. The subprojectile was 12.7cm in diameter with relatively thin walls and a shallow curvature from the nose to the shoulder. The base was streamlined. Three-piece discarding rings were fitted at the shoulder and the base—that at the base carrying a steel driving band. The filling was 4.05kg(8.93lb) of cast TNT, but, unfortunately, no other data is available on the shell's performance.
15cm Splitter-Beton Granate: details of fuze and weight not known.

Postwar investigation revealed that designs were in progress for a 15cm shell using a thin metal body enclosing a concrete lining in which metal fragments were embedded. The whole projectile was then filled with low-grade explosive, and it was claimed that detonation produced a fragment density and fragment range of comparable lethality to conventional shells, but with considerable economy of material. No further details are available, but it is known that this technique was adopted with some success in heavy mortar bombs

15cm Sprgr L/6.2m Hb: details of fuze and weight not known.

This was an experimental long-range shell still in the design stage when the war ended. With a length of 6.2 calibres, stabilisation by spin would have been marginal, and so it was built with a long hollow skirt at the rear to give additional drag stabilisation. A ballistic cap was fitted over the nose to give optimum head shape, but no performance figures are known.

15cm Flugelmine Klappleitwerk Geschoss: details of fuze and weight not known.

This, also revealed after the war and never a service round, was a Minengeschoss—a high-capacity over-length shell stabilised by fins that were carried in a forged-steel rear section and opened in jack-knife fashion to the rear after leaving the muzzle. A rotating sealing band, mounted on roller bearings, was fitted behind the fins.

15cm Hl/C mit Flugelminen Leitwerke: fuzed K1 AZ 40 Nb Pr, details of weight not known.

This was a similar design to the previous shell, but the head was filled as a hollow charge shell. No details of performance of either of these shells is known and the only specimen in existence is empty; a filled weight cannot therefore be given.

Note

It might be pointed out here that some reports have asserted that a smoothbore version of the 15cm s FH 18 was under development and adduce these fin-stabilised projectiles as evidence. The presence of the freely-rotating sealing band conclusively refutes this theory and points quite firmly to the intention that these shells were to be used in rifled weapons, obtaining stability of the extra length by the fins.

Propelling Charges

Charges 1 to 6 were in artificial silk bags contained in the cartridge case. Charges 7 and 8 were supplied separately in a metal canister, charge 7 being in a tubular silk bag some 215mm(8.46in) long, and 150mm(5.92in) in diameter; the charge 8 addition was held in a flat circular bag about 175mm(6.89in) in diameter. Charges 1 to 6 were made up by combining the bags up to and including the required charge number. The charge 7 bag replaced all the previous increments in the cartridge case, and for charge 8 the last bag was added.

Charge igniter: 550gm/19.40oz/1.21lb Nigl B1 P, used with all charges.

Charge 1: 62gm/2.19oz Digl B1 P.
Charge 2: 122gm/4.30oz Digl B1 P.
Charge 3: 124gm/4.37oz Digl B1 P.
Charge 4: 208gm/7.34oz Digl B1 P.
Charge 5: 312gm/11.00oz Digl B1 P.
Charge 6: 475gm/16.75oz/1.05lb Digl B1 P.
Charge 7: 2.39kg/5.26kg Digl R P.
Charge 8: 768gm/27.08oz/1.69lb Digl R P.

Primer

The percussion primer C/12nA was used.

Case Identification Number: 6350.

10·5cm schwere Kanone 18/40

10·5cm s K 18/40

The army had never been particularly impressed with the performance of the 10cm K 18, and before it had been in service for many years—some sources aver as early as the autumn of 1937—they were demanding a new model. Work began on a fairly low priority, and in 1941 both Krupp and Rheinmetall-Borsig produced models for test. But the time was not suitable for a change of production; the invasion of Russia had just begun and all available production facilities were committed to the manufacture of field howitzers and anti-tank guns. As a result the improved model, the 10.5cm s K 40 as the prototypes came to be known, was never made in quantity.

In order to produce a slight improvement, a small number of extemporary weapons were produced by placing the barrel of the s K 40 on a modified s K 18 carriage; the result was issued as the 10.5cm s K 18/40, a designation later changed to 10.5cm s K 42. The new barrel was eight calibres longer than the old and the chamber capacity was increased by about 25%, which increased the maximum range from 19075m(20860yd) to 21000m (22966yd). The rifling twist was lessened slightly at the breech to give less initial rotational velocity.

The carriage was modified by the substitution of hydropneumatic balancing-presses for the earlier spring pattern, by the adoption of a variable recoil system in place of the original fixed-length pattern; and by the replacement of the leaf springing with torsion bar suspension.

The sum of this activity was a weapon that weighed slightly more than the original and fired the same shell 1925m(2106yd) farther. In view of this marginal improvement it was not surprising that the army refused more than a handful, preferring to keep the old familiar model in the hope that something radically better would one day appear.

Data
Calibre: 105mm/4.13in.
Length of gun: 6300mm/248.03in/20.67ft.
Length of bore: 4849mm/190.91in/15.91ft.
Rifling: 36 grooves, right-hand increasing twist, 1/40 to 1/30.
Breech mechanism: horizontal sliding block, percussion fired.
Traverse: 56°.
Elevation: 0 to +45°.
Weight in action: 5680kg/12524lb/5.59ton.

Performance
Firing standard high explosive shell weighing 15.14kg(33.38lb).
Kleine Ladung: velocity 550mps/1805fps, maximum range 12725m/13916yd.
Mittlere Ladung: velocity 690mps/2267fps, maximum 15750m/17224yd.
Grosse Ladung: velocity 835mps/2740fps, maximum range 19075m/20860yd.
Firing smoke shell:
Grosse Ladung: velocity 827mps/2713fps, maximum range 18300m/20013yd.
Firing armour piercing shell.
Mittlere Ladung: 682mps/2238fps, maximum range 13850m/15146yd.
Grosse Ladung: 822mps/2697fps, maximum range 16000m/17498yd.

Ammunition
Separate-loading, cased charge.

Projectiles
The same projectiles as the s. 10cm K 18 were fired

Propelling Charges
A three-part charge was provided; the Kleine and Mittlere Ladungen were supplied in the cartridge case and the Grosse Ladung (Sonderkart 3), supplied separately, replaced the other two section in the case when required.
Ladung 1: 2.94kg/6.48lb Dgl R P.
Ladung 2: 1.01kg/2.23lb Dgl R P.
Sonderkart 3: 6.80kg/14.99lb Dgl R P.
As usual the Kleine Ladung consisted of Ladung 1; the Mittlere Ladung of Ladungen 1 and 2; and the Grosse Ladung of Sonderkart 2 alone.

Primer
The percussion primer C/12nA was used.

Case Identification Number: 6350: the case of the 15cm s FH 18 was used.

15cm schwere Feldhaubitze 13

15cm s FH 13

The 15cm s FH 13, relic of the Kaiser's army.

This weapon was produced by Krupp during World War 1 and was originally issued in 1917; with its long box trail, wooden wheels, curved shield and short barrel it was typical of its time. A small number of these horse-drawn equipments survived into World War 2 as reserve and training weapons, but it is extremely unlikely that any saw first line service.

It is amusing to note that the only data on this weapon available to Allied troops during the war were based on a British GHQ Intelligence summary written in August 1918.

Data
Calibre: 150mm/5.92in.
Length of gun: 2540mm/100in/8.3ft.

ength of bore: 2096mm/82.52in.
Rifling: 32 grooves, right-hand increasing twist, /45 to 1/22.4.
Breech mechanism: horizontal sliding block, percussion fired.
Traverse: 9°.
Elevation: −4° to +45°.
Weight in action: 2250kg/4961lb.

Performance
Firing standard high explosive shell weighing 42.00kg(92.61lb).
Maximum charge: velocity 381mps/1250fps, maximum range 8600m/9405yd.

Ammunition
Separate-loading, cased charge.

Projectiles
The following projectiles, described under the 15cm s FH 18, were also fired from the s FH 13:
15cm Gr 19 and variations.
15cm Sprgr 36 FES.
15cm Gr 19 Be.
15cm Gr 39 H1.
15cm Gr 19 Nb.

Propelling Charges
Seven charges were provided; the weight of the maximum charge was 1.35kg(2.98lb).

Primer
The percussion primer C/12nA was used.

Case Identification Number: 6303.

15cm schwere Feldhaubitze 36

15cm s FH 36

A 15cm s FH 36 in Poland, 1939. Note the mats beneath the wheels, intended to prevent sinking in soft ground.

In 1935 the army asked for a medium howitzer, lighter than the s FH 18, that could be drawn in one load by horses. The model eventually accepted in 1938 was a Rheinmetall-Borsig design in which the desired result was obtained by having a shorter barrel and a carriage largely made from alloy.

The barrel was some 1140mm(44.88in) shorter than that of the s FH 18 and was originally fitted with a cylindrical muzzlebrake with four rows of 13 slots though later models used the standard two-baffle pattern associated with the s FH 18. A quick-release connexion attached the breech-ring to the recoil system piston rods so that the gun could be disconnected and drawn back onto the cradle extension for travelling, although this facility rarely seems to have been used in practice—judging by photographs. The quick release system was interlocked, by means of a spring plunger, to the breechblock and prevented the block being opened or the firing pin being released if the gun was not securely locked to the recoil system.

The carriage was a split-trail type with two pressed-alloy wheels. For transport the trail ends were carried on a two-wheel limber with a spring-balanced draught pole. A folding seat above the right-hand gun wheel was provided on which a member of the detachment rode during transport, operating the gun handbrake at his side.

Owing to the shortage of light alloys and the increasing mechanisation of the army, production ceased in 1942 and few of these weapons remained by the end of the war.

Data
Calibre: 150mm/5.92in.
Length of gun: 3805mm/149.80in/12.48ft.
Length of bore: 2474mm/97.40in.
Rifling: 40 grooves, right-hand increasing twist 1/30 to 1/18.
Breech mechanism: horizontal sliding block, percussion fired.
Traverse: 56°.
Elevation: 0 to +45°.
Weight in action: 3280kg/7232lb/3.23ton.

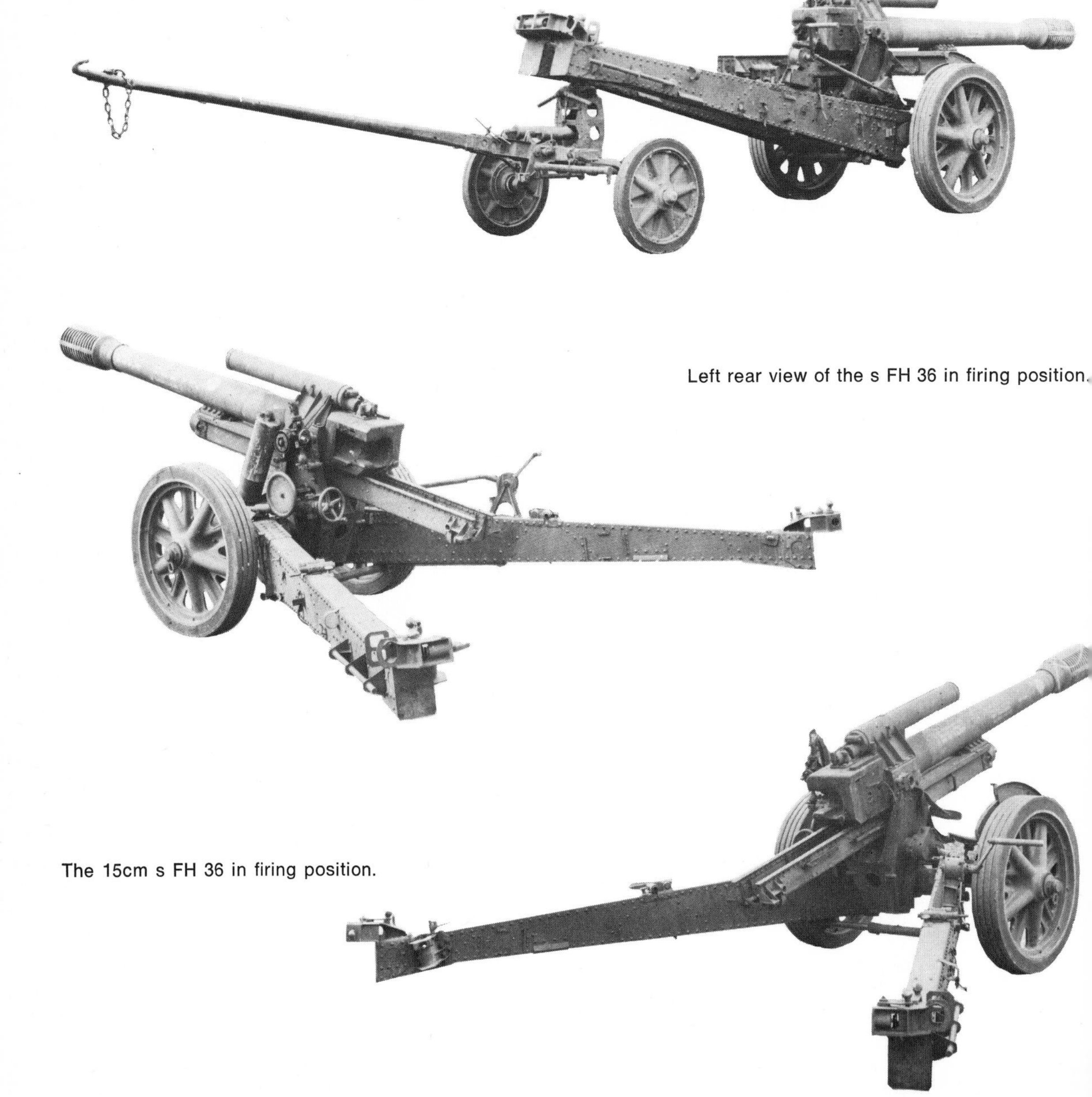
The s FH 36 limbered up for horse draught.

Left rear view of the s FH 36 in firing position.

The 15cm s FH 36 in firing position.

Performance
Firing the standard high explosive shell, weight 43.50kg(95.92lb).
Charge 1: velocity 210mps/689fps, range figures not available.
Charge 2: velocity 230mps/755fps, range figures not available.
Charge 3: velocity 250mps/820fps, range figures not available.
Charge 4: velocity 280mps/919fps, range figures not available.
Charge 5: velocity 320mps/1050fps, range figures not available.
Charge 6: velocity 400mps/1312fps, range figures

A 15cm s FH 36 with short barrel, apparently designed for single load horse draught, found at Hillersleben Proving Ground, July 1945.

Rear view of the short-barrelled s FH 36 at Hillersleben.

not available.
Charge 7: velocity 485mps/1591fps, maximum range 12300m/13450yd.

Ammunition
Separate-loading, cased charge.

Projectiles, Propelling Charges
The shells and propellant charges were those used with the s FH 18 except that charge 8 was no fired in the s FH 36.

Primer
The percussion primer C/12nA was used.

Case Identification Number:
6350

15cm schwere Feldhaubitze 40

15cm s FH 40

As with the s K 18, the army was not entirely satisfied with the performance of the FH 18 and requested a fresh design with both better performance and the ability to fire at high angles of elevation. Indeed, it is remarkable that the s FH 18 could only elevate to 45°, since the fundamental principle of a howitzer makes necessary the ability to fire at greater angles than that.

Prototypes, built by both Krupp and Rheinmetall-Borsig, were produced for test in 1941 but the weapons were not accepted for service, probably on the same grounds as those which negated the s K 40: shortage of production facilities.

Data
Calibre: 150mm/5.92in.
Length of gun: 4875mm/191.93in/15.99ft.
Length of bore: 3927mm/154.61in/12.88ft.
Rifling: 40 grooves, right-hand increasing twist, 1/30 to 1/18.
Breech mechanism: horizontal sliding block, percussion fired.
Traverse: 60°.
Elevation: 0 to +70°.
Weight in action: 5400kg/11907lb/5.32ton.

Performance
The full details of the weapon's performance are not known, but the range of muzzle velocities with the nine charges ran from 210mps(689fps) to 595mps(1952fps). The maximum range with the standard high explosive shell was 15400m (16841yd).

Ammunition
Separate-loading, cased charge.

Projectiles, Propelling Charges
The same projectiles used by the s FH 18 were intended to be used with this weapon, together with a new design of nine-part propelling charge of which no details are known.

15cm schwere Feldhaubitze 18/40

15cm s FH 18/40

The s FH 18/40 was a compromise similar to the s K 18/40. In an attempt to produce an improved weapon as cheaply as possible the barrel designed for the s FH 40 was mounted in a modified s FH 18 carriage. The improvements in the s FH 40 barrel were similar to those performed on the s K 40: the barrel length was increased by about three calibres and the chamber capacity was enlarged by some 32%. The muzzle brake designed for the s FH 40 was also fitted. These modifications allowed a more powerful charge to be fired but the delicate ballistic balance—between barrel length, rifling, charge and projectile—was unfortunately upset somewhere along the line and the accuracy was poor at short and medium ranges.

Only 46 of the s FH 18/40 were made, its demise probably being due to its lack of accuracy and the marginal improvement it offered over the existing s FH 18.

Data
Calibre: 150mm/5.92in.
Length of gun: 4875mm/191.93in/15.99ft.
Length of bore: 3297mm/129.80in/10.82ft.
Rifling: 40 grooves, right-hand increasing twist.
Breech mechanism: horizontal sliding block, percussion fired.
Traverse: 56°
Elevation: 0 to +45°.
Weight in action: 5720kg/12613lb/5.63ton.

Performance
Standard high explosive shell weighing 43.50kg(95.92lb)
Charge 9: veolcity 595mps/1952fps, maximum range 15100m/16513yd.

Ammunition, Projectiles, Propelling Charges
As s FH 18M but with a ninth charge of 6.81kg (15.02lb) of Digl RP replacing charges 1 to 8 when fired

15cm schwere Feldhaubitze 18/43

15cm s FH 18/43

The nomenclature leads one to expect yet another combination of an old carriage and a new barrel, but the s FH 18/43 was unusual in heralding a completely new trend in German gun design: one that had never before been successfully applied and one that gave the world's gun designers something to keep them occupied for many postwar years. The novelty was the introduction of a bag-charge loading system while retaining the mechanical simplicity of a sliding-block breech.

It has been previously mentioned, and discussed at length in Appendix 2, that the German designers were well aware of the shortage of cartridge case metal and of the production facilities needed to keep pace with the artillery's enormous appetite for cartridge cases; many ingenious designs were produced in order to economise. Good as this effort was, it was becoming obvious that this alone was insufficient and that other measures would have to be adopted. The designers began as a result to take a fresh look at bag-charge guns.

The usual—almost traditional—method of sealing the breech in this type of gun was the *De Bange system,* in which the breechblock was cylindrical with interrupted threads mating with similar threads in the breech ring, so that the block could be entered with its threaded portions passing along the cut-away sections of the ring. The block was then given a partial turn to bring all threads into engagement and so lock the block in place. Through the block passed an axial bolt terminating at the front in a *mushroom head,* slightly smaller than the entrance to the chamber. Between the mushroom head and the front face of the breechblock was a resilient pad, the circumference of which was sloped so that it mated (when the breech was closed) perfectly with a coned face at the chamber mouth.

When the charge was fired, the pressure on the mushroom head squeezed the pad against the face of the block and outwards against the gun chamber. From various considerations of unit pressure on the area of the mushroom head and on the area of the pad (which was smaller by the diameter of the axial bolt) it can be shown that the pressure exerted by the pad was always greater than the chamber pressure, so that, provided both the pad and the seating were undamaged, leaks never occurred.

It will be obvious from this brief description that manufacture of this type of breech demanded highly-specialised machinery for cutting the screws on the breechblock and in the gun breech-ring, producing the axial bolt and cutting the chamber face. Moreover, specialised firing mechanisms (which were fitted to the rear of the axial bolt) had to be designed and perfected, and—probably most vital of all—the composition and texture of the resilient pad had to be finalised, generally by a process of trial and error over a long period of time.

This system had been standard in British medium and heavy guns since the 1880s and it had been perfected over the years; factories specialising in breech-screw cutting and pad manufacture existed, and the development of a new gun on this system was a relatively straightforward affair. But Germany had never taken much interest in the system, preferring instead to use the sliding-block breech and the metallic cartridge case in every calibre, and there was consequently little expertise and little production capacity in the country that could have rapidly designed and produced a screw breech during the war years. It was therefore necessary to take the standard sliding-block breech and, as simply as possible, adapt it for use with a bag charge.

So the barrel of the standard s FH 18 was taken and the rear face of the chamber turned to give a flat and smooth surface (the original barrel had a sharp lip to hold the cartridge case rim so that the extractors could engage), around which the metal was recessed so that the prepared surface stood out. The front face of the breechblock was recessed in the form of a ring, matching the rear of the chamber, and into this recess fitted a number of metal rings: first, against the body of the block, a number of flat steel rings that were simply adjusting shims. Then came a ring in the shape of an inverted L, pierced with 52 radial holes, and then an L-shaped ring of plain steel that made contact with the barrel with one face and with the circumference of the breechblock recess with the other. The number of adjusting rings was chosen to ensure a tight sliding fit between the L ring and the chamber face when the breechblock was closed.

In addition to the rings in the breechblock, a second set of similar rings was fitted around the face of the chamber against the recessed portion of the barrel. The propellant gases generated on firing passed through the radial holes in the inverted L ring into the annular space between it and the outer L ring; this pressure then forced the outer ring forward into contact with the chamber face and outward into contact with the breechblock recess, thus effecting a seal. The gases that leaked past the seal initially (before sufficient pressure had been built up) were trapped in the chamber face rings, forcing the L ring around the chamber mouth into contact with the breechblock face to give a secondary seal.

The material of which the rings were made was obviously critical in this application and development of the system was still in progress when the war ended; the s FH 18/43 never saw service. It is interesting to note that the design was closely examined by Allied experts and designers after the war and formed the starting point for the British development of a successful similar system for their 120mm tank gun.

Data
All data as the s FH 18.

Performance
No performance figures are available owing to the fact that development was not completed; it can, however, be assumed that the performance would have been substantially the same as that of the s FH 18.

Ammunition
Separate-loading, bagged charge.

Projectiles
As the s FH 18.

Propelling Charges
A known specimen charge developed for this weapon was in the form of six flat circular bags held together in a bundle by four tapes attached to the charge 1 bag. This bag also had the igniter stitched to the base. The increments' constitution was:
Charge 1: 745gm/26.27oz/1.64lb Digl Bl P.
Charge 2: 115gm/4.06oz Gudol Bl P.
Charge 3: 145gm/5.11oz Gudol Bl P.
Charge 4: 210gm/7.41oz Gudol Bl P.
Charge 5: 355gm/12.52oz Gudol Bl P.
Charge 6: 495gm/17.46oz/1.1lb Gudol Bl P.
Charges 1, 3 and 5 had flash-reducing salts incorporated in a separate pocket in their bags. Charges 2 and 3 were semicircular bags, held together by light stitching to make a complete circle. This particular charge-set has the date of filling (24th September 1943) and is thus assumed to be an early trial model.

Charge Ignition
Ignition in bag charge guns is by a tube that resembles a blank cartridge for a rifle and is usually filled with coarse gunpowder. The tube fits into a firing lock at the rear of the axial bolt and when fired delivers a flash down the central vent to fire the igniter pad on the charge and thus initiate the cartridge. No details are available about tubes used with the s FH 18/43.

15cm schwere Feldhaubitze 43

15cm s FH 43

It will be recalled that the Russian campaign showed the army that new ideas of field howitzer design were required, and that as a result the development of the le FH 43 began. In a similar fashion demands were made for an improvement in the s FH 18 class of weapon to give all-round fire, high-angle fire and a range of at least 18000m (19685yd) in order to out-range the Soviet opposition.

Krupp, Skoda and Rheinmetall-Borsig all produced designs, the first two based on those that had been drawn up for the le FH 43 and having an extra trail leg under the barrel. The Krupp Entwurf 1 was then abandoned by them in favour of Entwurf 2, a simple cruciform platform that was being developed for the 12.8cm K 44 gun. This platform was redesigned so that it would accept either the K 44 gun or the s FH 43 ordnance interchangeably. The s FH 43 was to have had bag charges and ring obturation, as used by the s FH 18/43, but none of these designs was ever completed.

The Skoda model never even reached the mock-up stage, being still on the drawing board when the war ended. It appears to have been little more than a suitably enlarged version of the le FH 43. The known data is meagre, but what can be found is given below.

Data (Krupp Entwurf 2)
Calibre: 150mm/5.92in.
Length of gun: 6158mm/242.44in/20.20ft.
Length of bore: not known.
Rifling: not known.
Breech mechanism: horizontal sliding block, percussion fired.
Traverse: 360°.
Elevation: −5° to +70°.
Weight in action: 7500kg/16538lb/7.38ton (estimated).

Performance
Estimated figures, firing standard high explosive shell weighing 43.50kg(95.92lb).
Charge 1: velocity 250mps/820fps, range figure not available.
Charge 8: velocity 660mps/2165fps, maximum range 18000m/19675yd.

Ammunition
Separate-loading, bagged charge.

Projectiles, Propelling Charges
An eight-charge system was proposed, firing the standard range of 15cm s FH projectiles, but the details were never finalised.

Data (Skoda Entwurf)
Calibre: 150mm/5.92in.
Traverse: 360°.
Elevation: −5° to +65°.
Weight in action: 5950kg/13120lb/5.86ton (estimated).

Performance
Estimated by Skoda ballisticians; firing a shell weighing 43.50kg(95.92lb).
Maximum charge: velocity 600mps/1969fps, maximum range 15000m/16405yd.
Chamber pressure: 2700kg/cm², 38410lb/in², or 17.15ton/in².

Ammunition
Separate-loading, bagged charge.

Projectiles, Propelling Charges
It was probably intended to use the existing range of s FH shells; an eight-part charge of uncertain constitution was devised.

Wooden mock-up of the 15cm s FH 43, showing the firing position.

Wooden mock-up of the s FH 43 in travelling mode. Its resemblance to the 105mm models is easily seen.

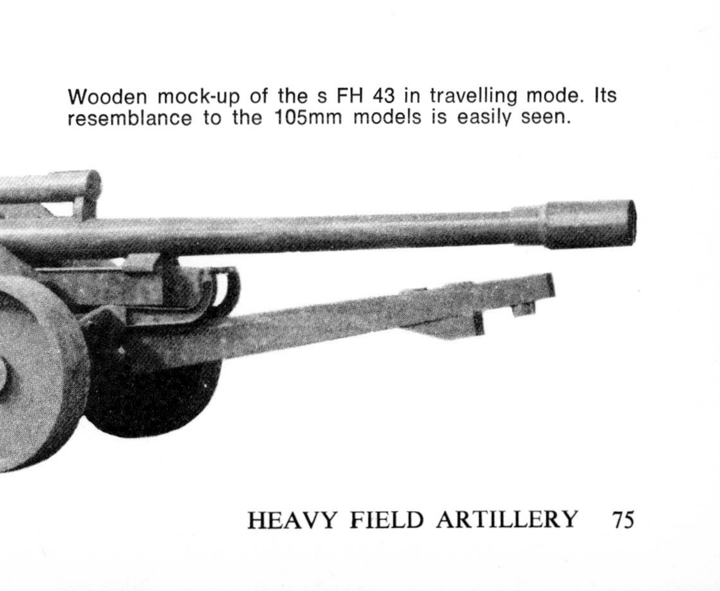

12·8cm Kanone 43

12·8cm K 43

By the middle of 1942 the army had been exposed to a variety of Soviet ordnance and had also captured a large number of them. They had been particularly impressed by the 12.2cm weapons, which seemed to give a useful blend of weight, range and shell power. The OKH therefore asked the designers for guns in either this or a similar calibre, taking care to include all the usual provisos about lightness, extra performance, ease of production and cheapness without which no weapon specification was complete. The calibre selected was 12.8cm, largely because this was already being used by various anti-aircraft and naval equipments and thus barrel-boring machinery was available.

Krupp and Skoda produced designs that were again largely based on the work they had already undertaken on the 10.5cm le FH 43. The Krupp version used a three-legged carriage (carrying the front leg under the barrel) from which the wheels were removed in action. The gun was a long high-velocity weapon with a 'pepperpot' muzzle brake. Its most unusual feature was to be a screw breech with De Bange obturation, owing to the shortage of cartridge case metal. This system has been discussed under the 15cm s FH 18/43, where it was pointed out that such a system is extremely demanding in machinery and expertise. While Krupp was probably the best firm in Germany to try it, since it had in the past produced a few screw breech weapons for export orders, there can be no doubt that successful development would have been a long process. Before the prototype stage was reached, however, the parallel development of the 12.8cm K 44 came to fruition, and

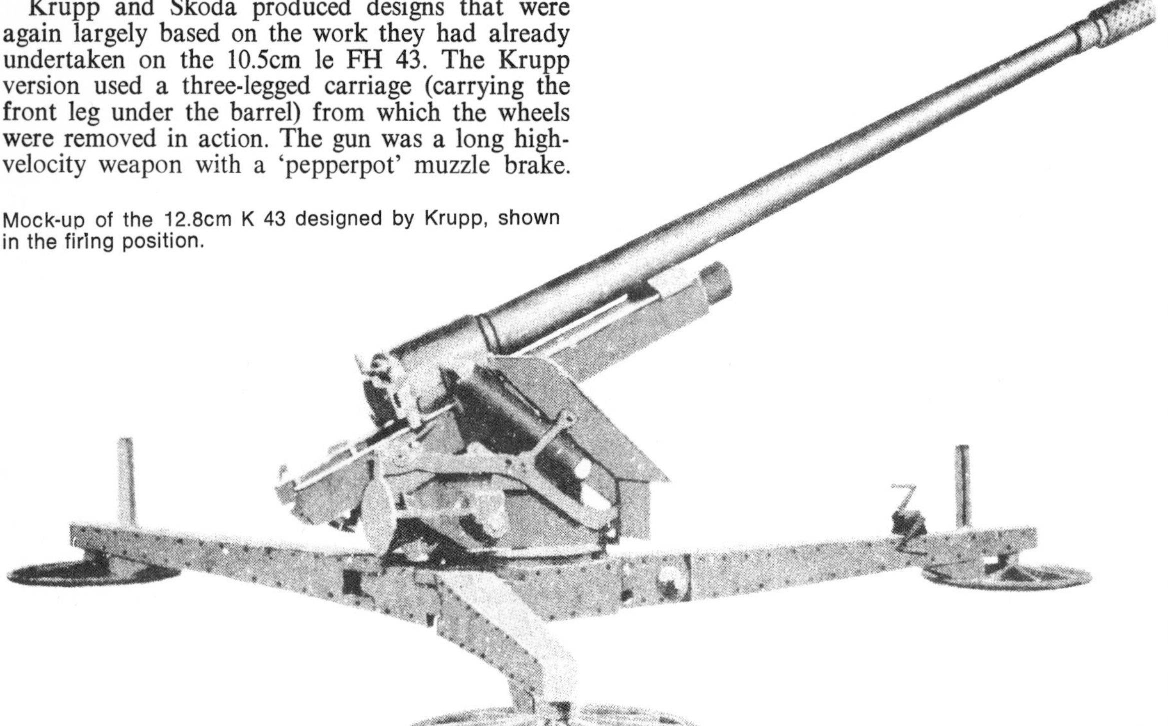

Mock-up of the 12.8cm K 43 designed by Krupp, shown in the firing position.

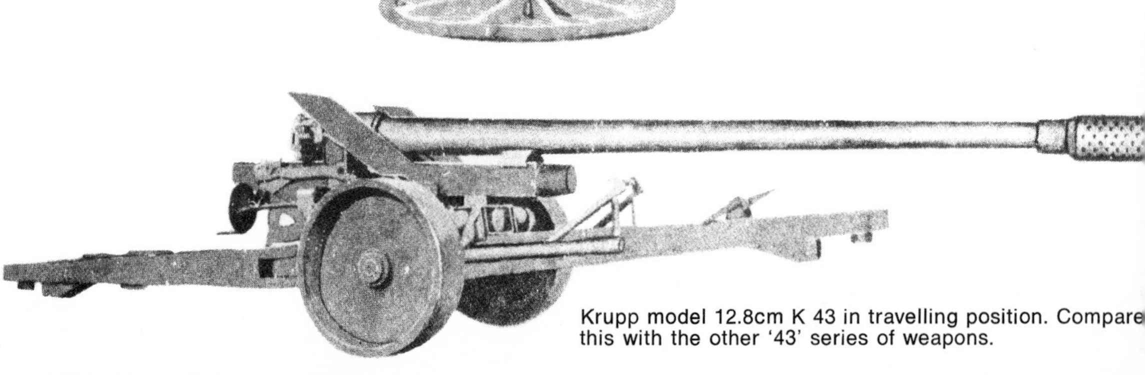

Krupp model 12.8cm K 43 in travelling position. Compare this with the other '43' series of weapons.

since this was a better gun in all respects the entire K43 project was dropped and the design staffs put to work on finalising the K44. Unfortunately no data on the K 43 has ever come to light; it is believed that all the drawings and specifications were destroyed, along with much more of the Krupp records, just before the war ended.

The Skoda model was also cancelled while still in the project stage. This was again to have been mounted on a four-legged carriage with firing pedestal. It is not known whether Skoda was developing it as a screw-breech weapon, though the firm was probably more familiar with this type of mechanism than was Krupp. What little data is known of the Skoda model is given below.

Data (Skoda Entwurf 25/940/S)
Calibre: 128mm/5.04in.
Traverse: 360°.
Elevation: −10° to +45°.
Weight in action: 6350kg/14002lb/6.25ton (estimated).

Performance
Skoda estimates, firing a shell weighing 25.00kg (55.131b).
Maximum charge: velocity 940mps/3084fps, maximum range 22000m/24059yd.

Ammunition
Separate-loading bagged(?) charge.

Projectiles
The planned projectile weight was 25.00kg(55.131b), but beyond that nothing is known of the shell or the charges by which it was fired.

12·8cm Kanone 44

12·8cm K 44

This equipment, considered by many authorities to be one of the most outstanding gun designs of the war years, was the outcome of combining the army's demand for a 12.8cm gun with Krupp's and Rheinmetall-Borsig's continuous development of anti-tank guns in larger and larger calibres.

The gun was 55 calibres long with a high efficiency muzzle brake. The breech mechanism was a semi-automatic sliding block using cased ammunition and the firing mechanism was an electric type. While the ordnance was the same, Krupp and Rheinmetall developed different carriages; the Krupp model had a cruciform platform with outriggers, carried on two two-wheel axles that could be swung from the ground as the platform was lowered by a simple hand-operated arc and pinion mechanism. The top carriage revolved on four rollers running around a racer plate on the lower carriage and was centred by a simple pivot.

The Rheinmetall carriage was also a cruciform type, carried on a two-wheel bogie at the front of the gun and a four-wheel bogie at the rear. The front bogie was removed completely on coming into action, while the rear bogie was raised from the ground but remained on the carriage to form part of the traversing mass and to add to the gun's stability. The top carriage was mounted on a roller race in the platform.

It was generally agreed that the Krupp design was the cleaner and better of the two, though critical examination showed that certain parts of the carriage—especially the wheel-raising gear and the traversing arrangements—were somewhat underweight for their tasks and might not have

Rheinmetall version of the K 44 in firing position.

Rheinmetall model K 44 in travelling position.

lasted long in service. Although prototypes were made, no complete weapons entered service though a number of gun barrels (51 according to some reports) were made and fitted to extempore carriages.

Data (Krupp Entwurf: data for Rheinmetall-Borsig's version was similar).
Calibre: 128mm/5.04in.
Length of gun: 7023mm/276.50in/23.04ft.
Length of bore: 6625mm/260.83in/21.74ft.
Rifling: 40 grooves, right-hand increasing twist, 1/27 to 1/24.75.
Breech mechanism: horizontal semi-automatic sliding block, electrically fired.
Traverse: 360°.
Elevation: −7°51 to +45°27'.
Weight in action: 10160kg/22403lb/10.00ton.

Performance
Firing standard high explosive shell weighing 28.00kg(61.74lb).
Reduced charge: velocity 750mps/2461fps, range figures not available.
Full charge: velocity 935mps/3068fps, maximum range 24410m/26695yd.

Ammunition
Separate-loading, cased charge.

Projectiles
12.8cm Sprgr Flak 40: fuzed AZ 23/28 or Dopp Z S/90, weight 26.00kg(57.33lb).
This, as its title implies, was originally a shell for the 12.8cm Flak gun and was supplied for the K 44 until stocks of specially-designed ammunition could be produced. Lighter than the standard shell, its maximum range was only 21030m (23000yd).
12.8cm Sprgr 5151 L/5.0: fuzed AZ 23/28 or Dopp Z S/60, weight 28.00kg(61.74lb).
This was the standard projectile that attained the maximum range. It is believed that this was originally a naval shell developed for the 12.8cm SK C/30, since some specimens are painted yellow —a standard naval colour—had naval acceptance stampings and were dated December 1943, before the K 44 design was finished. Like the Sprgr Flak 40, this shell had double driving bands and two grooves behind the bands indicating that it had started life as a component of a fixed round.
12.8cm Pzgr 43: fuzed Bd Z 5121, weight 28.30kg (62.40lb).
This was an armour piercing shell with penetrating and ballistic caps and a tracer pellet. Small variations in pattern were found in these projectiles, principally concerning the attachment of the ballistic cap: early models had a long cap that completely concealed the penetrating cap and was soldered on, while later models had a short cap that extended only half-way down the penetrating cap and was attached by six spot-welds.
12.8/9.6cm Fern Sprgr L/5.4 TS: fuzing not known, weight 15.20kg(33.52lb).
This was an experimental long-range shell that did not reach service. It consisted of a 9.6cm calibre subprojectile in a 12.8cm sabot. The sabot arrangements consisted of three cones at the shoulder of the subprojectile and a base cup held by shear pins. On firing, these pins broke, but the pressure of the propellant gas retained the base cup in contact with the shell. On leaving the muzzle the cones were thrown off by centrifugal force overcoming their attachment and the base cup was pulled clear by air drag. The payload was 1.40kg(3.09lb) of TNT. No details of performance are known.
12.8/10.5cm Fern Sprgr TS: fuzing not known, weight 19.20kg(42.34lb).
Another experimental long-range shell of differing dimensions. The sabot in this case was of pot type, the shell being held inside by three segments welded to the mouth of the pot and by a screw passing through the base of the pot into the shell base. On leaving the muzzle the segments were thrown clear by centrifugal force, while air drag forced the thin metal attachment of the base of the pot over the screw head and thus freed it from the shell. No performance details are known.

Propelling Charges
Two completely separate charges, each in its own case, were supplied: the reduced and the full charges. They both had the propellant enclosed in an artificial silk bag within the case, which was closed by a millboard cup; a label on the cup gave

Krupp model K 44 in travelling position.

Krupp version of the 12.8cm K 44 in firing position.

letails of the weapon and was overprinted in large ed letters SPRGR on the reduced charge and PZGR n the full charge—to emphasise the fact that rmour piercing projectiles were only to be fired vith the full charge. The make-up of the two harges was as follows:

Reduced charge: 12.55kg/27.67lb Digl R P.
ull charge: 15.30kg/33.74lb Gudol R P.

rimer

The electric primer C/22 St was used.
ase Identification Number: 6398.

A certain number of experimental cartridge cases for this weapon made their appearance after the war when various experimental and test establishments were examined. Two particularly interesting ones were bottle-necked, one 813mm(32.01in)—51mm(2.00in) shorter than the standard case—and marked *12.8cm Patrh 41 St.* The other was 1180mm(46.47in) long and was marked *I VII 30295 St 12.8cm Pz Jg K.* It appears from these that experiments were in progress to develop a fixed-ammunition version of the gun for use in self-propelled tank destroyers (*Panzerjäger* or Pz Jg)

12·8cm Kanone 81 series

2·8cm K 81, 81/1, 81/2

12.8cm Kanone 81 (12.8cm K 81).
The nomenclature K 81 was used in the development stages of the K 44, which has led to some confusion in the past. It was perpetuated in the names of two emergency equipments in which he K 44 gun was mated with captured French nd Russian gun carriages for troop trials and mergency combat use.

2.8cm Kanone 81/1 (12.8cm K 81/1).
This was the K 44 ordnance mounted on the ex-French 155mm gun Mle GPF-T carriage, the last of a series of guns based upon one originally developed during the 1914-18 war. This, a heavy split-trail pattern, had been modernised by fitting a four-wheel pneumatic-tyred bogie in place of the original two solid-tyred wheels. The gun was fitted into a German ring cradle placed on a simple pedestal top-carriage and appears to have been balanced by a large gunlayer's guard/counterbalance to make superfluous the need for equilibrators. The result was a high-set and cumbersome weapon that must have been awkward to use.

Data
Calibre: 128mm/5.04in.
Length of gun: 7020mm/276.38in/23.03ft.
Length of bore: 5533mm/217.83in/18.15ft.
Rifling: 40 grooves, right-hand increasing twist, 1/27 to 1/24.75.
Breech mechanism: horizontal sliding block, electrically fired.
Traverse: 60°.
Elevation: −4° to +45°.
Weight in action: 12150kg/26791lb/11.96ton.
Performance, Ammunition
See 22.8cm K 44.

12.8cm Kanone 81/2 (12.8cm K 81/2).
This was the K 44 mounted on the carriage of the ex-Russian 152mm howitzer model of 1937, another split-trail carriage with two solid tyred wheels although it was considerably modified by the Germans. The shield and balancing gear were removed and the traverse limited to 40° in place of the original 58°. The cradle and recoil system were discarded and the new gun was mounted in a ring cradle similar to that used on the 81/1, with a recoil system fitted on top. This mass effectively balanced the gun so that even without the original equilibrators the effort required to elevate and depress the barrel was very small. The K 81/2 was a more efficient weapon than the 81/1 but both designs appear to have been rushed and their execution imperfect, so that neither weapon was entirely trouble-free particularly with respect to the recoil systems which were poorly matched to the guns' power.

A second version of the K 81/2 was also built in which the original Russian equilibrators were retained and the gun mounted 583mm(22.95in) farther forward. This appears to have been a trial model since only one was ever found.

Data
As K 81/1 with the following exceptions.
Traverse: 40°.
Elevation: −4° to +45°.
Weight in action: 8200kg/18081lb/8.07ton.

Performance, Ammunition
See 12.8cm K 44.

An unusual 12.8cm K 81/2 fitted with equilibrators, found at a German proving ground in July 1945.

The more normal 12.8cm K 81/2 without equilibrators: Note the greater length of barrel behind the trunnions.

The 12.8cm K 81/1, using the ex-French 155mm gun carriage.

HEAVY
ARTILLERY

Most of the German Army's heavy guns had been taken over and destroyed by the Allied disarmament commissions after World War 1, and when the Wehrmacht rearmed, this class of weapon was high on the list of priorities. During the interwar years, heavy and super-heavy artillery was the cause of a great deal of contention. With the rise of air power—and the gradual increase in speed, bomb load and endurance of aircraft—it was often asked if heavy artillery was worth manufacturing and what, if any, advantage it had over aircraft. Many opinions voiced in the later 1920s and early 1930s visualised a force of aircraft at the army commanders' disposal, to be sent forth to deal with obstinate positions in the path of the advancing troops. The most voluble arguments of this type came—perhaps no surprise—from those who recalled the difficulties of moving enormous artillery weapons piecemeal through the mud of Flanders.

However there was one thing that the aeroplane could not at that time guarantee: round-the-clock, all-weather availability. Although the Germans accepted the idea of tactical air support, developing the well-known Junkers 87 *Sturmkampfflugzeug* ('Stuka') dive-bomber, they also decided to build conventional artillery.

When rearmament began the decision was taken to develop 17cm and 21cm guns and a 21cm howitzer, but a change of heart ensued and 24cm was selected as a more suitable calibre. Later still a 35cm howitzer was adopted for siege operations.

The heavy weapons of World War 1, notably the famous 42cm *Dicke Berthe* (strictly 'fat' or 'thick' Bertha, but generally known as 'Big Bertha') howitzers that had smashed the French and Belgian forts, were excellent weapons but had also been cumbersome to move and slow to emplace. The prime requirement for the new weapons, therefore, was ease and simplicity of transportation and assembly, made easier by contemporary techniques of suspension and motor traction. Towards the end of World War 2 plans were devised for transport on tracked chassis; these would have greatly improved the time-into-action figures, and also the cross-country performance, but few were properly developed before the war's end.

15cm Kanone 16

15cm K 16

This was a World War 1 equipment retained in post-war service, small numbers of which served on until 1945. Designed by Krupp and originally issued in 1917, it was a conventional design of its day with a box trail, steel wheels, and a curved shield. The axle was suspended by a transverse leaf spring. For transport the barrel could be detached from the recoil system and withdrawn on to a transport wagon, though for short moves the weapon generally travelled in its assembled form.

Data

Calibre: 150mm/5.91in.
Length of gun: 6410mm/252.36in/21.03ft.
Length of bore: not known.
Rifling: right-hand uniform twist, 1/25.
Breech mechanism: horizontal sliding block, percussion fired.
Traverse: 8°.
Elevation: −3° to +43°.
Weight in action: 10870kg/23968lb/10.70ton.

Performance

Firing the standard high explosive shell weighing 51.40kg(113.34lb).
Charge 1: velocity 555mps/1821fps, range figures not available.
Charge 2: velocity 696mps/2284fps, range figures not available.

The 15cm K 16, another relic of World War One

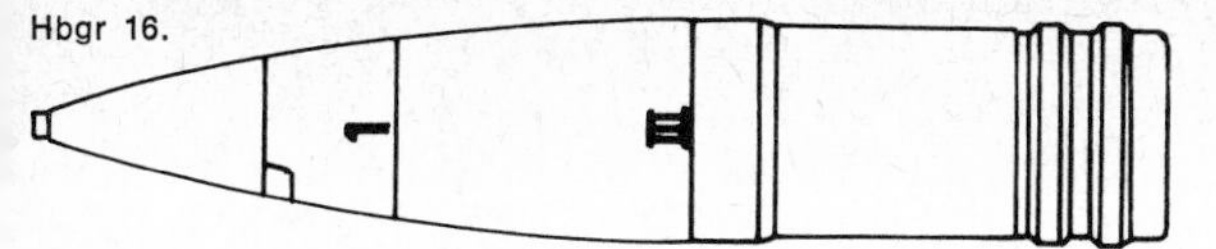

Charge 3: velocity 757mps/2485fps, maximum range 22000m/24059yd.

Ammunition
Separate-loading, cased charge.

Projectiles
15cm Hbgr 16: fuzed Hbgr Z 17/23, weight 51.40kg(113.34lb).
This was a nose-fuzed high explosive shell with a ballistic cap. The fuze, a modified First World War model, was only used with this equipment.
15cm Hbgr 16 umg: fuzed AZ Hbgr or Dopp Z S/60, weight 51.40kg(113.34lb)
This, basically similar to the previous shell, differed in the fuze-hole gauge and was thus adapted to the use of newer patterns of fuze.

Propelling Charges
A three-part charge of tubular propellant was provided in three bags. The charge 1 bag was issued in the cartridge case, the charge 2 bag replaced it completely when needed and the charge 3 bag could be slipped into the case alongside the charge 2 bag. A small circular igniter pad was secured to the bottom of the case by shellac cement.
Charge 1: 6.65kg/14.65lb Ngl R P.
Charge 2: 11.08kg/24.43lb Ngl R P.
Charge 3: 1.04kg/2.29lb Ngl R P.

Primer
The percussion primer C/12nA was used.

Case Identification Number: 6304.

15cm Kanone 18

15cm K 18

The K 18 was developed by Rheinmetall, commencing in 1933, to provide a replacement for the elderly 15cm K 16; it was eventually accepted into service in 1938. The K 18 was little improvement on its predecessor; it was almost two tons heavier, it still had to be dismantled for travelling, and the increase in range was a mere 2290m(2500yd).

In appearance the K18 was certainly more modern—a good example of the Rheinmetall's design style. The box trail was supported on a small limber for travelling and beneath it was slung a two-piece platform. The trail also carried a set of ramps for use during assembly, and for transport the barrel was removed to a transport wagon. The carriage unit, when it came into action, was drawn into the required position and the platform was lowered; the carriage was then pulled forward so that a supporting bracket, attached to the platform and to the axle, pivoted and raised the wheels from the ground. The ramps were then assembled to the trail and the barrel transporter was drawn up until the barrel could be slid into the cradle and connected to the recoil system. Once in action, the equipment was balanced so that it could be traversed relatively easily on the platform.

Data
Calibre: 150mm/5.91in.

The 15cm K 18 being brought into action: the ground platform has been lowered and the carriage is about to be pulled on to it.

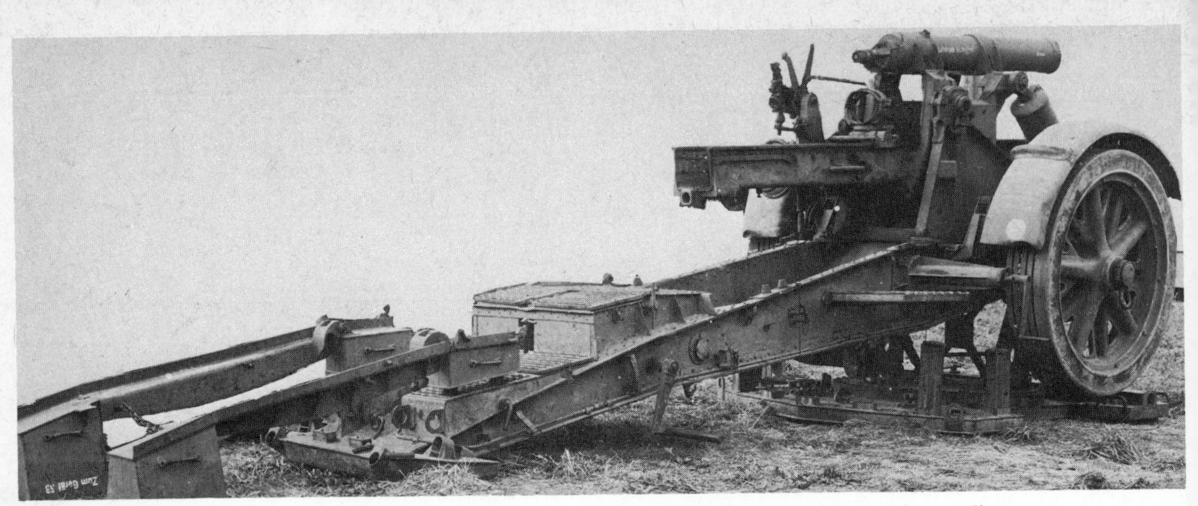

The carriage of the 15cm K 18 in position, ready for the barrel to be slid into place in the cradle.

Length of gun: 8200mm/322.83in/26.90ft.
Length of bore: 6432mm/253.23in/21.10ft.
Rifling: right-hand uniform twist, 1/30.
Breech mechanism: horizontal sliding block, percussion fired.
Traverse: 10° on the carriage, 360° on the turntable platform.
Elevation: −2° to +45°.
Weight in action: 12760kg/26136lb/12.56 ton.

Performance
Firing standard high explosive shell, weight 43.00kg(94.82lb).
Full charge: velocity 890mps/2920fps, maximum range 24500m/26793yd.

Ammunition
Separate-loading, cased charge.

Projectiles
15cm K Gr 18: fuzed AZ 23v(0.15), AZ 23v (0.25) or Dopp Z S/90, weight 43.00kg(94.82lb)
This, the standard high explosive shell, was of conventional pattern. Two copper driving bands were fitted and the filling was 5.65kg(12.46lb) of amatol 60/40.
15cm K Gr 42: fuzed AZ 1v(0.15) or Dopp Z S/90, weight 43.00kg(94.82lb).
Similar to the earlier model, this shell had two soft-iron (FEW) driving bands, set about 25mm (1in) farther forward on the shell, giving it a longer boat-tail. The walls were also slightly thinner, giving a capacity of 6.15kg(13.56lb) of amatol 50/50.
15cm Gr 19 Be rot: fuzed Bd Z f 15cm Gr Be, weight 43.50kg(95.92lb).
This was an anti-concrete shell with a truncated conical nose concealed by a bluntly-rounded ballistic cap; it was filled with 3.25kg(7.17lb) of TNT and was base fuzed.

Propelling Charges
It is known that three charges were provided, but no data of their constitution is available.

Primer
The percussion primer C/12nA was standard.
Case Identification Number: 6352.

The barrel of the 15cm K 18 on its transporter.

15cm Kanone 39

15cm K 39

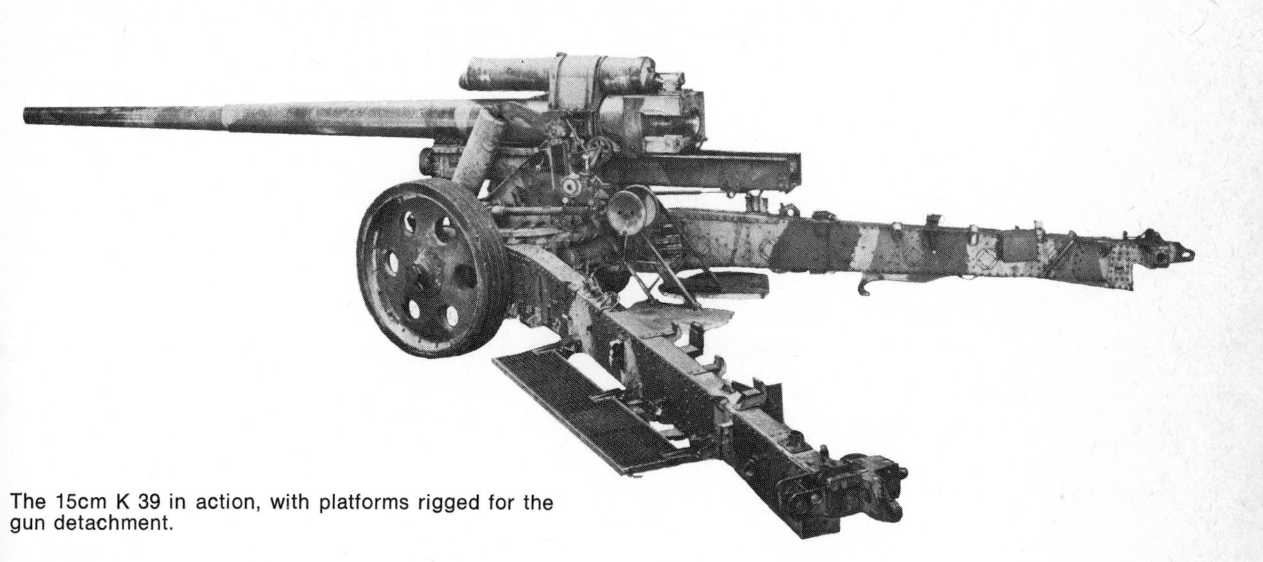

The 15cm K 39 in action, with platforms rigged for the gun detachment.

This was never demanded by the army but was one of Krupp's commercial products, designed and built in 1938 to fill an order from the Turkish Army. By September 1939 two weapons had been delivered, and the remainder of the order then being built was taken over by the German Army. Forty guns were thus acquired, issues of which commenced in 1940.

The K 39 was specifically designed as a dual-purpose weapon that was to be used in both the normal field role and, mounted on a special platform, as a coast defence gun. In common with the other 15cm guns the barrel was removed from the carriage for transport, and an additional transport wagon carried the ground platform when required.

The carriage was a split-trail type of modern appearance and had disc wheels suspended from leaf springs; hydropneumatic equilibrators were also fitted.

For coast use, the turntable platform was placed on the ground and twelve radial struts connected to it, the outer ends of which were then connected together by steel segments to form an outer circle. The whole unit was then firmly fixed in place by ground anchors. The gun went into action on the turntable with the trail legs locked together, the trail ends being fixed to a trolley riding on the outer circle of segments. The equipment was traversed by a hand-crank on the trolley that engaged a sprocket on one trolley wheel and gave coarse pointing; fine laying was then done by traversing the gun on the carriage in the usual way, although a movement of only 6° was available with the trail legs closed.

The whole idea seems to have been based on the American *Panama Mount* developed in the 1920s for the 155mm GPF gun, but the German version was in portable form. The later American *Kelly Mount* platform for the 155mm Gun M1, in turn, copied the German design.

Data

Calibre: 149.1mm/5.87in.
Length of gun: 8255mm/325.00in/27.08ft.
Length of bore: 7868mm/309.76in/25.81ft.
Rifling: right-hand increasing twist, 1/41 to 1/30.
Breech mechanism: horizontal sliding block, percussion fired.
Traverse: 60° on the carriage (trail legs open), 360° on the turntable.
Elevation: −3° to +46°.
Weight in action: 12200kg/26901lb/12.01ton.

Performance

Firing standard high explosive shell weighing 43.00kg(94.82lb).
Charge 1: velocity 620mps/2034fps, range figures not available.
Charge 2: velocity 780mps/2559fps, range figures not available.
Charge 3: velocity 865mps/2838fps, maximum range 24700m/27012yd.

The 15cm K 39 in marching order. Top: the barrel on its transporter. Centre: the carriage with limber. Below: the circular firing platform in pieces on its transporter.

The 15cm K 39 in place on its ground firing platform. This is one of the original Turkish guns, and the photograph was made in Krupp's assembly shop.

Ammunition
Separate-loading, cased charge.

Projectiles
15cm K Gr 18, 15cm Gr 19 Be rot.
These were the shells discussed under the 15cm K 18 (*qv*).
15cm Sprgr L/4.6: fuzed EK Zdr m V or Dopp Z S/60, weight 45.00kg(99.23lb).
This was the standard high explosive shell designed for Turkey and taken into use with the guns; when the stocks were used up, the shells of the 15cm K 18 were used.
15cm Halb Pzgr: base fused, weight 45.00kg (99.23lb).
This, a semi-armour-piercing shell for coast defence firing, was designed for Turkey. The term 'semi-armour-piercing' was not an official German designation but implied an armour piercing capability of about two-thirds of the shell's calibre. It was intended to attack lightly armoured vessels or the less well-protected upper-works of armoured warships with this shell.
15cm Pzgr: base fuzed, weight 45.00kg(99.23lb)
This was the third of the original Turkish shells: a genuine armour piercing projectile for use in the coast defence role but also effective as an anti-tank projectile. According to a German table it was fired at a velocity of 720mps(2362fps) and would penetrate 158mm (6.22in) of plate at 1000mm (1094yd), striking at a 30° angle.

Propelling Charges
There were three charges—Kleine, Mittelere and Grosse—obtained by combining four charge bags. The Kleine Ladung was a separate bag, the Mittelere Ladung was a combination of the Hauptkart bag and Vorkart 2, and the Grosse Ladung a combination of the Hauptkart and Vorkarten 2 and 3.
Kleine Ladung: 9.79kg/21.59lb Dgl R P.
Hauptkart: 14.50kg/31.97lb Dgl R P.
Vorkart 2: 2.30kg/5.07lb Dgl R P.
Vorkart 3: 2.13kg/4.70lb Dgl R P.
The Kleine Ladung and the Hauptkartusche had igniter pads stitched to the bottom of the bags.

Primer
The percussion primer C/12nA was standard.

Case Identification Number: 6318.

Rear view of the 15cm K 39 breech.

15cm Schiffskanone C/28 in Mörserlafette

15cm SK C/28M (Gladiole)

This was an extemporary equipment constructed by mounting the 15cm coast and naval gun SK C/28 on the carriage of the 21cm Haubitze 18. The carriage had been designed (as will be seen) for use interchangeably with either the 21cm howitzer or the 17cm gun, but production of carriages soon outpaced that of the guns. So, as an interim measure to provide the army with weapons (and also to enable units to become accustomed to the new carriages), the 15cm SK C/28 in Mrs Laf was devised. Only eight such hybrids were made in 1941, and as soon as an adequate supply of 17cm barrels became available they were reconverted to their designed calibre.

Further details of the weapon and its ammunition may be found in COAST ARTILLERY. The data given here refers only to the field version.

Data
Calibre: 149.1mm/5.87in.
Length of gun: 8291mm/326.42in/27.20ft.
Length of bore: 7815mm/307.68in/25.64ft.
Rifling: right-hand increasing twist, 1/50 to 1/30.
Breech mechanism: horizontal sliding block, percussion fired.

Traverse: 16° on the carriage, 360° on the platform.
Elevation: 0 to +50°.
Weight in action: 16870kg/37198lb/16.61ton.

Performance
Firing standard high explosive shell weighing 43.00kg(94.82lb).

Full charge: velocity 890mps/2920fps, maximur range 23700m/25918yd.

Ammunition
Separate-loading, cased charge.

Projectiles, Propelling Charges
See 15cm SK C/28.

15cm Hochdruckpumpe

Fleissige Liesel/Der Tausendfussler/Vergeltungswaffen-Drei

The 15cm HDP was the final flowering of one of the ideas that had hovered around the lunatic fringe of gunnery since the middle of the nineteenth century—the multiple-chambered gun. The basic idea is deceptively simple; a gun barrel of considerable length is made and additional lateral cartridge chambers are lead into the bore at periodic intervals, so that a plan view resembles a herring-bone. The projectile is loaded at the breech, complete with a propelling charge, and additional charges are loaded into the supplementary chambers. The first or conventional charge is fired, starting the shell on its way up the bore. At about the point where the rate of acceleration ceases to increase, the shell passes the mouth of the second chamber and as it does so the supplementary charge therein is fired to give a fresh quantity of propellant gas and further accelerate the shell. The same thing is done as each chamber is passed, until the desired velocity is achieved, after which the shell can be left to travel the rest of the bore before leaving the muzzle.

The principal ballistic objection to this is that the charges must be ignited at exactly the correct position of the projectile—literally to within an inch or two. The usual time-tolerance for electrical ignition of a charge is in the vicinity of 0.015sec, and since the desired bore velocities are in the order of 610–1220mps (2000–4000fps), this means that the position of the shell can only be guaranteed within something like 9-18m(30–60ft) when the supplementary charges are ignited. Another objection is that wear on the connecting ports leading to the bore from these chambers promotes still more irregularity, and the third bogey arises from the meeting of pressure waves in the bore giving rise to abnormal sporadic high pressures.

Patents were first granted on such an idea in the 1860s and the first practical attempt was the American *Lyman and Haskell gun,* fired experimentally in the 1880s. On trial this actually gave inferior performance to a conventional gun of the same calibre, although the pressures in the barrel reached alarming figures. The fault was found to be due to the propellant flash passing the shell in the bore and pre-igniting the supplementar charges so that they obstructed rather than rein forced the chamber pressure.

Like every other ordnance idea, the multi chamber gun reappeared from time to time; i was, for example, offered to the British Ordnanc Board in 1941. The board turned it down, pointin out that this was the third time it had bee presented since 1918. But at about the same tim in Germany Herr Cönders, who was the chie engineer of Röchling Stahlwerke AG, had als begun working on the idea. The Röchling com pany had, of course, developed the Röchling fin stabilised anti-concrete shell and it is apparen from Cönder's early descriptions that he wa looking for a way of delivering these projectile at long range and at high velocity. By May 194 he had sufficient faith in his ideas to persuade th company to build a 2cm prototype that seemed t work quite well. The next step was to obtai higher approval and, through Reichsministe Speer, Hitler was informed of the invention an its potential. By this time the end product ha been planned: a 50-barrel battery of 15 cm guns each with a barrel 150m(492ft) long, buried in a hillside at Mimoyèques (near Calais), and aime at London.

Speer's report, together with the grandios intention, captured Hitler's imagination, and th 15cm HDP forthwith became Vergeltungswaffendre (V3); on the Führer's authority contracts wer placed for the work necessary to construct th weapon and to build the massive emplacement— though neither a full-calibre gun nor a projectil had then been made. By the end of Septembe 1943 a short 15cm version had been built an installed at the Hillersleben artillery test range The gun was simply laid on a framework of stee girders set in concrete, and no recoil system wa used. The principal breech was a horizontal sliding block, while the supplementary chambers each had a simple screwed-block with a steel obturating ring. The original plan had been to electrically ignite the charges in the correct sequence, but this was abandoned; ignition was thereafter performed by the propellant flash as the shell passed up the bore. This in turn led straight to Lyman's

The rear end of the 15cm HDP long-range multiple-chamber gun at the Misdroy test installation. The side chambers can be seen in this view; the girder structure at the rear is part of a recoil-spreading arrangement of bracing.

and Haskell's troubles of premature ignition, but knowledge of sealing had improved in the intervening years and careful design of an obturating piston behind the shell eventually cured the fault. The original plan called for as many as 24 auxiliary chambers, but experiments showed that after the ignition of the first four or five the projectile was moving so fast that the remaining chambers had no time to produce a useful volume of gas; the design therefore settled on a smaller number of chambers.

The first firing trials disclosed faults in the special projectile: the fins had failed to open properly. These shells had used the wrap-around flexible fin system of the Röchling anti-concrete shell, but this type of fin assembly was not suited to the high velocities developed in the HDP. The design was changed to use rigid fins and shell production ensued.

The next stage was the assembly of a full-length 15cm barrel on a range at Misdroy on the Baltic, where final firing trials were undertaken and where the troops were trained to use the gun.

The Misdroy trials began in March 1944 and soon ran into trouble. The shells were unstable in flight and the sporadic high pressures in the barrel caused sections to be ruptured at frequent intervals. During all this time the Heereswaffenamt

(HWA), the ordnance department responsible for weapon design, had been excluded from the project by Hitler's express order; for he considered, probably justifiably, that these people were so reactionary that they would have thrown the idea into the wastebasket out of hand. They, too, would probably have been justified. After a good deal of political squabbling the HWA was called in to advise and under its guidance a stable shell, sub-calibre with rigid fins and a discarding support at the shoulder, was produced. In May 1944 a further series of trials were held, firing shells made by a variety of contractors—Röchling, Bochumer Verein, Wittkowitz and Skoda among them—and in spite of more burst barrels the predicted range of 150km(93mile) seemed to be in sight at last. During all this time work had been going ahead at Mimoyèques preparing the site and installing the ammunition hoists and gun barrels. At the same time, however, the Germans were busy installing V1 flying-bomb launching sites all over northern France and this activity drew the attention of the Allied airforces. In their efforts to bomb everything and anything that looked at all like a rocket installation, they found Mimoyèques and thoroughly bombed it; this naturally destroyed much of the engineering work and set the programme back considerably.

Eventually, while the firings at Misdroy continued in an attempt to perfect the projectile and solve the bursting barrel problem, the Allied invasion overran the Calais area, including Mimoyèques. After the position had been thoroughly examined by the Allies it was finally destroyed by the strategic application of 50 tons of blasting explosives.

The 15cm HDP, however, finally achieved active status when two short models were made and sent in December 1944 to assist the Ardennes offensive. One was assembled on a railway flatcar and the other emplaced on a hillside at Hermeskeil. The former opened fire against Antwerp and the latter fired against Luxembourg for a few days; they were then destroyed in the face of the Allied counterattacks. It is most unfortunate that little or no data has ever come to light on the performance of these two weapons: the figures that follow are collected from a variety of sources and their accuracy cannot be guaranteed.

Data (projected model).
Calibre: 150mm/5.91in.
Length of gun: 150m/492.15ft.
Breech mechanism: (primary) horizontal sliding block, electrically fired; (secondary) interrupted screw, flash fired.
Traverse: nil.
Elevation: fixed at 55° for optimum range.
Range (intended): 150000m/164040yd/93.20mile.

Performance
Firing a shell weighing 83.00kg(183.02lb).
Full charges: velocity 1463mps/4800fps, maximum range 88500m/96784yd/54.99miles.

Ammunition
Separate-loading.

Projectiles
15cm Sprgr 4481: weight 83.00kg(183.02lb), length as loaded 2345mm(92.32in).
This was an 8cm projectile with six full-calibre fins and a four-piece support sabot at the shoulder. At the base of the fins was a heavy pusher piston that, centred in the projectile by a spigot but not firmly connected, drove the shell up the bore and was allowed to fall clear after leaving the muzzle. The base of the piston was cupped to give a gas seal. The shoulder unit having been unlocked by setback on firing, was free to fall clear on ejection. The fuze fitted in the specimen shown is an inert dummy, and no information is available concerning the intended service fuze. The photograph shows a Wittkowitz designed projectile with the front supports in the unlocked position; the drawing shows a slightly different version made by Skoda.

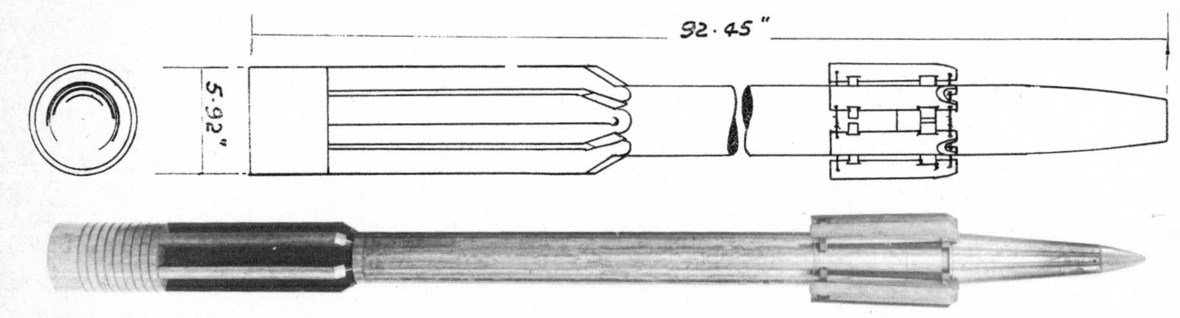

A projectile for the 15cm HDP. The forward sabot has been partly lifted from its place to show the method of discard, while the pusher piston is in place behind the tail fins.

Propelling Charges
The charges were all 5.00kg(11.03lb) in weight although the nature of propellant is not known.

Cartridge Case, Primer
The case was a standard 10.5cm le FH 18 case (6340) with an electric primer C/22.

17cm Kanone 18 in Mörserlafette

17cm K 18 in Mrs Laf (Matterhorn)

This, together with its partner piece the 21cm Mörser 18, was the mainstay of the German heavy artillery. The same carriage, designed by Krupp, was used for both weapons; for short-distance movement it remained in one piece but, for longer moves, it could be split into two loads. For such moves the barrel was carried on a separate transport wagon.

The 17cm Kanone 18 in Mörserlafette was introduced in 1941 to replace the 15cm weapons that by then had shown that their performance was insufficient for contemporary warfare. The gun itself was quite orthodox, but the carriage had a number of interesting features. A box-trail structure, it was one of the first—certainly the first in quantity production—to use the *dual recoil* system; in this design the barrel recoiled in its cradle in the usual way, but in addition the top carriage (which carried the gun and the cradle) was permitted to recoil across the basic carriage body. Both systems were of the usual hydropneumatic type and the normal recoil lengths were 860mm(33.86in) for the gun in its cradle and 1250mm(49.21in) for the top carriage. The effect of this dual system was to damp out the recoil stresses so effectively that, on firing, the gun platform was very steady.

The basic carriage carried an integral platform that could be lowered to the ground on going into action. The weight of the entire equipment was then transferred to the platform by jacking down three castor wheels that rode around its circumference, thus lifting the gun wheels from the ground. The trail end was supported on a spade float. To obtain large amounts of traverse the rear castor-wheel jack was operated to lift the trail and float clear of the ground, after which the whole weapon could easily be swung around the platform by two men.

Data
Calibre: 173mm/6.81in.
Length of gun: 8530mm/335.83in/27.99ft.
Length of bore: 8103mm/319.02in/26.58ft.
Rifling: 48 grooves, right-hand increasing twist, 1/50 to 1/30.
Breech mechanism: horizontal sliding block, percussion fired.
Traverse: 16° on the carriage, 360° on the platform.
Elevation: 0 to +50°.
Weight in action: 17520kg/38632lb/17.25ton.

Performance
Firing long-range high explosive shell weighing 62.80kg(138.47lb).
Charge 1: velocity 620mps/2034fps, maximum range 18300m/20013yd.
Charge 2: velocity 740mps/2428fps, maximum range 22700m/24825yd.

The 17cm K in Mrs Laf. in firing position.

K Gr 38 Hb.

The 17cm Kanone in Mörserlafette in the travelling mode.

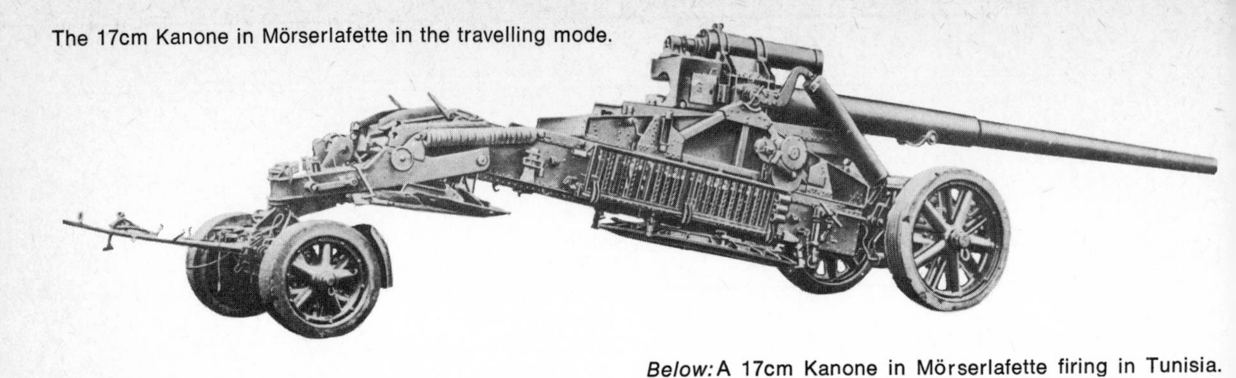

Charge 3: velocity 860mps/2822fps, maximum range 28000m/30621yd.
Charge 4: velocity 925mps/3035fps, maximum range 29600m/32371yd.

Ammunition
Separate-loading, cased charge.

Projectiles
17cm K Gr 39: fuzed AZ 35K or Dopp Z S/90K, weight 68.00kg(149.94lb).
The standard high explosive shell; the maximum range attained with this projectile was 28000m (30621yd).
17cm K Gr 38 Hb: fuzed Hbgr Z 35K or Dopp Z S/90S, weight 62.80kg(138.47lb).
This was a long-range shell fitted with a ballistic cap over the fuze; early models had two bimetallic driving bands, but after mid-1944 these shells were fitted with two sintered-iron bands.
17cm Pzgr 73: fuzed Bd Z f 17cm Pzgr, weight 71.00kg(156.56lb).
This, an armour piercing shell for anti-tank use, was restricted to use with charge 3 owing to its weight. The velocity attained using this charge was 830mps(2723fps) and the penetration at 1000m(1094yd) was 255mm(10.04in) at 30° impact.

Propelling Charges
This was a four-charge unit, assembled from various combinations of five bags:
Charge 1: Sonderkart 1 in the cartridge case.
Charge 2: Sonderkart 2 added, also in the case.

Below: A 17cm Kanone in Mörserlafette firing in Tunisia.

Charge 3: formed of the Hauptkart in the case, with Vorkart 3 loaded into the gun chamber ahead of it.
Charge 4: the Hauptkart, Vorkart 3 and Vorkart 4 pushed into an internal cavity in the centre of the Vorkart 3 bag; the fourth charge was only used with the Gr 38 Hb long range shell.
The various increments' constitution was:
Sonderkart 1: 14.98kg/33.04lb Digl R P.
Sonderkart 2: 4.89kg/10.78lb Digl R P.
Hauptkart: 16.00kg/35.28lb Digl R P.
Vorkart 3: 12.95kg/28.55lb Digl R P.
Vorkart 4: 1.35kg/2.98lb Digl R P.

Primer
The percussion primer C/12nA was standard.
Case Identification Number: 6324.

Lange 21cm Mörser

Lg 21cm Mrs

This was another Krupp design of World War 1, having been introduced in 1916. In its original form the weapon was designed for horse draught in two loads, the barrel and the carriage, but between the wars it was modified for vehicle draught by replacing the old steel-spoked wheels by solid rubber-tyred disc wheels and providing a rubber-tyred limber to carry the trail end.

The carriage was a box-trail pattern typical of its day, complete with shield (sometimes discarded in the Reichsheer), and was easily recognised by the unusual sheet-metal shield over the hydro-pneumatic recuperator above the barrel. The hydraulic buffers were mounted in the cradle in the usual way and a single spring balancing-press supported the muzzle preponderance.

The design was obsolescent in 1939 and few saw active service.

Data
Calibre: 211mm/8.31in.
Length of gun: 3063mm/120.59in/10.05ft.
Length of bore: 2296mm/90.39in.
Rifling: not known.
Breech mechanism: horizontal sliding block, percussion fired.
Traverse: 4°.
Elevation: −6° to +70°.
Weight in action: 6680kg/14729lb/6.58ton.

Performance
Firing standard high explosive shell weighing 113.00kg(249.17lb).
Charge 1: velocity 247mps/810fps, range figures not available.
Charge 2: velocity 269mps/883fps, range figures not available.
Charge 3: velocity 290mps/951fps, range figures not available.
Charge 4: velocity 310mps/1017fps, range figures not available.
Charge 5: velocity 335mps/1099fps, range figures not available.
Charge 6: velocity 359mps/1178fps, range figures not available.
Charge 7: velocity 393mps/1289fps, maximum range 11100m/12140yd.

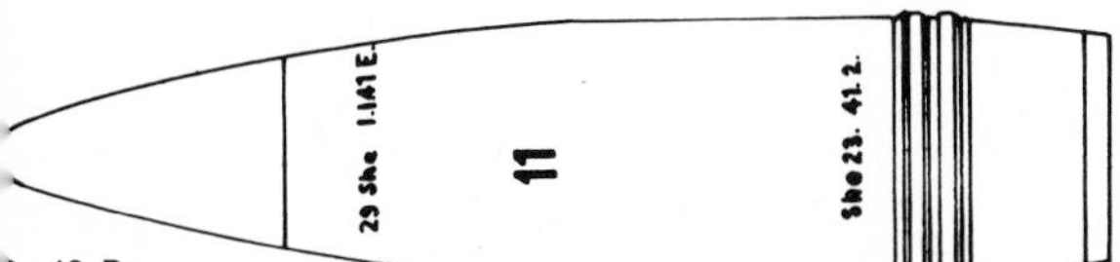

Gr 18 Be.

Ammunition
Separate-loading, cased charge.

Projectiles
21cm Gr 18: fuzed AZ 23v(0.15) or Dopp Z S/90, weight 113.00kg(249.17lb).
This, the standard high explosive shell, had two bimetallic driving bands; the filling was TNT. An alternative was the 21cm Gr 18 Stg manufactured of cast-steel.
21cm Gr 18 Be: fuzed Bd Z f 21cm Gr Be, weight 121.40kg(267.69lb).
A concrete-piercing shell with a ballistic cap and a base fuze, this was fitted with two bimetallic driving bands (very close together) and filled with 11.61kg(25.60lb) of TNT.

Propelling Charges
No details are available.

Primer
The percussion primer C/12nA was used.
Case Identification Number: 6305.

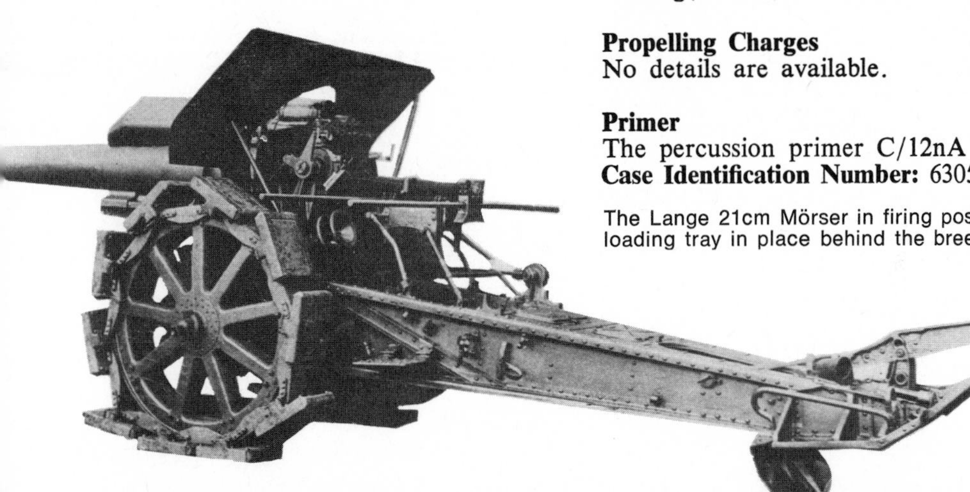

The Lange 21cm Mörser in firing position, with the shell loading tray in place behind the breech.

The Lange 21cm Mörser in action. The shield has been removed from this weapon.

21cm Mörser 18

21cm Mrs 18 (Brümmbar)

This Krupp design was intended to replace the 21cm Langer Mörser, and issue began in 1939. It was a vast improvement in every respect, since the carriage was the 'dual recoil' model with 360° traverse already described under the 17cm Kanone in Mörserlafette. The only difference was that, since this design was a howitzer, it was capable of elevation to 70°, while the gun was only operable to 50°.

The 21cm Mörser 18, good as the weapon was, was not in the army's view good enough to warrant volume production, especially as the 17cm Kanone had almost twice its range. In 1942, therefore, the production programme was cancelled so that more 17cm weapons could be produced; with this move the army virtually abandoned 21cm as a viable calibre, concentrating instead on 24cm weapons.

Gr 18.

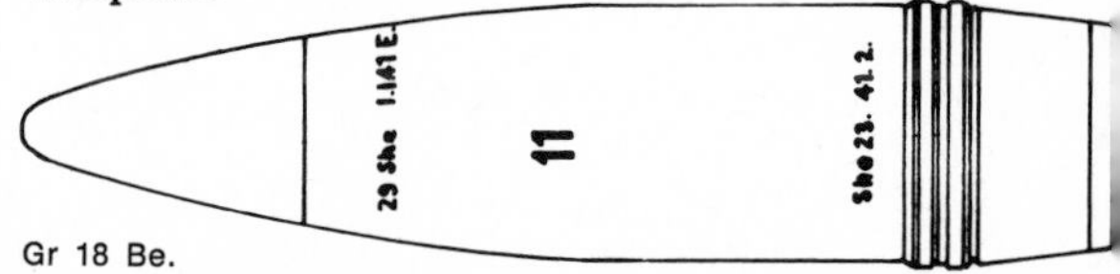

Gr 18 Be.

The 21cm Mörser 18 goes into action. The barrel transporter is at the right of the picture, and the barrel has been slid into place on the carriage.

A 21cm Mörser 18 with the barrel at maximum elevation.

A 21cm Mrs. 18 in action. This is the issue version, using single solid-tyred wheels instead of the dual bogie.

Above: The carriage of the 21cm Mrs 18. *Below:* A 21cm Mörser 18 positioned on its firing table.

Data
Calibre: 211mm/8.31in.
Length of gun: 6510mm/256.30in/21.36ft.
Length of bore: 6070mm/238.98in/19.91ft.
Rifling: 64 grooves, right-hand increasing twist, 1/35 to 1/30.
Breech mechanism: horizontal sliding block, percussion fired.
Traverse: 16° on the carriage, 360° on the platform.
Elevation: 0 to +70°.
Weight in action: 16700kg/36824lb/16.44ton.

Performance
Firing standard high explosive shell weighing 113.00kg(249.17lb).
Charge 1: velocity 225mps/739fps, maximum range 4650m/5085yd.
Charge 2: velocity 255mps/837fps, maximum range 5850m/6398yd.
Charge 3: velocity 290mps/951fps, maximum range 7325m/8011yd.
Charge 4: velocity 355mps/1165fps, maximum range 9800m/10717yd.
Charge 5: velocity 440mps/1444fps, maximum range 12500m/13670yd.
Charge 6: velocity 565mps/1854fps, maximum range 16700m/18263yd.
Firing anti-concrete shell weighing 121.40kg (267.69lb).
Charge 1: velocity 218mps/715fps, maximum range 4350m/4757yd.
Charge 2: velocity 247mps/810fps, maximum range 5500m/6015yd.
Charge 3: velocity 281mps/922fps, maximum range 7000m/7655yd.
Charge 4: velocity 344mps/1129fps, maximum range 9600m/10499yd.
Charge 5: velocity 426mps/1398fps, maximum range 12400m/13561yd.
Charge 6: velocity 550mps/1805fps, maximum range 16725m/18290yd.

Ammunition
Separate-loading, cased charge.

Projectiles
21cm Gr 18 or Gr 18 Stg: fuzed AZ 23umg M2V or Dopp Z S/90, weight 113.00kg(249.17lb). This, the standard high explosive shell, was fitted

with two bimetallic driving bands; the 'Stg' model was of cast-steel with soft-iron driving bands.

21cm Gr 18 Be: fuzed Bd Z f 21cm Gr Be, weight 121.40kg(267.69lb).

An anti-concrete shell of the usual ballistic-capped type, with a base fuze.

21cm Gr 37: fuzed AZ 23umg (0.15), weight 120.30kg(265.26lb).

This was similar to the Gr 18 model but was fitted with only one wide sintered-iron driving band.

21cm Rö Gr 42 Be: weight 192.00kg(423.36lb), length 2591mm(102.01in).

This was a special Röchling anti-concrete shell. An 'over-long' projectile, it was provided with tangentially-folding fins at the rear, covered by a metal case that was discarded shortly after leaving the muzzle; the shoulder of the shell had a multi-groove three-part sabot that was also discarded at the muzzle. At high elevations these discards were a hazard to the detachment. Penetration into concrete was quoted as being 4000mm (157.48in) in official manuals, though incomparably better results were obtained on trial firings and this low figure may have been deliberately printed on security grounds. The explosive content was only 2.85kg(6.28lb) and the maximum range attainable was 11275m/12330yd.

21cm Rö Gr 44 Be: weight 113.00kg(247.17lb) length 1677mm(66.02in).

This was a much smaller Röchling shell, thoug of the same basic design. This had a much bette performance insofar as accuracy and effect wer concerned, since the filling was 8.00kg(17.64lb) o TNT/montan wax. Penetration figures quote 2200mm(86.61in) as the optimum figure, but agai much better figures were obtained on trials. It i doubtful whether any of these shells were eve used.

21cm Minengeschoss mit Klappleitwerk: no detail of weight or fuzing available.

This projectile, a fin-stabilised high-capacity shel based on much the same design as that for th 15cm s FH 18, was under development in 194 at the factory of Faserstoff und Spinnerei Fürsten-berg AG. No details of performance are know and, indeed, it is not certain that the shell got a far as the firing stage.

21cm Minengeschoss: no details of weight o fuzing available.

Under development by Krupp in 1945, this wa a spin-stabilised high-capacity shell. So far as i known it never got beyond the drawing board stage before the war ended.

21cm Mörser 18s—a display of captured weapons in Russia.

Side view of the 21cm Mrs. in action.

A 21cm Mörser transporter being tested in deep snow.

Another transporter design for the 21cm Mörser.

Propelling Charges

Two types of charge were provided; one for the normal projectiles and one for the Röchling pro-ectiles. The normal charge was in six bags, plus an igniter; charges 1 to 5 were in the cartridge case, and charge 6 was in a separate bag that when used completely replaced the other five. The charge 1 unit was in a double bag, each ection carrying a different propellant granulation or ballistic reasons. Charges were made up from Gudol, Ngl or Digl powders; the example given here is the Digl charge.

Charge 1: 1.00kg/2.21lb Digl B1 P plus 1.37kg/3.02lb Digl Rg P.
Charge 2: 0.527kg/1.16lb Digl Rg P.
Charge 3: 0.697kg/1.54lb Digl Rg P.
Charge 4: 1.480kg/3.26lb Digl Rg P.
Charge 5: 2.124kg/4.68lb Digl Rg P.
Charge 6: 15.537kg/34.26lb Digl R P.

The special charge for Röchling projectiles was a single bag, issued in the standard cartridge case, containing 13.04kg(28.75lb) of Digl R P. The charge bags were conspicuously marked in red *Nür fur 21cm Rö Gr 44 Be und 21cm Rö Gr 42 Be* and the extra-large letters *Rö*.

Primer

The percussion primer C/12nA was standard in both types of cartridge.

Case Identification Number: 6341.

21cm Kanone 38

21cm K38

After the development of the 21cm Mörser 18, the OKH asked for a 21cm gun of similar mobility, and Krupp undertook the development against a contract calling for the delivery of 15 equipments by 1940. By 1943 only eight had been produced, one of which had been sent to Japan, but by then the army had decided that 21cm was an unsuitable calibre in terms of shell-power, range and mobility; the contract was consequently terminated without the remainder of the guns being completed.

The mounting was basically similar to that used on the 21cm Mörser 18, although it was considerably improved by the use of inclined undersurfaces at each end that rode on the transport limbers. By means of a hand winch (or the power-winch of the towing tractor) the limbers were winched apart and the inclined surfaces allowed the mounting to drop quickly into action. When it was necessary to move the gun, the limbers were positioned at each end of the mounting and winched together—thus raising the mounting into the travelling position as the inclined surfaces rode up on to the limbers. A central platform and three jacks allowed all-round traverse, in common with the Mörser mounting. The weapon's barrel could be unshipped and carried on a transport wagon when necessary.

Data
Calibre: 211mm/8.31in.
Length of gun: 11620mm/457.48in/38.12ft.
Length of bore: 11075mm/436.02in/36.34ft.
Rifling: 56 grooves, right-hand increasing twist, 1/40 to 1/33.
Breech mechanism: horizontal sliding block, percussion fired.
Traverse: 17° on the carriage, 360° on the platform.
Elevation: 0 to +50°.
Weight in action: 25300kg/55787lb/24.90ton.

Performance
Firing standard high explosive shell weighing 120.00kg(264.60lb).
Kleine Ladung: 680mps/2231fps, range figures not available.
Mittelere Ladung: 796mps/2612fps, range figures not available.
Grosse Ladung: 905mps/2969fps, maximum range 33900m/37073yd.

Ammunition
Separate-loading, cased charge.

Projectiles
21cm K Gr 38: fuzed Hbgr Z 35K or M Dopp Z 28K, weight 120.00kg(264.60lb).
This, the standard high explosive shell, was fitted with a ballistic cap over the nose and carried three soft-iron driving bands.

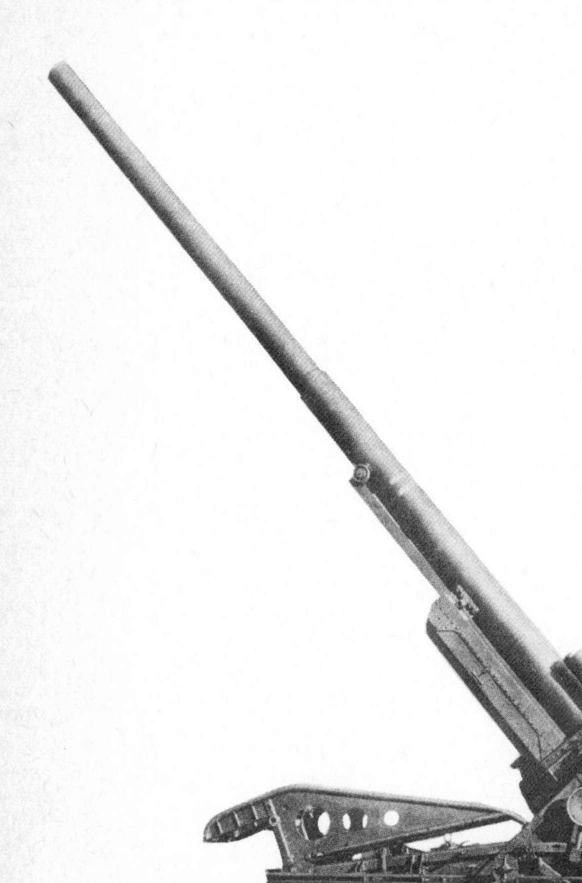

21cm Kanone 38 in action.

ropelling Charges
'his consisted of three bags, one for each charge. ombinations of bags were not used: each com-letely filling the case.
leine Ladung: 34.00kg/74.97lb Digl R P.
Mittelere Ladung: 42.20kg/93.05lb Digl R P.
Grosse Ladung: 60.20kg/132.74lb Digl R P.

Primer
The percussion primer C/12nA was standard.

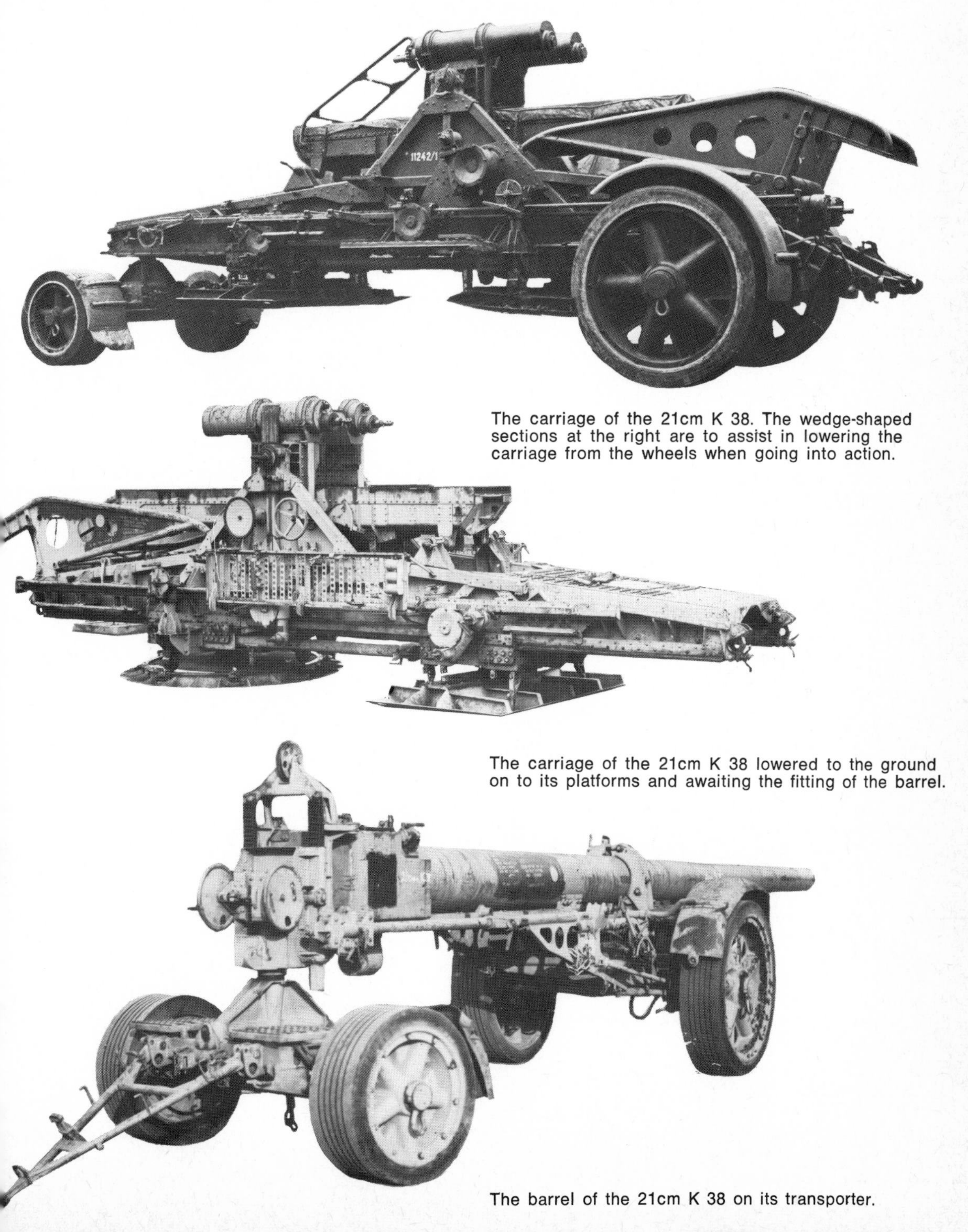

The carriage of the 21cm K 38. The wedge-shaped sections at the right are to assist in lowering the carriage from the wheels when going into action.

The carriage of the 21cm K 38 lowered to the ground on to its platforms and awaiting the fitting of the barrel.

The barrel of the 21cm K 38 on its transporter.

21cm Kanone 39

21cm K 39

This weapon was originally designed and built by the Czechoslovakian Skoda-Werke firm for a Turkish order originating in prewar days. The Skoda designation was K52. It is probable that two guns were actually delivered to Turkey before the war intervened, after which the German Army took the balance of the contract. Some slight alterations were made to suit the new owners and the designation K 39/40 was adopted. The design was then modified once more, by the addition of a muzzle brake, and the designation was changed to K 39/41. The German Army contracted for 50 of the latter, but only 13 were delivered before the war ended. Most of the weapons were used on the Eastern Front, reports of their employment elsewhere being exceptional.

The gun was unusual in German service in that it was a bag-charge gun using De Bange obturation. It was also a *monobloc auto-frettaged gun,* another unusual feature. In this form of construction the gun barrel was a single tube of steel that, during manufacture, was radially expanded under hydraulic pressure to place the metal in a state of initial compression; this assisted it, when fired, to resist the explosive stresses from within.

The mounting was a box-trail structure (carrying the saddle, the cradle and the gun) that revolved on a ballrace on a ground platform. For transportation the equipment was divided into three loads—the barrel, the carriage, and the ground platform with the turntable—each on a pneumatic-tyred transport wagon. The K 39 took from 6 to 8 hours to emplace, a large part of which was devoted to digging in and anchoring the platform.

Data (K 39)
Calibre: 210mm/8.27in.
Length of gun: 9530mm/375.20in/31.27ft.
Length of bore: not known.
Rifling: uniform right-hand twist, 1/25.
Breech mechanism: interrupted screw, De Bange obturation, percussion fired.
Traverse: 360°.
Elevation: −4° to +45°.
Weight in action: 33800kg/74529lb/33.27ton.

Performance
Firing standard high explosive shell weighing 135.00kg(297.68lb).
Grosse Ladung: velocity 800mps/2625fps, maximum range 30000m/32808yd.

Ammunition
Separate-loading, bagged charge.

Projectiles
21cm Gr 39 (t): fuzed AZ SKHZR and Bd DZR, weight 135.00kg(297.68lb).
This was the original Czech shell fitted with Czec fuzes; the AZ SKHZR was a nose fuze wit optional delay, while the DZR was a base fuz with an optional delay time. The filling wa 18.80kg(41.45lb) of TNT.
21cm Gr 40: fuzed AZ 35K or Dopp Z S/9 weight 135.00kg(297.68lb).
This was the German equivalent of the Gr 39 (t it differed only in the fuze-hole gauge and in th fact that it was not fitted with a base fuze. Bot these shells were unusual in the appearance of single heavy copper driving band set well forwar on the shell, and in the fact that the parall section behind the band was covered in a shi metal casing filled with a graphite mixtur intended as a wear reducer and a bore lubrican The Gr 40 was filled with 21.70kg(47.85lb) of TN
21cm Gr 39 Be: fuzed Bd Z DVER, weig 135.00kg(297.68lb).
An anti-concrete shell, of Czech design and fitte with a Czech base fuze. It was originally designate Halb Panzergranate (semi-armour-piercing), b when the shell was taken into German use th nomenclature was dropped in favour of the wor 'Beton'. It had a long ballistic cap, a large coppe driving band and the additive sleeve. It was fille with 8.10kg(17.86lb) TNT.
21cm Pzgr 39: fuzed Bd Z f 21cm Pzgr, weig 135.00kg(297.68lb).
This was a German-manufactured anti-tan armour-piercing shell of which little is know except that it was filled with 2.80kg(6.17lb) o PETN/wax.

Propelling Charges
The K 39 used a three-part charge, the constitu tion of which was as follows:
Kleine Ladung: 21.5kg/47.41lb Ngl Str P, with a igniter stitched to the base.
Vorkart 2: 10.15kg/22.38lb Ngl Str P.
Vorkart 3: 5.85kg/12.90lb Ngl Str P.
The two increments, Vorkarten 2 and 3, were i separate bags lightly stitched together at the tops and enclosed in another bag—tied at th mouth and with an igniter at the base. The thre charges were combined thus:
Kleine Ladung single bag as above.
Mittlere Ladung: Kleine Ladung and Vorkart only in the separate bag.
Grosse Ladung: Kleine Ladung, Vorkart 2 an Vorkart 3—the increments both contained withi the 'overall' bag. The two Vorkarten were loade ahead of the Kleine Ladung.

Primer
None: being a bag-charge gun the K 39 was fired by a percussion tube, the 11mm Zundhülse M 40.

Data (K 39/41 Steinpilz).
The data for this weapon is that of the K 39 except for:
Length of gun with muzzle brake: 11462mm/451.26in/37.60ft.
Weight in action: 39800kg/87759lb/39.18ton.

Performance
Firing standard high explosive shell weighing 135.00kg(297.68lb).
Grosse Ladung: velocity 860mps/2822fps, maximum range 33000m/36089yd/20.51mile.

Ammunition, Projectiles, Propelling Charges
See 21cm K 39, except that the propelling charge was larger—the total weight being 55.00kg (121.28lb) instead of 37.50kg(82.69lb).

24cm Haubitze 39

24cm H 39

The top carriage, cradle and recoil system of the 24cm Haubitze 39 on its transport limbers.

Turkey had an extremely frustrating time when the war broke out: this is yet another heavy artillery piece that they had ordered beforehand—two of which were delivered but the rest of which were taken by the German Army. The H 39 was another Skoda design, a companion piece to the 21cm K 39, and also used a bagged charge. The mounting and transport arrangements were practically identical. The Skoda designation for the howitzer was vzor (model) 166/600, indicating a projectile of 166kg(366lb) and a velocity of 600mps (1969fps). An improved model, the 21cm H 39/40, is sometimes mentioned in reports but (so far as is known) the changes were purely manufacturing alterations intended to simplify production. The performance and data figures were the same as the basic H 39.

Data
Calibre: 240mm/9.45in.
Length of gun: 6765mm/266.34in/22.19ft.
Length of bore: not known.
Rifling: not known.
Breech mechanism: interrupted screw, De Bange obturation, percussion fired.
Traverse: 360°
Elevation: −4° to +70°.
Weight in action: 27000kg/59535lb/26.58ton.

Performance
Firing standard high explosive shell weighing 166.00kg(366.03lb).
Charge 5: velocity 600mps/1969fps, maximum range 1800m/19685yd.

Ammunition
Separate-loading, bagged charge.

Projectiles
24cm Gr 39 (t): fuzed AZ SKHZR and Bd Z DZR, weight 166.00kg(366.03lb).
This was the standard Czech-designed high

explosive shell, fuzed at both the nose and the base in common with the 21cm model. It contained 23.66kg(52.17lb) of TNT and the two copper driving bands had deep grooves packed with a graphite anti-wear compound.

24cm Gr 39 umg: fuzed AZ 23 umg(0,15) or Dopp Z S/90, weight 166.00kg(366.03lb).

This, a German version of the original Czech shell, differed in using a German fuze at the nose. There was no base fuze, soft-iron driving bands were used and the shell contained slightly less explosive—22.90kg(50.49lb) of TNT. The graphite anti-wear composition was retained.

24cm Gr 39 Be: fuzed Bd Z DVZR, weight 166.00kg(366.03lb).

This Czech-designed anti-concrete shell was less sharply pointed than the 21cm model; it had two wide copper driving bands packed with graphite composition.

Propelling Charges

These consisted of five numbered bags, Teilkarten 1 to 5, enclosed in a larger bag that had the mouth tied with tape and an igniter stitched to its base. To prepare a charge for firing, the bag was untied, the unwanted charge increments removed, the bag tied and loaded into the chamber. The charges' make-up was as follows:

Charge 1: 8.75kg/19.29lb Digl R. P.
Charge 2: 10.30kg/22.71lb Digl R P.
Charge 3: 11.30kg/24.92lb Nz Str P.
Charge 4: 11.00kg/24.26lb Ngl Str P.
Charge 5: 11.00kg/24.26lb Ngl Str P.

Primer

None: being a bag-charge gun the H 39 was fired by a percussion tube, the 11mm Zundhulse M 40 or M 40 St.

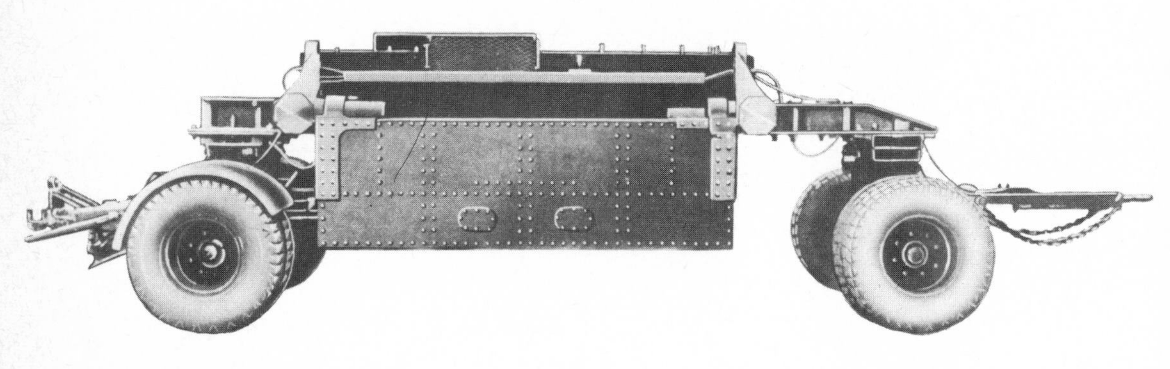

Lower carriage assembly of the 24cm H 39.

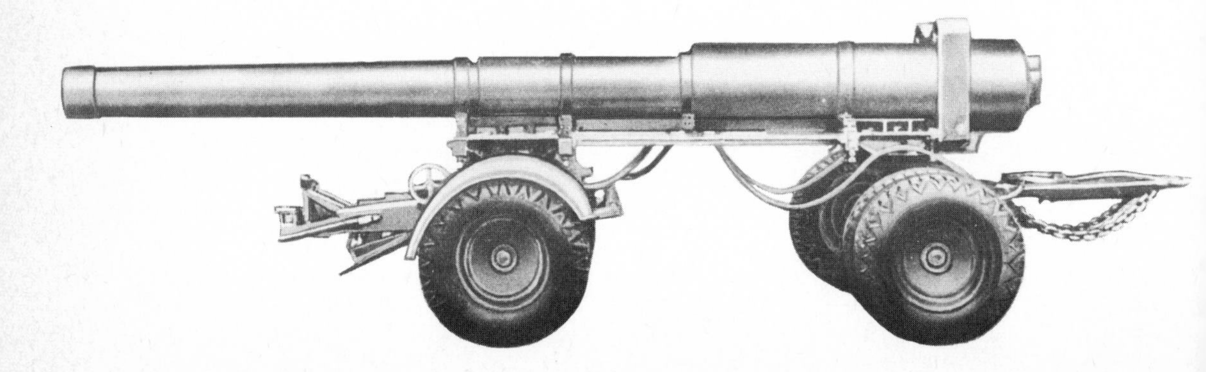

The barrel of the 24cm H 39.

24cm Kanone L/46

24cm K L/46

This Krupp design was introduced in 1937 but only a very few were ever made; only one unit, I. Batterie of Artillerie-Regiment 84, was ever armed with them. The general design was very similar to a scaled-up 15cm K 39, although a box trail replaced the earlier gun's split-trail type. The same type of ground platform for coast emplacement was provided and the K L/46 carried electric data transmission dials for the gunlayer. This was apparently the normal method of laying (even in the field), using data from a central predictor, but should this system have failed normal field artillery sights were also provided.

For transport the weapon divided into three or four loads. In the three-load configuration the barrel, the carriage and the ground platform each travelled on their own transport wagon. In the four-load arrangement the breech-ring and the breechblock were unscrewed from the barrel and carried on a fourth transport wagon.

Details of this weapon are scarce, since none apparently survived to the end of the war, but from what accounts there are it seems to have been more than usually cumbersome for its job.

Data
Calibre: 238mm/9.37in
Length of barrel: 10948mm/431.02in/35.92ft
Length of bore: not known
Rifling: not known
Breech mechanism: horizontal sliding block, percussion fired
Traverse: 360° on the platform
Elevation: −4° to +45°
Weight in action, without platform: 29600kg/65268lb/29.14ton
Weight in action with platform: 45200kg/99666lb/44.49ton.

Performance
Firing standard high explosive shell weighing 180.00kg(396.90lb)
Kleine Ladung: velocity 550mps/1805fps, maximum range 17000m/18591yd
Mittlere Ladung: velocity 700mps/2297fps, maximum range 23500/25700yd
Grosse Ladung: velocity 850mps/2789fps, maximum range 32000m/34995yd.

Ammunition
Separate-loading, cased charge.

Projectiles, Propelling Charges
The total weight of the propelling charge was 50.00kg(110.25lb); no other details are known.

Primer
Probably the percussion primer C/12nA.

24cm Kanone 3

24cm K 3 (Petersdorf)

The K3 was a Rheinmetall-Borsig design, commenced in 1935 and introduced to service in 1938, although most of the production models were actually built by Krupp. The weapon was a dual-recoil carriage equipment of quite outstanding design, transported in six loads—the firing platform, the carriage, the cradle, the barrel, the breech, and an electric generator. The total weight on the road was some 83tons.

The method of attaching the breech-ring to the barrel was rather unusual; a revolving interrupted collar was fitted inside the breech-ring, and after the ring was slid into place on the barrel the collar was revolved by a crank and gear train. This locked the two together without the detachment revolving either of them by hand. Furthermore, safety interlocks were included so that unless the barrel and the breech were correctly assembled and locked to the recoil system the breechblock could not be opened.

Another notable feature was the effort made by the designers to render the gunners' work easier. Assembly could be done without cranes or gins by an ingenious system of inclined ramps, guide rails, and runways. Power for the assembly work was provided by the electric generator driving winches integral with the gun, through direct haulage by the towing vehicles, or (in the last resort) by hand winches. Great pains had also been taken to provide numerous safety devices to prevent accidents should a winch rope break during the assembly work.

The carriage was of box-trail pattern with a four-wheel bogie at the front. Beneath this was the pivot seated on a rectangular platform. A rear spade-plate carried the trail end, riding on a wheeled trolley that allowed rearward movement during carriage recoil; the dual-recoil system allowed the barrel to recoil in the cradle and then the carriage body to recoil across the platform.

The standard gun, for which data is given below, used a 64-groove conventionally-rifled barrel but—in addition—a small number of 8-groove barrels were made to fire splined projectiles. The ballistic performance showed that there was little advantage to be gained from this form of construction and the project was not taken further.

Experiments were also undertaken with a variety of muzzle-squeeze attachments under the direction of Dr Banck of Rheinmetall-Borsig, but the technical difficulties were so great that no design had been satisfactorily completed before the war ended.

These experiments into ballistic improvement were due to the army's complaint that, good as the K 3 was, it was not good enough; 25 men working for 1½hr to get it into action was felt to be wasteful of time and manpower, the transport arrangements were cumbersome, and the performance was not considered to be commensurate with the size of weapon.

Data
Calibre: 240mm/9.45in.
Length of gun: 13102mm/515.83in/42.99ft.
Length of bore: 12480mm/491.34in/40.95ft.
Rifling: 64 grooves, right-hand uniform twist, 1/30.
Breech mechanism: horizontal sliding block, percussion fired.
Traverse: 6° on the carriage, 360° on the platform.
Elevation: 0 to +56°.
Weight in action: 54866kg/120980lb/54.01ton.

Performance
Firing standard high explosive shell weighing 151.40kg(333.84lb).

The 24cm K 3.

Full charge: velocity 970mps/3183fps, maximum range 37500m/41010yd.

Ammunition
Separate-loading, cased charge.

Projectiles
24cm Gr 35: fuzed AZ 35K, weight 151.40kg (331.84lb).
This was the standard high explosive shell; no further details are known.
Taper or Squeeze Bore Projectiles.
Many varieties of these were developed for an equally wide variety of muzzle adaptors. The degrees of squeeze proposed were 24/21cm (with which 500 trial rounds were fired), 24/18cm, 24/17.5cm and 24/17cm, with which groups a total of 600 trial rounds were fired; 24/16.5cm designs were also drawn up but never reached firing trials. Finally a 24/15cm design showed considerable promise, increasing the range to 60km (37.28mile), using a projectile with collapsing bolt-centering devices and a sintered-iron skirt band. The 24/21cm project had given an 83.00kg (183.02lb) shell a velocity of 1100mps(3609fps) to reach a range of 50000m(54680yd). Most of the projectiles were based on standard issue shells of the lesser calibre, adapted by the addition of bolts and skirt bands.
Discarding Sabot Projectiles.
Concurrently with the squeezebore development, there was also a number of trials held to discover the feasibility of using discarding sabot techniques to improve the range. Most of this work was done by Krupp, because Rheinmetall was specialising in the squeeze-bore problem. Among the many patterns tried were cage, ring and pot sabots of 24/17cm, 24/16.5cm and 24/21cm calibres. The most successful appears to have been the *24/17cm Sprgr L/4.6 m Triebspiegel.* This was a cage sabot design weighing 77.00kg(169.79lb) when loaded, with a 58.00kg(127.89lb) subprojectile that carried a payload of 7.00kg(15.44lb) of high explosive. Unfortunately, no reliable figures on the performance of these shells are available.
Peenemünder Pfeilgeschosse.
These vaned discarding sabot projectiles are discussed at greater length elsewhere, and they are not usually associated with this weapon. There is evidence, however, that a smoothbore version of the K3 was made and at least three companies—Maschinenfabrik Niedersachsen AG of Spenge, Hessische Industriewerk of Herne-Westfalen and Wittkowitzer Bergbau- und Eisenhüttenwerkgeschaft of Morovska-Ostravia—were all engaged in production of projectiles as late as January 1945, though no details of their performances are known.

Propelling Charges
Beyond the fact that there were two charges no details are known.

24cm Kanone 4

24cm K 4

When the army decided that the K 3 did not come up to its requirements, the OKH drew up a specification for a new 24cm gun, demanding much better mobility, a range of 48–49km(29.83–30.45mile) with a 160kg(353lb) shell, and that it must move as a single unit (or, if that was quite impossible, in not more than two loads).

Krupp, having been involved in the production of the K 3, decided to show Rheinmetall—the designers of the K 3—how it should be done, and began the task of designing two prototypes, one a two-load model with the barrel and cradle on a transport wagon, and the other a single-load model. The latter design was from all accounts a highly advanced concept, and was to mount either a 24cm gun or a 30.5cm howitzer on a box-trail mounting with a turntable. The ends of the mounting were to be run on to fifth-wheel connectors on modified Panzerkampfwagen VI Tiger chassis, and with both tank chassis working in tandem the whole weapon could then be moved in one piece. (This concept later showed concrete results when applied to the US army's 280mm gun.) Rheinmetall-Borsig also began work on a two-load design but, so far as is known, the only result of all this work was the construction by Krupp of an experimental two-load model; this was severely damaged in an air raid on Essen and work on the project was then abandoned.

Krupp also considered developing a further gun known as the 24cm Kanone 4 in Selbstfahrlafette (24cm K 4 Sf), a self-propelled gun running on a full-track chassis. The gun was mounted in a cradle on a limited-traverse mount in the chassis well, and could be drawn to the rear for travel. In action, coarse laying was achieved by pivoting the chassis—in the fashion of a tank—after which the chassis body was lowered to the ground to provide a stable firing platform. Fine laying was then done by the limited on-mount traverse. The whole weapon, in concept if not in execution, bore some resemblance to the 60cm Mörser Gerät 040; although drawings of the K 4 Sf are known to exist there is no evidence that one was made.

The following figures are Krupp's estimates for the two-load version.

Data (24cm K 4, Krupp 2-load project)
Calibre: 240mm/9.45in.
Length of gun: 17280mm/680.31in/56.69ft.
Breech mechanism: horizontal sliding block, percussion fired.
Traverse: 16° on the carriage, 360° on the platform.
Elevation: 0 to +55°.
Weight in action: 55000kg/121275lb/54.14ton.

Performance
Firing a shell weighing 160.00kg(352.80lb).
Full charge: velocity 1100mps/3609fps, maximu range 49000m/53586yd/30.47mile.

Ammunition
Separate-loading, cased charge.

Projectiles, Propelling Charges: No known details

28cm Haubitze L/12

28cm H L/12

This was an old Krupp equipment dating back to pre-World War 1 days. A few were still on the army's inventory during World War 2, but they were usually statically emplaced as defensive weapons—largely owing to the considerable time (3 to 4 days) required to emplace them. A massive ground platform had to be assembled and du in, and the weapon was then literally built on to of it using winches and gins. The H L/12 wa the only bag-charge gun of German design i service until the ring obturation experiment began in 1943–44.

Data
Calibre: 283mm/11.14in.
Length of gun: 3396mm/133.70in/11.14ft.
Breech mechanism: horizontal sliding block, per cussion fired.
Traverse: 360°.
Elevation: not known.
Weight in action: 50300kg/110912lb/49.51ton.

Performance
Firing standard high explosive shell weighin 350.00kg(771.75lb).
Full charge: muzzle velocity 350mps/1148fps maximum range 10400m/11373yd.

Ammunition
Separate-loading, bagged charge.

Projectiles
28cm Sprgr L/3.5: fuzed Bd Z f 28cm Sprgr H weight 350.00kg(771.75lb).
This was a pointed shell of antedeluvian design with a short-curve ogive and the single coppe driving band right at the base.

Propelling Charges
No details are known except that a seven-par charge was used, the full weight of which wa 17.30kg(38.15lb).

Left:
A 28cm H L/12 being assembled.

Above. right:
The barrel of the 28cm Haub. L/12 being lowered to the mounting at the Krupp proving ground, Meppen.

Below right:
The 28cm Haubitze L/12 ready to fire.

35·5cm Haubitze M1

35·5cm H M1

This was a Rheinmetall-Borsig design, development of which commenced in 1936 in response to an army demand for a super-heavy howitzer. The H M 1 was introduced into service in 1939 and was a thoroughly up-to-date equipment (although only about five were ever built), using the dual-recoil system and a two-part carriage on a platform giving 360° traverse. The gun also broke into six loads that were carried on wheeled trailers for high-speed transport. The six towing vehicles were 18-ton three-quarter-tracked artillery tractors, while a seventh tractor towed an assembly gantry. By and large the design might be best described as a logical enlargement of the 24cm K 3.

The six transport loads were the cradle, the barrel, the top carriage, the lower carriage, the front platform and the turntable, and finally the rear platform. On arrival at the gun position, the gantry (electrically powered from a generator on the towing tractor) was erected and used to assemble the weapon, an operation that took about two hours.

The gun's elevating gear and the ammunition hoist were also operated by electric power from the generator, although hand operation was available in cases where the power supply failed.

The barrel recoiled inside a ring cradle and was controlled by a hydropneumatic system. The carriage recoiled across the ground platforms, controlled by another hydropneumatic system the cylinders for which were within the carriage structure.

Data
Calibre: 356mm/14.02in.
Length of gun: 9585mm/377.36in/31.45ft.
Length of bore: 8050mm/316.93in/26.41ft.
Rifling: 96 grooves, uniform right-hand twist, 1/36.
Breech mechanism: horizontal sliding block, percussion fired.
Traverse: 6° on the carriage, 360° on the platform.
Elevation: +45° to +75°.
Weight in action: 7500kg/165375lb/73.83ton.

Performance
Firing standard high explosive projectile weighing 575.00kg(1267.88lb).
Ladung 4: velocity 570mps/1870fps, maximum range 20000m/21872yd.

Ammunition
Separate-loading, cased charge.

Projectiles
35.5cm Gr Be, 35.5cm Gr Be Stg: fuzed Bd Z 21cm Gr Be, weight 575.00kg(1267.88lb).
This was the standard high explosive shell for the weapon, and was a pointed anti-concrete projectile of conventional design with a ballistic cap. Two copper driving bands were fitted and the filling was 7.94kg(17.50lb) of TNT/montan wax.

Propelling Charges
A four-part propelling charge was provided, in which each unit was fired separately to give charges 1, 2, 3 and 4. The required charge was placed in the cartridge case prior to loading. Their constitution was as follows:
Ladung 1: 33.40kg/73.65lb Dgl R P.
Ladung 2: 43.40kg/95.70lb Dgl R P.
Ladung 3: 6.40kg/133.18lb Dgl R P.
Ladung 4: 93.4kg/205.95lb Dgl R P.

Cartridge Case
No details of the case are available.

The 35.5cm Haubitze M 1 prepares to fire.

42cm Gamma Haubitze

42cm Gamma H

This weapon cannot really be considered as a service weapon of World War 2, but its survival is not without interest. The howitzer was originally built by Krupp c.1906, the forerunner of the 42cm Dicke Berthe—a lighter and more mobile version of 'Gamma'. According to some reports 10 complete Gamma howitzers with eight spare barrels were made, but there is a strong suspicion that this figure includes the 'Big Bertha' weapons and that only one of the former was actually built. The gun was later dismantled and played no part in World War 1. 'Gamma' then avoided the eyes of the postwar disarmament commissions; in the 1930s it was resurrected, assembled at Krupp's Meppen proving ground, and used as a trials weapon in connexion with the development of anti-concrete shells. If the need had ever arisen, the gun could have been dismantled and moved on ten railway flatcars.

Data
Calibre: 420mm/16.54in.
Length of gun: 6720mm/264.57in/22.05ft.
Rifling: right-hand increasing twist, 1/45 to 1/19.8.
Breech mechanism: horizontal sliding block, percussion fired.
Traverse: 46°.
Elevation: +43° to +75°.
Weight in action: 140000kg/308700lb/137.81ton.

Performance
Firing standard concrete-piercing shell weighing 1003.00kg(2211.62lb).
Full charge: velocity 452mps/1483fps, maximum range 14200m/15530yd.

Ammunition
Separate-loading, cased charge.

Projectiles
42cm Sprgr Be: fuzed Bd Z f 21cm Gr Be, weight 1003.00kg(2211.62lb).
An example of this shell showed manufacturing marks dated July 1944, so it would seem that shells were prepared for the weapon in case it ever became necessary to use it in action. The 42cm Sprgr Be was a conventional anti-concrete shell with a ballistic cap over the tip. A single copper driving band was fitted, very close to the base.

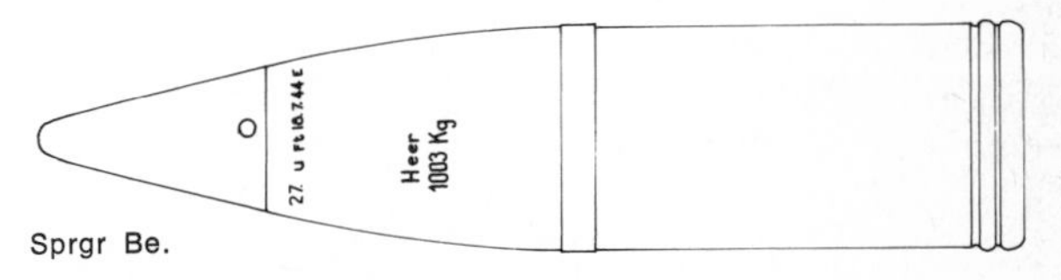

Sprgr Be.

'Gamma' in the loading position, with breech open and a round of ammunition ready to be hoisted up.

The 'Gamma' Mörser. A sequence of photographs taken at Meppen Experimental Range about 1912, to demonstrate the assembly sequence. Here, the basic structure is being positioned by the travelling hoist.

The top carriage is lowered into place.

The cradle, with recoil system and elevating arc, is lowered into the trunnions

The barrel is inserted into the cradle to complete the assembly

Propelling Charges
The propelling charge for the 'Gamma' howitzer was of the conventional howitzer pattern—a basic charge with additional increments. The basic charge was contained in the cartridge case and the increments were loaded into the chamber as required, ahead of the case.
Grundladung: 52.30kg/115.32lb Dgl R P.
Vorkart 2: 6.00kg/13.23lb Dgl R P.
Vorkart 3: 7.50kg/16.54lb Dgl R P.
Vorkart 4: 12.00kg/26.46lb Dgl R P.
This gave a total weight for the fourth charge of 77.80kg/171.55lb.

Cartridge Case
No details of this are known.

The 42cm 'Gamma' Mörser in action.

Front view of 'Gamma'.

RAILWAY ARTILLERY

The railway gun has always been particularly attractive to a Continental army, since it allows heavy support weapons to be moved rapidly across the country in time of need. World War 1 saw the first large-scale use of railway guns and their utility was not lost on the German Army. During the interwar years, too, there was a widespread opinion that this type of weapon would form a useful addition to coast defences; groups of guns could then be held at convenient rail centres and rapidly deployed to a threatened coast area.

Railway guns generally came in two types: those in which the gun was pivot-mounted, to fire in any direction relative to the line of track, and those in which the gun was rigidly aligned in its mounting and was capable only of a very small amount of traverse by moving the mounting bodily across the supporting bogies. The first type required stabilising outriggers to resist the firing stress and to prevent the mounting tipping over when firing across the track. The second type—by and large those above about 20cm/8in calibre—required either a curved track or a track turntable to allow them to point over a wide arc. Pushing the gun mounting along a curved track obviously changed the direction of fire and this was done for coarse pointing, the fine laying being done by the small on-mounting traverse. A turntable mounting was self-explanatory. Both these systems demanded that special preparation, whether laying the curved track or assembling the turntable, was done before the gun could operate. Moreover it was usually necessary to construct track from the commercial railway system to the gun's chosen location.

It will be seen in the following pages that all these systems were used by the German guns, plus an innovation or two of their own. A point usually made in arguments against railway guns was the very fact that they relied on tracks, either commercial or specially-laid, and that such tracks were particularly vulnerable to air attack. This was quite true, but the track could also be easily and quickly repaired and one of the design features of a railway gun was that the suspension could negotiate indifferent and hastily-laid track without mishap.

The *Vogele Drehscheibe* (Vogele turntable) was developed by the Germans during the late 1920s as a necessary and vital accessory for the consequent employment of railway guns, and it was perfected in good time for extensive use during the war. The turntable gave all-round traverse to all railway guns and was a standard item of equipment. Many German positions along the captured French and Belgian coasts were equipped with these turntables, ready to receive guns whenever needed for defence and thus speeding reaction time.

German railway guns fell into two broad groups, those that were the result of long-term development and those that were hurriedly produced as a result of the so-called Sofort-Programm ('crash programme') initiated in 1936 with the object of providing a sizeable force of railway guns by the summer of 1939. One weapon fell into neither of these groups: the 80cm K(E) Gustav Gerät was developed outside both programmes by Krupp, in its early stages more or less as a private venture.

The long-term programme was principally concerned with the slow development of very-long-range guns for bombardment. In this the memory of the Paris-Geschütz ('Paris gun') of 1918 played a part. The Sofort-Programm was begun when it became obvious that the long-term development was not going fast enough to give time to the development of smaller modern weapons, and so the products of the 'crash-programme' were elderly naval weapons that could be obtained from store and mounted on modifications of World War 1 carriages (the drawings for which were still in the Krupp files). It is an odd fact that all German railway guns were Krupp products; Rheinmetall-Borsig did design two models, one of calibre 15cm and one of 24cm, but neither was accepted for service or even built in prototype form.

15cm Kanone in Eisenbahnlafette

15cm K (E)

Although introduced in 1937 this was actually a long-term design and was the first modern equipment to enter service with the Wehrmacht. The design bore some resemblance to the American 8in Mk VI Mod 3A2 that, introduced at about the same time, had been announced in prototype some years earlier. The 15cm K(E) was on a well-base flatcar with four outriggers, mounted on two six-wheel bogies. In action the outriggers were swung out and jacks took the recoil stress, further jacks locked the spring suspension, four more bore on the surface of the rails, and screw clamps gripped beneath the rails to provide additional security.

The gun mounting revolved on a ballrace in the truck-well and carried a working platform for the detachment. The gun itself was the 15cm SK C/30 (naval) gun.

The 15cm K(E) was a very efficient design, but 15cm was really too small a calibre to be worth the trouble of a railway mounting. Eight were issued in 1937 and a further 10 in 1938, but with that the design was dropped in favour of heavier weapons.

The 15cm K (E)—battery in action.

Data

Calibre: 149.3mm/5.88in.
Length of gun: 5960mm/234.64in/19.55ft.
Length of bore: 5571mm/219.33in/18.28ft.
Rifling: 44 grooves, right-hand increasing twist, 1/45 to 1/25.5.
Breech mechanism: vertical sliding block, percussion fired.
Traverse: 360°.
Elevation: +10° to +45°.
Weight in action: 74000kg/163170lb/72.84ton.
Length over buffers: 20100mm/791.34in/65.94ft.

Performance

Firing standard high explosive shell weighing 43.00kg(94.82lb).
Kleine Ladung: velocity 600mps/1969fps, range figures not available.
Mittlere Ladung: velocity 725mps/2379fps, range figures not available.
Grosse Ladung: velocity 805mps/2641fps, maximum range 22500m/24606yd.

Ammunition

Separate-loading, cased charge.

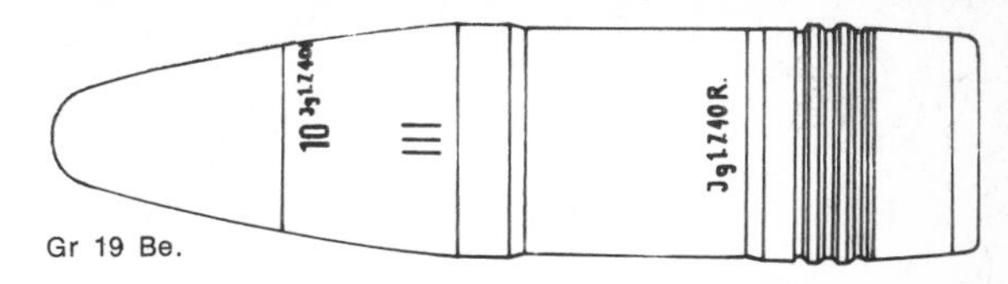

Gr 19 Be.

Projectiles

15cm K Gr 18: fuzed AZ 23v(0.15) or Dopp Z S/90, weight 43.00kg(94.82lb).
The standard projectile, this was a nose-fuzed high explosive shell of normal construction containing 5.68kg(12.52lb) of TNT.
15cm Gr 19 Be: fuzed Bd Z f 15cm Gr Be, weight 43.50kg(95.92lb).
This was an anti-concrete shell fitted with a base fuze and with a filling of 4.80kg(10.58lb) of TNT in pre-pressed blocks; the shell had a sharp conical point covered by a rounded sheet-steel ballistic cap.

Propelling Charges

Three charges were provided, each made up from the basic charge and three increments. The

The 15cm K (E), showing the outriggers and rail clamps.

increments' constitution was as follows:
Grundladung, basic charge: 100gm/3.53oz NZ Man P, 400gm/14.11oz Nigl R P.
Sonderkart 1, first increment: 7.20kg/15.88lb Ngl R P.
Teilkart 2, second increment: 11.80kg/26.02lb Ngl R P.
Teilkart 3, third increment: 1.50kg/3.31lb Ngl R P
The three gun charges were made up thus:
Kleine Ladung: Grundladung and Sonderkart 1.
Mittlere Ladung: Grundladung, Sonderkart 1 and Teilkart 2.
Grosse Ladung: Grundladung, Sonderkart 1, Teilkarten 2 and 3.

Primer
The percussion primer C/12nA was used.
Case Identification Number: 6372.

17cm Kanone in Eisenbahnlafette

17cm K (E)

This weapon was produced with the intention of replacing the 15cm K(E) by a heavier weapon, though in fact no more than six were ever built and issued in 1938. Although the 17cm K(E) was an improvement over the 15cm, so far as shell weight and range were concerned, it was still too little gun for too much mounting—and finally convinced the army that if railway guns were to be built at all they might as well be big ones.

The mounting was the same as that of the 15cm K(E), a well-base flatcar on two six-wheel bogies with the gun pivot-mounted. The mounting only required slight modifications to make it suitable for the gun selected; this, the 17cm Schiffskanone L/40 naval and coast gun, was an elderly design but one that was readily available; the guns, dating from c.1901/2, had been designed as the casemate guns of the Deutschland class pre-dreadnoughts.

Data
Calibre: 173mm/6.81in.
Length of gun: 6900mm/271.65in/22.64ft.
Length of bore: 4992mm/196.54in/16.38ft.
Rifling: right-hand increasing twist, 1/50 to 1/30.
Breech mechanism: horizontal sliding block, percussion fired.
Traverse: 360°.
Elevation: +10° to +45°.
Weight in action: 80000kg/176400lb/78.75ton.
Length over buffers: 20100mm/791.34in/65.94ft.

Performance
Firing standard high explosive shell weighing 62.80kg(138.47lb).
Grosse Ladung: velocity 875mps/2871fps, maximum range 27200m/29746yd.
Minimum range owing to 107° minimum elevation: 13350m/14600yd.

mmunition
eparate-loading, cased charge.

rojectiles
7cm Sprgr L/4.7 KZ m Hb: fuzed EK Zdr f prgr or Dopp Z S/90, weight 62.80kg(138.47lb) 'he standard high explosive shell with a fuze tted beneath a ballistic cap. The bursting charge 'as 6.40kg(14.11lb) of TNT in a cardboard conainer. The same shell was used with these guns 1 the coast artillery role.

'ropelling Charges
)nly one charge was provided, but this was available in a number of different propellant types and weights—all of which were adjusted to give the same ballistics. The charge was enclosed in a bag carried in the cartridge case, and the options were: 22.60kg(49.83lb) R P C/12, or 20.50kg (45.20lb) R P C/12 of different dimensions, or 23.60kg(52.04lb) R P C/32, or 25.20kg(55.56lb) R P 38 Bu.

Primer
The percussion primer C/12nA was used.

17cm K (E) prepared for travelling, outriggers folded.

20cm Kanone in Eisenbahnlafette

20cm K(E)

In 1938, with the 1936 programme under way, a number of 20.3cm gun barrels were under construction at Krupp's Essen factory, destined for heavy cruisers of the *Blücher* class. Eight of these were surplus to OKK's (Oberkommando der Kriegsmarine) requirements at the time and so the army took them instead, and asked Krupp to provide a suitable railway mounting. The OKH asked of Krupp that the eight completed equipments be delivered by the end of 1941. Krupp delved into its archives and came up with the drawings for World War 1's 21cm SK L/40 railway guns that had used naval guns taken from the disarmed armoured cruisers SMS *Prinz Adalbert* and SMS *Friedrich Karl*. These, with slight adjustments here and there, could be made to do the job.

Shortly after work had begun, the army belatedly realised that acceptance of these weapons would mean that they had introduced a new calibre to the artillery—and that the eight guns would be the only weapons of their calibre, an unnecessary and undesirable logistic complication. To try to avoid this Krupp was asked if it could bore-out the barrels to 21cm, a standard army calibre, but by that time it was too late: the guns were built and rifled, and breech mechanisms had been installed. Stripping everything down to rebuild the guns in a new calibre would have been impractical, and so they were completed in the original form and delivered—well ahead of time—in the middle of 1940.

Once the guns had been delivered, plans were drawn up for the manufacture of eight replacement barrels in 21cm calibre; these were to be built at Essen by Krupp, on a low priority, and fitted to the weapons as the original barrels wore out. The work progressed slowly until by the middle of 1944 four barrels had been completed and the other four were well ahead in their construction. But then, in late 1944, six of the guns were captured by the Allies in Normandy, and as the two remaining guns thereafter had two spare barrels apiece the remainder of the programme was abandoned.

The gun was a long-barrelled weapon mounted in a ring cradle trunnioned to the side girders of the mounting. The mounting itself was a simple box-girder construction carried on two eight-wheel bogies. A portable turntable was provided with each weapon, since there was no provision on the mounting for traverse.

Data
Calibre: 203mm/7.99in.
Length of gun: 12150mm/478.35in/39.86ft.

The 20cm K (E) on its turntable, prepared for firing.

The 20cm K (E) ready to fire

Length of bore: 11587mm/456.18in/38.02ft.
Rifling: 64 grooves, right-hand increasing twist, 1/50 to 1/30.
Breech mechanism: horizontal sliding block, percussion fired.
Traverse: none on the carriage, 360° on the turntable.
Elevation: +10° to +47°.
Weight in action: 86100kg/189850lb/84.75ton.
Length over buffers: 19445mm/765.55in/63.80ft.

Performance
Firing standard high explosive shell weighing 122.00kg(269.01lb).
Maximum charge: velocity 925mps/3035fps, maximum range 37000m/40463yd/22.99mile.
Minimum range owing to 10° minimum elevation: 13700m/14982yd.

Ammunition
Separate-loading, cased charge.

Projectiles
20.3cm Sprgr L/4.7 m Hb: fuzed KZ C/27 or Dopp Z S/28K, weight 122.00kg(269.01lb).
This was the standard high explosive shell, with either a percussion or a time and percussion fuze beneath a ballistic cap; three copper driving bands were fitted.
20.3cm Sprgr L/4.7 m BdZ m Hb: fuzed Bd Z C/38, weight 124.00kg(273.42lb)
Similar to the foregoing shell but pointed, with a ballistic cap and fitted with a base fuze; employed as an anti-concrete shell.

Propelling Charges
Two charges, normal and reduced, were provided. The reduced charge (Hauptkartusche) was issued in the cartridge case, and the full charge increment (Vorkartusche) was separately packaged.
Hauptkartusche: 30.50kg/67.25lb R P 38.
Vorkartusche: 20.70kg/45.64lb R P 38 Bu.

Primer
The percussion primer C/12nA was used.

Case Identification Number
None: the cartridge case was identified by the stamping W KARTH C/34 on the base.

21cm Kanone 12 in Eisenbahnlafette

21cm K 12 (E)

The 21cm Paris Geschütz (Paris gun) of 1918 had been developed by Krupp at the request of the German navy, and it was manned and controlled during its short but spectacular life by naval personnel. The army was never very happy about the sailors' invasion of their domain (showing them how it should be done), and in the early 1920s set about preparing plans for a high-velocity long-range gun, which would show the navy that the soldiers were quite capable of bettering the seamen's efforts. During the remainder of the 1920s and early 1930s a great deal of theoretical research work was done, and the Vogele Drehscheibe (portable turntable) was designed and perfected.

Eventually, with all the paperwork done and the political indications favourable, work began on the actual gun. The great problem was to

Top view of the 21cm K 12 (V), showing the barrel bracing.

achieve the very high velocity that would put the shell into the stratosphere, there allowing it to travel against much less air resistance and so attain a very long range, the same technique that had been employed with the Paris gun. The 1918 weapon had, however, worn out at an incredible rate—to such a degree that shells of gradually increasing diameter, serially numbered, had to be made to suit the rate of wear; the barrel could sustain no more than 50 shots before having to be replaced. Moreover there is reason to believe, though it has never been officially confirmed, that one Paris gun (eight were made) was destroyed by a premature explosion in the bore owing to loading an oversize shell out of its serially-numbered order, and this sort of hazard had to be avoided. One of the principal difficulties was spinning the shell; a conventional copper driving band had to be massive if it was to deliver the rotational acceleration to the shell without shearing at the pressures involved, and before such a band set up into the rifling there was considerable gas-wash around it. This, of course, soon led to excessive wear.

In view of this it was decided to rifle the barrel with a few deep grooves and to make the shell with an equivalent number of curved ribs or splines on its outer surface. These would then engage the rifling and deliver the rotational thrust with a much more even distribution over the entire shell wall. The gas sealing would be done by a copper band in the place usually occupied by a driving band, backed with an asbestos and graphite packing to give a good seal before the copper took up the task. To test this theory a number of small barrels with eight grooves, known as 10.5cm K 12 M, were made and fired with experimental projectiles. To provide comparative data a normally rifled barrel, the 10.5cm K 12 MKu, was also made and fired. The tests took place in 1935 and showed that the eight-groove barrel was the right solution; work then began on manufacturing a full-sized 21cm eight-groove barrel.

Meanwhile the design of the carriage was under way. This was a relatively simple box-girder structure carried on two subframes which were in turn mounted on double bogies, the front subframe on two ten-wheel and the rear on two eight-wheel bogies. To absorb the recoil the gun was mountec in a ring cradle with a hydropneumatic recoi system and the mounting incorporated two more hydro pneumatic systems connected to the tw subframes, so that the entire girder section wa capabe of recoiling some 980mm(38.58in) rearwards across the subframes. Provision was made to disconnect the gun from its recoil system anc pull the barrel back some 1500mm(59.06in) ir the cradle, reducing the overall length and improving the weight distribution, so that when travelling the entire equipment was manoeuverable within the standard loading gauge and track curvature.

The gun itself posed one or two problems. It wa exceptionally long (33.30m/109.25ft) and requirec to be braced throughout its length to prevent i bending under its own weight. It was moreove considered impossible to balance such a preponderance and so the trunnions were set forwarc

The 21cm K 12 (V) elevated. It is no yet in the firing position, the main carriag having yet to be jacked up from the bogies

to obtain as much weight as possible at the breech. This in turn meant that the breech came perilously close to the track when the gun was elevated, and so it became necessary to design and instal a hydraulic jacking system to lift the whole mounting structure from the subframe by 1.00m (3.28ft) before firing; this allowed the breech room to recoil. The jacking process had to be repeated for every round, as it was impossible to load the gun when the mounting was raised.

The K 12 was fired from a curved track, a turntable or a special firing-track assembly that was carried in prefabricated parts on the gun train, which included a special crane wagon. This allowed a T-shaped track to be laid at any convenient spot, whereupon the gun was pushed up by a locomotive until the front bogies were at a crossover at the top of the T. The front bogie units were then jacked up and turned with the subframe through 90°, and lowered on to the cross-stroke of the T. The gun was then traversed by driving the front bogies along the track by electric motor drive to the wheels and, once laid in this way, the equipment was then clamped to the track for firing.

This weapon, completed in 1938 and issued to the army in March of 1939, was known as the 21cm K 12 V. It was a success, but the complicated business of jacking it up and down between shots was not well received by the army and the designers embarked on a major redesign. Much research was done into the question of balancing the immense barrel length, until it was found that hydropneumatic balancing-presses could be made to work at much greater weights and pressures than had previously been believed possible. The mounting was consequently redesigned with the barrel as far forward as possible and with a single hydropneumatic balancing-press. The whole equipment was also made slightly longer, and the recoil stroke of the gun mounting was increased to 1500mm(59.06in).

This equipment, called the 21cm K 12 N, was issued to service in the summer of 1940. No more were ever made, but Krupp's designers are said to have expressed the opinion that—although as a practical weapon it was a waste of time—as a technical exercise the K 12's development was worth every penny spent on it.

Details of the employment of these two guns are not known, but an interesting sidelight is thrown by a British report dated February 1941 referring to a German shell that had landed at Rainham (near Chatham) in Kent late in 1940. The point of impact was 88km(55miles) from the nearest point on the French coast. Similar fragments were recovered from the areas of Dover and Eastbourne, and so it seems likely that both were employed as cross-Channel bombardment guns. The report went on to detail the fragments found, and from them built up a theoretical picture of the shell. From this were deduced the possible ballistics of the gun: the final answers arrived at proved remarkably close to the true values.

Data (21cm K 12V[E])
Calibre: 211mm/8.31in.
Length of gun: 33300mm/1311.02in/109.25ft.
Length of bore: 32112mm/1264.25in/105.35ft.
Rifling: 8 grooves, uniform right-hand twist, 1/20.
Breech mechanism: horizontal sliding block, percussion fired.
Traverse: 0° 25′ on the mounting, 360° on the turntable.
Elevation: +25° to +55°.
Weight in action: 302000kg/665910lb/297.28ton.
Length over buffers: 41300mm/1625.98in/139.50ft (the K 12 N was the same except: weight, 318000kg/701190lb/313.03ton, length 44945mm/1769.49in/147.46ft).

Performance
Firing standard high explosive shell weighing 107.50kg(237.04lb).
Standard charge: velocity 1500mps/4922fps, maximum range 115000m/125765yd/71.46miles.
Minimum range owing to 25° minimum elevation: 45000m/49210yd/27.96miles.

Ammunition
Separate-loading, cased charge.

The 21cm K 12 V being traversed on its cross-track.

Projectiles
21cm Gr 35 m Hb: fuzed Hbgr Z35K and BdZ C/36, weight 107.50kg(236.50lb).
This was the standard, indeed the only, high explosive shell for the weapon. It had eight external splines, together with a copper sealing band. A nose percussion fuze was fitted beneath the ballistic cap and a base fuze was also fitted.

Propelling Charges
A single charge was provided, divided for ease of handling into three components. The cartridge case contained the Grundladung, and the two Vorkerten were provided in bags that were loaded into the chamber ahead of the cased portion.
Grundladung: 75.00kg/165.38lb Gudol R P.
Vorkart 1: 83.00kg/183.02lb Gudol R P.
Vorkart 2: 83.00kg/183.02lb Gudol R P.
This gave a total charge weight of 241.00kg/531.41lb. A report on German propellants states that a third Vorkart was developed, containing 23.00kg(50.72lb) and intended to boost the muzzle velocity to 1625mps(5332fps), but there is no record of this charge ever being used in service.

24cm Kanone in Eisenbahnlafette 'Theodor Bruno'

24cm Th Br K (E)

This was a 1936 Programme gun based on the 24cm SK L/35 barrel, a naval and coast artillery piece dating back to about 1910. It was a Krupp design remarkable for its breechblock, which was half-cylindrical in shape. The gun was mounted in a rectangular cradle, built from cast-steel plates and containing the recoil system cylinders above and below the barrel.

The mounting was largely based on a World War 1 design and consisted of a box-girder structure supported on two eight-wheel bogies. Hinged handrailed platforms were provided for the detachment on each side of the mounting. On-carriage traverse was applied by sliding the rear of the mounting across the bolster of the rear bogie by a hand-operated nut-and-screw mechanism.

Six of these guns were manufactured and delivery was completed in January 1939.

Data
Calibre: 238mm/9.37in.
Length of gun: 8400mm/330.71in/27.56ft.
Length of bore: 7800mm/307.09in/25.59ft.

A battery of 24cm 'Theodor Bruno' K (E) being brought into action. The position is obviously one which has been prepared in advance, since all guns are on turntables and there appear to be ammunition magazines and blast walls surrounding the turntables.

The 24cm 'Theodor Bruno' K (E) in firing position.

Rifling: not known.
Breech mechanism: horizontal sliding block, percussion fired.
Traverse: 1° on mounting.
Elevation: +10° to +45°.
Weight in action: 94000kg/207270lb/92.53ton.
Length over buffers: 20700mm/814.96in/67.91ft.

Performance
Firing standard high explosive shell weighing 148.50kg(327.44lb).
Full charge: velocity 675mps/2215fps, maximum range 20200m/22091yd.
Minimum range owing to 10° minimum elevation: 10000m/10936yd.

Ammunition
Separate-loading, cased charge.

Projectiles
24cm Sprgr L/4.2 m Bd Z u KZ m Hb: fuzed KZ C/27 (or Dopp Z S/90) and Bd Z C/28, weight 148.50kg(327.44lb).
This was the standard projectile, a high explosive shell with base and nose fuzes and a ballistic cap. Fitted with two copper driving bands, it carried a filling of 16.40kg(36.16lb) of TNT.
24cm Pz Sprgr L/4.5 m Bd B m Hb: fuzed Bd Z f Sprgr K, weight 150.50kg(331.85lb).
This was a coast and naval piercing shell with

penetrating and ballistic caps and a base fuze. It was employed with the railway gun as an anti-concrete projectile. The filling was 8.18kg(18.04lb) of TNT/montan wax.

Propelling Charge
A two-part charge, giving full and reduced charges, was used. The reduced-charge section was supplied in the cartridge case, the full charge increment in a separate bag.
Hauptkartusche: 37.50kg/82.69lb R P C/32.
Vorkartusche: 6.90kg/15.21lb R P C/32.

Primer
The percussion primer C/12nA was used.

Case Identification Number
None: the case was identified by the base-stamping KARTH F TH BR K(E).

24cm Kanone in Eisenbahnlafette 'Theodor'

24cm Theodor K (E)

Another 1936 Programme equipment utilising the 24cm SK L/40 gun, another ex-naval and coast artillery piece: such was the Theodor-Kanone that differed from the Theodor Bruno principally in its length (which was five calibres more), and in the adoption of the more orthodox rectangular shape for the breechblock. The cradle was of the more common ring type and carried a large counter-weight, to balance the gun without the need for balancing-presses.

The mounting, although of somewhat different appearance, was basically the same as that used with Theodor Bruno: a box structure on two eight-wheel bogies with the rear of the mounting allowed a limited degree of traverse across the rear bogie bolster.

This equipment had originally been called Theodor Karl, but this had led to some confusion with another project and the name Karl had been dropped. Three were built and issued in 1937.

A 24cm 'Theodor' gun fired from its turntable.

)ata
:alibre: 238mm/9.37in.
.ength of gun: 9550mm/375.98in/31.33ft.
.ength of bore: 8900mm/350.39in/29.20ft.
ɫifling: right-hand increasing twist, 1/50 to 1/30.
}reech mechanism: horizontal sliding block, per-
:ussion fired.
Traverse: 1°.
:levation: +10° to +45°.
Veight in action: 95000kg/209475lb/93.52ton.
.ength over buffers: 18450mm/726.38in/60.53ft.

'erformance
'iring standard high explosive shell weighing
48.50kg(327.44lb).
'ull charge: velocity 810mps/2658fps, maximum
ange 26750m/29254yd.
Minimum range owing to 10° minimum elevation:
13700m/14982yd.

Ammunition
Separate-loading, cased charge.

Projectiles
24cm Sprgr L/4.2 m Bd Z u KZ m Hb.
See 24cm Theodor Bruno.
24cm Pz Sprgr L/4.1 m Bd Z m Hb: fuzed Bd Z f Sprgr K, weight 151.00kg(332.96lb).
This was similar to the shell for the Theodor Bruno but contained 14.90kg(32.85lb) of high explosive.

Propelling Charges
A two-part charge giving reduced and full charges was used:
Hülsenkartusche: 34.50kg/76.07lb R P C/12.
Vorkartusche: 7.50kg/16.54lb R P C/12.

Primer
The percussion primer C/12nA was used.
Case Identification Number
None: the case was identified by the base-stamping TH KAN (E) C/95.

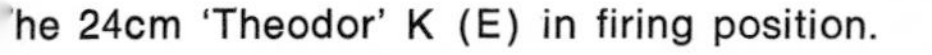

'he 24cm 'Theodor' K (E) in firing position.

28cm Kanone in Eisenbahnlafette 'kurz Bruno'

28cm Kz Br K (E)

This 1936 Programme gun was one of a series of our of the same calibre that differed principally n barrel length and were named accordingly; his was the shortest (kurz, or short) of the four. The gun was the 28cm SK L/40 naval gun nounted in a ring cradle with the hydropneumatic ecoil system underneath.

The mounting was of much the same design as hat of the 24cm Theodor Bruno, suitably :nlarged: a box-girder structure into which the ;un was trunnioned. Folding platforms and hand-ails were fitted and the assembly was mounted on two ten-wheel bogies. A limited degree of raverse was available by moving the mounting across the rear bogie bolster, but the gun was usually emplaced on a portable turntable. Eight guns of this type were built and issued in 1937–8.

Data
Calibre: 283mm/11.14in.
Length of gun: 11200mm/440.94in/36.75ft.
Length of bore: not known.
Rifling: 80 grooves, right-hand increasing twist, 1/50 to 1/30.
Breech mechanism: horizontal sliding block, percussion fired.
Traverse: 1° on the carriage.
Elevation: +10° to +45°.
Weight in action: 129000kg/284445lb/126.98ton.
Length over buffers: 22800mm/897.64in/74.80ft.

'kurz Bruno' on turntable, with camouflage netting covering the running gear.

Front end of a 24cm 'kurz Bruno' on Vogele turntable, showing the turntable recoil mechanism.

Performance
Firing standard high explosive projectiles weighing 240.00kg(529.20lb).
Standard charge: velocity 820mps/2690fps, maximum range 29500m/32261yd.
Minimum range owing to 10° minimum elevation: 14300m/15638yd.

Ammunition
Separate-loading, cased charge.

Projectiles
28cm Sprgr L/4.1 m KZ u Bd Z m Hb: fuzed KZ C/27 (or Dopp Z S/90) and Bd Z C/38, weight 240.00kg(529.20lb).
This was a ballistic-capped shell with base and nose fuzes; the filling was 18.70kg(41.23lb) of TNT in pre-pressed blocks.

Propelling Charges
A single-charge bag contained in a cartridge case. The charge consister of 67.00kg(147.73lb) of R P C/32 or 64.00kg(141.12lb) of R P C/12.

Primer
The percussion primer C/12nA was used.

Case Identification Number
None: the case was identified by the base-stamping W KARTH D KZ BR K C/95.

ringing up a fresh round to 'kurz Bruno', using a small trolley running on a track from the magazine car.

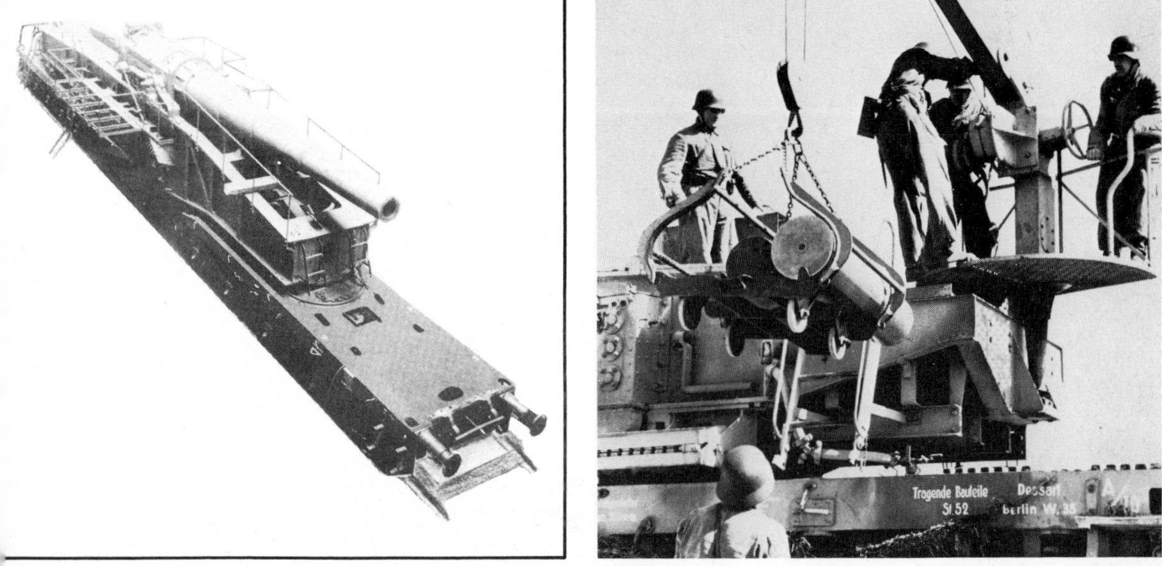

'he 24cm 'kurz Bruno' K (E).

Hoisting shell and cartridge up to the loading platform.

28cm Kanone in Eisenbahnlafette 'lange Bruno'

?8cm lg Br K(E)

The second of the 1936 series of 28cm guns, this ad the long barrel and was thus called lange 3runo ('long Bruno'). The ordnance was the '8cm SK L/45, another ex-naval weapon. Only hree weapons were built in 1937.

The mounting was the same as that used with the hort model, a box-girder body riding on two ten-vheel bogies. The lange Bruno was slightly lighter han the shorter kurz Bruno, because although the barrel was longer it was also of thinner section.

Data

Calibre: 283mm/11.14in.
Length of gun: 12735mm/501.38in/41.78ft.
Length of bore: not known.
Rifling: right-hand increasing twist, 1/50 to 1/30.
Breech mechanism: horizonal sliding block, per-

ussion fired.
Traverse: 1° on the carriage.
Elevation: +10° to +45°.
Weight in action: 123000kg/271215lb/121.08ton.
Length over buffers: 22800mm/897.64in/74.80ft.

Performance
Firing standard high explosive shell weighing 284.00kg(626.22lb).
Standard charge: velocity 875mps/2871fps, maximum range 36100m/39479yd/22.43mile.
Minimum range owing to 10° minimum elevation: 16800m/18372yd.

Ammunition
Separate-loading, cased charge.

Projectiles
28cm Sprgr L/4.4 m KZ m BdZ m Hb: fuzed KZ C/27 (or Dopp Z S/90) and Bd Z C/38, weight 284.00kg(626.22lb).
This was a ballistic-capped high explosive shell fuzed at nose and base; the bursting charge was 22.90kg(50.49lb) of TNT in pre-pressed blocks.

Propelling Charges
A single charge bag was supplied in the cartridge case; it consisted of 106.00kg(233.73lb) of R P C/12.

Primer
The percussion primer C/12nA was used.

Case Identification Number
None: the case was identified by the base-stamping LG U S BR K(E).

Left: The 28cm 'lange Bruno' firing.

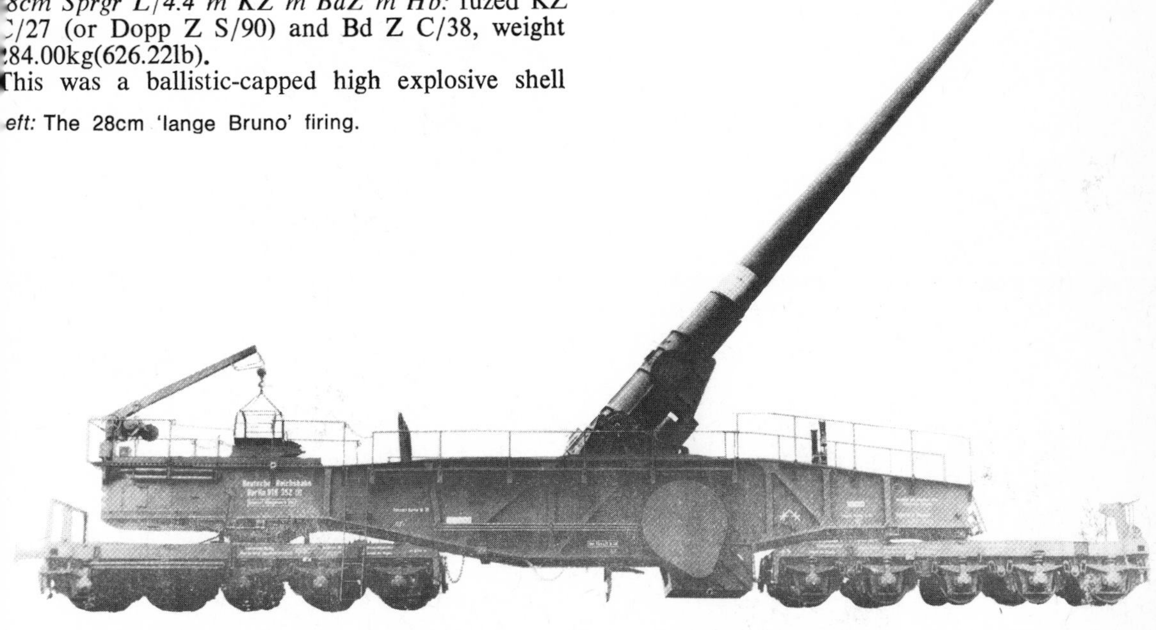

28cm 'lange Bruno' K (E) in firing position.

28cm Kanone in Eisenbahnlafette 'schwere Bruno'

28cm s Br K(E)

The third 1936 gun in 28cm calibre 'heavy Bruno' was based on the ordnance of the 28cm Kusten Kanone L/42, a weapon that had been superseded in coast defence but two of which were available from old stock. The mounting was the same as that used for the other Bruno guns, and the two equipments were built and issued in 1938.

Data
Calibre: 283mm/11.14in.
Length of gun: 11930mm/469.69in/39.14ft.
Length of bore: 11084mm/436.38in/36.36ft.
Rifling: 80 grooves, right-hand increasing twist, 1/60 to 1/45.
Breech mechanism: horizontal sliding block, percussion fired.
Traverse: 1° on the carriage.
Elevation: +10° to +45°.
Weight in action: 118000kg/260190lb/116.15ton.
Length over buffers: 22800mm/897.64in/74.80ft.

Performance
Firing standard high explosive shell weighing 284.00kg(626.22lb).

A 28cm 'schwere Bruno' being rolled into the firing position.

28cm 'schwere Bruno' K (E). Although still hooked u to its train, the service platforms have been rigged ready for firing.

Standard charge: velocity 860mps/2822fps, maximum range 35700m/39042yd/22.18mile.
Minimum range owing to 10° minimum elevation: 16800m/18372yd.

Ammunition, Projectiles, Propelling Charges
See 28cm lange Bruno.

The 28cm 'schwere Bruno' fires—the vibration of the camera, due to the discharge, has blurred the picture.

28cm Kanone in Eisenbahnlafette 'Bruno neue'

28cm Br N K (E)

In the spring of 1938, while the earlier series of Bruno guns were reaching completion, the army reviewed their performance and—deciding it was insufficient—asked if improvements could be made. After studying the designs Krupp replied that, since the army had specified that the programme was to be completed by 1939, modification involving the design and manufacture of new barrels could not be done in the time. The army accepted this and instructed Krupp to proceed with the design of a new equipment, the delivery date for which was not finalised. Eventually three weapons were manufactured: one delivered in November 1940, one in July 1941 and the last in February 1942. It had been intended to build more but the better performance of the 28cm K 5 (E), together with a ballistic irregularity that defied solution, caused the project to be cancelled after the third delivery.

Whereas the earlier Bruno series had been converted naval guns, the neue Bruno was a completely new piece, which accounted for its name. The barrel was 58 calibres long and mounted in a ring cradle with an unusual outer casing that concealed the recoil cylinders. The mounting was based on those of the earlier models but was of much 'cleaner' appearance and was supported on two ten-wheel bogies. Power assistance was provided for elevation and ammunition hoisting, and the muzzle preponderance was balanced by two hydropneumatic presses.

Firing could be done from either a curved track or a turntable; it is also believed that this weapon introduced the *controlled carriage recoil system* that was later applied to most guns firing from turntables. In this system the gun was connected to the turntable front by a hydropneumatic recoil cylinder and was thereafter allowed to recoil slightly on the turntable track.

Data

Calibre: 283mm/11.14in.
Length of gun: 16400mm/645.67in/53.81ft.
Length of bore: 15247mm/600.28in/50.02ft.
Rifling: 80 grooves, right-hand increasing twist, 1/50 to 1/35.
Breech mechanism: horizontal sliding block, percussion fired.
Traverse: 1° on the carriage.
Elevation: 0 to +50°.

Weight in action: 150000kg/330750lb/147.66ton.
Length over buffers: 24880mm/979.53in/81.62ft.

Performance
Firing standard high explosive shell weighing 265.00kg(584.33lb).
Standard charge: velocity 995mps/3265fps, maximum range 36600m/40026yd/22.74mile.

Ammunition
Separate-loading, cased charge.

Projectiles
28cm Gr 39 m Hb: fuzed Hbgr Z 35K, weight 265.00kg(584.33lb).
This was a ballistic-capped high explosive shell fitted with a nose fuze. It had three copper driving bands and was prepared at the base with a threaded hole for a tracer, a most unlikely fitting for a long-range gun. The shell contained 34.30kg (75.63lb) of TNT and TNT/wax in pre-pressed blocks.

28cm 'Bruno neue' K (E), showing its extremely clean design.

Propelling Charges
A single charge of 163.80kg(361.18lb) of Gudol R P was supplied in the cartridge case.

Primer
The percussion primer C/12nA was used.
Case Identification Number: None.

28cm Kanone 5 in Eisenbahnlafette

28cm K 5 (E)

This weapon, one of the best railway guns ever made, became the standard army railway gun. Design of the K 5 began in 1934, concurrently with the design of the 21cm K 12; the first gun entered service in 1936 and from then until the end of the war the K 5 was in regular production, some 28 weapons having been made by 1945.

The design of the K 5 and the K 12 overlapped to some extent, as both were intended as super-long-range weapons employing deep-grooved barrels and splined projectiles. The K 5 barrel was made with 12 grooves 10mm(0.39in). A 15cm experimental barrel, known as the 15cm K 5M, was first made and tested, and as with the K 12 a normally-rifled barrel (the 15cm K 5 MKu) was built for comparative trials. By 1936 a full-size barrel had been made and proof-fired successfully at Krupp's Meppen test-range, and by 1937 a complete equipment had been built and tested. Production then began and by 1940 eight were in service. Then a sudden spate of split barrels occurred; an investigation produced no definite conclusions but, more or less at hazard, the depth of the rifling grooves was reduced to 7mm(0.28in). This appears to have been the correct solution since the trouble never occurred again; the resulting guns were called K 5 Tiefzug 7mm.

The mounting was a straightforward box-girder assembly carried on two twelve-wheel bogies. The gun was fitted into the usual ring cradle and trunnioned directly to the mounting's side-girders. It was originally intended to brace the barrel, in similar fashion to the K 12, but trials proved that bracing was unnecessary.

The wartime development of iron driving bands gave Krupp's designers hope that it might be possible to produce a normally-rifled K 5 barrel to work with FEW-banded shell. Towards the end of 1943, after successful completion of their experiments, a production multi-grooved barrel was issued. This was known as the K 5 Vz (*Vielzug*, many grooves) and about six were manufactured.

Consideration had meanwhile been given to extending the range. The first project was to develop a rocket-assisted shell that was eventually issued as the *Raketen Granate 4331* (R Gr 4331) and carried a cast-propellant rocket motor in the nose section. This was ignited by a time fuze in the nose after 19sec flight. The rocket efflux passed down a central blast pipe to the base of the shell, and the high explosive payload was packed around the blast pipe. Two special graze percussion fuzes were mounted in the transom between the rocket motor and the high explosive. A similar projectile with a conventional driving band, known as the *R Gr 4341*, was developed for the K 5 Vz.

The next step was to adapt the gun to fire Peenemünder Pfeilgeschosse (Peenemünde arrow shells), and to do this the barrel was bored-out to become a 31cm calibre smoothbore. These guns, two of which were completed (one made by Krupp and the other by Hanomag), were known as the K 5 Glatt.

In addition to the four types that entered service —K 5 Tiefzug 10mm, K 5 Tiefzug 7mm, K 5 Vielzug and K 5 Glatt—several other projects were mooted at various times during the war. In 1943 a contract was let to develop a screw-breech model to fire bagged charges; the development was done by Krupp but trials of the proposed system ended in failure. By that time the work on sliding-block breeches for bag charges was beginning to show promising results, and further work on the modified K 5 was shelved to await further research. Another project was the provision of a muzzlebrake in order to increase performance, but after the initial enthusiasm wore off this also fell by the wayside.

A most interesting project was begun in 1943 at the instigation of the army. It was decided that, owing to the increasing intensity of Allied air attacks, a railway gun should be developed that was capable of cross-country detours around points at which the track had been destroyed. The gun itself was also intended to carry an integral turntable platform so that it could be lowered to the track and the bogies run clear, leaving the weapon ready to fire from the platform with 360° traverse. This idea resembled the American 14in M1920 railgun, but the idea was then carried further by a suggestion that it should then be possible to partly dismantle the K 5 and transport it across country on special transporters based on the chassis and running gear of the Pz Kpfw VI (Tiger tank). In this, one transporter was to carry the breech mechanism, two were to carry the barrel between them, two were to take the gun-carriage and one was to move the platform. The mounting was also to be designed to take either the barrel of the 28cm K 5 or a new 38cm howitzer with a planned range of 25000m(27340yd)

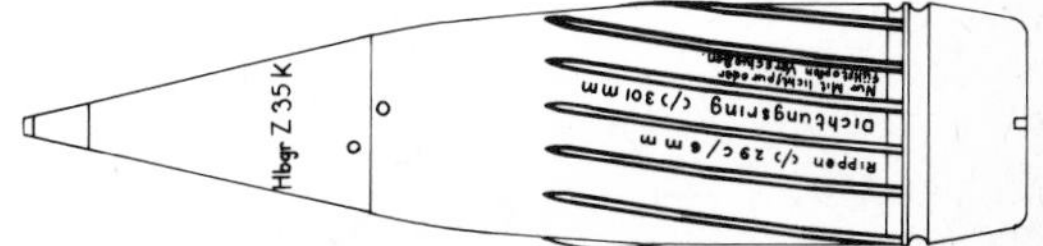

Gr 35.

The 28cm K 5 (E) firing.

with an 800kg(1764lb) shell. The whole project received a great deal of thought and would no doubt have been successfully completed in due course, but it was still in the planning stage when the war ended.

Data (K 5 [E] Tiefzug 7mm)
Calibre: 283mm/11.14in.
Length of gun: 21539mm/840.91in/70.08ft.
Length of bore: 20548mm/808.98in/67.41ft.
Rifling: 12 grooves, right-hand uniform twist, 1/36.
Breech mechanism: horizontal sliding block, percussion fired.
Traverse: 1° on the carriage.
Elevation: 0 to +50°.
Weight in action: 218000kg/480690lb/214.59ton.
Length, including barrel overhang: 41234mm/1623.39in/135.28ft.

Performance
Firing standard pre-rifled shell weighing 255.50kg (563.38lb).
Grosse Ladung: velocity 1128mps/3701fps, maximum range 62180m/68000yd/38.64miles.
Firing pre-rifled rocket-assisted shell weighing 248.00kg(546.84lb).
Grosse Ladung: velocity 1130mps/3708fps, maximum range 86500m/94596yd/53.75miles.
Firing conventional shell from K 5 Vz, weighing 255.50kg(563.38lb).
Grosse Ladung: velocity 1128mps/3701fps, maximum range 62180m/68000yd/38.64miles.
Firing Peenemünder Pfeilgeschoss (from K 5 Glatt) weighing 136.00kg(299.88lb).
Grosse Ladung: velocity 1524mps/5000fps, maximum range 151000m/165135yd/93.83miles.

Ammunition
Separate-loading, cased charge.

Projectiles
28cm Gr 35: fuzed Hbgr Z 35K, weight 255.50kg (563.38lb).
This was the standard shell and was fitted externally with 12 soft-metal ribs, curved at 5° inclination to match the rifling. At the rear of these ribs was a soft copper sealing band of thin section, and a deep groove into which an asbestos and graphite sealing ring (Dichtungsring) was tamped before firing. The shell had a ballistic cap with a light alloy tip and the nose fuze was beneath this cap. The original design had the base fuze Bd Z 35K fitted in addition to the nose fuze, but this was later omitted and the base fuze cavity closed with a sealing plug. Time and percussion fuze Dopp Z 45K, which had a running time of 125sec, could be fitted as an alternative to the percussion fuze. The bursting charge was 30.50kg (67.25lb) of high explosive.
28cm Gr 35 (Ei): fuzed Hbgr Z 35K, weight 255.50kg(563.38lb).
This was the ranging shell (Einschiessgeschoss) used in conjunction with the Gr 35. It was o similar appearance and ballistic performance bu had a special filling of 9.50kg(20.95lb) of hig explosive together with an additional compositio that gave a thick column of black smoke fo observation at long-range.
28cm Gr 42: fuzed Hbgr Z 35K, weight 255.50k (563.38lb).
This was the standard projectile for the mult groove barrel K 5 Vz. It was of the same genera construction and appearance as the Gr 35 bu instead of the external splines it was fitted with large soft-iron driving band.
28cm Gr 42 Ei: fuzed Hbgr Z 35K, weigh 255.50kg(563.38lb).
The ranging shell for the K 5 Vz gun, similar t the Gr 35 Ei but conventionally banded.
28cm Sprgr L/5.2 m Hb: fuze unknown, weigh 190.00kg(418.95lb).
A new design of long-range shell was unde development in 1944 by Krupp. It had a hollo tail section to give additional stabilisation by dra and a high-efficiency driving band for use with th K 5 Vz gun. It was to contain 27.00kg(59.54lb of high explosive, and was to be fitted with a nos fuze beneath a ballistic cap. A number of exper mental models were fired in trials but the desig was not completed before the war ended.
28cm R Gr 4331: fuzed two AZ 4331 and on Zeit Z S/30, weight 248.00kg(546.84lb).
This was a splined shell of similar appearance t the Gr 35. It was fitted with a time fuze in th nose to initiate the rocket motor and two specia internal graze fuzes to detonate the high explosiv filling. The blast pipe exit in the base was seale by a heavy plug that prevented the propellan flash igniting the rocket prematurely; the plu was blown clear by the rocket blast after ignition landing about 13–15km(8–9.5miles) in front of th gun. The time fuze was always set to give ignitio after 19sec of flight, at which time the shell wa almost at the vertex of its trajectory. The she contained 19.50kg(43.00lb) of rocket propellan and 14.00kg(30.87lb) of high explosive. It accuracy was such that at the maximum rang 50% of the shots fired fell into a longitudina rectangle 3400m × 200m(3718yd × 218yd).
28cm R Gr 4341: fuzed two AZ 4331 and on Zeit Z S/30, weight 248.00kg(546.84lb).
This was the rocket-assisted shell for the K 5 V gun. It was constructed exactly as the R Gr 433 except that it was conventionally banded instea of splined, with the addition of two narro centering bands at the shoulder; its operation wa exactly the same.
28cm Gr 39/42, 28cm Gr 39/44 (Ei).
References to these shells have been seen but n confirmed details are known. It is believed tha they were conversions of Gr 39 bodies to con ventional banding by removing the splines.
31cm Sprgr 4861: fuzed AZ 41 and Bd Z 512 weight 136.00kg(299.88lb).

The Peenemünde Pfielgeschosse for the 31cm K 5 Glatt. The fuze is missing from this specimen.

This was the Peenemünde arrow shell—Peenemünder Pfeilgeschoss or Flugstabilisierte treibringgeschoss. It was of 12cm calibre and 1911mm (75.23in) long, with a 31cm diameter three-piece discarding ring sabot at the waist and four fins at the rear. (Some early models had six fins.) On firing, from the K 5 Glatt smoothbore gun, the ring was discarded and fell about 2km(1.25 miles) in front of the gun, leaving the fin-stabilised projectile to fly to the target. Development began in February 1940 and the long-range trials, fired at the Rugenwalde range, gave a maximum range of 151.00km(93.83miles). The high explosive content was 25.00kg(55.13lb).

Propelling Charges
The propelling charge was of four separate units that could be combined to give two charges, the Kleine and Grosse Ladungen:
Hauptkartusche: 60.50kg/133.40lb Dgl R P.
Vorkart 1: 46.25kg/101.98lb Dgl R P.
Vorkart 2: 46.25kg/101.98lb Dgl R P.
Vorkart 3: 21.00kg/46.31lb Dgl R P.
The charge composition was as follows:
Kleine Ladung: Hauptkart plus Vorkarten 1 and 2, a total of 152.50kg/336.26lb.
Grosse Ladung: Hauptkart plus all three Vorkarten, a total of 173.50kg/382.57lb.
The Hauptkart was carried in the cartridge case, the Vorkarten being separately supplied and loaded ahead of the case. These charges were used with the splined and conventional barrels. The smoothbore K 5 Glatt, less highly stressed than the rifled guns owing to the absence of resistance that was due to the rifling, fired a heavier charge—four parts adding up to a total weight of 250.00kg(551.25lb).

Primer
The percussion primer C/12nA was used.

Case Identification Number: 6309.

38cm Kanone in Eisenbahnlafette 'Siegfried'

38cm Siegfried K(E)

By 1938 Krupp felt that, with the 1936 Programme almost complete and the K 12 and K 5 designs finished, they had amassed sufficient experience of railway gun design to warrant trying something better, and so design work began on three super-heavy weapons. To conserve time two were built around existing barrels that were under construction for naval use, the 38cm SK C/34 being selected for the first. This had already been ear-marked for use as a coast artillery weapon and had been modified for the role by enlarging the chamber and developing a long-range shell; it was this modified barrel that Krupp was to use. By the middle of 1939 all design work had been completed and approved, and the army ordered eight equipments to be built. But it was the summer of 1943 before the first was delivered and only three were completed before the war ended.

The ordance was quite conventional, though it appears that it was felt necessary to brace it against droop—something that had not been found necessary in the coast application. The breech mechanism was electrically interlocked to the elevating motors so that the gun could only be elevated and depressed if the breech was closed. For travelling, the gun was disconnected from the recoil system and run back 6.00m(19.69ft) in its cradle.

The mounting was a box-girder structure riding on two sixteen-wheel bogies; the gun, in a ring cradle, was trunnioned directly to the side plates. No traverse was available on the mounting as it was intended to use a turntable, but where no turntable was available the gun could be fired from a curved track (when pointing was done by electrically driving the bogie wheels).

Owing to the long wheelbase of the bogies and the requirement that railway guns were to be capable of moving on emergency tracking, only two axles on each eight-axle bogie were rigidly mounted in the frames; the outer axles were pivoted, the next pair in were rigid and the inner four were permitted a large amount of sideways movement.

Data
Calibre: 380mm/14.96in.
Length of gun: 19630mm/772.83in/64.40ft.
Length of bore: 18405mm/724.61in/60.38ft.

Rifling: 90 grooves, right-hand increasing twist, 1/36 to 1/30.
Breech mechanism: horizontal sliding block, percussion fired.
Traverse: nil.
Elevation: 0 to 45°44′.
Weight in action: 294000kg/648270lb/289.41ton.
Length over buffers: 31320mm/1233.10in/102.76ft.

Performance
Firing long-range projectile weighing 495.00kg (1091.48lb).
Kleine Ladung: velocity 920mps/3019fps, maximum range 40000m/43744yd/24.85mile.
Grosse Ladung: velocity 1050mps/3445fps, maximum range 55700m/60914yd/34.61mile.
Firing shell weighing 800.00kg(1764.00lb).
Grosse Ladung: velocity 820mps/2690fps, maximum range 42000m/45931yd/26.10mile.

Ammunition
Separate-loading, cased charge

Projectiles
38cm Sprgr L/4.6 m KZ m Hb: fuzed KZ C/27, weight 800.00kg(1764.00lb)
This was the standard high explosive shell fitted with a nose fuze and a ballistic cap
38cm Sprgr L/4.5 m Bd Z m Hb: fuzed Bd Z C/38, weight 800.00kg(1764.00lb)
This was a naval semi-armour-piercing shell with penetrating and ballistic caps; it was employed with the railway gun as an anti-concrete shell
38cm Sprgr L/4.5 m KZ u Bd Z m Hb: fuzed Hbgr Z 40K (or Dopp Z 45K) and Bd Z 40K, weight 495.00kg(1091.48lb)
The lightweight long-range *Siegfried Granate* shell of Army design, it carried its nose fuze beneath a ballistic cap and was also provided with a base fuze. The bursting charge was 69.00kg(152.15lb) of TNT
38cm R Gr L/4.6: fuze unknown, weight 570.00kg (1256.85lb)
This was a rocket-assisted shell of similar design to the 28cm R Gr 4341. The rocket motor ignited after 16sec flight and the maximum range was

The 38cm 'Siegfried' ready to fire.

The 38cm 'Siegfried' on its Vogele turntable.

57.80km(42.13mile). The muzzle velocity with a special charge was 980mps(3215fps) and the rocket motor consisted of 45.00kg(99.23lb) of solid propellant. The shell was under development early in 1943 but it appears that it never reached production; no performance details are known.

Propelling Charges
Two charges were provided, one for use with the 800.00kg(1764.00lb) shells and one for use with the 495.00kg(1091.48lb) Siegfried Granate. The standard charge was divided into two portions for convenience in loading but was not normally fired as a two-part charge, though the base portion was sometimes used as a practice charge:
Hauptkartusche: 110.0kg/242.55lb R P C/38.
Vorkartusche: 101.0kg/222.71lb R P C/38.
The special Siegfried Ladung was also supplied in two sections, but this was divided for firing into Kleine or Grosse Ladungen:
Hauptkart 'Siegfried Ladung': 133.00kg/293.27lb Gudol R P.
Vorkart 'Siegfried Ladung': 123.00kg/271.22lb Gudol R P.

Primer
The percussion primer C/12nA was used.

Case Identification Number
None: the case was identified by the base-stamping 38CM–34.

40·6cm Kanone in Eisenbahnlafette 'Adolf'

40·6cm Adolf K(E)

This was the second Krupp design of superheavy gun and used the ex-naval 40.6cm SK C/34 that was also employed as a coast artillery weapon. The mounting was the same as that for the 38cm Siegfried gun with some modifications, principally to strengthen it for the heavier 40.6cm weapon. Production was delayed by the need to make further changes in order to get the finished equipment past the loading gauge. In fact the documented history of this weapon is scant and contradictory, and little definite information has ever emerged. It is believed only one was built.

Data
Calibre: 406mm/15.98in.
Length of gun: 20300mm/799.21in/66.60ft.
Length of bore: not known.
Rifling: not known.
Breech mechanism: horizontal sliding block, percussion fired.
Traverse: nil.
Elevation: 0 to 45°.
Weight in action: 323000kg/712215lb/317.95ton.
Length over buffers: 31320mm/1233.07in/102.76ft.

Performance
Firing standard high explosive shell weighing 1030.00kg(2271.15lb).
Grosse Ladung: velocity 810mps/2658fps, maximum range 42800m/46806yd/26.59mile.
Firing long-range shell weighing 610.000kg(1345lb).
Kleine Ladung: velocity 970mps/3183fps, maximum range 46700m/51070yd/29.02mile.
Grosse Ladung: velocity 1050mps/3445fps, maximum range 56000m/61242yd/34.80mile.

Ammunition
Separate-loading, cased charge.

Projectiles
40.6cm Sprgr L/4.8 m KZ m Hb: fuzed KZ C/27, weight 1030.00kg(2271.15lb).
This was standard high explosive shell fitted with a nose fuze under a ballistic cap.
40.6cm Sprgr L/4.6 m Bd Z m Hb: fuzed Bd Z C/38, weight 1030.00kg(2271.15lb).
A naval semi-armour-piercing shell with a base fuze and a ballistic cap, used in this gun as an anti-concrete projectile.
40.6cm Adolf Granate L/4.2 m Bd Z u KZ m Hb: fuzed Hbgr Z 40K (or Dopp Z 45K) and Bd Z 40K, weight 610.00kg(1345.05lb).
This was a special long-range shell developed by the army, carrying 78.00kg(171.99lb) of TNT; it had a nose fuze under a ballistic cap and a base fuze. Three copper driving bands were fitted at the base and a copper centering band appeared at the shoulder.

Propelling Charges
Two charges were provided, one for the 1030kg (2271lb) projectiles and one for the 610kg(1345lb) *Adolf Granate.* The standard charge was supplied in two portions for convenience in handling and loading, the Hauptkart in the cartridge case and the Vorkart in a bag; they were never fired separately:
Haupkart: 149.00kg/328.55lb R P/40 Bu.
Vorkart: 152.00kg/335.16lb R P/40 Bu.
The Adolf Ladung was also in two sections but could be split to fire reduced or full charges:
Hauptkart 'Adolf Ladung': 160.00kg/352.80lb Gudol R P.
Vorkart 'Adolf Ladung': 203.80kg/449.38lb Gudol R P.

Primer
The percussion primer C/12nA was used.

Case Identification Number
None: the case was identified by the base-stamping 40.6 w34 ST.

80cm Kanone in Eisenbahnlafette 'Gustav Gerät'

80cm K(E)

The third gun whose production occupied Krupp's designers after 1937 was this 80cm monster. In common with most superweapons many legends have grown up around the 80cm K(E), and with the passing of the years it is becoming increasingly difficult to sort the wheat from the chaff; the following information appears to approximate to the truth and is substantiated by examination of documents and drawings, statements by Krupp employees and correspondence with eyewitnesses.

The weapon was conceived some time in 1935 partly as a serious project and partly as a propaganda stunt, when the Heereswaffenamt (army weapons office) enquired of Krupp what size of weapon would be needed to defeat the fortifications of the Maginot Line by direct assault. In response to this, ballistic data was calculated for hypothetical guns of 70, 80 and 100cm calibre and sent to the army. There the matter rested until a visit by Hitler in March 1936 to the Krupp works. There he apparently asked the same question and was given the same figures; he was also told that although manufacture of such a weapon would be difficult it would not be impossible. No definite committment was made by Hitler, but Gustav Krupp von Böhlen und Halbach—knowing his man—gave instructions for design work to commence on the 80cm model and early in 1937 drawings were laid before the Heereswaffenamt. They were approved and manufacture began in the summer of the same year.

The production of such a monster was not easy (particularly the forging and machining of the barrel, jacket and cradle), and it was soon apparent that it would not be ready by the Spring of 1940 in accordance with the original estimate. The Maginot Line was overcome by other means, but when the French campaign was over Hitler reportedly carpeted the Krupp management and demanded results. Whether this had any effect is doubtful, but the gun barrel was successfully built by the end of 1940 and fired at proof early in 1941. Finally, early in 1942, the complete equipment was assembled at the Rugenwalde firing range and underwent its final tests in the presence of Hitler himself.

The finished weapon was code-named *Gustav Gerät* by the Krupp management in honour of Gustav Krupp, and was duly presented to Hitler as Krupp's gift to the war effort. The German gunners—somewhat irreligiously—christened it Dora, and this dual terminology has since led to the belief that two such weapons existed.

After its test firing the 80cm K(E) was shipped to the siege of Sevastopol to make its first appearance in action. There it fired a small number of rounds, variously reported between 36 and 55, some of which caused immense damage to the Russian installations. The gun was then removed and sent to Leningrad, but before it could be emplaced there the Red Army began advancing and it was hastily withdrawn. Its only other recorded appearance, oddly enough, was near Warsaw in 1944 when (or so it is reported by former members of the Polish Underground) it was used to fire a few rounds into the city during the abortive rising. It then vanished completely, never to be seen again. Three different versions of its fate have been published. One states that the 80cm K(E) was returned to Essen and there cut up by the Allies, which is not substantiated by the reports on the examination of the Essen works after their capture; one avers that two wrecked equipments were found in the Russian zone of Germany, and the last that it was found in Bavaria by US Army troops, neither of which statements stands up to critical examination. It can only be assumed that the railgun was dismantled and scrapped some time in late 1944. When the Hillersleben proving ground was examined in April and May 1945 by Allied technical intelligence teams, a proof mounting and some ammunition was found: no other trace of the weapon has ever been found.

The construction of such a large equipment obviously had to be in sections in order to transport the components within the loading gauge; when assembled the gun was 42976mm(141.00ft) long, 7010mm(23.00ft) wide and the maximum height was about 11600mm(38.06ft). For movement the unit dismantled into the following sections: breech-ring and breechblock, barrel (in halves), jacket, cradle, trunnions and trunnion bearings, all of which were carried on special separate flatcars. The remainder of the mountings—comprising the upper carriage, the lower carriage and the bogie units—was split longitudinally so that, as well as being dismantled from the top down, each section was divided into halves. These pieces were carried in a number of trains using more special flatcars, together with the bogie units on their own wheels, ammunition wagons, coaches for the crews and a dismantled large gantry crane.

On arrival at the chosen position a four-rail double track was laid for the gun, together with two outer tracks on which the travelling crane was erected. The right and left halves of the bogies were then shunted into place on the gun tracks and connected together. The remainder of the components then arrived piece by piece and the mounting was erected with the aid of the crane.

The 80cm 'Gustav' in position at Sebastopol and being prepared for firing.

The barrel was then assembled by inserting the rear half into the barrel jacket and connecting the front half, which was thereafter locked in place by a massive joint nut. The assembled barrel fitted to the cradle, and the whole assembly was lifted on to the mounting. The breech was then lifted and fixed to the barrel by another joint nut. The whole process of preparing the site and erecting the gun took up to three weeks, and a force of 1420 men (commanded by an officer holding the rank of Generalmajor) was occupied in the task.

Further projects involving this weapon were considered after its successful debut at Sevastopol. It was intended to produce a 52cm gun known as Lange Gustav to fit the same mounting; this was to fire a 1420kg(3131lb) projectile to a range of 110km(68.35mile), a 52/38cm sabot shell to 150km (93.21mile), or a 52/38cm rocket-assisted sabot shell to 190km(118.06mile). It was considered that the gun would then make a good cross-Channel bombardment gun. Had this ever been done it would have given a large part of England a severe shock: sited on Cap Griz Nez the weapon would have commanded an arc running from Portsmouth through Henley-on-Thames, Luton and Cambridge to Lowestoft (though it is doubtful whether it would have fired more than once before the inevitable air retaliation arrived). Indeed it may be that the prospect of attempting to conceal such a weapon was enough to stop the plan. As an interim measure designs were drawn up for a Peenemünder Pfeilgeschoss (Peenemünde arrow shell) that could be fired from the 80cm barrel (presumably smooth-bored); two suggestions were an 80/32cm model ranging to 140km(86.99mile) or an 80/30.5cm model ranging to 160km(99.42 mile), but none of these projects ever passed the planning stage.

After all is said and done, it has to be admitted that the 80cm K(E) was a gross waste of time, money, material and men. Far better results would have been obtained had all the wasteful dissipation of raw material and time been put—for example—into another five or six 38cm Siegfried guns. But the Gustav Gerät nonetheless remains the largest gun ever seen by the world (not the largest *calibre* gun) and is likely to remain so.

Data
Calibre: 800mm/31.50in
Length of gun: 32480mm/1278.74in/106.56ft

Length of bore: 28957mm/1140.04in/95.00ft.
Rifling: 96 grooves, right-hand twist.
Breech mechanism: horizontal hydraulically operated sliding block, percussion fired.
Traverse: Nil, fired only from a curved track.
Elevation: +10° to +65°.
Weight in action: 1350000kg/2976750lb/1328.90 ton.
Length over buffers: 42976mm/1691.97in/141.00ft.

Performance
Firing high explosive shell weighing 4800kg (10584lb/4.73ton).
Full charge: velocity 820mps/2690fps, maximum range 47000m/51400yd/29.20mile.
Firing concrete-piercing shell weighing 7100kg (15656lb/6.99ton).
Full charge: velocity 710mps/2330fps, maximum range 38000m/41557yd/23.61mile.

Ammunition
Separate-loading, cased charge.
Projectiles
80cm Sprgr: fuzed Hbgr Z 40K, weight 4800kg (10584lb/4.73ton).
This was a ballistic-capped shell of conventional design, with the nose fuze beneath the cap and an extended striker rod connecting the fuze mechanism with a plug at the tip of the cap. Three double driving bands of sintered-iron were fitted, with a single soft-iron sealing ring of larger diameter behind them. The explosive content was approximately 400.00kg(882.00lb).
80cm Gr Be: fuzed Bd Z C/38, weight 7100kg (15656lb/6.99ton).
This was of similar appearance to the high explosive shell but was base fuzed, the shell having a concealed hardened point beneath the ballistic cap. The explosive content was approximately 200.00kg(441.00lb).

Propelling Charges
Two charges were provided, one for the high explosive shell and one for the anti-concrete shell. The charge was split into three sections, the Hauptkart in a cartridge case, and Vorkarten 1 and 2 in cloth bags. The Hauptkart was common to both shells, but the Vorkarten were of different weights for the different shells and were prominently marked FUR SPRGR or FUR GR BE accordingly. It appears that the standard charge was the Hauptkart and both Vorkarten; some reports have spoken of a reduced charge for short-range firing, presumably the Hauptkart and one Vorkart, but there is no confirmation of this.
Hauptkart: 1050kg/2326lb Gudol R P.
Vorkart 1 (Sprgr): 535kg/1180lb Gudol R P.
Vorkart 1 (Gr Be): 465kg/1025lb Gudol R P.
Vorkart 2 (Sprgr): 655kg/1444lb Gudol R P.
Vorkart 2 (Gr Be): 585kg/1290lb Gudol R P
Total weight of charge fired with HE shell: 2240kg/4939lb.
Total weight of charge fired with anti-concrete shell: 2100kg/4631lb.

Primer
The percussion primer C/12nA was used.
Case Identification Number.
None: no case mark was used, for presumably none was necessary. The case was 1300mm (51.18in) long with a base diameter of 960mm (37.80in) and was difficult to confuse with any other.

The 80cm 'Gustav' completely assembled.

ANTI-AIRCRAFT
ARTILLERY

The German anti-aircraft armoury contained less variety of equipment than some of the other classes of artillery, but what it lacked in diversity it made up in numbers. At the outbreak of war the Luftwaffe Flak gun strength totalled 8950 weapons, 6500 of which were smaller than 5cm calibre. In June 1944 (the time of maximum strength) the total was 45550 guns, 30463 of which were light weapons. The priority accorded to their emplacement is indicated by the allocation to the western defences—against British and American bombers—compared to that to other fronts: the western defences of the Reich absorbed 33345 guns, no less than 73% of the total strength.

The early history of the Flak organisation has already been outlined in previous pages, and it only remains to remark on the technical aspects. As will be seen, the Luftwaffe was well aware of the rapid improvement of aircraft performance and as early as 1935 the OKL (Oberkommando der Luftwaffe) was preparing to deal with the bombers predicted for 1945. In some cases, however, the OKL's solutions demanded ballistics that were difficult to achieve, and in some cases the performance of the aircraft advanced so quickly that the guns were obsolete before they were even built. It was eventually realised that conventional gunnery was not going to be the complete solution and, from about the middle of 1943, more and more effort went into developing a variety of unconventional projectiles that were intended to reduce the time of flight of the shell to the target. This was consequently expected to improve the chance of hitting, to increase the ceiling of the gun and thus force the enemy to fly higher (thus reducing the accuracy of his bombing) and to cut the barrel-wear rate that was an economic and production problem of major proportions. Discarding sabot, squeeze-bore and fin stabilisation were all tried throughout the entire range of weapons in the medium and heavy classes (5cm calibre and above) and a great deal of useful knowledge of the high-velocity performance of guns and projectiles was acquired, though the end of the war came before any of it could be put into practice.

From the middle of 1944, though, another factor entered the anti-aircraft world—the guided missile. Germany spent little time or energy on the deployment of simple free-flight anti-aircraft rockets and instead threw massive resources into the more sophisticated designs, one or two of which actually entered service in limited numbers towards the latter days of the war. Since these pages are concerned with artillery no further space will be devoted to this fascinating subject, but it has to be kept in mind for (after September 1944) more and more design and experimental staff were diverted from work on artillery to reinforce the missile programme. This in turn helps to explain why so few of the artillery developments, many of which had good starts, failed to reach satisfactory conclusions.

An interesting tactical/technical concept wa explored by the German Flak during the war Ever since the first anti-aircraft guns were pro duced in the early 1900s it was accepted that since the chance of a direct hit was so slender time-fuzed ammunition was the only possible solution. With the original shrapnel shells thi was indisputable, and the same reasoning was carried over to the high explosive shell when i became the standard projectile. The 8.8cm shell carrying just under 900gm(2lb) of explosive, had a lethal burst radius of about 9.14m(30ft): or, in other words, the shell had to burst within 9.14m (30ft) of the aircraft to damage it. Assuming tha perfect results were obtained from the predictor so that the course of the aircraft and the path of the shell coincided, there was one facto that could make nonsense of everything—the fuze The clockwork fuzes used by the Flak guns were probably the best of their kind, but even so they had a tolerance in their timing which can be assumed to be about 0.5% of the flight time. So assuming that the target was at a height demand-ing 20sec flight, this half per cent meant that at the speed the shell was travelling the fuze was liable to function anywhere within a 61m(200ft) section of the trajectory, above or below the air-craft, with no control over the precise point o detonation.

When the development of subcalibre projectiles began, the standard high explosive filling was se at 500g(17.63oz), since this was theoretically lethal to a four-engined bomber. Diminution of the explosive content in turn reduced the lethal radius, which then decreased the chances of a hit It was left to Dr Voss, a research scientist in the Reichsluftministerium, to take this idea to its logical conclusion. In a paper written in 1944 he showed that the chance of putting a shell close enough to the aircraft to damage it was very little different from the chance of obtaining a direct hit; from this it followed that fitting the shells with impact fuzes would, by removing one error source in the fuze zone and another in the possible setting device, and by speeding up the rate of fire and cutting down the time lapse between com-puting and firing would in effect improve the chances of a direct hit—to such a degree that impact-fuzed ammunition showed a considerable theoretical superiority over time-fuzed shells.

This was difficult for the OKL staff to accept but Voss's figures were so persuasive that the Luftwaffe asked a number of other scientists to examine the question and a series of firing trials were also organised in which the bursts of the shells were filmed. The results proved that Voss had—if anything—been understating the case, and as a trial a number of Flak batteries were instructed to use time and percussion fuzes set at maximum time (in effect converting them into percussion fuzes). The gunners in their turn were sceptical, but the method gave some remarkably good results. On 20th March 1945 the Luftwaffe finally gave orders to abandon the use of time fuzes with high explosive shells and to use percussion fuzes exclusively. But this was so late in the war that conclusive figures for the method's effectiveness was never acquired.

Other fields of experiment were the development of highly-effective incendiary shrapnel and of high capacity *Minengeschosse,* both of which will be discussed later. One item of equipment that was of inestimable value to the Allied anti-aircraft guns was the proximity fuze which, sensing when an aircraft was within lethal burst distance, automatically detonated the shell. Had such a fuze been available to the Luftwaffe Dr Voss's paper might never have been written, but except for two low-priority projects all the German development work in this field was directed towards the guided missiles.

Two technical terms peculiar to anti-aircraft weapons must be explained here: ceiling and self-destruction. The 'ceiling', in British practice always quoted in feet, is the height to which the gun fires. There are, however, three ceilings—the maximum, the practical and the effective. The maximum ceiling is the height to which, ignoring everything except gravity, the gun can propel a shell. This is never reached by a gun in service because (1) it rarely points vertically, and (2) the running time of the shell's time fuze expires and the shell detonates before reaching that altitude. The height at which the fuze runs out of time is therefore the practical ceiling, but this again assumes that the gun fires at 90° elevation; at any other elevation trigonometry. shows that the practical ceiling will be less. Thus one finally arrives at the effective ceiling; this varies in accordance with contemporary aircraft performance and tactical thinking, but in 1944–5 it was taken to be the height at which an aircraft flying at 485kph(300mph) could be engaged for twenty seconds.

Self-destruction was installed into anti-aircraft shells to make sure that, should they miss their target, they burst in the sky and did not return to earth armed and live. Since setting a time fuze automatically gives a self-destruction capacity, such devices were confined to impact-fuzed light guns. They were usually pyrotechnic delays in the fuzes, ignited on firing, or were incorporated in tracers that—after burning for a given time—ignited gunpowder booster pellets which then exploded and destroyed the shells. A later development consisted of a centrifugal mechanism (built into the fuze) that, when the spin-rate dropped towards the end of the useful trajectory, allowed a detonator to fire and thus initiated the shell filling. The main preoccupation of the anti-aircraft artillery during the war was to get more performance out of their heavy guns and more firepower out of their light ones. By way of an introduction to the guns, it is worth studying a letter written in 1944:

> *Führerhauptquartier*
> 4th November 1944
>
> SECRET
> The enemy, in his terroristic attacks on the Reich, speaks of the hell of the German anti-aircraft defence. Many of his intentions have been frustrated by our concentrated anti-aircraft defence.
>
> It is important to strengthen the firepower of the anti-aircraft defence in every conceivable way in order to make use of this psychological and tactical moment.
>
> I therefore command the immediate increase of the anti-aircraft weapons and ammunition programme, although the notice given is short.
>
> This affects the heavy, medium and light guns, including the corresponding ammunition, radar and predictor apparatus
>
> At the same time all current problems of development referring to the increase of efficiency of guns and shells and other developments for anti-aircraft defence are to be carried out energetically and with accelerated effort.
>
> No withdrawal of the labour forces employed on these programmes may take place for the armed forces, for trench works, air raid precautions and security services outside their works, technical emergency corps, Geilenberg programme, etc. The members of the companies who belong to the Volkssturm are to be enrolled for the second appeal.
>
> All the reserved forces of labour in active employment of these programmes are to be exempt until further notice from all 'call-up groups' under reservation orders.
>
> All arms and ammunition factories including preliminary, immediate and subcontractors must mobilise additional capacities for these tasks and concentrate all their efforts on this purpose within their works.
>
> Owing to the unusual urgency of this order, besides the obvious support required from all offices of the Party, armed forces and State, I expect the *Gauleiters* especially to make it their duty to provide every possible assistance for these programmes in addition to the high production of high efficiency aircraft.
>
> *Adolf Hitler*

It was easy to command: it was not so easy to achieve.

2cm Flugabwehrkanone 30

2cm Flak 30

This was a Rheinmetall design developed at Solothurn during the late 1920s and early 1930s, and it entered production in 1934 for the German Navy. In 1935 it was taken into use by the Luftwaffe as a field-service anti-aircraft weapon. The Flak 30 had a box magazine and was recoil operated: it was really little more than an overgrown machine-gun firing from an open bolt, which is just what it was—an enlarged Solothurn-MG30. Two triggers were used; the left trigger gave automatic fire and the right gave single shots.

The mounting was a highly mobile trailer (the Sonderanhänger 51) that could be towed by almost any vehicle. Upon this trailer fitted the mounting proper; this could be removed simply by withdrawing a shackle pin, tipping the trailer to disengage two anchoring lugs, and pulling it clear to leave the mounting on the ground. It could then be levelled by the three adjustable fee the gunlayer climbed into the seat and the gu was ready for action. It could also, in emergency be fired from the trailer.

The sight originally fitted was known as th Flakvisier 35, a reflecting mirror sight with a integral mechanical course-and-speed calculator Although it was an excellent sight, it demanded high quality of manufacture, maintenance an operation: things not always forthcoming during war. In 1941 the Flakvisier 35 was replaced by th Linealvisier 21, a simple open course-and-spee sight stamped out of sheet metal and clamped t the gun's sight bar. Later still it was replaced by th Schwebekreisvisier 30, a 'cart-wheel' open sight.

Although some Flak 30 guns remained i service throughout the war, most were replace by the Flak 38.

A high-explosive round (Sprgr Patr L'Spur) for the 2cm Flak 30. The explosive charge fills the front portion of the shell, the tracer the rear. The propelling charge is contained in a silk bag.

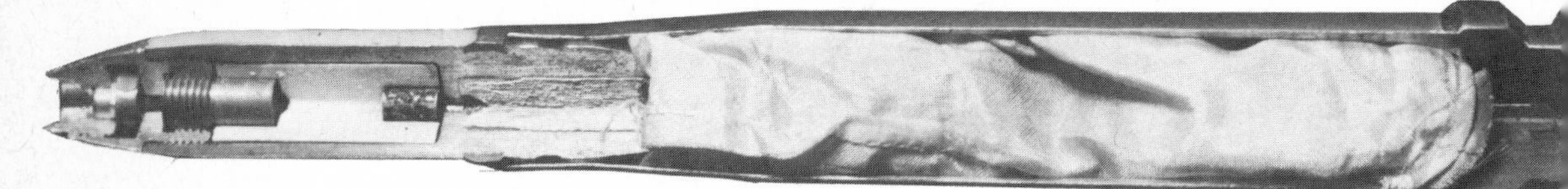

The 2cm Flak 30 dismounted from trailer to ground platform.

Data

Calibre: 20mm/0.79in.
Length of gun: 2300mm/90.55in.
Length of bore: 1300mm/51.18in.
Rifling: 8 grooves, right-hand uniform twist, 1/36.
Breech mechanism: recoil-operated bolt, percussion fired.
Traverse: 360° on the platform, 40° on the trailer.
Elevation: −12° to +90°.
Weight in action: 483kg/1065lb.
Rate of fire: 280rpm(cyclic), 120rpm(practical).

Performance

With Flakvisier 35.
Target speed: 25kph/16mph to 435kph/270mph.
Effective ceiling: 299m/981ft to 2000m/6562ft.
Ground range: 2695m/2947yd.
With Linealvisier 21.
Target speed: 38kph/24mph to 540kph/336mph.
Effective ceiling: 100m/328ft to 1645m/5397ft.
Ground range: 1600m/1750yd.

Ammunition

Fixed rounds; cartridge case length 137mm(5.39in).

1. *2cm Patr Sprgr L'spur:* fuzed AZ 5045, complete round weight 305gm(10.76oz).
A high explosive shell with self-destroying tracer; velocity 900mps(2953fps).
2. *2cm Sprgr Patr L'spur mit Warmeübertragung:* fuzed AZ 5054, weight 300gm(10.6oz).
As above, but the self-destruction element was initiated by heat transfer from the tracer through a steel diaphragm instead of by direct flame contact. This was a safer system, insuring against faulty tracer fillings that gave premature bursts.
3. *2cm Br Sprgr Patr L'spur W:* fuzed AZ 5045, weight 291gm(10.26oz).
As *2* but with an explosive/incendiary filling.
4. *2cm Br Sprgr Patr vk L'spur:* fuzed Kpf Z Zerl Fg.
As *3* but with a short-burning tracer and with self-destruction achieved by a spin decay unit in the fuze.

The 2cm Flak 30 on its trailer.

5. *2cm Br Sprgr Patr o L'spur:* fuzed Kpf Z Zerl Fg.
As *4* but without the tracer.
6. *2cm Br Sprgr Patr vk L'spur W:* fuzed AZ 1504.
As *4* but with a heat relay self-destroying tracer.
7. *2cm Pzgr Patr L'spur m Zerlegung.*
An armour piercing/high explosive/incendiary shell with a heat relay self-destroying tracer and no fuze; the velocity of this round was 830mps (2723fps).
8. *2cm Pzgr Patr 40 L'spur.*
An armour piercing shot with a tungsten core; the penetration at 100m was 40mm at 0° (1.57in at 109yd).
9. *2cm Sprgr Patr L'spur (Ub).*
This was an empty practice shell with a dummy tracer and a dummy fuze; the velocity was 995mps (3265fps). The propelling charge was adjusted to give a specific velocity with each shell, but was about 40gm(1.41oz) of nitrocellulose powder.

Sectioned rounds for the 2cm Flak:

High explosive:

Practice tracer:

Practice inert:

Drill round with wooden bullet:

The 2cm Flak 30 on its trailer.

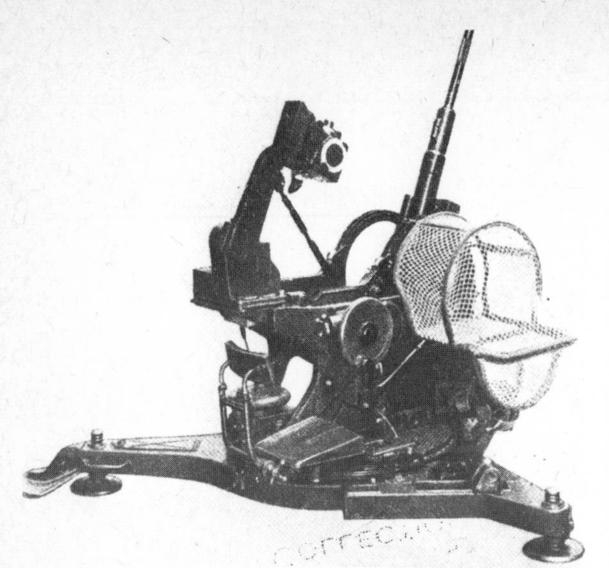

2cm Flak 30 showing net cage for catching empty cases.

The Flakvierling goes to sea, mounted in an armoured

2cm Flugabwehrkanone 38

2cm Flak 38 (Erika)

The Flak 30 gave a good performance in the 1939 Polish campaign but experience there, together with reports from Spain where the Condor Legion had taken a few to the Civil War (1936–9), convinced the Luftwaffe that a higher rate of fire would materially improve the gun's effect. Since Rheinmetall-Borsig were now busy with other weapons, the Luftwaffe called in Mauser-Werke and asked them to attempt a redesign of the weapon to double the rate of fire.

The redesign involved little change; the bolt mechanism, the accelerator and the return spring were replaced by fresh components, but apart from that there was nothing new and the gun remained outwardly identical to the earlier model. The same mounting was used and the equipment came into service early in 1940, thereafter gradually replacing most of the Flak 30. By the end of the war there were 17589 2cm guns in use.

The mountain and the airborne units of the army and the Luftwaffe had been demanding an anti-aircraft gun for some time and so later in 1940 the Flak 38 was mounted on a lightweight two wheeled carriage with folding tubular legs and called the 2cm Geb Flak 38 (*Zugspitze*). As well as its primary anti-aircraft role, the Flak 38 had its uses as a light support weapon when fired with the mounting legs folded. The development trend was always towards putting more metal into the sky, and this led to the production of the 2cm Flakvierling 38 (*Distelfink*, gun, *Kindersegen*, mounting) late in 1940. This was a quadruple arrangement of guns on a platform and carriage (Sonderanhänger 52) similar to that of the single gun but enlarged and strengthened. This was a highly effective and successful equipment tha remained in use throughout the war, a total o 3851 being made. Later versions were fitted with radar, in which case a parabolic reflector wa carried between the gun barrels.

The sight of the Flak 38 was originally th Flakvisier 38, an electric computing sight with a reflecting-mirror optical system. It was electricall linked with the gun's elevation and traverse gears so that as the layer followed an aircraft the sigh automatically calculated 'aim-off' and displace the graticule of the optical sight accordingly. Thi was later replaced by the Flakvisier 38A, a simila apparatus but of modular 'black box' constructio to simplify repair in the field. This was still late replaced by the Linealvisier 21 used by the Fla 30, and finally with the Schwebekreisvisier 30/58 also used by the Flak 30. The four-barrelle equipment began with the Flakvisier 40, a modi fication of the 38 to suit the quadruple mountin but this, too, was later replaced by the mor simple types of sight.

Data (2cm Flak 38)
Calibre: 20mm/0.79in.
Length of gun: 2251mm/88.62in.
Length of bore: 1299mm/51.14in.
Rifling: 8 grooves, right-hand uniform, 1/36.
Breech mechanism: recoil-operated bolt, per cussion fired.
Traverse: 360°.
Elevation: −20° to +90°.
Weight in action: 406kg/895lb.

ebel ferry.

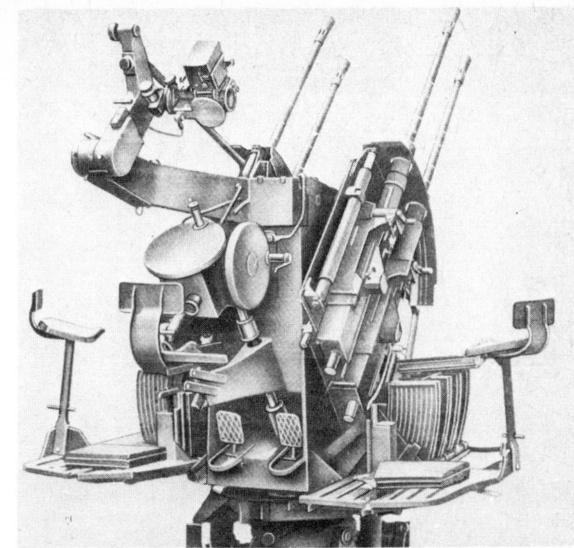

The 2cm Flakvierling—four barrels on one mounting.

he 2cm Gebirgs Flak 38, mountain version of Flak 30.

The 2cm Gebirgs Flak 38.

elow: The 2cm Flakvierling dug-in as a dual-purpose weapon, capable of ground or anti-aircraft fire.

Rate of fire: 420–480rpm cyclic, 180–220rpm practical.

Data (2cm Geb Flak 38)
As above, except.
Weight in action: 332kg/732lb.

Data (2cm Flakvierling 38)
As above, except:
Elevation: −10° to +100°.
Weight in action: 1520kg/3352lb.
Rate of fire: 1680–1920rpm cyclic, 700–800rpm practical (all barrels combined).

Performance, Ammunition
See Flak 30.

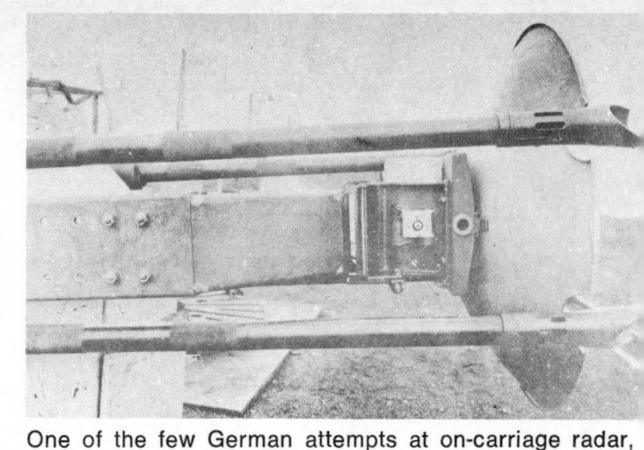
One of the few German attempts at on-carriage radar, this was an experimental mounting on a Flakvierling.

3cm Flugabwehrkanone 103/38

3cm Flak 38 (Jaboschreck)

This was a hastily arranged marriage between the 3cm Maschinenkanone 103 (MK 103), a Rheinmetall-Borsig design of aircraft cannon, and a modified 2cm Flak 38 mounting. It was developed in mid-1944 to augment the standard weapons in view of the increasing amount of Allied low-level air attacks after the 1944 invasion. Rheinmetall-Borsig were given a contract to produce 2000 guns and Gustloffwerke of Suhl were to produce 1000, all of which were to be completed by March 1945—though it is doubtful if anything near this number were actually built. A four-barrelled version, the 3cm Flakvierling 103/38, was also produced in limited numbers. In addition to the Rheinmetall contract, two other companies were also engaged in developing an anti-aircraft version of the MK 103; Mauser-Werke produced a model identical to that of Rheinmetall and Brunserwerke AG produced a longer-barrelled version that, naturally enough, achieved a higher muzzle velocity. It also showed a much heavier recoil below—1200kg compared to 900kg for the Rheinmetall gun—which ruled it out for assembly to the Flak 38 mounting, and so the project was dropped. Skodawerke of Pilsen were also involved in developing a twin-barrel version, but it is open to doubt whether this ever got past the drawing-board stage.

The equipment was not conspicuously successful; the 3cm gun was a much more powerful weapon than the older 2cm guns and the firing stress set up vibrations in the mounting that caused damage, and which also gave the layer difficulty in aiming. Various expedients were applied to cure the trouble; a muzzle brake helped to reduce the recoil force, the carriage was strengthened and the sight was modified to be a spring-suspended pattern that was intended to damp out the vibrations. These helped, but it remained a fault-prone weapon.

The gun itself was a fully-automatic model, gas operated with the breech locked at the moment of firing by lock plates on the bolt that engage in recesses in the barrel extension, basically the same system used by some contemporary German machine-guns. Feed was by a disintegrating-link belt and the sight was a modification of the Schwebekreisvisier.

Data
Calibre: 30mm/1.18in.
Length of gun: 2318/91.25in.
Length of bore: 1338mm/52.67in.
Rifling: 16 grooves, right-hand uniform twist 1/30.
Breech mechanism: gas-operated bolt, locked breech, electrically fired.
Traverse: 360°.
Elevation: −10° to +80°.
Weight in action: 619kg/1363lb.
Rate of fire: 400rpm cyclic, 250rpm practical.

Performance
Firing standard Minengeschoss shell:
Muzzle velocity: 900mps/2953fps.
Maximum ceiling: 4700m/15420ft.
Effective ceiling: 1500m/4922ft.
Maximum ground range: 5730m/6266yd.

Ammunition
Fixed rounds; cartridge case length 184mm (7.24in).
3cm Sprgr Patr L'spur El o Zerl: fuzed AZ 1504 complete round weight 815gm(28.74oz/1.80lb). This was a conventional high explosive shell with

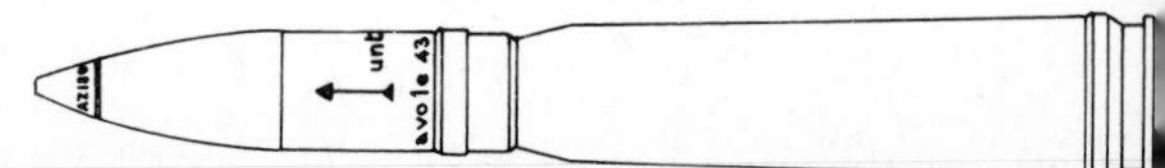
Practice round for the MK 103.

a tracer and a percussion fuze, but without a self-destruction element. This was the original aircraft projectile for ground-attack use and was retained with the gun for ground shooting. The 'El' in the nomenclature denoted the use of an electric primer, since certain 3cm aircraft cannon used percussion-primed rounds of otherwise similar nomenclature and appearance.

3cm M–Gesch Patr L'spur El o Zerl: fuzed AZ 1504.

This was a 'Minengeschoss' projectile, a high-capacity high explosive shell. It was formed by deep-drawing and was a technically interesting innovation; it carried twice as much explosive as a conventional shell and it was considered that three or four hits with these shells would be sufficient to destroy the heaviest aircraft. There were four varying designs of M–Geschoss: Rheinmetall, DWM, Tonshoff and Rheinmetall base-fuzed. The Rheinmetall design was conventional in shape but the DWM model had a hemispherical base. Both were nose fuzed and were in service. The Tonshoff model had been designed by the Luftwaffe research unit at Rechlin and was on the way to production by Tonshoff Werke as the war ended. This shell was of conventional appearance, its particular features being matters of production convenience. The Rheinmetall base-fuzed model carried a 100gm(3.53oz) charge of RDX/TNT/aluminium, the large amount being due to the fact that the walls could be made extremely thin since they no longer had to support

Left side of the 3cm Flak 103/38.

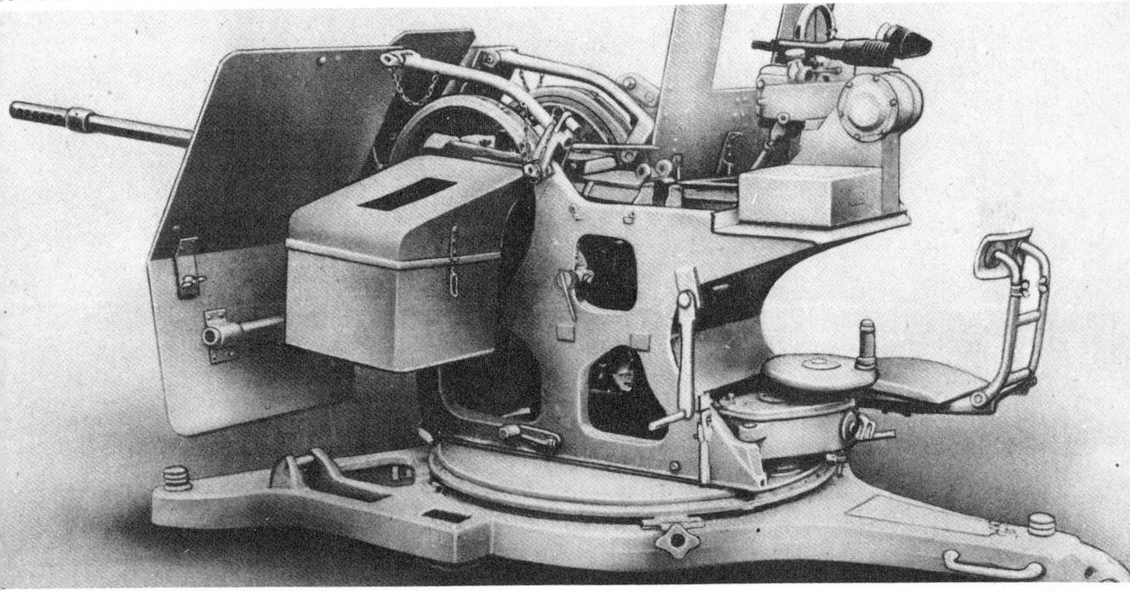

The 3cm Flak 103/38, right side.

The 3cm Flakvierling 103/38.

the weight of the fuze. This shell passed its trials in January 1945 and was to be produced by Polte-Werke of Magdeburg, but it is unlikely that many were made. A fifth variation was developed by HASAG (Hugo Schneider AG of Leipzig), based on the DWM shell but with a pellet of incendiary material in the base which—it was hoped—would be launched by inertia through the hole blown by the shell and so ignite fuel and other combustible material within the aircraft. It was still undergoing trials when the war ended.

3cm Pz Sprgr Patr El L'spur o Zerl.

This, an armour-piercing shell with a small explosive filling and a base fuze, had a muzzle velocity of 800mps(2625fps).

3cm Pz Br Sprgr Patr L'spur El o Zerl.

An armour-piercing shell similar to the foregoing, this had the addition of an incendiary component to the filling.

Propelling Charge

The propelling charge for the foregoing rounds varied in small amounts from batch to batch, but was nominally in the region of 30gm(1.06oz) of nitrocellulose powder.

Primer

The electric primer C/23 was standard.

3·7cm Flugabwehrkanone 18

3·7cm Flak 18 (Altvater)

This, developed by Rheinmetall in the early 1930s and first issued in 1935, was little more than an enlarged version of the 2cm FlAK 30, and was of similar recoil operation, aided by accelerator in the same way. The ammunition was also an enlarged version of the FlAK 30 round, using the distinctive Solothurn belted cartridge case pattern. The mounting was a cruciform platform carried on two two-wheeled limbers and the sight, Flakvisier 33, was similar to the Flakvisier 35.

A 3.7cm Flak 18 looking for targets during the Polish campaign in 1939.

The weapon—introduced, as has been said, in 1935—had a short life. After being thoroughly tested on battle manoeuvres held in the same year, it was rejected as too cumbersome for its calibre and a new design was demanded; a few more were built, to make use of components already made, but production stopped completely in late 1936.

Data
Calibre: 37mm/1.46in.
Length of gun: 3626mm/142.76in/11.90ft.
Length of bore: 2112mm/83.15in.
Rifling: 20 grooves, right-hand increasing twist, 1/50 to 1/40.
Breech mechanism: gas-operated bolt, percussion fired.
Traverse: 360°.
Elevation: −8° to +85°.
Weight in action: 1748kg/3854lb.
Rate of fire: 160rpm (cyclic), 80rpm (practical).

Performance
Firing standard high explosive shell weighing 635gm(22.39oz/1.40lb).
Muzzle velocity: 820mps/2690fps.
Maximum ceiling: 4800m/15749ft.
Effective ceiling: 2000m/6562ft.
Maximum ground range: 6585m/7201yd.

Ammunition
Fixed rounds; cartridge case length 265mm (10.43in).
3.7cm Sprgr Patr L'spur 18: fuzed Kpf Z Zerl P or FG, projectile weight 635gm(22.39oz), complete round weight 1.50kg(3.31lb).
This was the standard round for the weapon. The shell was fitted with two copper driving bands, and was filled with about 24gm(0.85oz) of PETN/wax. The propelling charge was 185gm(6.52oz) of Digl R P. The percussion fuze carried a self-destruction unit; Kpf Z Zerl P used a powder-burning delay and proved to be unreliable in use, while Kpf Z Zerl FG used a centrifugal mechanism relying on spin decay. This was more reliable and became the standard fuze.
3.7cm Br Sprgr Patr L'spur: fuzed Kpf Z Zerl P or FG.
This was similar to the previous round but with the addition of an incendiary composition to the

The 3.7cm Flak 18 in firing position.

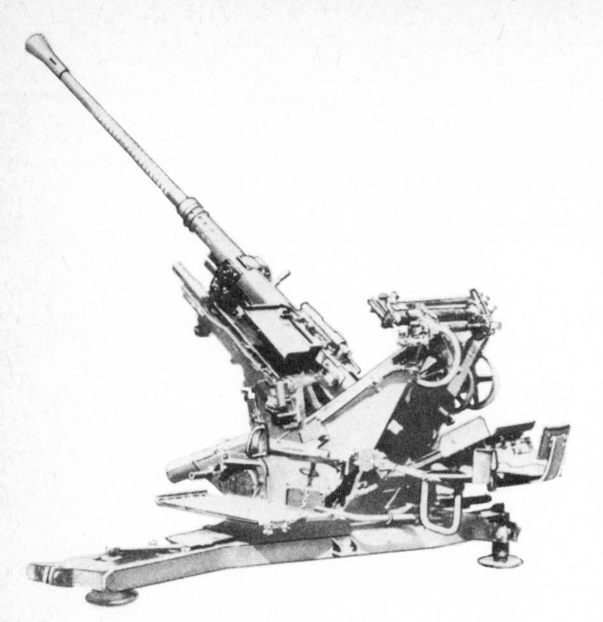

A 3.7cm Flak 18 mounted on a half-track.

shell filling.
3.7cm Br Sprgr Patr o L'spur.
As above but without the tracer.
3.7cm Br Sprgr Patr vk L'spur.
As above but with a tracer burning for 5sec instead of the 6.5sec delay in the previous models
3.7cm Pzgr Patr 18: fuzed Bd Z 5103, projectile weight 0.68kg(1.50lb), round weight 1.54kg(3.40lb) This was a pointed base-fuzed armour piercing shell of normal type, for use against armoured vehicles. The tracer burned for only 2sec.

Propelling Charge
A charge of 189gm(6.67oz) of Digl R P was contained in the cartridge case.

Primer
The percussion primer C/13nA was standard.

3·7cm Flugabwehrkanone 36 und 37

3·7cm Flak 36 and 37 (Westerwald)

This, the redesign demanded by the army, consisted of the Flak 18 gun on an improved two-wheeled carriage. This in its turn was little more than an enlarged and improved version of that used with the 2cm Flak guns and consisted of a two-wheeled trailer, *Sonderanhänger 52*, carrying a three-legged mounting. The resulting combination was introduced in 1938 as the Flak 36 and became the standard light anti-aircraft weapon. In 1940, with the shortage of copper fast approaching, the double driving-band shell was declared obsolete and replaced by one with a single soft-iron band. In order to accommodate the modified shell the guns were altered by slightly shortening the chamber, such modification being indicated by V for *verkurzt* (shortened) stamped on the rear of the barrel.

The original Flakvisier 36 sight, a modification of the Flakvisier 33 to suit the new carriage, was soon replaced by a mechanical computing sight driven by clockwork and called the *Uhrwerkvisier* (or *Flakvisier 40*). The gun's elevation and traverse were fed in and the clockwork mechanism, regulated both by these factors and by an estimate of range fed in by the gunlayer, displaced the sight graticule to compensate for the target's speed and angle of approach. It was intended that this sight should replace the FV36, but considerable modification was found necessary to the carriage and thus—when the Uhrwerkvisier was fitted—the nomenclature changed to Flak 37. Only a limited number of weapons were so converted, for by that time an improved gun was reaching production and the available supplies of Uhrwerkvisiere were allotted to the new weapon.

Data
As 3.7cm Flak 18 except:
Weight in action: 1544kg/3405lb.

Performance, Ammunition
See 3.7cm Flak 18.

The 3.7cm Flak 36 ready for travelling.

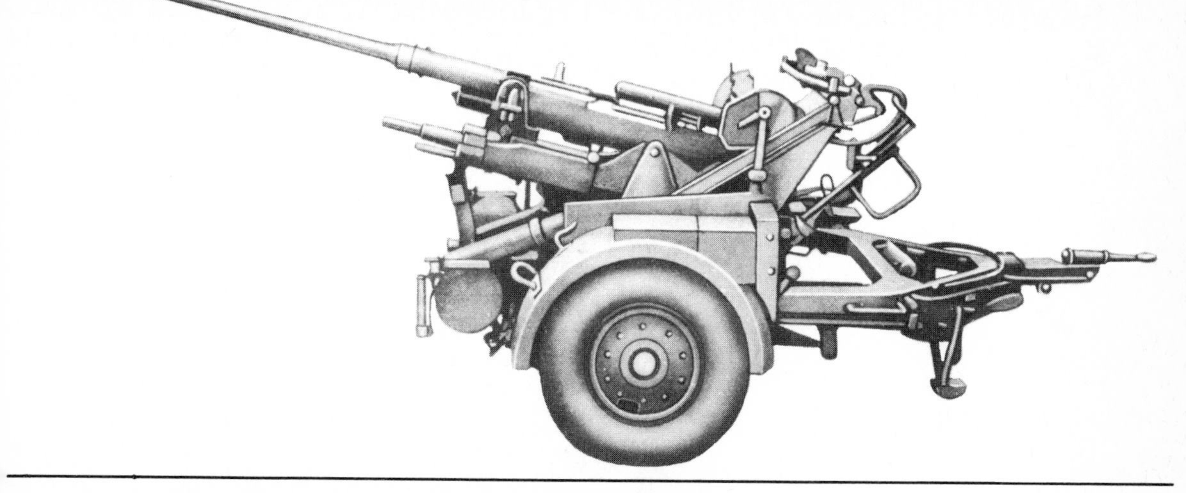

3·7cm Flugabwehrkanone 43

3·7cm Flak 43 (Schwarzwald)

This was a Rheinmetall-Borsig development that was essentially the gas-operated mechanism of the MK103 (MK—maschinenkanone, machine cannon) enlarged and fitted to the body of the Flak 36. The barrel was slightly longer than that of the Flak 36 and the rifling was changed to a much steeper pitch, to obtain a longer time to self-destruction using the spin-decay mechanism in the Kpf Z Zerl FG fuze. Another innovation was the addition of outsize trunnions, positioned around the feed opening, so that the the feed position remained the same at all angles of elevation. The weight of the ammunition feed was also applied to the centre of balance, so that aim was not disturbed by replenishment of the loading tray.

The mounting was a simple three-legged platform upon which the gun revolved (basically similar to the earlier models), and a new trailer—the Sonderanhänger 58—carried it into action.

The 3.7cm Flak 43.

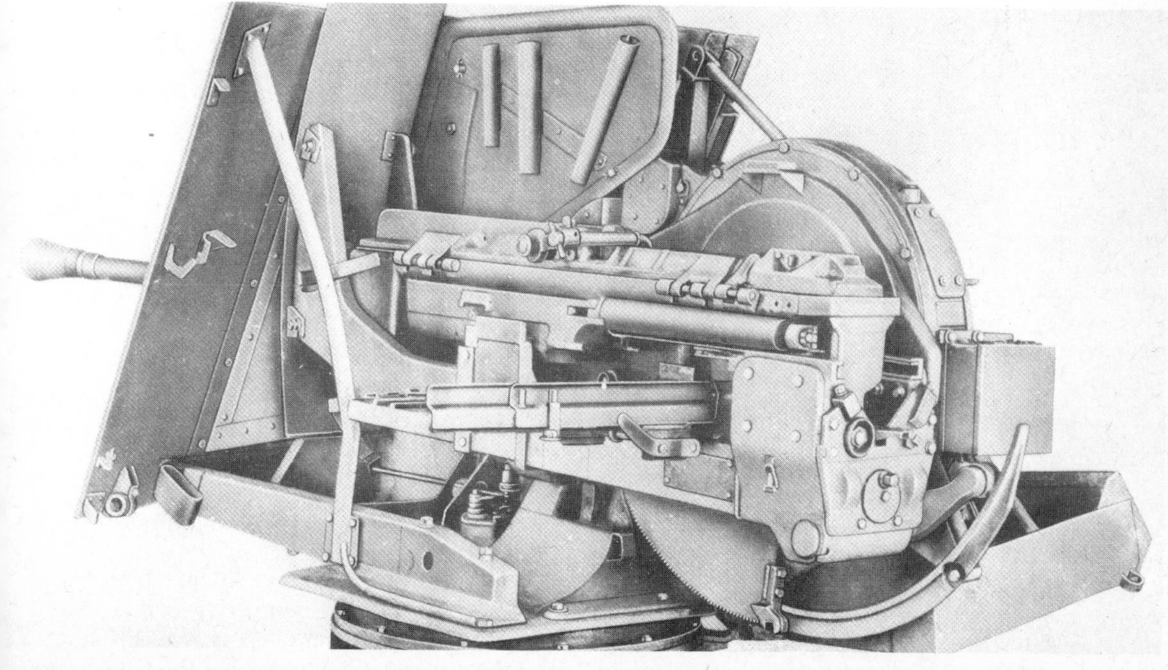

The 3.7cm Flakzwilling 43 ready for action, showing the system of ammunition feed through the trunnions.

The gun's muzzle heaviness was balanced by a large clock-type coiled spring.

Shortly after the introduction of the Flak 43 a two-barrelled version was produced, the 3.7cm Flakzwilling 43. This consisted of a heavier and stronger mounting carried on two two-wheel bogies (Sonderanhänger 106), and mounted the two guns one above the other. This was a highly ingenious and effective design, 390 of which were in service in 1945.

The gun was originally provided with the Uhrwerkvisier sight, ultimately renamed the Flakvisier 43, but this was replaced in mid-1944 by the Schwebekornvisier, a simple course-and-speed sight developed from the earlier Schwebekreisvisier. The principal difference was that it catered for higher target speeds.

Data
Calibre: 37mm/1.46in.
Length of gun: 3300mm/129.92in/10.83ft.
Length of bore: 2130mm/83.86in.
Rifling: 20 grooves, right-hand increasing twist, 1/18 to 1/13.
Breech mechanism: gas-operated bolt, percussion fired.
Traverse: 360°.
Elevation: −7° 30′ to +90°.
Weight in action: 1248kg/2752lb.
Rate of fire: 250rpm (cyclic), 180rpm (practical).

Data (3.7cm Flakzwilling 43)
As above, except.
Elevation: −8° to +90°
Weight in action: 2796kg/6165lb.
Rate of fire: 500rpm (cyclic), 360rpm (practical).

Performance
Firing high explosive shell.
Muzzle velocity: 820mps/2690fps.
Maximum ceiling: 4800m/15755ft.
Effective ceiling: 4200m/13780ft.
Maximum ground range: 6585m/7201yd.
The improvement in effective ceiling stemmed from a combination of longer time to self destruction and better sights.

Ammunition
See Flak 18 and 36; only the single driving band projectiles were used, the earlier double-banded designs being obsolete before this gun was introduced.

Another view of the Flak 43, showing the feed slot.

ƽcm Flugabwehrkanone 41

ƽcm Flak 41

'he Germans were probably the first to realise hat there was a gap in the sky between the naximum effective ceiling of the light weapons nd the minimum of the heavy guns; they were ertainly the first to try to plug it. As early as 935 Rheinmetall were given a development contract for a 5cm gun, and in 1939 a similar contract was passed to Krupp. Eventually, in November 1940, the former's design was accepted for service as the FlAK 41 but only limited numbers—less than 200 including the pre-production series—were made.

he 5cm Flak 41 ready to travel.

The gun mechanism was gas-operated but used a vertical sliding breechblock with multiple bearing surfaces instead of the strengthened machine-gun mechanism of the smaller guns. The mounting was a triangular platform with two folding outriggers carried on two two-wheel axles (Sonderanhänger 204). To put the gun into action the mounting was lowered from the axles by winch gear, the legs were lowered and the platform was roughly levelled by screw-jacks. It was then accurately levelled by screws in the base-ring of the gun pedestal; this was a weak point in the design, since it added complication and weight. The sight was the Flakvisier 41, an electric tachymetric computing sight using an optical mirror sighting-head.

After some months of service the Luftwaffe concluded that the design was a failure. It was unstable when fired, the centre of gravity was so high that the gun was also unstable when being towed, it was difficult to conceal, it could not track targets fast enough, and the sight was too complicated and a poor calculator into the bargain. Despite the catalogue of woe, the Flak 41 had been a useful test bed for the concept of an 'intermediate' light-to-medium gun and it showed that a weapon of this class was desirable.

Data
Calibre: 50mm/1.97in.
Length of gun: 4686mm/184.49in/15.37ft.
Length of bore: 3418/134.57in/11.21ft.
Rifling: 20 grooves, right-hand increasing twist, 1/36.5 to 1/30.
Breech mechanism: gas-operated vertical sliding block, percussion fired.
Traverse: 360°.
Elevation: −10° to +90°.
Weight in action: 3100kg/6836lb.
Rate of fire: 130rpm (practical).

Performance
Muzzle velocity: 840mps/2756fps.
Maximum ceiling: 9000m/29529ft.
Effective ceiling: 5600m/18374ft.
Maximum ground range: 12400/13561yd.

Ammunition
Fixed rounds; cartridge case length 532mm (20.94in).
5cm Sprgr Patr 41 L'spur: fuzed 5cm Kpf Z Zerl P, projectile weight 2.20kg(4.85lb), complete round weight 4.28kg(9.44lb).
The standard high explosive shell, this was fitted with a tracer burning from 8 to 10sec. The self destroying fuze was special to this gun and was unusual in having two settings: short initiating destruction after 5 to 8sec, and long giving destruction after 14 to 18sec. The bursting charge was of TNT. The propelling charge was 690gm (24.33oz/1.52lb) of Digl R P K.
5cm Br Sprgr Patr 41 L'spur: fuzed 5cm Kpf Z Zerl P, projectile weight 2.20kg(4.85lb), complete round weight 4.28kg(9.44lb).
This was similar to the previous round, but included an incendiary pellet in the explosive filling.
5cm Pzgr Patr 42: fuzed Bd Z 5103, projectile weight 2.34kg(4.92lb), complete round weight 4.35kg(9.59lb).
An armour-piercing shell of conventional design this was made of chromium steel. The driving band was of soft iron and the bursting charge was PETN/wax. A tracer, burning for 2sec, was also fitted. This round was issued as an anti-tank round for ground use, and was in fact the normal

Right side of the 5cm Flak 41.

cm PAK projectile fitted to the Flak case
cm Sprgr Patr 41 Ub: fuzed Ersst 5cm Kpf Z 2 Zerl P.
This was identical to the Sprgr 41 round but had an inert shell and fuze, and was used for training. The propelling charge was 671gm(23.66oz/1.48lb) of Digl R P K.

Primer
The percussion primer C/12nA was standard for all rounds.

Case Identification Number
None: the case was identified by the base-stamp 5CM FLAK 41.

5cm Flak 41 in march order.

Left:
The rear of the 5cm Flak 41 ready for action, showing the ammunition feed tray.

Right:
The 5cm Flak 41 ready for action.

5cm Flugabwehrkanone 214

5cm Flak 214 (Neckartal)

Since the 5cm Flak 41 was a comparative failure and the 5.5cm replacement some way off, the Luftwaffe searched in 1944 for something suitable to fill the gap until the 5.5cm gun entered service.

When the 5cm PAK 38 anti-tank gun had been superseded, a large number was taken by the Luftwaffe with the intention of fitting them to aircraft for use as tank and submarine attack weapons. In order to suit the guns to the airborne task, Mauser-Werke had developed a drum-fed automatic loading gear that was quite effective. It was proposed to take 50 of the original guns, to fit them with the automatic feed and to mount them on a slightly modified version of the carriage designed for the 5.5cm gun. This would then be known as the 5cm Flak 214.

None was ever produced, since the 5.5cm carriage programme fell behind schedule. Had the design staff working on the Flak 214 been left to proceed with the 5.5cm weapon, they might have got one gun into service: as it was they finished neither.

5·5cm Gerät 58 Flugabwehrkanone

5·5cm Flak Ger 58 (Stammgericht)

After the Flak 41 had been tried and found wanting, a fresh specification was issued, owing much not only to the shortcomings in the 5cm weapon but also to an 'agonising reappraisal' of the contemporary anti-aircraft problem as it affected the German defences. Sufficient had been seen of the tactical use of the 5cm Flak 41 to enable a 'medium anti-aircraft theory' to be put forward, which insisted that a medium gun was only justified in defensive areas where it was vital to destroy 100% of the attacking aircraft, situations where even a single aircraft getting through could cause a disaster—such as the raid on the Möhne Dam. If a gun guaranteed this 100% success no price was too high to pay for it, and the solution deduced was to employ a six-gun battery (remotely controlled from a predictor) with a high rate of fire.

Working from this, a new specification called for what would today be called a *weapons system* in which the radar, the predictor, the displacement corrector and the guns were all tailored to each other and formed a cohesive package.

The development of the 5.5cm gun was a logical consequence of the 5cm weapon, conditioned partly by the Flak 41's shortcomings and the tactical concept outlined above, and partly by Rheinmetall-Borsig's discovery early in 1942 that the 5cm calibre was ballistically unsuitable: it was impossible to produce a shell of the required destructive power that would also be stable at the high velocities demanded. The destructive power was based on a ruling that the explosive content was to be 500gm(17.63oz/1.10lb), which had been proved by experiment to be the minimum amount necessary to guarantee the destruction of a heavy bomber with one shot. The velocity demanded was high, to reduce the time of flight and thus improve both the accuracy and the chance of hitting. Rheinmetall proposed the 5.5cm calibre and, after considerable delay while the whole medium anti-aircraft problem was evaluated, the Luftwaffe finally agreed and issued the specification. 1943 was spent largely in perfecting the ammunition and designing the various other components of the system. By the spring of 1944 prototype ammunition and guns had been fired and the results gave rise to a good deal of rethinking. Several different designs of shell were then tried in turn, together with various twists of rifling, but the question of what was finally to be the service standard was never settled before the war ended.

The 5.5cm Flak Gerät 58 in travelling mode.

The gun itself was little more than a slightly enlarged version of the 5cm Flak 41 using the same basic mechanism, but in order to improve stability an old idea was resurrected. This was the principle of *differential recoil,* a theory that apparently reappears once every thirty years or so. It had a brief heyday before World War 1 when the French and Austrians employed it in mountain guns, it was used here by the Germans in 1944, and in 1970 it re-emerged in the USA

The Gerät 58 prepared for action.

3 024239

under the title of *soft recoil*. Call it what you will, the principle remains the same: the gun is pulled back to the limit of the recoil stroke and held. It is then loaded and released, allowing it to run forward—driven by the recuperator. It is fired a microsecond or two before it reaches the fully forward position. Thus the explosion and the subsequent recoil thrust has first to overcome the inertia of the forward-moving mass before starting it on its recoil stroke again; the nett result is a considerable reduction in the recoil stress transmitted to the mounting.

The mounting was also an enlargement of the two-axle Flak 41 design under the title Sonderanhänger 206, but it was also intended to develop static and self-propelled mountings in due course in addition to a twin-gun version. A notable feature of both the gun and the mounting design was the extensive use of stamped sheet-metal components in order to simplify production. In early 1945 a project was begun to attach a squeeze bore muzzle unit to the gun.

The long delay in the ballistic development, together with the late start of the project and its ambitious ancillaries, was unfortunate. Although three prototype guns were built, the remainder of the programme never reached the production stage before the war ended. It is thought in some quarters that the Soviet 57mm anti-aircraft gun of 1950 represents the final version of the work begun by Rheinmetall-Borsig in 1943.

Data (5.5cm Flak Gerät 58, Versuchsmodell 3, third prototype).
Calibre: 55mm/2.17in.
Length of gun: 6150mm/242.13in/20.18ft.
Length of bore: 4211mm/165.79in/13.82ft.
Rifling: 20 grooves right-hand increasing twist 1/90 to 1/25.5.
Breech mechanism: gas-operated vertical sliding block, percussion fired.
Traverse: 360°.
Elevation: −5° to +90°.
Weight in action: 3500kg/7718lb.
Rate of fire: 140rpm (practical).

Performance
Muzzle velocity: 1050mps/3445fps.
Maximum ceiling: no figures produced.
Effective ceiling: no figures produced.
Maximum ground range: no figures produced.

Ammunition
Fixed rounds; belted rimless case, length 452mm (17.80in). Numerous experimental shells were designed. A representative specimen examined weighed 2.03kg(4.48lb), carried 485gm(17.10oz/1.07lb) of high explosive and the cartridge carried a 1.10kg(2.43lb) charge of Gudol R P. The fuze was Zerl 18V, a new design of self-destroying fuze developed for this gun that was expected to give self destruction at a range of 4800m, giving a practical ceiling of 15750 feet.

The 5.5cm Gerät 58 in action, with wheels removed.

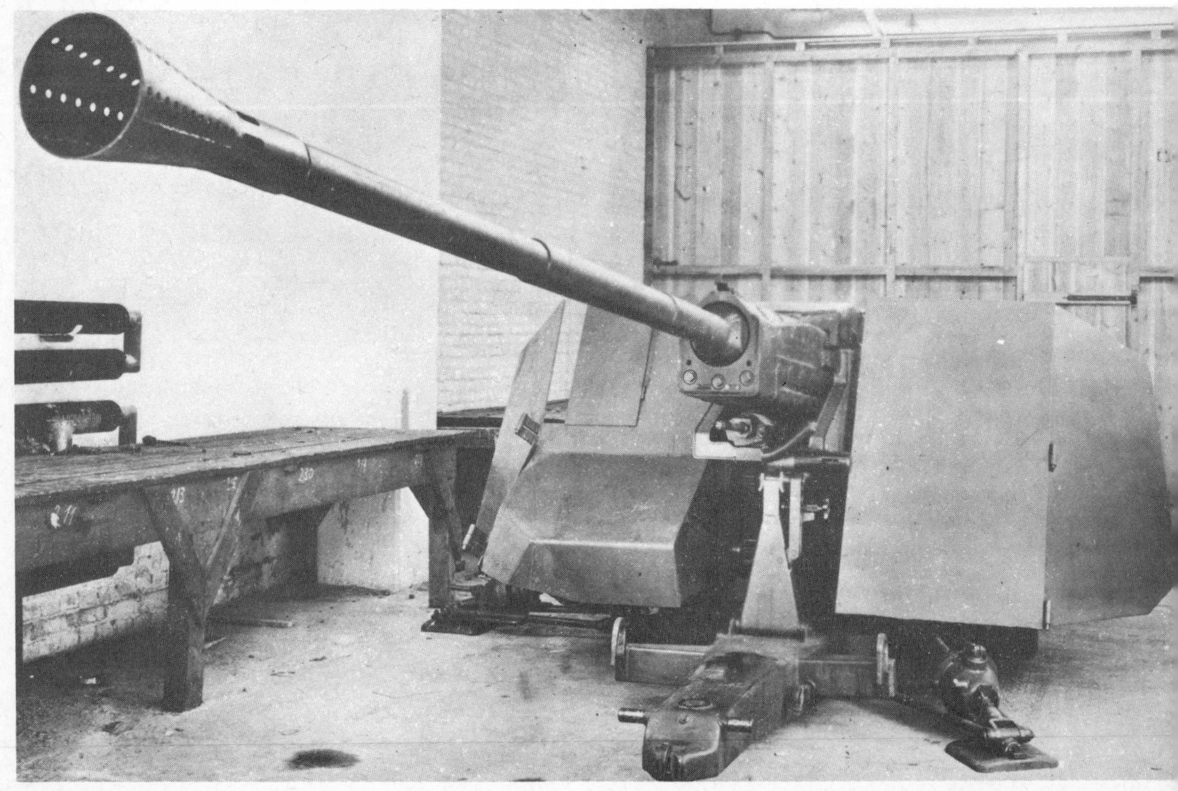

'he 5.5cm Gerät 58 in action on its wheels, with steadying jacks extended.

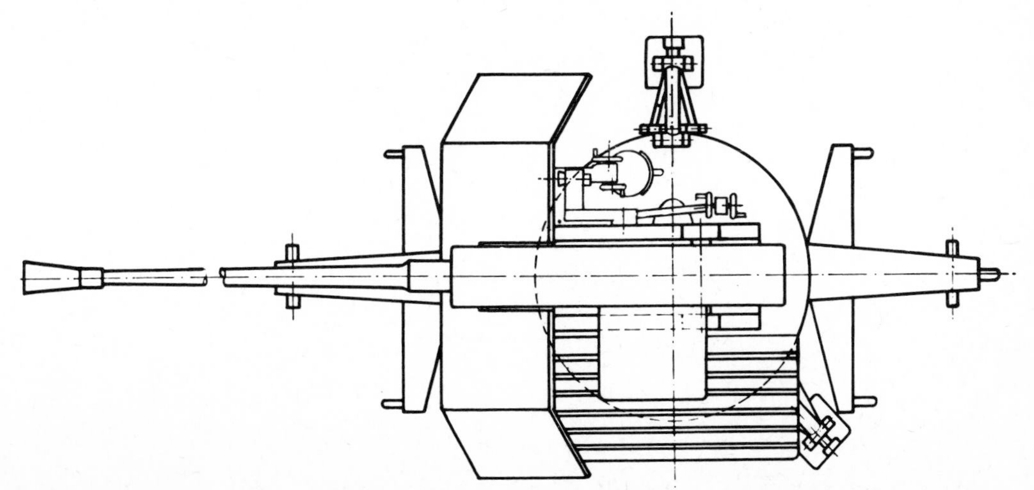

ʼlanufacturer's plan of the Gerät 58 .

8·8cm Flugabwehrkanone 18,36 und 37

8·8cm Flak 18, 36 and 37

The German 8.8cm anti-aircraft guns were probably the best-known weapons of the war, largely because of their use as field and anti-tank guns. Any loud bang was likely to be heralded as an '88' by Allied troops; an idea of its all-pervading mental image may be gained from a cartoon in the *Stars and Stripes* showing a US intelligence officer interrogating prisoners and reassuring a nearby GI 'Don't worry; if I find the one wot invented the 88 I'll let you know'.

There is no doubt that the 8.8cm Flak was an effective gun, but it must also be said that it was skilfully publicised and magnified into an all-conquering super weapon—which it certainly was not. As an anti-aircraft gun it was no better than its contemporaries, as the following figures show:

	muzzle velocity (mps/fps)	shell weight (kg/lb)	effective ceiling (m/ft)	fire rate (rpm)	weight in action (kg/lb)
8.8cm Flak 36 (auf Sonderanhänger 202)	820/2690	9.07/20	7925/26000	15	8199/18078
British 3.7in Mk 3	792/2600	12.70/28	9755/32000	20	9316/20541
US 90mm M1 (on Mounting M1A1)	823/2700	10.43/23	9755/32000	20	8617/19000

The basic fact about the '88' was that the German forces had plenty of them at a time when the Allies had little or nothing comparable in the anti-tank field; it was this fortunate circumstance that gave rise to all the legends.

It has been stated that the 8.8cm was developed in a continuing process from the 8cm and 8.8cm guns developed during World War 1, and the similarity of mountings has been noted in support of this theory. There is no foundation for this, however; anti-aircraft guns as a class tend toward similar mountings, and a great deal more resemblance can be found between the 8.8cm Flak of 1918 and the British 3inch 20cwt of 1916—though no one, to my knowledge, has tried to draw any conclusions from that. 88mm had been a standard German calibre for many years, and there is no more connexion than that.

The 8.8cm Flak 18 had its beginnings in 192 when the army decided that 7.5cm was the smallest practical calibre for a heavy anti-aircraft gun. Krupp and Rheinmetall were asked to produce the prototypes that were tested in 1929/3 but neither was satisfactory and, except for impressed weapons of commercial pattern and captured guns, no 7.5cm anti-aircraft gun was ever in German service during the war. Owing to the repressive provisions of the Versailles Treaty a team of Krupp designers had gone to work at the Bofors factory in Sweden, where—among other things—they spent considerable time designing an anti-aircraft gun around a 20lb 8.8cm shell that promised adequate lethality. The drawings were taken back to Germany in 1931 whereupon a prototype gun was built and demonstrated to the army. It was immediately approved and entered production, being introduced to service in 1933 as the 8.8cm Flak 18.

The gun as issued, was of single-tube barrel construction within a jacket, with an ingenious semi-automatic breech operating for both opening

The 8.8cm Flak 18, fresh from the factory.

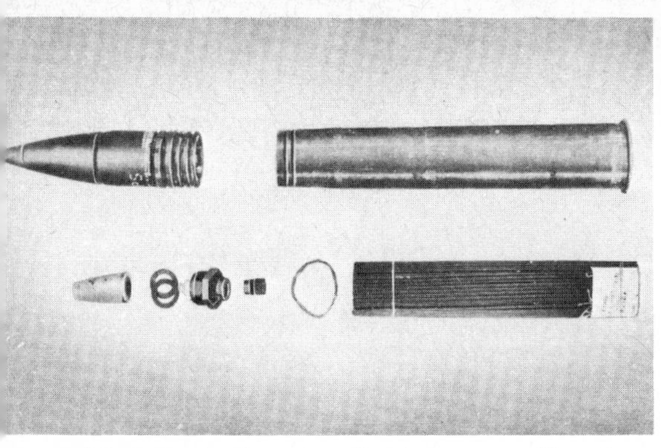

complete round of armour-piercing ammunition for ne 8.8cm Flak 18, stripped into its component parts.

nd closing, under the pressure of clock-type prings, a system that gave positive and constant ction irrespective of the length of recoil or the harge used—but which also demanded close olerances in the manufacture of cartridges cases, nd a multiplicity of parts in the breech nechanism.

The carriage was a cruciform platform carried n two two-wheel limbers (Sonderanhänger 201) hat could be removed after lowering the platform y hand winches. Four outriggers were then unolded to give stability and the pedestal was inally levelled on the platform.

Sighting was arranged for either gun or preictor control, with additional sights for use in he ground role. The gun control sight was a imple telescopic apparatus, Flakzielfernrohr 20, hat was rarely (if ever) used. The predictor ring system was the Ubertragungs 30, which was f a rather unusual pattern. The receiver units consisted of three concentric rings of electric bulbs, with three mechanical pointers of different lengths. When data was transmitted to the gun, the appropriate bulbs lit up and the gunlayers operated elevation or traverse until the three pointers revolved and covered the bulbs with their tips. The ground shooting sight was the Rundblickfernrohr für Flak, a typical dial sight, which was also used for the initial orientation of the gun on arriving in action.

An 8.8cm Flak 18 fitted with a shield.

After some practical experience had been gained with the new weapon it was decided that, in some respects, it could be improved to make it easier both to produce and to operate. The principal changes were in the mounting; the basic platform was changed from its original octagonal shape to a square, the front and rear outriggers were made identical, the barrel support was duplicated at each end so that the gun could be towed in either of two positions, the front and rear bogies were made both identical and interchangeable and had twin wheels (only the rear had previously carried twin wheels), and minor improvements were made to the levelling arrangements and to the transmission system cable connexions. The new carriage was known as Sonderanhänger 202. The gun was also improved in an unusual way; instead of the one-piece barrel that had to be withdrawn and changed when worn (anti-aircraft guns wear out their barrels at a fast rate) the new design had the barrel in three pieces—a chamber section, a centre section and a muzzle section. This method of construction demanded precision in manufacture and considerable care in assembly, but it conferred three advantages. The three sections could firstly be made of different steels, to economise on the higher quality materials and thus confine their use to where it was really needed. Secondly, gun-barrel wear is usually confined to the first part of the rifling, and the rest of the barrel often has considerable useful life remaining; by replacing only the worn part considerable economy was effected. Thirdly, by making the barrel in short sections it became no longer necessary to confine manufacture to specialist companies with large lathes and boring machines; the short sections could be made on smaller machines that were more readily available.

The old and new barrels were ballistically th same, although the newer model had a differen twist of rifling and slightly shallower riflin grooves. The three-piece liner was held togethe by a double jacket and a locking ring. The ne weapon was put into production in 1936 an entered service as the 8.8cm Flak 36 but, sinc the barrels were dimensionally and ballisticall alike, it was not unusual to find a one-piece barre on a '36' carriage or a three-piece barrel on a '18' carriage. One can almost hear the quarte masters saying: 'Why worry? It fits, does it not' Two final changes were made before the outbrea of war. The Ubertragung 30 had proved unsatis factory on trial and work had been going on fo some time to find an improved system. In 193 the Ubertragung 37 was perfected and issued, system based on Selsyn synchronous motors; th receiver dials were provided with two sets o pointers, one electrically operated by transmissio from the predictor and the other mechanicall linked to the gun. The gunlayer then operated hi controls so that his pointers matched the positio

A later version of the Flak 18, with a spring rammer added to the left of the breech.

An 8.8cm Flak 18 ready for action.

The Flak 18 with shield, ready for travelling.

An 8.8cm Flak 18 in action in the North African campaign. Notice that it is being fired from its wheels, one outrigger having been hastily dropped to give some stability.

Sprgr Patr L/4.5.

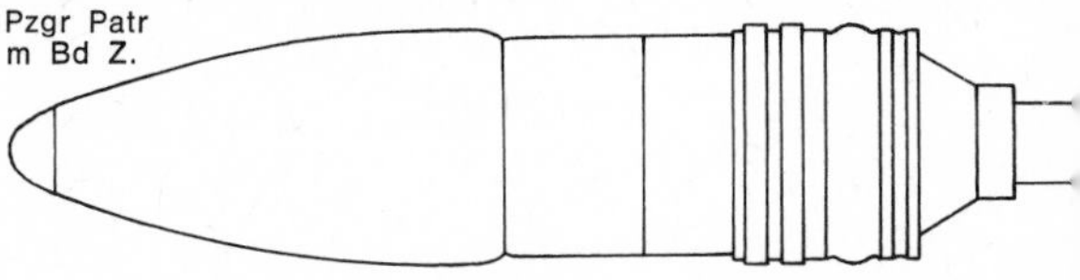

of the predictor-operated pointers, and so the gun was laid. The method gave finer control, smoother following of data, and was easier to operate and maintain. With this system fitted, the guns took the nomenclature 8.8cm Flak 37 (Rauschgeld). The other change lay in the simpler construction of the barrel; where, on the three-piece barrel, the joint between the chamber and the centre section fell there was an erosive tendency, and cartridge cases sometimes expanded into this joint and gave rise to trouble in extraction. So a final version of the barrel was produced in which the liner was in two pieces: the chamber and commencement of rifling, and the remainder of the bore.

The anti-tank capabilities of the gun had been observed during the Spanish Civil War (1936–9), when a small number of guns had accompanied the Condor Legion. To accommodate the gun to this role a telescopic direct sight (the Zielfernrohr 20) was fitted; and shortly after the outbreak of war, shields began to be fitted to a number of guns. But as an anti-tank weapon the 8.8cm saw little use in the early battles of World War 2, and its full potential as an anti-tank gun was not exploited until the Libyan campaign of 1941–2.

Data (8.8cm Flak 18).
Calibre: 88mm/3.46in.

Under new management—an 8.8cm Flak 18 complete with its towing tractor, captured before it could be got into action.

Another oddity is this self-propelled Flak 18. The side walls could be dropped to form an extended platform and permit all-round fire.

Length of gun: 4930mm/194.09in/16.17ft.
Length of bore: 4686mm/184.49in/15.37ft.
Rifling: 32 grooves, right-hand increasing twist, 1/38 to 1/30.
Breech mechanism: horizontal semi-automatic sliding block, percussion fired.
Traverse: 720°.
Elevation: −3° to +85°.
Weight: 4985kg/10992lb.
Rate of fire: 15rpm.

Data (8.8cm Flak 36 and 37).
As for Flak 18 except.
Rifling: 32 grooves, right-hand increasing twist, 1/40 to 1/30.

Performance
Muzzle velocity: 820mps/2690fps.
Maximum ceiling: 9900m/32482ft.
Effective ceiling: 8000m/26248ft.
Maximum ground range: 14815m/16202yd.

Ammunition
Fixed rounds; cartridge case length 570mm (22.44in).
8.8cm Sprgr Patr L/4.5: fuzed AZ 23/28 or Zeit Z S/30, projectile weight 9.40kg(20.73lb), complete round weight 14.40(31.75lb).
This was the standard high explosive shell. It contained 0.87kg(1.92lb) of TNT or amatol and had two bimetallic driving bands. When used in the anti-aircraft role it was fitted with the time fuze, the percussion fuze being used only in the ground role. The propelling charge was 2.41kg(5.31lb) of Digl R P. Later production of this shell used two sintered-iron driving bands.
8.8cm Sprgr Patr L/4.5 Gerillt: fuzed Zeit Z S/30 Zn.
This was the same round as above, but the shell was engraved with 15 longitudinal grooves (120mm/4.72in) on the parallel portion of the body. This was introduced in 1944 in an attempt to control fragmentation of the shell, so that large fragments (which would do more damage to an airframe) would be produced on detonation. The idea was not particularly successful; it was one of the first attempts at fragment control and subsequent experiments showed that to have any effect at all the grooving had to be on the inside surface—which was impractical.
8.8cm Sch Sprgr Patr L/4.5: fuzed Zeit Z S/30 Kurz, projectile weight 10.06kg(22.18lb), complete round weight 15.06kg(33.21lb).
This shell used a form of incendiary shrapnel attributed to one Oberst Knublauch. It was not strictly a shrapnel shell but a high explosive shell body with a central core of explosive surrounded by steel segments, each containing an incendiary mixture. This was an attempt to increase the lethal area and damaging effect, but apparently

The fire controls for the 8.8cm anti-aircraft gun, the Uberträgung 37 'follow-the-pointer' system.

The breech of the 8.8cm Flak 18.

few were made since it was quickly superseded by an improved design.

8.8cm Br Sch Gr Patr L/4.5: fuzed Zeit Z S/30 Kurz, projectile weight 9.58kg(21.12lb), complete round weight 14.58kg(32.15lb).

This was a normal nose-ejection shrapnel shell filled with a large number of cylindrical metal pellets each carying a firing pin, a detonator and a charge of barium-nitrate/magnesium incendiary mixture. A million of these shells were ordered and the design entered use in February 1944, but it proved to be less successful than forecast since the shells tended to be unstable in flight and many of the incendiary pellets misfired owing to striking broadside-on. The shell was to be replaced by one with a new design of pellet that was aerodynamically stable and which carried a charge of PETN/wax/aluminium; 72 were to go into the shell. This model, however, had not reached production when the war ended, All the anti-aircraft shrapel shells were distinctively coloured; the Sch Sprgr was yellow from the tip to the shoulder and blue from there to the base, while the Br Sch Gr was red from the tip to the shoulder and blue thereafter.

8.8cm Pzgr Patr: fuzed Bd Z f 8.8cm Pzgr, projectile weight 9.50kg(20.95lb), complete round weight 15.40kg(33.96lb).

This was an anti-tank projectile of the usual type with penetrating and ballistic caps, a bursting charge of 155gm(5.47oz) of PETN/wax and a base fuze. The propelling charge was 2.52kg(5.56lb) of Digl R P. The penetration was claimed as 105mm at 1000m at 30°(4.13in at 1095yd).

8.8cm Pzgr Patr 39: fuzed Bd Z f 8.8cm Pzgr.

This differed very little from the previous round except that the projectile had two soft-iron driving bands instead of two copper ones, and the ballistic cap was slightly more pointed.

8.8cm Pzgr Patr 40: projectile weight 7.50kg (16.54lb), complete round weight 13.80kg(30.43lb).

This was a tungsten-cored shot. Penetration claimed was 103mm at 1000m at 3°(4.06in at 1095yd), which illustrates the fact that at longer ranges this type of shot showed no advantage over plain-steel projectiles. At shorter ranges, however, the advantage showed itself; at 500m (547yd) the Pzgr Patr penetrated 110mm(4.33in), while the Pzgr Patr 40 achieved 126mm(4.96in). The muzzle velocity with this lighter projectile was 935mps(3068fps).

8.8cm Hl Gr Patr 39 Flak L/4.7: fuzed AZ 38,

Another variation on the quick action theme: in this case there was enough time to disengage the wheels, but not enough to allow them to be removed before opening fire.

:eady to repel boarders. This 8.8cm Flak 18 is being carried from Italy to Tunisia on a Siebel ferry, and is pparently expected to earn its keep should the vessel be attacked. Notice in the background armoured towers vith 2cm Flakvierlings covered by canvas shrouds.

›rojectile weight 7.20kg(15.88lb), complete round veight 10.65kg(23.48lb).
This was an anti-tank hollow charge shell of con-ventional design. It carried two sintered-iron driving bands. The penetration was claimed as 65mm at 1000m(6.50in at 1095yd).
.8cm Leuchtgeschoss L/4.4: fuzed Zeit Z /60nA, projectile weight 9.50kg(20.95lb), com-plete round weight 13.90kg(30.65lb).
This was a naval shell adapted for use with the Flak gun by simply fitting it to the appropriate cartridge case. It was of the usual base ejection pattern carrying a parachute-suspended illuminat-ing unit. The propelling charge was 2.09kg 4.61lb) of Digl R P.

Experimental Ammunition

n addition to the foregoing service rounds, a multitude of experimental rounds was produced at various times in attempts to improve the gun's performance. Among those of particular interest, or which drawings and specimens have been xamined, were:
.8/7cm Sprgr Triebspiegel L/4.8: weight of sub-projectile 4.90kg(10.80lb).
This discarding sabot projectile used a solid base with a fibre driving band and a hollow sheet-metal upporting sabot at the shoulder.
.8/6.5cm Sprgr TS: weight of subprojectile 3.90kg 8.60lb).
Another discarding sabot high explosive projectile

A rare photograph of the 8.8cm Flak 36/43, a Flak 41 barrel mounted on a Flak 36 carriage.

similar to the 8.8/7cm model.
8.8/5.5cm Sprgr TS: weight of subprojectile 2.60kg (5.73lb).
This was also on similar lines to the previous models. All these discarding sabot shells were designed with the intention of increasing velocity and thus reducing the time of flight.

8.8/7cm Sprgr TS L/4.2: weight of subprojectil 3.70kg(8.16lb).
This model used a hollow base unit discarded b gas pressure and a three-piece shoulder suppor unit. It contained 0.41kg(0.90lb) of explosive an is said to have attained a velocity of 1135mp (3724fps) on trial.

8·8cm Flugabwehrkanone 41

8·8cm Flak 41 (Eisenerz)

Even while the FlAK 36 was entering service the Luftwaffe began to look ahead. From what they knew of their own aircraft it was obvious that the speed and height of bombers was bound to increase, eventually reaching a point where the Flak 36 would no longer be able to deal with them. The muzzle velocity and the rate of fire would have to be increased, and, as it seemed that an anti-tank capability might also be needed, the weapon wanted to be of low silhouette. Under the title of Gerät 37 a specification was issued in the autumn of 1939 calling for a gun weighing not more than 8000kg, firing 25 rounds per minute at 1000mps. Rheinmetall-Borsig was given the contract and their first prototype was ready for trial in early 1941. The title 'Gerät 37' was causing some confusion with the existing Flak 37 gun, and so the new project was officially called the 8.8cm Flak 41. Shortly before the appearance of the prototype the Luftwaffe, hearing that all was not well with Rheinmetall's development, issued another contract to Krupp in the hope that they might develop a competitive gun. The Krupp project became Gerät 42, but (although it showed some promise) it was dropped early in 1943 whe the Luftwaffe asked for even more performanc

The Rheinmetall-Borsig design was a very goo one indeed. Instead of the Flak 18's pedestal th gun was mounted on a turntable and trunnione well back, to be as low-set as possible. Th ballistics were greatly improved, and a powere roller loading mechanism—drawing its powe from a hydropneumatic piston operated on reco —speeded up the rate of fire. The most adven turous part of the design was the barrel, but her (in the opinion of many authorities) Rheinmetall' designers overreached themselves. The barrel wa divided into three bore sections with a sleeve, jacket and a locking collar to hold everythin together, plus a complicated arrangement of retaining collar and a ring holding the breech-rin in place. This was all very well on paper, but i practice it gave a good deal of trouble owing t the cartridge case failing to extract. Part of th trouble was due to the fact that the joint betwee the first and second sections of barrel fell exactl at the cartridge case bottleneck: steel case expanded into this joint and became stuck. Specia

The 8.8cm Flak 41 in draught.

rass cases were developed, which overcame the rouble to a large degree, but it periodically re-urred; this was probably due to the high chamber ressures involved. The design was eventually hanged to a two-section liner with a jacket and sleeve. The 152 guns issued with the original aree-piece liner were marked with a yellow band round the barrel and a yellow M painted on the reech-ring, indicating that they were only to be sed with ammunition having brass (Messing) artridge cases. A further 133 guns were then sued with two-piece barrels, but the trouble per-sted—though to a smaller degree—and was argely due to the different expansion factors of ie chamber and cartridge case when under evere pressure. The design was again changed to heavier two-piece barrel with a jacket and no eeve, and the remainder of production (some 71 guns) used the third type of barrel. In spite f all this trouble the Flak 41 was a good weapon, nd specimens were still used by the Czecho-ovakian army until the early 1960s.

ata

'alibre: 88mm/3.46in.
.ength of gun: 6545mm/257.68in/21.47ft.
.ength of bore: 6302mm/248.11in/20.68ft.
Rifling: 32 grooves. First section of barrel of right-and increasing twist, 1/44 to 1/34. Muzzle ection of right-hand uniform twist, 1/34.
Breech mechanism: horizontal semi-automatic liding block, electrically fired.
'raverse: 360°.
Elevation: −3° to +90°.
Veight in action: 7800kg/17199lb.
Rate of fire: 20rpm.

erformance

Auzzle velocity: 1000mps/3281fps.
Aaximum ceiling: 15000m/49215ft.
Effective ceiling: 10675m/35025ft.
Aaximum ground range: 19735m/21582yd.

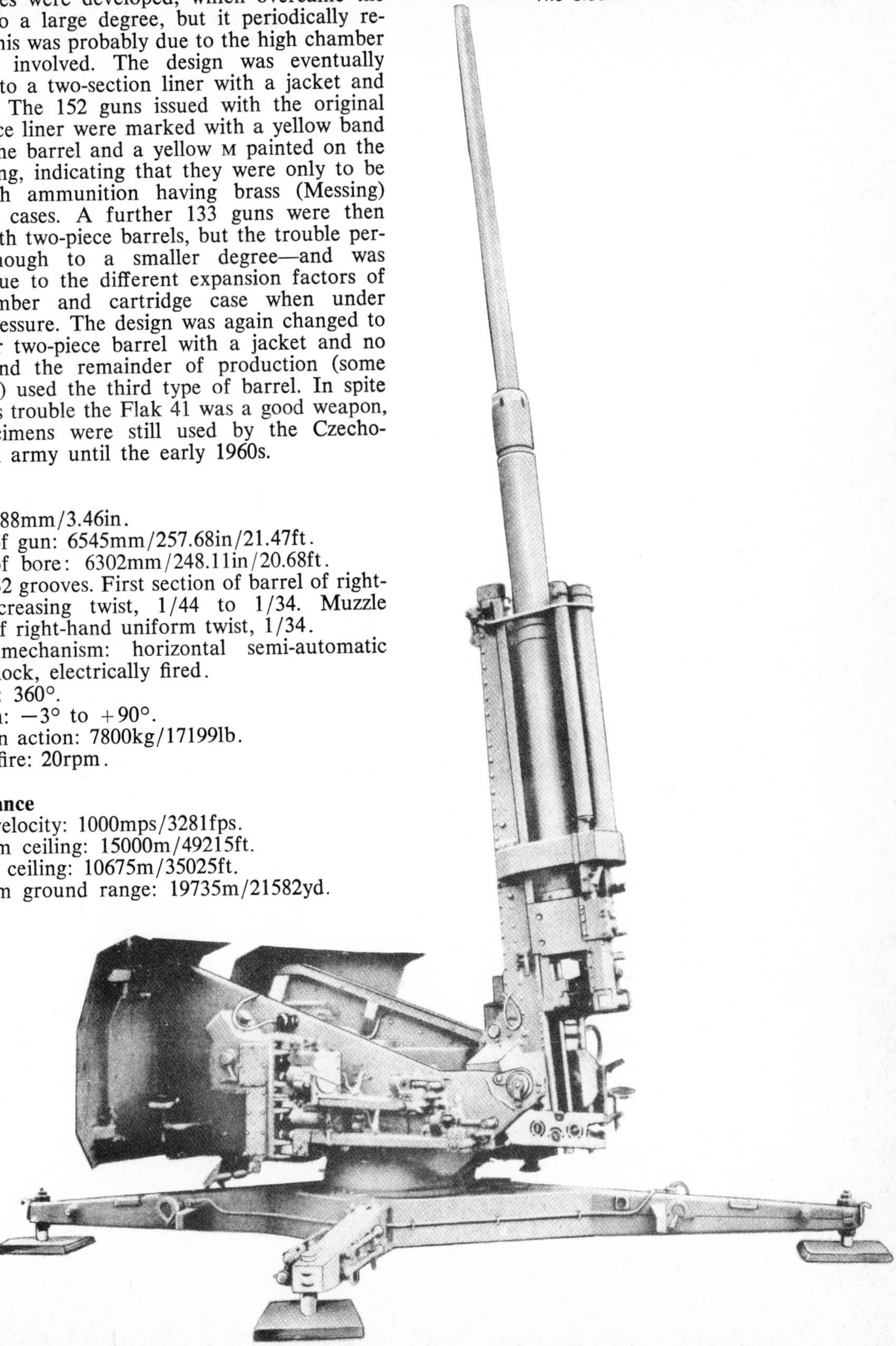

The 8.8cm Flak 41 at maximum elevation.

Another view of the Flak 41 in action, illustrating the low silhouette obtained by using a turntable instead of a pedestal.

Ammunition
Fixed rounds; cartridge case length 859mm (33.82in).
8.8cm Sprgr Patr Flak 41: fuzed Zeit Z S/30 or AZ 23/28, projectile weight 9.40kg(20.73lb), complete round weight 20.40kg(44.98lb).
This was a conventional high explosive shell fitted with two driving bands. It was very slightly longer than the shell for the Flak 36 and had a streamlined base. The explosive content was 0.86kg (1.90lb) of amatol, and the propelling charge was 5.12kg(11.29lb) of Gudol R P.
8.8cm Sprgr Patr Flak 41 Gerillt.
This, like its Flak 36 equivalent, was the standard high explosive shell grooved in an attempt to improve fragmentation.
8.8cm Pzgr Patr 39/1 Flak 41: fuzed Bd Z f 8.8cm Pzgr.
This was the same projectile used with the Flak 36 but assembled with the Flak 41 cartridge case. The propelling charge was 5.42kg(11.95lb) of Gudol R P, giving a muzzle velocity of 980mps (3215fps) and a claimed penetration of 202mm at 1000m at 3°(7.95in at 1095yd).
8.8cm Pzgr Patr 40 Flak 41.

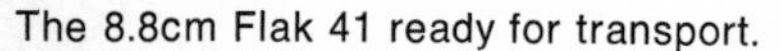

The 8.8cm Flak 41 ready for transport.

This was again the same projectile as that used with the Flak 36. The propelling charge was of Gudol R P giving a velocity of 1150mps(3773fps).

Primer
The electric primer C/22 was used with all Flak 41 cases.

8.8cm Flugabwehrkanone 37/41
(8.8cm Flak 37/41).
In the spring of 1942, when better performance was being demanded, an extemporary weapon was developed to fill the gap until the Flak 41 was in full production. This consisted of a new barrel, based on the FlAK 37 type but with an enlarged chamber and a muzzlebrake, fitting the Flak 36/37 jacket and thus capable of being assembled to the '36' or '37' carriage. It was hoped that the addition of the muzzlebrake would allow the more powerful ammunition of the Flak 41 to be safely fired from the older carriage. The enlarged chamber unfortunately gave rise to considerable trouble with faulty extraction, and only for production.
12 barrels were ever built; the design was rejected

Diagram of the breech mechanism of the 8.8cm Flak 41, showing the operation of the roller ramming gear.

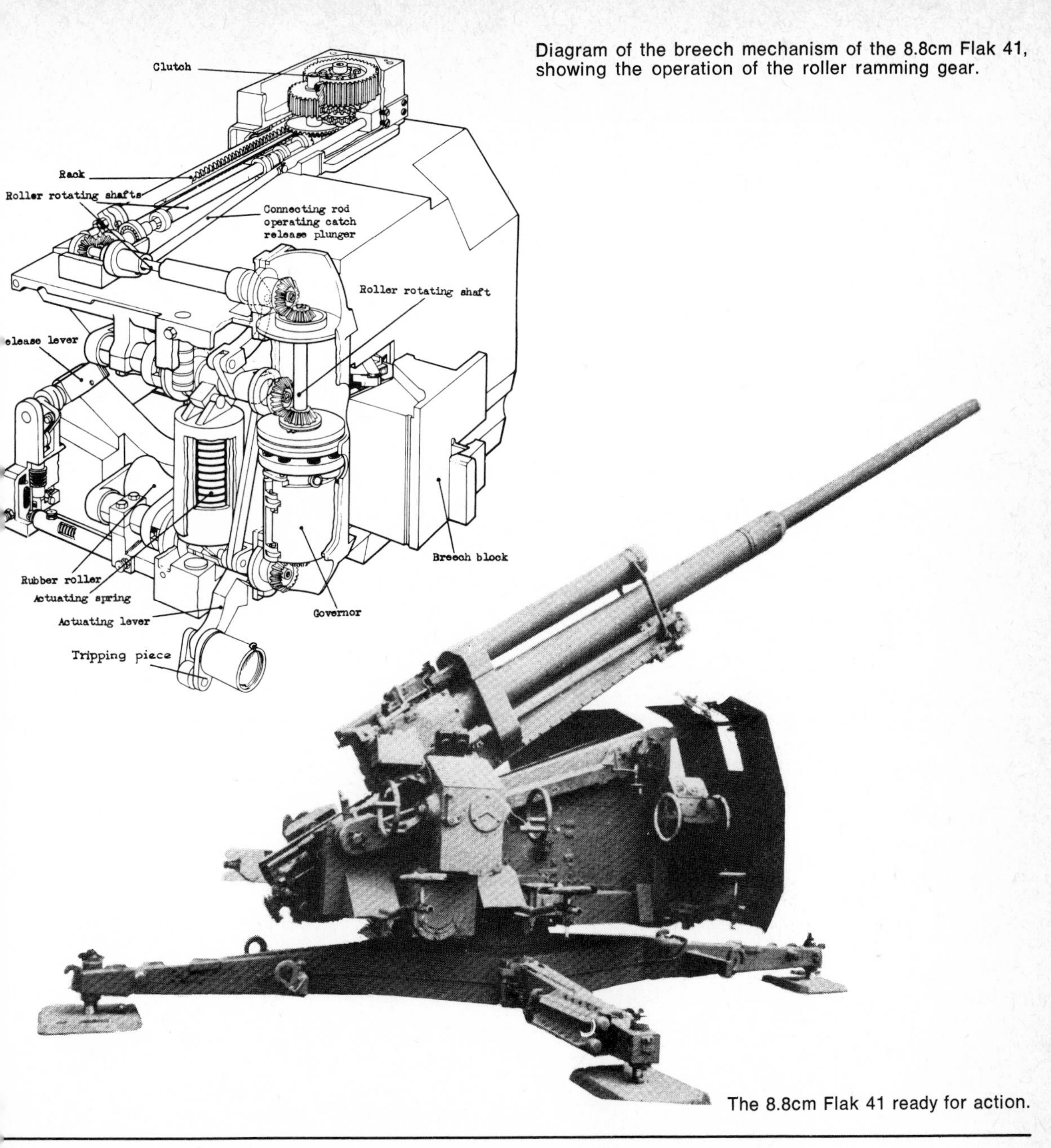

The 8.8cm Flak 41 ready for action.

10·5cm Flugabwehrkanone 38 und 39

10·5cm Flak 38 and 39 (Regenbegen)

When the 8.8cm series of guns was first introduced the Luftwaffe considered that, while the Flak 18/36/37 promised to be an excellent mobile weapon, it was as well to insure against the rapidly improving performance of aircraft by beginning the development of a heavier weapon for static sites. Since the contemporary state of the ballistic art precluded velocities much above 900mps (c.3000fps), owing to the restrictions imposed by hot propellants and copper driving bands, the only way to achieve a greater ceiling was to adopt a larger calibre. So, at the end of 1933, a specification for a 10.5cm gun (provisionally called Gerät 38) was issued and contracts were given to both Krupp and Rheinmetall. The brief demanded full-power operation, a high rate of fire, good stability and good road mobility. Each company was asked to produce two prototypes, followed by a further four pre-production guns with which experimental units were formed to undertake extended trials. One prototype was to use hydraulic power and the other was to be electrically operated.

By mid-1935 the prototypes had been put through a succession of tests that had resulted in a number of modifications being made, and in 1936 the trial batteries carried out extensive field trials. In October of 1936 the Rheinmetall design fitted with Pittler-Thoma hydraulic power-control was selected as the production weapon, and it entered service the following year as the 10.5cm Flak 38.

In 1939 some further changes were made, in the light of experience. The electric power supply (which drove the four motors on the carriage that provided power for the hydraulic motors) was changed from direct to alternating current so that commercial and domestic power supplies could be used in static sites; the original power supply had been from a 220v 24kw DC motor-generator forming part of the troop equipment. The gun barrel, originally a single tube, was changed to a five-piece design with the bore in three sections (as on the 8.8cm guns) and the Ubertragung 30 data transmission system was changed to the Ubertragung 37. With these changes the weapon took the new title of 10.5cm Flak 39.

The mounting was a cruciform platform with outriggers of the usual pattern, similar to that used with the 8.8cm guns but—naturally—bigger and stronger. Two interconnected loading trays, a mechanical fuze-setter and roller-loading gear were fitted—so that, to load, the gunner dropped a round into the first loading tray, where it was fed to the fuze setter. With the fuze set, the tray then rocked and transferred the round to the second tray, which also rocked and presented the nose of the shell to the rollers. These contracted, gripped the shell and propelled the round into the breech. As the cartridge case left the tray, its rim tripped a cam that returned the tray; the breech then closed automatically and the gun fired. All in all the 10.5cm Flak was a most effective weapon, the only criticism levelled at it being of its weight (13.8ton on the move) and of the fact that it took something like 20 minutes of hard work to get the gun into action. Since it was primarily intended for static defence, neither drawback was particularly serious.

An interesting development lay in the mounting of 10.5cm anti-aircraft guns on railway trucks so that they could be rapidly moved to marshalling yards and city areas. By the end of 1944 there were 116 of these railway mountings in use, plus 877 fixed and 1025 mobile equipments.

Towards the end of the war numerous developments were undergoing trials, with the intention of improving the gun's performance. In addition to a variety of sabot projectiles, new barrels with different rifling better suited to unconventional projectiles were being tested; these included rifling twists of 1/35, 1/20 and 1/22.5, as well as a smoothbore barrel for firing Peenemünde arrow shells. Other projects involved the fitting of muzzle-squeeze attachments, but none of these developments came to fruition before the war ended.

Data
Calibre: 105mm/4.13in.
Length of gun: 6648mm/261.73in/21.81ft.
Length of bore: 5547mm/218.39in/18.20ft.

The Krupp mock-up of the 10.5cm Flak in its original form.

The 10.5cm Flak 39 as finally produced.

The 10.5cm Flak 39 ready for action.

Rifling: 36 grooves, right-hand increasing twist, 1/48 to 1/36.
Breech mechanism: horizontal semi-automatic sliding block, electrically fired.
Traverse: 360°.
Elevation: −3° to +85°.
Weight in action: 10224kg/22544lb/10.06ton.

Performance
Muzzle velocity: 881mps/2891fps.
Maximum ceiling: 11400m/37403ft.
Effective ceiling: 9450m/31005ft.
Maximum ground range: 17600m/19247yd.

Ammunition
Fixed rounds; cartridge case length 766mm (30.16in).
10.5cm Sprgr L/4.4: fuzed Zeit Z S/30 or S/60, projectile weight 14.80kg(32.63lb), complete round weight 26.50kg(58.43lb).
This was the standard high explosive shell of conventional pattern fitted with two sintered iron or bimetallic bands. The high explosive filling was 1.50kg(3.31lb) of amatol. The propelling charge was 5.63kg(12.41lb) of Digl R P.
10.5cm Sprgr L/4.4 Pr Zugz
This was identical to the foregoing, but the shell was made of forged steel drawn from a billet and stencilled to that effect: PR ZUGZ for *press-stahl Zugezogen.* The only example seen of this shell was dated January 1944 and it is thus presumed to be a wartime manufacturing expedient.
10.5cm Sprgr L/4.4 Gerillt
This was the standard shell, modified by 24 grooves milled in the external surface for fragmentation control.
10.5cm Pz Sprgr Patr Flak: fuzed Bd Z f 10cm Pzgr, projectile weight 15.45kg(34.07lb), complete round weight 27.00kg(59.54lb).
This, an armour-piercing shell of conventional pattern, had penetrating and ballistic caps and a single bimetallic driving band. The propelling charge was 4.90kg(10.80lb) of Digl R P giving a velocity of 860mps(2822fps) and a penetration of 140mm at 1000m at 30°(5.51in at 1095yd).
10.5cm Sprgr Patr C/32 L/4.9 Br: fuzed EK Zdr C/28
This was a naval projectile taken into Luftwaffe

Close-up of the operating side of the 10.5cm Flak. Compare this with the clean lines of the original mock-up!

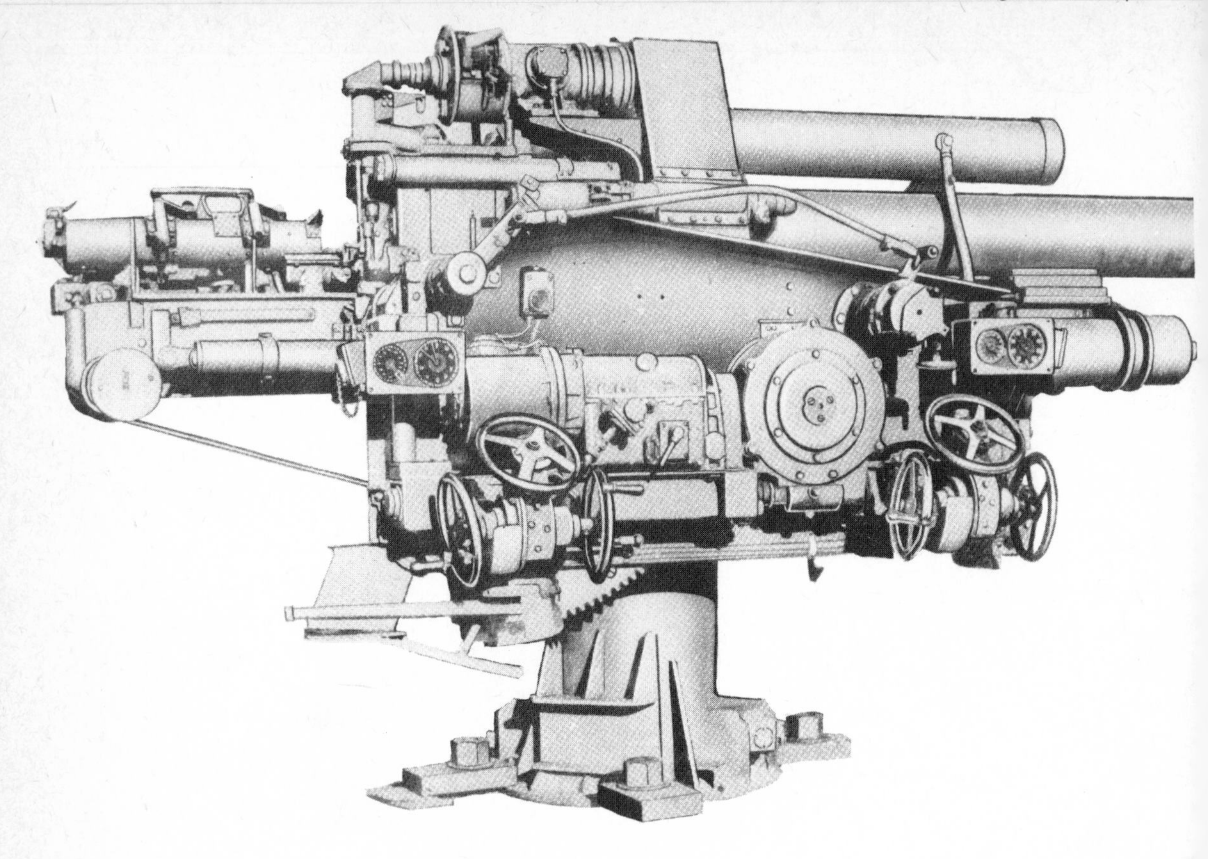

service on a trial basis late in 1944. It contained an explosive charge of TNT surrounding a core of thermite incendiary pellets. The shell had two sintered iron driving bands and was fitted with a tracer in the base.

10.5cm R Gr: projectile weight 14.00kg(30.87lb) This was an experimental rocket-assisted shell to be fired from the standard gun in an attempt to increase the ceiling. It was fitted with two copper driving bands and a blow-out plug on the base; the rocket motor was in the rear section. No details are known of its ignition system or performance.

10.5cm Sprgr Pfeilgeschosse

Numerous experimental patterns of this projectile existed; three have been examined and drawings of others studied. All are very similar but exhibit small differences in such things as the weight, the fin contour, the nose contour, and the attachment of driving rings. A representative specimen weighed 9.30kg(20.51lb) and the subprojectile was 4.5cm(1.77in) in diameter. The driving ring sabot was divided into three sections and held in place by papier-mâché adhesive bonding. Four tail fins were welded to the rear. The subprojectile weighed 7.15kg(15.77lb) and was reputed to have attained a velocity of 952mps(3124fps).

10.50cm Spitzgeschoss 'Haack'

This experimental shell was designed according to various ballistic theories developed by Professor Haack. His principal concern, to put it in a nutshell, was to develop the best possible shape for the shell's flight and then make it fit the bore by means of sabots. Weighing 14.00kg(30.87lb) it was sharply tapered and rounded at the base, with a wide sintered iron driving band and three-piece discarding centring sabot at the shoulder. No figures are known concerning its performance.

10.5cm Triebspiegelgeschosse

Numerous examples of these were also developed. The 10.5/8.8cm pot type was said to achieve 1065mps(3495fps) in a 1/35 rifled barrel, while a 10.5/7.5cm shell with base and shoulder discards fired in a barrel rifled 1/20, achieved 1350mps (4430fps).

10.5cm K–Geschosse

These projectiles were fired from a normal gun with a muzzle-squeeze attachment that reduced the calibre to 8.0cm. They were of the usual type with a perforated front skirt and a rear skirt band that folded back under the squeeze action, or with soft metal studs at the shoulder. Examples seen weighed between 6.10kg(13.45lb) and 7.80kg (17.20lb); velocities in the region of 1160mps (3806fps) were reached on trials.

12·8cm Flugabwehrkanone 40 und 45

12·8cm Flak 40 and 45 (Havelland)

In 1936, with the 10.5cm Flak project under way, the Luftwaffe once again reviewed the situation and decided that even larger guns would be needed at some time in the future, since the aircraft seemed to be advancing faster than the gun designs. As a result of these opinions, specifications were drawn up for a 12.8cm gun and for a 15cm gun; that of the 12.8cm model called for a velocity of about 1000mps(3280fps), a shell weighing about 27.5kg(60lb), and full power assistance. Rheinmetall-Borsig was given the contract and the new project was called Gerät 40.

The prototype was ready in the second half of 1937 and passed its trials with flying colours; it then went into production as the 12.8cm Flak 40. In its original form the gun was very similar to an enlarged 10.5cm, mounted on the usual type of cruciform carriage with outriggers and carried on two two-wheel limbers. Unfortunately, owing to its weight, the barrel had to be unshipped and carried on a separate transport wagon. While this method of transportation had been written into the specification and approved on trial, a short period of practical use soon showed that such an arrangement was ill-suited to an anti-aircraft gun. Late in 1938 a number of manufacturers were circularised by the Luftwaffe to see if they could develop a one-load transport system. A suitable system, devised by Waffen Prüf 10 and executed by the Meiller company, was eventually approved. In this the platform was a simple girder construction with the gun pedestal bolted to it and four support horizontally-folding legs were attached to the corners. At each end of the platform a cantilever arm was attached by a boss and a hydraulic ram. The outer ends of these arms rode on a four-wheel limber that was independently sprung by swinging half-axles and leaf springs. Lock pins were removed to lower the platform and the pressure in the hydraulic rams was released. Hydraulic pressure was applied by hand pumps to raise the platform.

While this was a good technical solution, the result was cumbersome to move—since the carriage was 15m(49ft) long and weighed about 26450kg/(26ton), the limbers weighed 4570kg (4.5ton) apiece, and the wheelbase was 11.73m (38.5ft). By comparison the equivalent British transportable anti-aircraft gun, the 4.5in, weighed 17270kg(17ton) with a 3.66m(12ft) wheelbase.

In the event, few of these mobile equipments were built. Those of the original pattern were few in number, and by the time the 12.8cm gun came into full production (in 1942) the production of mobile guns above 10.5cm was prohibited—so few of the Meiller transporters were built either. The vast majority of the 12.8cm guns were statically emplaced by simply bolting the pedestal down in concrete.

The standard mounting was, of course, fully power-operated. Owing to the size of the weapon, platforms were provided for the gunner; an interesting feature was the coupling of these platforms to the left gun trunnion, so that they moved as the gun was elevated and depressed and so kept the gunners in the same position relative to the loading apparatus and other controls. Another unusual feature was the absence of a breech-mechanism lever; the breech was opened by pulling a wire lanyard from a drum, thus driving a pinion gear-train that rotated the actuating crank to slide the breechblock open. Only in this way could sufficient mechanical advantage be obtained to open the breech against the pressure of the semi-automatic closing spring.

In the search for effective anti-aircraft defences within Germany, it was decided in 1940 to build Flak towers (Flaktürme) for the defence of major cities. These citadels were intended to mount the 15cm anti-aircraft guns and to be so placed that, by virtue of their height and location, they were able to fire in all directions without being restricted by buildings. This might otherwise have been the case on a ground level site in a built-up area. Since the 15cm gun was unlikely to be available for some time, the 12.8 was proposed as an emergency substitute; a single 12.8cm gun, however, would have been an uneconomic employment of the towers and so a twin-gun equipment, the 12.8cm Flakzwilling 40 (Innsbruck), was developed and installed. The first was erected in Berlin in 1942, and by the war's end 34 such twin guns had been installed in the towers.

In these ways the Flak 40 was assimilated into the air defences, but in late 1943 it was decided to try and improve the weapon's performance. In the usual way a variety of discarding sabot projectiles was tried, plus a 12.8/10.5cm squeeze-bore attachment. In addition a new gun with a larger chamber, a longer barrel and a muzzle brake was designed to fit the original mountings. This was the 12.8cm Flak 45 and it is believed that a prototype was built just before the war ended. Not only was this to fire a slightly-heavier conventional shell but sabot projectiles were also proposed; so, too, were a 'squeeze' muzzle-attachment and a smoothbore barrel to fire Peenemünde arrow shells. Unfortunately, no further details are known of its performance.

An interesting development under way as the war ended was the lining-down of a 12.8cm gun to take the 10.5cm Flak 39 shell propelled by the

12.8cm Flak 40 cartridge. The result was known as the 10.5cm Flak 39/40 but, so far as is known, it never reached even the prototype stage. Rifled 1/25.5, it was hoped to achieve a velocity of 1090mps(3576fps) with the standard shell and plans were drawn up for a 10.5/8.8cm discarding sabot incendiary shrapnel shell that would reach 1405mps(4610fps). Such a solution would probably have increased the effective ceiling by about 30–35%, but it would also have brought severe wear problems in its train.

Data
Calibre: 128mm/5.04in.
Length of gun: 7835mm/308.46in/25.71ft.
Length of bore: 7490mm/294.88in/24.57ft.
Rifling: 40 grooves, right-hand increasing twist 1/54 to 1/32.5.
Breech mechanism: horizontal semi-automati sliding block, electrically fired.
Traverse: 360°.
Elevation: −3° to +88°.
Weight in action: 13000kg/28665lb/12.80ton.
Rate of fire: 12rpm.

Data (12.8cm Flakzwilling 40).
As above, except:
Weight in action: 27000kg/59535lb/26.58ton.
Rate of fire: 25rpm.

Performance
Muzzle velocity: 880mps/2887fps.

12.8cm Flakzwilling 40, the twin mounting designed for use in flak towers.

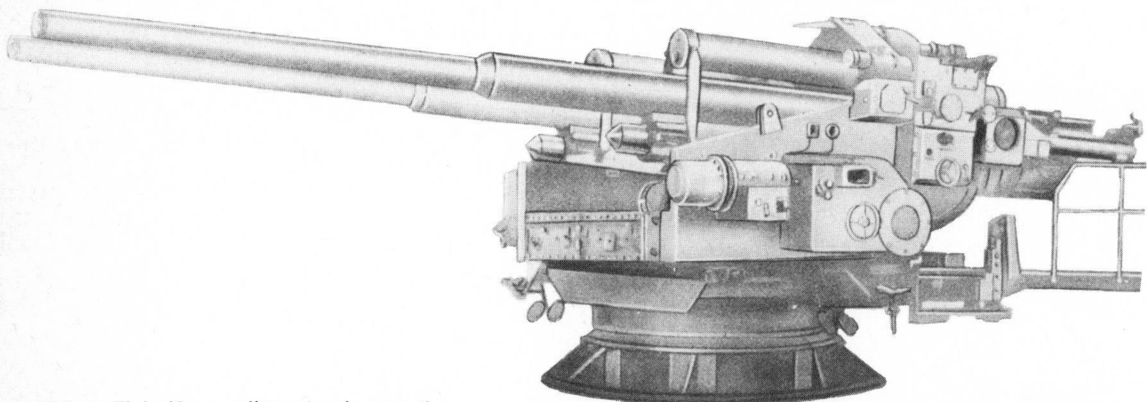

A 12.8cm Flak 40 on railway truck mounting.

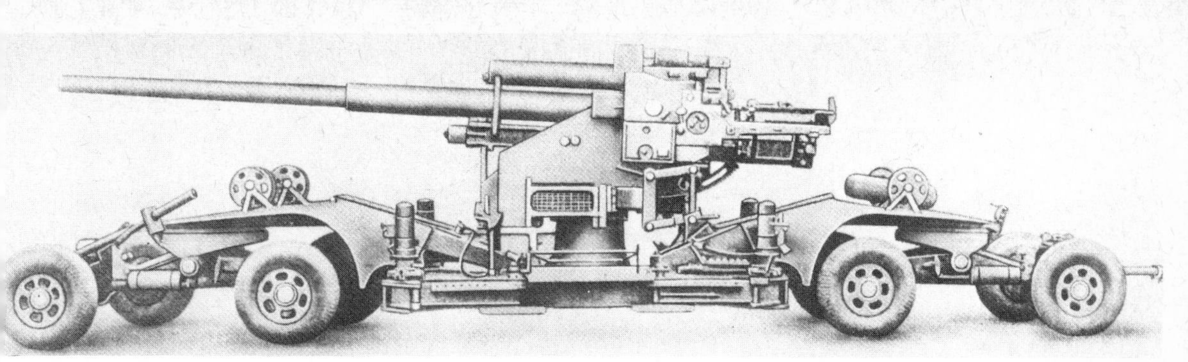

A 12.8cm Flak 40 on its transporter.

Another view of the 12.8cm Flakzwilling.

Side view of the 12.8cm Rail Flak, showing the clamps used to hold the truck firmly to the track during firing.

Maximum ceiling: 14800m/48559ft.
Effective ceiling: 10675mm/35025ft.
Maximum ground range: 20475m/22391yd.
The maximum ground range is a purely theoretical figure; the gun was never fired in this role.

Ammunition
Fixed rounds; cartridge case length 959mm (37.76in).
12.8cm Sprgr Patr L/4.5 Flak 40: fuzed Zeit Z S/30 or EK Zdr C/28, projectile weight 26.02kg (57.31lb), complete round weight 45.51kg(100.25lb)
This was the standard shell and was of conventional design, fitted with two soft iron driving bands. The filling was 3.40kg(7.51lb) of amatol and the propelling charge was 9.62kg(21.25lb) of Digl R P.
12.8cm Br Schr Flak 40: fuzed Zeit Z S/30, projectile weight 25.25kg(55.5lb), complete round weight 44.25kg(97.5lb).
This incendiary-shrapnel shell was developed late in the war and issued in small quantities in 1945, the only specimen seen being dated 6th March 1945. It contained 124 incendiary pellets, each carrying its own detonator. The propelling charge was 9.73kg(21.5lb) of Digl R P.
12.8cm Pzgr Patr Flak 40: fuzed Bd Z 5121, projectile weight 26.50kg(58.5lb), complete round weight 42.50kg(95.94lb).
This was a capped piercing shell with a base fuze and a bursting charge of 670gm(1.5lb) of Ethylenediamine dinitrate/cyclonite/wax (46/18/36) in pre-pressed blocks. Two versions existed, an early model with two bimetallic driving bands and a later one with two sintered iron bands. The propelling charge was 8.25kg(18.6lb) of Digl R P. The purpose of these rounds is somewhat puzzling; it was extremely unlikely that these weapons would ever be called on to shoot as anti-tank guns, and it must be assumed that these shells were issued as part of a general policy to provide every weapon with an armour-defeating round—irrespective of the likelihood of it ever being used. Specimens seen have been dated 1942 and 1944, and there is a possibility that they were originally produced for the self-propelled 12.8cm K 40 and the refitted to the 12.8cm Flak cases in order to use them up.
12.8cm R Gr H/65: fuzed AZ 25/28, projectile weight 21.50kg(48.5lb).
This was an experimental rocket-assisted shell, externally almost identical to the L/4.5 model but with a propulsion unit carried in the rear half and venting through a central hole in the base. No details of its performance are known.

Experimental projectiles
No valuable purpose would be served by individually detailing the many experimental projectiles developed towards the end of the war. By and large they were similar to the 10.5cm Flak varieties and included 12.8/10.5cm sabot shells (both high explosive and incendiary shrapnel), and 12.8/10.5cm squeeze-bore projectiles for versions of the 12.8cm Flak 40 with rifling twists varying from 1/33 to 1/18. The Flak 45 was proposed with rifling varying from 1/30 to 1/18, a 12.8/9.6cm explosive shell, a 12.8/9.6cm squeeze-bore incendiary-shrapnel shell and 12.8/7.3cm Peenemünder Pfeilgeschosse. Velocities of up to 1530mps(5020fps) were forecast for some of these projectiles.

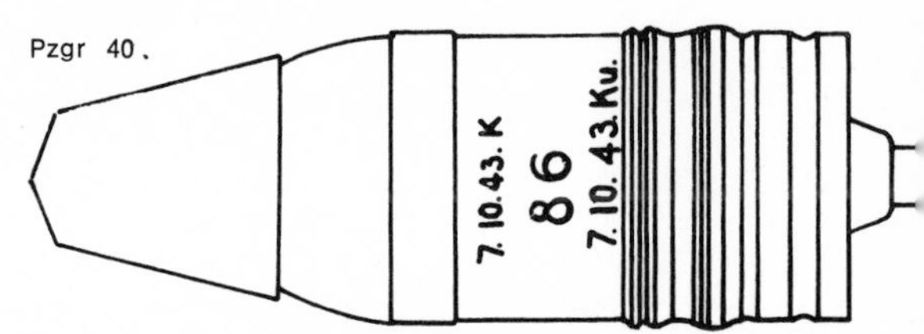

The 12.8cm Flak 40 in action.

Super-Heavy Flak Weapons

When the Luftwaffe initiated the demand for the 12.8cm gun in 1936, they also issued a specification for a 15cm super-heavy gun and a contract was given to Krupp, whose weapon was known as the Gerät 50. Shortly afterwards Rheinmetall-Borsig was also given a contract for a weapon to be known as the Gerät 55.

The Rheinmetall gun was ready first, in May of 1938, little more than an enlarged 12.8cm with the addition of an electric hoist to feed ammunition to the loading tray. The equipment was transported in three loads—the gun, the mounting and the platform—on three transporters.

The Krupp design appeared in September 1938, its slower development owing to two innovations. Firstly, in an attempt to alleviate the ever-present problem of wear, a new form of rifling was introduced in which the depth of the rifling groove gradually decreased towards the muzzle; this was to be fired together with a special shell having a centering band at the shoulder. Secondly, to speed up loading, Krupp had developed a ten-round magazine that fitted behind the gun. This was hand-loaded prior to an engagement and then fired semi-automatically. The Gerät 50 travelled in four loads—the gun, the cradle and the top carriage, the pedestal, and the platform—and, by way of a bonus, Krupp had also designed a railway mounting that could take either the Gerät 50 or the Gerät 55.

Trials of both weapons soon showed some fundamental defects. Most important was the fact that the performance was no better than that of the 12.8cm gun, and the multi-part transportation was undesirable. A redesign accordingly began to lengthen the barrels, to increase the propelling charge, and to try and develop one-load transportation using two six-wheel limbers (a similar solution to that used for the 12.8cm gun). But after about a year of work it became obvious that there was no hope of improving the performance of either 15cm gun to any useful degree and so, in January 1940, the whole project was abandoned.

While discarding the Gerät 50 and the Gerät 55, the Luftwaffe produced a fresh specification that called for a 15cm gun to fire a 42kg(92lb) shell at 960mps(3150fps), to use a muzzle brake,

The 15cm Flak Gerät 60F, basically the same as the 50 but more cumbersome, since it was to be statically sited.

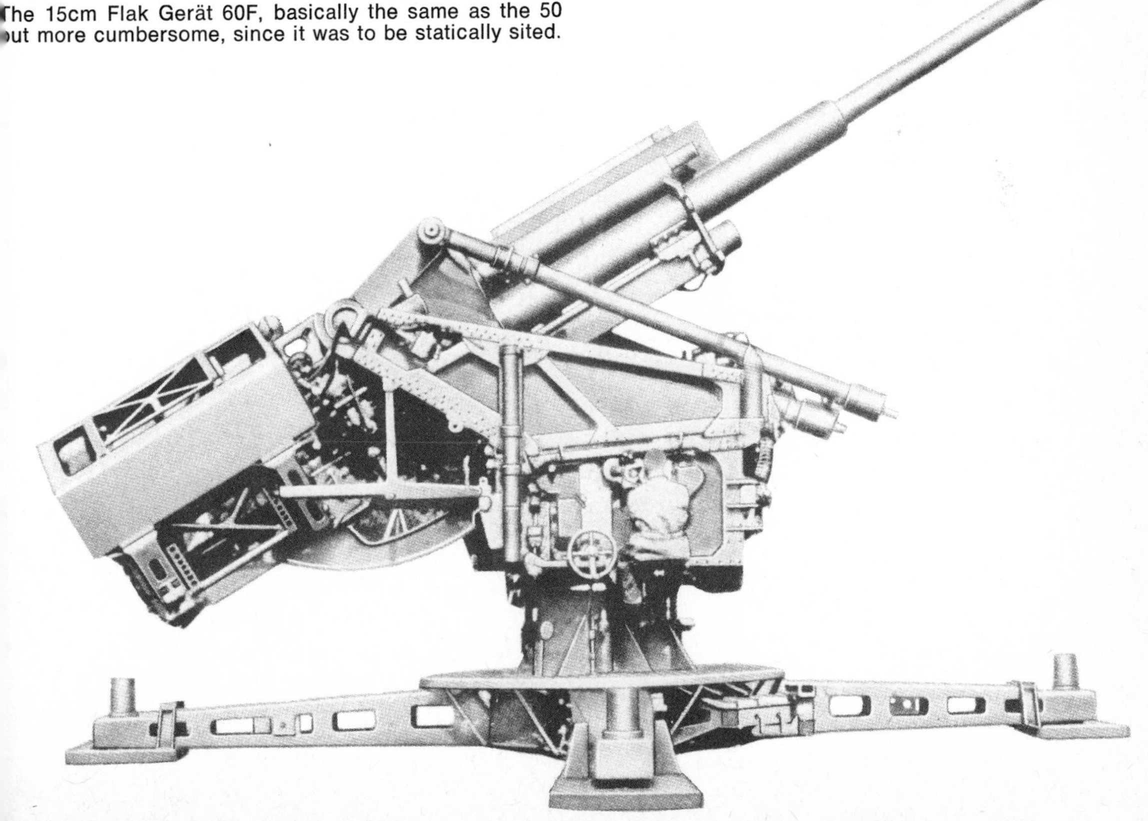

and to be transportable in one load. The contracts duly went to Krupp and Rheinmetall, the new project being known as Gerät 60 and Gerät 65 respectively. By early 1942 the first gun was ready for proof firing. It used a five-section barrel of similar construction to those of the 8.8 and 10.5cm guns, and encountered trouble when the steel cartridge cases failed to eject. This, it was hoped, could be cured by a rolled-steel cartridge case, but as an insurance a design of monobloc barrel was begun. In October 1942 the production of heavy mobile guns was terminated to enable the production capacity to be devoted to more static equipments. Krupp and Rheinmetall, informed of this decision, were asked if they could wring any more performance out of their designs by static-mounting them. Although it meant starting all over again, an increase in velocity to 1200mps (3925fps) was forecast; this was accepted and the projects were renamed Gerät 60F and Gerät 65F —F for *fest* or static. It was hoped that prototypes would be ready by mid-1944 and that the guns would be in service by the Spring of 1945.

Fate, however, was against the 15cm guns. In September 1943, just as Krupp was about to start proof firings with a new barrel, the Luftwaffe cancelled all work on anti-aircraft guns above 12.8cm calibre so that more effort and production capacity could be devoted to aircraft and missile designs. As a sop, the gunmakers were allowed to continue developing barrels and ammunition as research projects into high-velocity firing, since this would possibly be helpful in other areas; apart from this the 15cm anti-aircraft gun had come to the end of the line.

These, though, were not the biggest guns pro jected. In the summer of 1941 the Luftwaffe while contemplating the performance of the 15cm gun, decided to reach further and drew u specifications for both 21cm and 24cm weapons The 21cm gun was to fire a 123kg(270lb) shell a 1040mps(3410fps) to a ceiling of 18000m(59000ft) and was to do this at a rate of ten rounds minute. The 24cm gun was to fire a 198kg(435lb shell at 1000mps(3280fps) to the same altitude a eight rounds a minute. In the light of contem porary ballistic development one can only con clude that these were pious hopes. In the cours of discussions on these projects, however, th Luftwaffe discovered that the navy was als conferring with the gunmakers in the hope o obtaining two superheavy anti-aircraft guns fo dockyard defence. Their specifications called fo a 20.3cm gun firing a 110kg(242lb) shell a 1000mps(3280fps) to 16700(55000ft), and a 24cm gun firing a 177kg(390lb) shell at 965mp (3165fps) to the same altitude. These guns wer to be in twin turret-mounts to produce rates o fire of 20 and 16 rounds per minute respectively

Unusually, for the German war effort wa generally a tale of conflicting requirements fight ing for priorities, the armament ministry steppe in and persuaded the Luftwaffe and the navy tha they might stand a better chance of getting a gun if they settled on a common specification. Such a radical suggestion took some time to sink in, but

Front view of the 15cm Gerät 60F.

ventually—in the late summer of 1942—it was greed to produce a weapon based on the uftwaffe 24cm gun in the navy's 24cm twin urret. Krupp and Rheinmetall-Borsig received ontracts, the projects being named Gerät 80 and Gerät 85 respectively. It appears that Rheinmetall vere reluctant to take the idea seriously, since the nly designs that ever appeared were those of Krupp, and even these got little further than rtist's impressions and general arrangement rawings. Within a few months further work was uspended until the 15cm Gerät 60F and 65F projects showed some results, since it was thought that these might give useful information. The 1943 edict finally put an end to the 24cm project, as it did to the 15cm guns.

It is doubtful whether these massive weapons would have been cost-effective, to use the modern phrase. The 12.8cm Flak gun had a barrel life of 700 rounds, and it was not particularly highly stressed; the British 3.7in Mark 6, more powerful, had a life of 500 rounds. It is thus a reasonable supposition that had the 24cm gun been built, and achieved the ballistics demanded by the

he 15cm Flak Gerät 55, showing the rear-mounted nagazine.

services, the barrel life would have been in the region of 200–300 rounds. This amount of ammunition could easily have been fired in a single night of heavy air-raids, and hence the resupply problem with this gun would not have been ammunition: it would have been new gun-barrels—daily.

One cannot leave the German anti-aircraft gun scene without a passing glance at the most incredible project of all—the Electric Gun *(Electricitäts Gewehr).* The idea of projecting a missile by electricity was nothing new for, as soon as the solenoid had been invented, patents had appeared adapting it to missile-throwing; the available power, however, was far too small to allow a practical weapon to be built. The first serious move was by a Frenchman, Fauchon-Villeplé, who developed a system using two bus-bars and a winged projectile connecting them—the forerunner of what is today known as the linear motor. In 1918 he attempted to interest the French War Office in his ideas and actually assembled a working model, but the war ended before anything more could be done.

As far as the Third Reich was concerned the electric gun was first put forward by an electrical engineer named Otto Muck, a consultant to Siemens, who wrote a paper outlining a coil-type gun and forwarded it in May 1943 to Reichminister Speer. His idea was on the grand scale; a gun with a 'barrel' 100m(328ft) long was to be installed in a shaft sunk in the ground on the edge of the Lille coalfield and pointed at London. This was supposed to hurl a 15cm fin-stabilised shell weighing 200kg(450lb) at a velocity of 1640mps(5260fps) to a range of 250km(155miles), thus effectively bombarding Greater London. The gun's location was vital to the whole scheme, since Muck envisaged firing 500000 shells a month; to develop the necessary electrical power 54000 tons of coal would be needed each month. The power demand was estimated at 100000kW.

It is of no value to pursue Muck's idea through the volume of paperwork that attached itself to it during the time in which the concept shuffled around various ministries. It was shown by a number of eminent scholars that some of Muck basic assumptions were invalid, and that the whol thing—even if it *was* possible—would involv collossal expense. However, independently of Muc (whose report had been graded top secret and file away) another company, the *Gesellschaft fi Gerätbau* had taken an interest and had begun b examining Fauchon-Villeplé's work. By Octobe of 1944 sufficient had been done to enable publication of the 'Preliminary Report on the Electri Gun', promising an anti-aircraft weapon with muzzle velocity of 2000mps(6560fps) and a rate c fire of 6000rpm from a multi-barrel installatio This was studied by the Luftwaffe authorities, wh were sufficiently impressed to issue a contract fo the development of a 4cm prototype. The projectile was intended to contain 500gm(1.10lb) c explosive, and six-gun batteries (each firing 1 rounds per barrel per minute) were to b connected to a common power supply. Th apparatus was to be built on a 12.8cm Flak 4 mounting.

The full treatment of the Hänsler Electric Gu (named after its proposer) ran to several pages o abstruse mathematics, but the conclusion reache was that each gun needed a power of 3900kW Since this was readily available from standar generators all seemed well, and work began i February 1945. But before very much could b done the war ended, and the electric gun ende with it.

As might be supposed, such a revolutionar idea took the fancy of the Allied investigators i their postwar examination of German munition developments, and the whole project was examine very closely—particularly in Britain where anti aircraft performance was still under investigation After long and exhaustive studies, the Britis scientists finally reported in 1947 that (attractiv as the idea sounded) it was not practical. It *coul* be made to work, but the power required was s great that the six-gun battery would have neede its own power station to be able to operate! S far as is known, there has been no proposal sinc then to revive the electric gun.

Drawings of proposed projectiles for the Hänsler Electric 4cm Flak gun.

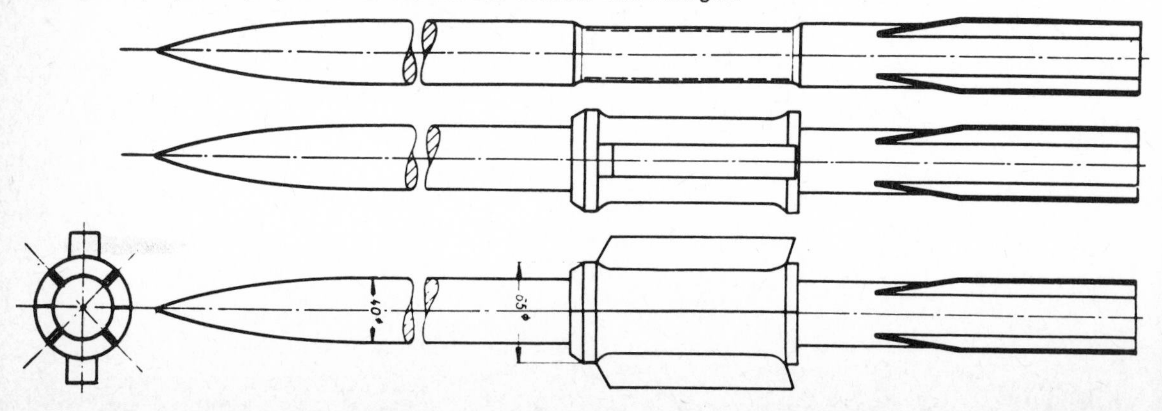

ANTI-TANK ARTILLERY

German anti-tank artillery followed much the same pattern of improvement as its British and American equivalents, but did so that much quicker and consequently led the field for most of the war years. The story of tank and anti-tank has always been one of leapfrog activity between the gun and the enemy tank, with the ammunition designers being periodically called on either to extend the life of an old weapon or to wring more performance out of a new one.

All the combatants in the 1939–45 war started on the same level. The 1930s concept of an anti-tank gun was a light weapon that could be manhandled and concealed easily and, in view of the armour thickness of contemporary tanks, the common calibre was in the region of 37–40mm (1.46–1.57in), firing a projectile of 0.68–0.91kg (1.50–2.00lb). These weapons were generally allotted to the infantry, although Britain elected to man hers with artillerymen, and were supported by anti-tank rifles—shoulder-fired weapons of (at the time they were introduced) high power and adequate performance.

The rapid improvements in tank armour and mobility soon led the German Army to contemplate still heavier weapons: in 1938 development contracts were issued for a 5cm gun, followed in 1939 by a specification for a 7.5cm gun. In similar fashion Britain planned a 5.7cm gun in 1938 but, since production capacity was not available, it had to wait; the delay was to cost her dearly in the Desert campaign.

At the same time, plans for coned and squeeze bore guns were devised and the subsequent appearance of these weapons introduced to the field the efforts of the ammunition designers. Prior to this the standard German anti-tank projectile had been the armour-piercing shell, but the successful development of flanged tungsten-cored shot for the coned bore guns paved the way for work on arrowhead and discarding sabot projectiles: subjects which have already been discussed in detail and which need not be repeated here.

The progress of the war soon showed that, on occasion, any and every gun might be called upon to fight tanks, and so almost every gun in the German armoury was provided with some sort of anti-tank projectile. These were originally piercing shells, but the issue was soon supplemented by hollow charge projectiles; even some genuine anti-tank guns were provided with hollow charge shells in addition to their standard high-velocity ammunition.

Another feature of German anti-tank gun development paralleled by other nations—notably Britain—was the close relationship between the anti-tank gun and the contemporary tank armament. In many cases the design and development of the two were inseparable (though the tank gun often appeared in different barrel lengths, with different breech arrangements or even different chamber dimensions); the same range of projectiles was generally used in both.

The anti-tank gun's size increase was proportional to that of the tank it had to defeat. The British army entered the war with their 40mm 2pdr and finished with a 76.2mm 17pdr (a 94mm 32pdr was also in the final development stages). The German Army, in similar fashion, began with a 37mm gun and ended with a 12.8cm weapon about to enter production. But with such massive weapons the practical limits of manoeuvrability, handiness and concealable bulk had been reached and the designers were instead turning to other systems to restore lightness and mobility to the weapon without impairing its ability to destroy tanks. Germany, as discussed elsewhere, had developed the recoilless gun and it was to this class of weapon that Britain turned in 1944 to develop a lighter weapon, taking advantage of new ideas in explosive anti-tank ammunition. The German Army, though, was dissatisfied with the recoilless guns developed for its use, since they were short-barrelled and relatively inaccurate at short ranges—and, an important item in the latter months of the war, such guns consumed disproportionate amounts of propellant. All this led to the development of an anti-tank gun using the high-low pressure system of ballistics, and a remarkably cheap, simple and efficient weapon ensued.

Although they do not fall within the scope of this book, it must also be remembered that Germany was prominent in the development of a variety of lightweight recoilless guns and rocket launchers capable of being operated by one or two men. The various Panzerfaust models, Püppchen, Hammer, Ofenrohr and a wide variety of rifle grenades were extremely effective. They replaced the outmoded anti-tank rifles as the soldiers' personal anti-tank defence in cases where the enemy tanks evaded the 'proper' anti-tank guns. This class of weapon has been considerably researched and developed since the war, to the point where the heavy anti-tank gun has lost its former importance and more reliance is placed on simple but deadly devices. 1944 foresaw another postwar development when Dr Kramer proposed his *Rotkappchen* (or X-7), a wire-guided winged rocket missile with a hollow charge head for anti-tank use. Another similar weapon, *Steinbock*, used infra-red homing and another, *Pfeifenkopf*, used television guidance. All of these were in the test stage by late 1944: between them and the high-powered anti-tank guns, the tank/gun pendulum would have made a very decisive swing during the summer of 1945 had the war not ended when it did.

2·8cm schwere Panzerbüchse 41

2·8cm s PzB 41

This weapon, although called a schwere Panzerbüchse (heavy anti-tank rifle), was a gun in everything but calibre. It was the first weapon based on the Gerlich principle of a tapering bore to reach the battlefield, and although the projectile was tiny its penetration and velocity certainly vindicated Gerlich's theories. It has been said that this was the first German 'secret weapon' to be revealed and there is some justification for this claim, because its existence was unknown to the allies until a specimen was captured in the Western Desert in the late summer of 1941. Only a few months before, one British authority—confronted with a suggestion for a squeeze bore weapon—admitted that such things had been discussed, that one or two people were known to have been experimenting with them before the war, but that 'neither weapon nor ammunition are within measurable distance of employment in the war'.

The gun was conventional enough in appearance, with a simple muzzle brake and a normal sliding-block breech, but the bore tapered from 28mm(1.10in) at the commencement of rifling to 20mm(0.79in) at the muzzle. The carriage was an equally simple split-trail unit, with two wheels suspended from a transverse leaf spring and a small shield. Because neither elevating nor traversing gear was fitted, the laying was done by one man sitting behind the sights and grasping a machine-gun type of spade grip to direct the gun. A hydropneumatic recoil system was carried in the cradle.

A lightweight carriage was produced for use by airborne troops (Ausführung für Fallschirmjäger); this was a simple pole trail of tubular steel running on two small aircraft-type wheels, suspended from rubber mounted Dubonnet-type suspension arms. The light version had no shield.

The 2.8cm s PzB 41. Notice the double shield and the small auxiliary shield in front of the gun sight.

Data (standard version)
Calibre: 28mm/1.10in, tapering to 20mm/0.79in.
Length of gun: 1714mm/67.48in.
Length of bore: 1358mm/53.46in.
Rifling: 12 grooves, right-hand increasing twist.
Breech mechanism: horizontal sliding block, percussion fired.
Traverse: 90° at zero elevation, 30° at 45° elevation.
Elevation: −5° to +45°.
Weight in action: 229kg/505lb.
Airborne version as above except
Weight in action: 118kg/260lb.
Performance
Firing standard projectile weighing 131gm (4.62oz).
Muzzle velocity: 1400mps/4593fps.
Penetration at 100m: 0° 94mm/3.70in, 30° 69mm/2.72in.
Penetration at 500m: 0° 66mm/2.60in, 30° 52mm/2.05in.

Ammunition
Fixed rounds; cartridge case length 188mm(7.40in).
2.8cm Pzgr Patr 41: projectile weight 131gm (4.62oz), round weight 630gm (22.22oz/1.39lb). This was the standard anti-tank projectile and consisted of a tungsten core inside a lead sleeve carried in a body made of a soft iron alloy with a magnesium-alloy nose cap; this gave a bright flash on impact with a hard target, thus indicating the point of strike to the gunner. The body was flanged to fit the 2.8cm calibre and the front flange was pierced with five holes to allow the escape of between-flange air during the squeezing action. The propelling charge was 152gm(5.36oz) of Nz P P.
2.8cm Sprgr Patr 41: fuzed AZ 5072, projectile weight 85gm(3.00oz), complete round weight 577gm(20.35oz/1.27lb).
This was a high explosive shell round. The projectile was machined from a steel bar to give a tubular body with sloping flanges, the front flange being pierced. The bursting charge was a pellet of PETN/wax weighing 5gm(0.18oz/77.1gr) and the shell was fitted wih a percussion fuze. The propelling charge was 150gm(5.29oz) of Nz R P. The ballistics of this round were the same as those of the piercing projectile, the maximum engagement range still being 800m(875yd).

A captured 2.8cm PzB 41.

'he 2.8cm schwere Panzerbuchse 41, taper-bore gun.

'ase Identification Number

'345; this was actually the case manufacturer's ode number, but since it was on this case and ever found on artillery-type cases it serves as an identification number.

Primer

The percussion primer C/13nA St was standard.

3·7cm Panzerabwehrkanone 36

3·7cm Pak 36

'his was the standard German anti-tank gun at he outbreak of war. It was developed by Rhein-netall in 1933 and was first issued in 1936. Small umbers were sent to Spain for field trials in the 'ivil War (1936–9), and it was also sold to Soviet Russia in some quantity until 1940. The PAK 36 vas a sound design that was extensively copied by ther nations, and while its penetrative perform-nce was quickly found a little disappointing its nobility more than compensated for any defect. n later years, when it was outmatched by newer anks, the PAK 36's useful life was extended by he provision of an unusual spigot bomb; over 0000 guns had been issued by the middle of 1941, nd so it was essential to find a way of utilising hem.

The gun itself was of conventional type and was arried on a two-wheel split-trail carriage of ubular construction with a small sharply-sloped hield. A hydrospring recoil system was carried n the cradle and the wheels were suspended by oil springs.

Data

'alibre: 37mm/1.46in.
Length of gun: 1665mm/65.55in.
Length of bore: 1567mm/61.69in.
Rifling: 16 grooves, right-hand increasing twist, /44 to 1/33.
Breech mechanism: horizontal sliding block, percussion fired.
Traverse: 60°.
Elevation: −5° to +25°.
Weight in action: 432kg/953lb.

Performance

Firing standard piercing projectile weighing 0.68kg (1.50lb).
Muzzle velocity: 762mps/2500fps.
Penetration at 100m: 0° 65mm/2.56in, 30° 50mm/1.97in.
Penetration at 500m: 0° 48mm/1.89in, 30° 36mm/1.42in.
Firing tungsten-cored projectile weighing 0.35kg (0.78lb/12.49oz).
Muzzle velocity: 1030mps/3379fps
Penetration at 100m: 0° 79mm/3.11in, 30° 68mm/2.68in.
Penetration at 500m: 0° 50mm/1.97in, 30° 40mm/1.57in.

Ammunition

Fixed rounds; cartridge case length 249mm(9.80in).
3.7cm PAK Pzgr: fuzed Bd Z 5103, projectile weight 0.68kg(1.50lb), complete round weight 1.32kg(2.91lb).
This was the standard piercing-shell round introduced with the weapon. The shell was uncapped

Below left: A PAK 36 on prewar manouevres, with rudimentary camouflage. *Above:* A PAK 36 in action

Below: 3.7cm PAK 36. *Above right:* A PAK 36 loaded with the 3.7cm Steilgranate stick bomb

A PAK 36 captured by the British Army near Abbeville in 1940.

and was fitted with a single copper driving band. The explosive filling was 13gm(0.46oz) of PETN/wax. The base fuze carried a tracer at its rear. The propelling charge was 175gm(6.17oz) of Digl R P.

3.7cm PAK Pzgr 40: projectile weight 0.35kg (0.78lb/12.50oz), complete round weight 0.97kg (2.14lb).

This was a tungsten-cored composite rigid projectile of the 'arrowhead' type. It resembled a taper-bore projectile in having a sub-calibre body supported on skirts, but the skirts did not collapse and this particular type of projectile could be easily distinguished by the absence of holes in the front flange. It consisted of a tungsten core supported in a two-piece body, the rear portion of which was made of steel and the nose section of magnesium alloy. A tracer cavity was formed in the rear section. The propelling charge was 150gm(5.29oz) of Ngl R P.

3.7cm Sprgr Patr: fuzed AZ 39, projectile weight 0.61kg(1.35lb), complete round weight 0.97kg (2.14lb).

This was the standard high explosive round, provided for use against personnel and light vehicles. The shell carried a large tracer element, occupying all the space behind the driving band. The explosive filling was a 25gm(0.88oz) pressed-pellet of TNT. The propellant charge was 164gm(5.78oz) of Digl R P.

3.7cm Stielgranate 41 (also known as 3.7cm Aufsteck Geschoss): fuzed AZ5075 and Bd Z 5130, projectile weigh 8.60kg(18.96lb).

This oddity was an attempt to extend the useful life of the weapon by providing it with a hollow charge projectile. Since a 3.7cm diameter hollow charge would have been useless, an over-calibre head was developed—carried on a long finned tail boom. Inside this perforated tail was a solid rod that slipped into the muzzle of the gun, allowing the tail unit to pass over the outer surface of the barrel. A separate-loading cartridge was used to fire the bomb. The tail unit had six fins, and the central rod had three gas-check cannelures at its end in order both to extract the maximum performance from the propellant gases and to prevent too much blow-by. The hollow charge head had a conical liner, behind which was a shaped charge of 2.42kg(5.34lb) of cyclonite/TNT and a base fuze. A nose fuze was also fitted, one of the few cases on record where a double fuzing system was used with a hollow charge. The performance

The lightness of the PAK 36 made it an early candidate for self-propelled mountings. This is the SdKfz 251/10.

of this unit was quite formidable for its day; it could penetrate 180mm(7.09in) of plate at any range, though its low muzzle velocity—110mps (361fps)—restricted its use to ranges of 300m (328yd) or less in combat. Its absolute maximum range was about 800m(875yd). A special propelling charge was contained in the normal case, closed at the mouth by a cork plug and consistin of 217gm(7.65oz) of Ngl R P with the customar primer.

Primer
The percussion primer C/13nA was standard.
Case Identification Number: 6331.

4·2cm Panzerjägerkanone 41

4·2cm PJK 41 or Pak 41

This was the second taper-bore weapon to be used, entering service shortly after the 2.8cm PzB 41. Although nominally 4.2cm calibre, the actual calibre was 4.06cm(1.60in) at the commencement of the rifling—tapering evenly to 2.94cm(1.16in) at the muzzle.

The gun was mounted on the 3.7cm PAK 36 carriage; the two weapons are difficult to distinguish at a distance, since they are outwardly very similar. The breech mechanisms, although of similar pattern, have slight differences in detail. The only major changes to the carriage were the replacement of the coil spring suspension by a laminated torsion bar and the fitting of a double-skin shield.

Owing to shortages of manganese (used in some alloy carriage components) and tungsten (for the ammunition), production of this weapon terminated in the summer of 1942.

Data
Calibre: 40.6mm(1.60in) tapering to 29.4mm (1.16in).
Length of gun: 2350mm/92.52in.
Length of bore: 2114mm/83.23in.
Rifling: 12 grooves, right-hand increasing twist.
Breech mechanism: horizontal sliding block, pe cussion fired.
Traverse: 60°.
Elevation: −8° to +25°.
Weight in action: 642kg/1416lb.

Performance
Firing standard piercing projectile weighin 336gm(11.85oz).
Muzzle velocity: 1265mps(4150fps).
Penetration at 100m: 0° 120mm/4.73in, 30 90mm/3.54in.
Penetration at 500m: 0° 87mm/3.43in, 30 72mm/2.83in.
Penetration at 1000m: 0° 60mm/2.36in, 30 53mm/2.09in.
Maximum engagement range: 1000m/1094yd.

Ammunition
Fixed rounds; cartridge case length 348mm (13.70in).
4.2cm Pzgr Patr 41: projectile weight 336gr

he 4.2cm PAK 41, the second taper-bore gun to enter service. It can be distinguished from the 3.7cm PAK by its ›nger barrel.

(11.85oz), complete round weight 1.52kg(3.35lb) 'his was the standard tungsten-cored projectile. t resembled that of the 2.8cm s Pz B 41 in being anged, the front having ten air expulsion holes. 'he cap was of magnesium alloy that provided a ash on impact. The propelling charge was 435gm 15.34oz) of Gudol R P.

.2cm Sprgr Patr 41: fuzed AZ 5072, projectile 'eight 280gm(9.87oz), complete round weight .34kg(2.95lb).

'his was the high-explosive shell round—a skirted rojectile similar to that used in the 2.8cm weapon. The front flange was pierced with only four holes and the propelling charge was 310gm (10.93oz) of Digl R P. (It should be noted that with this and the 2.8cm guns the ammunition was loaded to give a specific velocity, and thus the actual charge weight varied from batch to batch of propellant.)

Primer

The percussion primer C/13nA was standard.

Case Identification Number: 6329.

he 4.2cm PAK 41 in firing position.

The breech of the 4.2cm PAK 41. (From the German handbook: d1 is the firing push, and b31 the re-cocking handle for use in cases of misfire.)

5cm Panzerabwehrkanone 38

5cm Pak 38

The 5cm PAK 38 was the first gun to lift the anti-tank gun out of the tiny two-man class into the realm of full-sized artillery. Although developed by Rheinmetall-Borsig from 1938, the gun was not available for the campaigns of 1940 but was issued later in that year to replace the 3.7cm PAK 36. Heavier weapons eventually supplanted the 5cm gun, but it was never completely replaced and large numbers remained in service throughout the war. In postwar years several were used by the Bulgarian Army.

The gun itself was of conventional pattern, fitted with a muzzlebrake and a semi-automatic breech. The carriage was of the split-trail type with tubular legs and solid-tyred disc wheels. Torsion bars were used in the suspension and a double-skin shield was fitted.

The weapon was also used by the Luftwaffe as a stop-gap anti-aircraft gun under the nomenclature of 5cm Flak 214.

Data
Calibre: 50mm/1.97in.
Length of gun: 3187mm/125.47in/10.46ft.
Length of bore: 2824mm/111.18in.
Rifling: 20 grooves, right-hand increasing twist 1/36 to 1/32.
Breech mechanism: horizontal semi-automati sliding block, percussion fired.
Traverse: 65°.
Elevation: −8° to +27°.
Weight in action: 986kg/2174lb.

Performance
Firing standard piercing shell weighing 2.25k (4.96lb).
Muzzle velocity: 823mps/2700fps.
Penetration at 250m: 0° 88mm/3.46in, 30° 67mm 2.64in.
Penetration at 500m: 0° 78mm/3.07in, 30° 61mm 2.40in.
Penetration at 1000m: 0° 61mm/2.40in, 30 50mm/1.97in.
Firing tungsten-cored projectile weighing 0.85k (1.87lb).
Muzzle velocity: 1198mps/3931fps.
Penetration at 250m: 0° 141mm/5.55in, 30 109mm/4.29in.
Penetration at 500m: 0° 120mm/4.72in, 30 86mm/3.39in.

A captured 5cm PAK 38 on display at Aberdeen Proving Ground Museum, USA.

5cm PAK in action at Stalingrad.

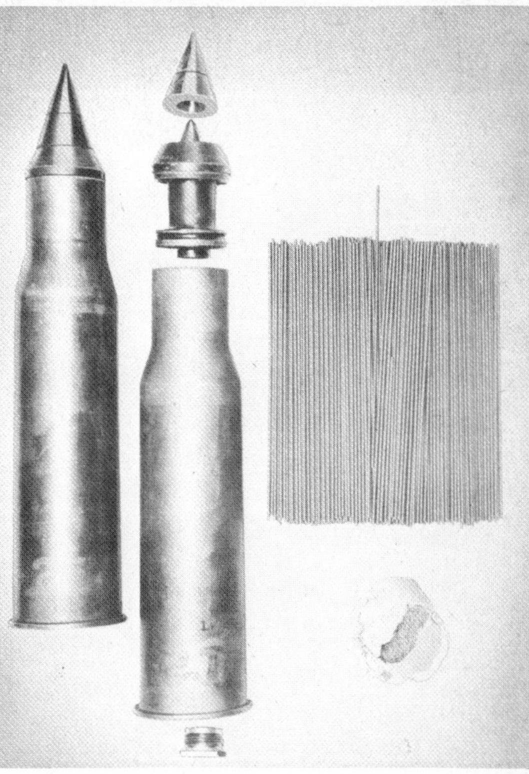

A round of Pzgr 40 Arrowhead ammunition for the 5cm PAK 38, dismantled to show the various components.

elow: A 5cm PAK being ferried across a Russian river. The towing vehicle is a captured Russian T-27.

Penetration at 1000m: 0° 84mm/3.31in, 30° 55mm/2.17in.
Firing high explosive shell weighing 1.96kg (4.32lb).
Muzzle velocity: 550mps/1805fps.
Maximum range: 2650m/2898yd.

Ammunition
Fixed rounds; cartridge case length 419mm (16.50in).
5cm Pzgr Patr 38: fuzed Bd Z 5103, projectile weight 2.05kg(4.52lb), complete round weight 4.13kg(9.11lb).
The original piercing projectile for the gun, this was a plain-steel uncapped shell with a bursting charge of 25gm(0.88oz) of PETN/wax and a base fuze. A single iron driving band was fitted and the fuze carried a tracer element. The propelling charge was 882gm(31.10oz/1.94lb) of Digl R P

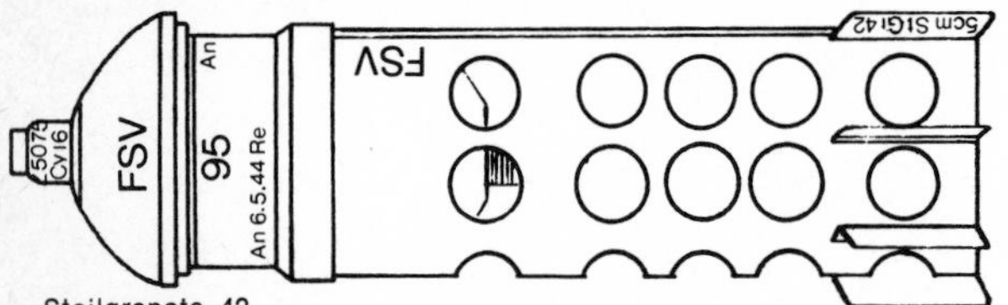

Steilgranate 42.

5cm Pzgr Patr 38 umg: fuzed BdZ 5103.
This round was basically similar to the previou one but with the addition of a penetrating ca to the shell to improve its performance agains face-hardened armour. The filling and fuzing wer the same.
5cm PAK 38 Pzgr 40: projectile weight 0.85k (1.87lb), complete round weight 2.73kg(6.02lb)
This was the tungsten-cored arrowhead sho similar to that produced for the 3.7cm gun; th propelling charge was 688gm(24.26oz/1.52lb) o Digl R P.
5cm Sprgr Patr PAK 38: fuzed AZ 39, projecti weight 1.78kg(3.92lb), complete round weigh 3.28kg(7.23lb).
This was the standard high explosive shell fo anti-personnel use. It contained a filling of 165gn (5.82oz) of pressed TNT, with a smoke-box fitte below the fuze, and the driving band was of sof iron. The propelling charge was 280gm(9.88oz) o Gudol R P.
5cm Steilgranate 42: fuzed AZ 5075, projectil weight 8.20kg(18.08lb).
This was another hollow charge stick bomb similar to that developed for the 3.7cm gun. I the 5cm version the tail unit was the sam

Front view of a 5cm PAK 38, showing the auxiliary shield lowered.

A 5cm PAK in action in the early stages of the Russian campaign.

Breech end of the 5cm PAK 38.

Barrel, locking bus and breech ring c the 5cm PAK 3

The 5cm PAK 38 in the travelling position.

liameter as the head in order to leave sufficient space around the muzzle stick for the tail to pass over the gun's muzzle brake. The warhead contained 2.33kg(5.14lb) of cyclonite/TNT and the special cartridge carried a charge of 770gm (27.15oz/1.70lb) of Ngl R P. It was capable of penetrating 180mm(7.09in) of plate and the recommended maximum engagement range was 150m(165yd).

Primer

The percussion primer C/13nA was standard.

Case Identification Number: 6360.

7·5cm Panzerabwehrkanone 40

7·5cm Pak 40 (Hünengrab)

In 1939, anticipating the inevitable increase in tank armour, the army had placed contracts with Krupp and Rheinmetall-Borsig to develop a 7.5cm anti-tank gun. The priority accorded these contracts appears to have been low at first, but the invasion of Russia in 1941 and the appearance of Russian heavy tanks soon showed that the 5cm PAK was operating at the limit of its performance, and so the 7.5cm designs' progress was accelerated; the first guns were issued in late November 1941.

The PAK 40 was the Rheinmetall-Borsig model and was virtually an enlarged 5cm PAK 38, using a similar split-trail carriage and a double-skinned shield. It became the standard anti-tank gun, remaining in service for the remainder of the war; and in postwar days it could be found on the inventories of many European armies—including those of Albania, Bulgaria, Czechoslovakia, Hungary and Rumania. The PAK 40 was a powerful and effective anti-tank gun, but its weight was rather high. This led to instances in Russia where guns had to be abandoned because their crews could not manhandle them in bad ground conditions caused by the winters' snow and the springs' thaw, and because the towing tractors were too conspicuous and unarmoured. A German report of January 1944 stated that, owing to this, a change of position in daylight was almost impossible.

The PAK 40 was incorporated in some formations as a divisional artillery weapon, and when so employed was redesignated 7.5cm FK 40.

Data

Calibre: 75mm/2.95in.
Length of gun: 3702mm/145.75in/12.15ft.
Length of bore: 3201mm/126.02in/10.50ft.
Rifling: 32 grooves, right-hand increasing twist, 1/24 to 1/18.
Breech mechanism: horizontal semi-automatic sliding block, percussion fired.
Traverse: 65°.
Elevation: −5° to +22°.
Weight in action: 1425kg/3142lb.

Performance

Firing standard piercing shell weighing 6.80kg (14.99lb).
Muzzle velocity: 792mps/2600fps.
Penetration at 100m: 0° 148mm/5.83in, 30° 120mm/4.72in.
Penetration at 500m: 0° 132mm/5.20in, 30° 104mm/4.09in.
Penetration at 1000m: 0° 116mm/4.57in, 30° 89mm/3.50in.
Penetration at 1500m: 0° 102mm/4.02in, 30° 76mm/2.99in.
Maximum engagement range: 1800m/1968yd.
Firing tungsten-cored projectile weighing 3.18kg (7.01lb).
Muzzle velocity: 990mps/3250fps.
Penetration at 100m: 0° 175mm/6.89in, 30° 135mm/5.31in.
Penetration at 500m: 0° 154mm/6.06in, 30°

Pzgr 39

92 202 CWgZ 43

Side view of the 7.5cm PAK 40.

Rear of a 7.5cm PAK 40 captured in Tunisia.

115mm/4.53in.
Penetration at 1000m: 0° 133mm/5.24in, 30° 96mm/3.78in.
Penetration at 1500m: 0° 115mm/4.53in, 30° 80mm/3.15in.
Maximum engagement range: 1800m/1968yd.
Firing standard high explosive shell weighing 5.80kg(12.79lb).
Muzzle velocity: 548mps/1798fps.
Maximum range: 7680m/8399yd.

Ammunition
Fixed rounds; cartridge case length 715mm (28.15in).
7.5cm Pzgr Patr 39: fuzed Bd Z 5103, projectile weight 6.80kg(14.99lb), complete round weight 12.00kg(26.46lb).
This was a conventional piercing shell with ballistic and penetrating caps, a 16gm(0.56oz) charge of cyclonite/wax, and a base fuze with an integral trace. A bimetallic driving band was originally fitted, but later production used soft iron. The propelling charge was 2.75kg(6.06lb) of Digl R P.
7.5cm Pzgr Patr 40: projectile weight 3.20kg (7.04lb), complete round weight 9.55kg(21.09lb).
This, the tungsten-cored shot, differed considerably from the Pzgr 40 designs that had gone before. Instead of arrowhead-shot type it was externally the same shape as a standard steel-capped shell, the tungsten core being carried in a full-calibre body made of plastic and steel. A soft-iron driving band was fitted, and there was a tracer at the rear. The only external distinction was a white tip to the ballistic cap and the white stencilling PZGR *40* on the base of the cartridge case. The propelling charge was 3.80kg(8.38lb) of Gudol R P. Few of these rounds survived the war, since the 1942 ban on tungsten put an end to their production.
7.5cm Sprgr Patr 34: fuzed Kl AZ 23, projectile

A 7.5cm PAK 40 on show at Aberdeen Proving Ground.

weight 5.80kg(12.79lb), complete round weight 9.15kg(20.18lb).
This was the standard high explosive shell, of conventional design, filled with a bursting charge of 640gm(22.57oz/1.41lb) of amatol. The propelling charge was 780gm(27.51oz/1.72lb) of Gudol R P.
7.5cm Patr H1/B: fuzed AZ 38, projectile weight 4.65kg(10.25lb), complete round weight 8.00kg (17.64lb).
This hollow charge shell was issued for a short time after the discontinuance of the Pzgr 40 projectile, but its ballistics were not well suited to the weapon and its low muzzle velocity (450mps/1476fps) made accurate shooting at moving targets very difficult. It was a normal 'B' type hollow charge shell with a conical liner and a central tube leading to an exploder at the rear. A single FES driving band was fitted. The propelling charge was 900gm(31.74oz/1.98lb) of Gudol R P.
7.5cm Pzgr PAK Patr TS 42: projectile weight 2.74kg(6.04lb).
In an endeavour to improve the PAK 40's anti-tank performance, this discarding sabot projectile was developed. It was a 'pot' sabot in which the pot was made of aluminium and was retained about the subprojectile by two spring-steel rings. These allowed the sections of the pot to spread under centrifugal force after leaving the muzzle, whereupon air resistance pulled the pot away and allowed the 6cm calibre sub-projectile to depart. The subprojectile was a steel shot of conventional type with a long ballistic cap of light alloy. No details of its performance are known, but with a suitable charge it should have achieved a velocity in excess of 1000mps(3280fps).
7.5cm Sprgr 38 H1/C Klappleitwerk: fuzed AZ 385, projectile weight 6.80kg(14.99lb).
This fin-stabilised hollow charge projectile was developed towards the end of the war; as with others of its type it was an attempt to produce an unspun projectile that could be fired from a

Breech end and layer's controls of a 7.5cm PAK 40.

Front view of 7.5cm PAK 40.

rifled gun. The sealing ring at the rear was free to rotate with the rifling, and the rear portion of the shell body carried six fins connected to a plunger that fitted tightly into a cylinder in the body. A fine hole was drilled through the plunger to give access to the cylinder. When fired, propellant gas passed through the hole and filled the cylinder's free space with gas at chamber pressure —about 3150kg/cm²(20ton/in²). Nothing happened in the bore (since the same pressure existed outside the piston), but when the shell left the muzzle and entered an area of atmospheric pressure—about 7.03kg/cm²(14.7lb/in²)—the gas in the cylinder, unable to escape quickly through the smallbore hole, expanded and forced the plunger out: this, by means of the connexion, swung the fins out into the airstream. A spring-catch on the plunger ensured that, when the gas pressure was exhausted, the fins were locked in the open position.

No details of performance are known. A report of the Waffen-Entwicklungsbüro (weapon development bureau) noted in October 1944 that development was slow owing to the difficulty of getting accurate results in trials. This was largely on account of the poor fit of the blades and the fact that they tended to open prematurely, thus fouling the muzzlebrake. According to the general staff, however, Hitler had authorised the manufacture of 40000 shells, the parts for which were being made at seven different factories; final assembly was the task of DWM at Lübeck. But, in spite of all this, development was never successfully completed.

Primer
The percussion primer C/12nA was standard.

Case Identification Number
6340. The cartridge case used with this equipment was 715mm(28.15in) long and stamped *7.5CM PAK 40 6340* on the base, but a number of rounds were assembled with a case 667mm(26.26in) long and stamped *7.5CM* PAK *44* RH *6340* ST on the base. The PAK 44 was a different weapon whose development failed to bear fruit, as will be seen later. Cartridge cases which had been produced for this gun were then used up, slightly modified as necessary, in the PAK 40 and in the 7.62cm PAK 36(r) guns. The correct nomenclature of the weapon for which the shells were intended was stencilled on the side of the case. As can be imagined, the discovery that cases stamped PAK *44* were being used by two totally different guns gave the Allied intelligence agencies some entertaining blind alleys to explore before the mystery was unravelled.

7·5cm Panzerabwehrkanone 41

7·5cm Pak 41

The 7.5cm anti-tank gun developed by Krupp, in response to the 1939 specification, was vastly different from the Rheinmetall-Borsig model that became the 7.5cm PAK 40. The principal difference was the combination of a coned bore and tungsten-cored ammunition to give high velocity and massive striking power. The PAK 41 was a well-designed and most successful gun, but after 150 had been made production was stopped because of the restrictions placed on the use of tungsten. This apart, it is highly likely that the PAK 41 would have become the standard weapon instead of the PAK 40. The few guns produced were largely issued to selected special-duty units. After the ammunition supply had been exhausted the guns were withdrawn and most of them were scrapped, though it is believed that some of the carriages were modified to mount PAK 40 barrels.

The PAK 41's gun was a conventional rifled weapon for most of its length, the design being a 'squeeze' rather than a taper bore. The barrel itself was 2950mm(116.14in) long and then a 950mm(37.40in) tapered section was attached by a screwed collar. As the projectile entered the squeeze it first passed through a section tapered at 1 in 20 for about 270mm(10.63in), then through a section tapered at 1 in 12 for 170mm(6.69in) and finally into a parallel section for the remainder of its travel. The whole unit was smoothbore and a muzzlebrake was attached to the front; its effective life was only some 500 rounds but, when necessary, it could be quickly and easily changed in the field.

The carriage was an equally novel design. The principal feature was the use of the shield as a structural member rather than as a sheet of metal added as an afterthought. The gun was carried in a cradle and the whole assembly was then suspended in the shield by a gimbal-like arrangement of horizontal and vertical trunnions. The trail legs and the torsion-bar suspended axles and wheels were attached directly to the shield. The result was a very low and easily-concealed gun that was remarkably light for its size.

Data
Calibre: 7.5cm(2.95in) squeezed to 5.5cm(2.17in).
Length of gun: 4320mm/170.08in/14.17ft.
Length of bore: 2950mm/116.14in.
Length of squeeze unit: 950mm/37.40in.
Rifling: 28 grooves, right-hand increasing twist, 1/26 to 1/20.
Breech mechanism: horizontal semi-automatic sliding block. Percussion fired.
Traverse: 60°.

he 7.5cm PAK 41, the cone-bore gun.

:levation: −12° 30′ to +16° 45′.
Veight in action: 1356kg/2990lb.

erformance
'iring standard tungsten-cored projectile weighing .59kg(5.71lb).
Muzzle velocity: 1125mps/3691fps.
'enetration at 250m: 0° 226mm/8.90in, 30° 85mm/7.28in.
'enetration at 500m: 0° 209mm/8.23in, 30° 71mm/6.73in.
enetration at 1000m: 0° 177mm/6.97in, 30° 45mm/5.71in.
'enetration at 1500m: 0° 149mm/5.87in, 30° 22mm/4.80in.
enetration at 2000m: 0° 124mm/4.88in, 30° 02mm/4.02in.

mmunition
'ixed rounds; cartridge case length 544mm 21.42in).
5cm Pzgr 41 HK (HK—Hartkern, hard core): rojectile weight 2.59kg(5.71lb), complete round eight 7.76kg(17.11lb).

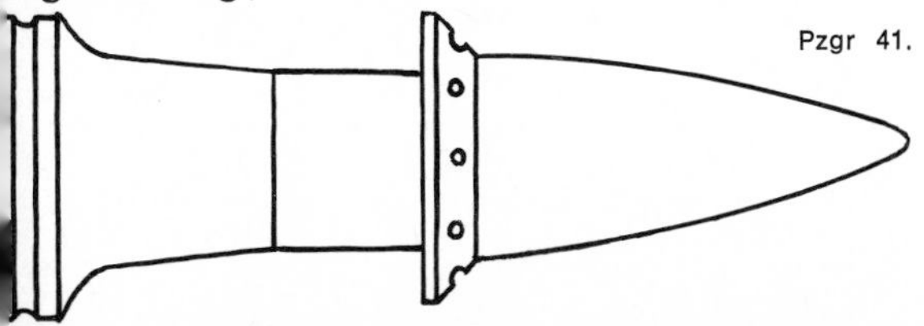

Except for its size this projectile was the same as those of the 2.8cm and 4.2cm guns. The forward flange was pierced with ten holes and a tracer was fitted at the rear. The complete round differed from those of the other calibres in that the rim of the casemouth was pressed into a groove on the rear flange; in the smaller rounds the case was pressed into the forward band. Thus the 7.5cm projectile was exposed, while the smaller ones were concealed (except for their front caps) by the case. The propelling charge was 2.58kg (5.69lb) of Digl R P.
7.5cm Pzgr 41W (W—Weicheisen, soft iron): projectile weight 2.59kg(5.71lb), complete rounds weigh 7.70kg(16.98lb).
This, a practice projectile, was a simple soft-metal shot with skirts formed integrally with the body; a ballistic cap was added to give the correct shape and distribution of weight. The projectile, however, had no penetrative capability. A tracer was fitted at the rear, and the outer surfaces of the skirt bands were treated with a graphited lubricant in order to minimise bore wear. The propelling charge used was 2.67kg(5.89lb) of Digl R P, which gave a velocity of 1210mps(3970fps)—somewhat in excess of that of the service round.

Primer
The percussion primer C/12nA St was used.
Case Identification Number: 6344.

wo views of the 7.5cm PAK 41, showing the 'ball and ocket' assembly of the barrel to the shield.

7·5cm Panzerabwehrkanone 97/38

7·5cm Pak 97/38

When confronted by the heavy Soviet tanks in the late summer of 1941, the German army rapidly realised that the contemporary production of anti-tank guns was insufficient, and that their performances were also in need of improvement. One problem was overcome by speeding the service introduction of the 7.5cm PAK 40 and PAK 41, but, in order to strengthen the defences, numbers of captured guns were also pressed into service. Among these was the venerable French 75mm gun model of 1897, vast numbers of which —in various modifications—had been taken from the French in 1940. The barrels of these were removed from their original field mountings and fitted into modified 5cm PAK 38 carriages. A cage-type muzzle brake was fitted to reduce the recoil stresses arising from the 'up-gunning' of the carriage, and a hollow charge round was provided.

The gun was not particularly successful owing to its low muzzle velocity, and it was also unpopular with the troops because of an inherent instability when fired and a high failure rate amongst the carriages. Although the PAK 97/38 was soon superseded on the Eastern Front, numbers were retained for use in the West Wall defences.

Data
Calibre: 75mm/2.95in.
Length of gun: 2721mm/107.13in.
Length of bore: 2489mm/97.99in.
Rifling: 24 grooves, right-hand uniform twist, 1/25.6.
Breech mechanism: Nordenfelt eccentric screw percussion fired.
Traverse: 60° degrees.
Elevation: −8° to +25°.
Weight in action: 1190kg/2624lb.

Performance
Firing high explosive shell.
Muzzle velocity: 577mps/1893fps.
Maximum range: 3000m/3281yd.
Firing armour piercing shell.
Muzzle velocity: 570mps/1870fps.
Maximum range: 1300m/1422yd.
Firing hollow charge shell.
Muzzle velocity: 450mps/1476fps.
Maximum range: 1900m/2078yd.
(The quoted ranges are anti-tank engagemen ranges.)

Ammunition
Fixed rounds; cartridge case length 336mm (13.23in).

7.5cm Sprgr Patr 230/1(f), 7.5cm Sprgr Pat 231/1(f), 7.5cm Sprgr Patr 233/1(f), 7.5cm Sprg Patr 236/1(f).

These were standard French rounds fitted wit high explosive shells of various patterns, impac fuzed; all were captured stocks and all wer issued with the guns for anti-personnel employ ment or for use against light vehicles.

7.5 K Gr Pz Patr (p).

This was a piercing shot that had been part o the Polish army stocks, since the Poles also use the French 75mm gun.

Camouflage-painted 7.5cm PAK 97/38 at Aberdeen Proving Ground.

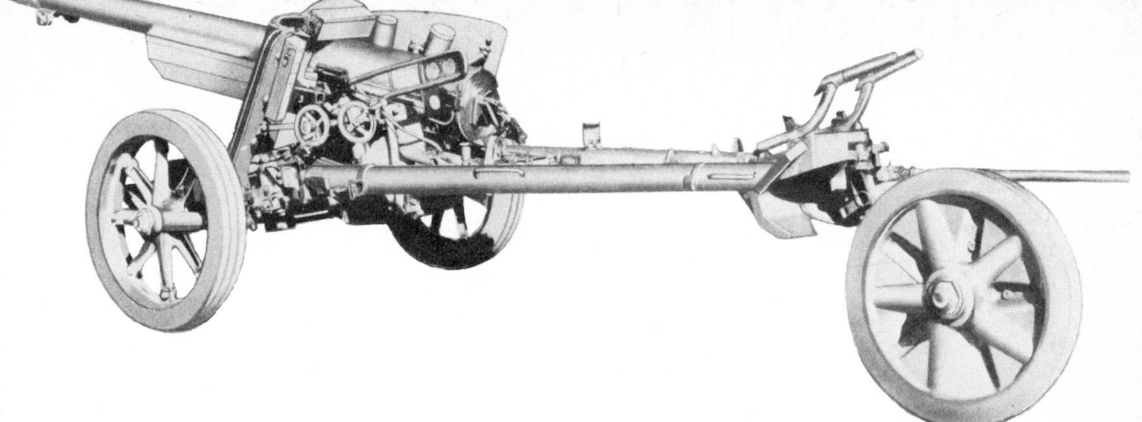

The 7.5cm PAK 97/98 fitted with a 'dolly wheel' for manhandling.

7.5cm Gr Patr 97/38 H1/B: fuzed AZ 38, projectile weight 4.54kg(10.01lb), complete round weight 5.98kg(13.19lb).
This was a German-designed and German-manufactured round, except that the case and the charge were captured French stocks. The shell was a normal B type hollow charge design and was, in fact, the 7.5cm FK 38 shell with the substitution of a copper driving band for the sintered-iron one used with the German gun. The propelling charge was 349gm(12.31oz./0.77lb) of French 'Poudre BC'.

Primer
French percussion primers were used.
Case Identification Number
The case could be identified by the base stamping '75'.

In a Russian dump of captured equipment a PAK 97/38 stands in front of a 7.5cm PAK 40.

A train-load of PAK 97/38 guns en route to the Eastern Front.

The 7.5cm PAK 97/38, modification of the ex-French 75mm field gun model of 1897.

7·5cm Panzerabwehrkanone 44

7·5cm Pak 44

This was a Rheinmetall-Borsig design of coned-bore weapon that never reached service. Work began in 1942 on the design of a gun in which a normal chamber was followed firstly by a smooth-bore coned section and then by a normally-rifled parallel barrel. The coned section gave no trouble but the rifled portion was prone to excessive wear: trial barrels never managed to last more than 200 rounds without severe scoring and stripping of the lands, although many variations of rifling twist were tried. In an endeavour to find an easy solution, the rifled section was modified so as to be readily changed in the field. The muzzle velocity with tungsten-cored shot was 1300mps (4265fps) and penetration at 2500m(2734yd) was claimed to be 120mm(4.72in).

The carriage was an ingenious design of split trail in which the trail legs rotated as they closed and raised the axle height for travelling. At the same time the centre of gravity of the weapon moved forward and made handling easier. To close the trail legs it was necessary only to depress the gun slightly and pull down on the muzzle, whereupon the legs came together to be locked. The whole design was commended by the army but it was too late to be adapted to other weapons.

None of the prototypes, so far as is known, survived the war and no further data is available.

Krupp's wooden mock-up of the 7.5cm PAK44, later modified to become the PAK 41.

7·5cm Panzerabwehrkanone 50

7·5cm Pak 50

This was another 1944 development of which little is known, particularly what motivated its design. The gun consisted of a shortened 75mm PAK 40 barrel, with a large muzzle brake, mounted on the carriage of the 5cm PAK 38. Two types of muzzle brake have been seen with this weapon, one with three baffles and one with five. It appears likely that the object was to produce a weapon with a performance approximating to the PAK 40 but lighter, more easy to handle, and more easy to conceal. Some reports have claimed that a small quantity were built and issued late in 1944 but this cannot be positively confirmed. No German ammunition data tables give any data for the weapon, and so it is highly unlikely that the PAK 50 ever saw service.

Data
Calibre: 75mm/2.95in.
Length of gun: 2245mm/88.38in.
Length of bore: 1435mm/56.50in.
Rifling: 32 grooves, right-hand increasing twist, 1/32 to 1/20.
Breech mechanism: horizontal semi-automatic sliding block, percussion fired.
Traverse: 65°.
Elevation: −8° to +27°.
Weight in action: approximately 1100kg/2425lb.

Performance, Ammunition
No details available.

The 7.5cm PAK 50.

7·62cm Panzerabwehrkanone 36(r)

7·62cm Pak 36(r)

In the early weeks of the Russian campaign, the German Army captured vast numbers of Soviet guns and huge stocks of ammunition. Prominent among the booty was the standard Soviet field gun, the 76.2mm 1936 model. These weapons were immediately assimilated into German use under their Fremdengerät name FK 296(r). It was then decided that the design was potentially a good anti-tank gun if a few simple changes were made. These involved reaming-out the chamber to suit a standard German cartridge case (that of the 7.5cm PAK 40), moving the elevating handwheel to the left side of the carriage to allow one-man laying, and adding a muzzle brake. With these modifications the weapon became the 7.62cm PAK 36(r) and was used on all fronts for the remainder of the war, a successful and efficient weapon.

Data
Calibre: 76.2mm/3.00in.
Length of gun: 4201mm/165.39in/13.78ft.
Length of bore: 2934mm/115.51in.
Rifling: 32 grooves, right-hand uniform twist, 1/25.
Breech mechanism: vertical semi-automatic sliding block, percussion fired.
Traverse: 60°.
Elevation: −6° to +25°.
Weight in action: 1730kg/3815lb.

Performance

Firing standard piercing shell weighing 7.54kg (16.63lb).
Muzzle velocity: 740mps/2426fps.
Penetration at 500m: 0° 120mm/4.72in, 30° 98mm/3.86in.
Penetration at 1000m: 0° 108mm/4.25in, 30° 88mm/3.46in.
Penetration at 1500m: 0° 97mm/3.82in, 30° 79mm/3.11in.
Penetration at 2000m: 0° 87mm/3.43in, 30° 71mm/2.80in.
Firing tungsten-cored shot weighing 4.05kg (8.93lb).
Muzzle velocity: 990mps/3248fps.
Penetration at 500m: 0° 158mm/6.32in, 30° 118mm/4.65in.
Penetration at 1000m: 0° 130mm/5.12in, 30° 92mm/3.62in.
Penetration at 1500m: 0° 106mm/4.17in, 30° 71mm/2.80in.
Penetration at 2000m: 0° 84mm/3.31in, 30° 55mm/2.17in.
Firing high explosive shell weighing 6.20kg (13.67lb).
Muzzle velocity: 550mps/1805fps.
Maximum range: 9000m/9842yd.

Ammunition

Fixed rounds; cartridge case length 715mm (28.15in).

7.62mm Pzgr Patr 39 rot: fuzed Bd Z 5103, projectile weight 7.54kg(16.63lb), complete round weight 12.81kg(28.25lb).

This was a conventional piercing shell with ballistic and penetrating caps. The explosive filling was 17gm(0.60oz) of cyclonite/wax and the

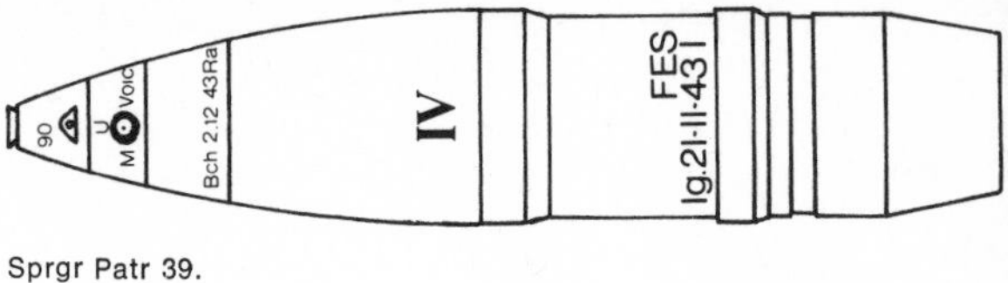

Sprgr Patr 39.

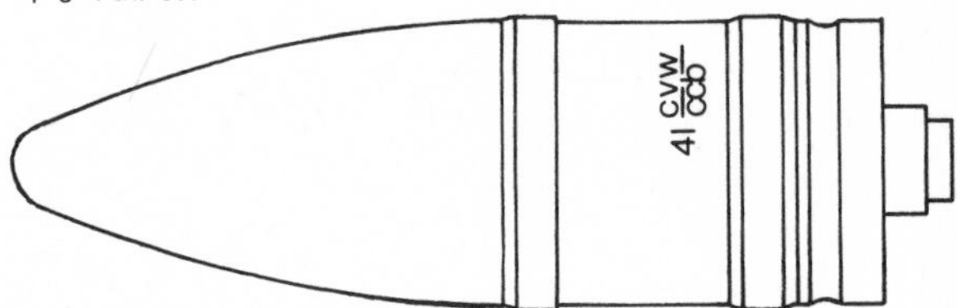

Pzgr Patr 40.

PAK 36(r) on display at Aberdeen Proving Ground. This model is without a shield, a frequent modification.

Side view of the 7.62cm PAK 36(r).

The 76.2cm PAK 36(r), the ex-Soviet field gun made over into a German anti-tank gun.

base fuze carried a tracer. The single driving band was either bimetallic or of sintered iron. The propelling charge was 2.48kg(5.47lb) of Digl R P.

7.62cm Pzar Patr 40: projectile weight (8.82lb), complete round weight 8.88kg(19.58lb) This was a full-calibre tungsten-cored projectile. The core was carried in a plastic and steel body covered in light sheet-steel that formed a ballistic cap. The driving band was bimetallic and a tracer was fitted. The propelling charge was 2.07kg (4.56lb) of Gudol R P.

7.62cm Sprgr Patr 39: fuzed Kl AZ 23, projectile weight 6.30kg(13.89lb), complete round weight 10.00kg(22.05lb).

This was a conventional German-made high explosive shell, fitted with a single bimetallic driving band and fitted with 550gm(19.40oz/1.21lb) of amatol. The propelling charge was 775gm(27.33oz/1.71lb) of Gudol B1 P. In addition to the normal 6340 case, these rounds were assembled with cases stamped PAK *44* RH owing to the use of stocks ordered in advance of the PAK 44.

Primer

The percussion primer C/12nA. was fitted.

Case Identification Number

6340 (7.5cm PAK 40 case): see also 7.62cm Sprgr Patr 39 (above).

7·62cm Panzerabwehrkanone 39(r)

7·62cm Pak 39(r)

This was another conversion of a captured Russian weapon . The Soviet fieldgun of 1939 was an improved model of the 1936 pattern; the two differed very little. The principal change was a shortening of the barrel by 710mm(27.95in) and a simplification of the carriage design which saved about 250kg(551lb) in weight. Owing to the shorter barrel the velocity of the PAK 39(r) was slightly less than that of the PAK 36(r), but for all practical purposes the performance data of the PAK 39 was the same as that of the PAK 36. The ammunition was identical.

76.2cm PAK 39(r) an improved version of the 36(r).

8cm Panzerabwehrwerfer 600

8cm PAW 600(Elfenbein) later known as the 8cm PWK 8H63

The German Army was less than completely satisfied with the various recoilless guns that had been developed, owing to their relative inaccuracy as anti-tank guns, the problems raised by the back-blast, and their appetite for propellant. An infantry anti-tank gun was still needed—in spite of the rapid development of a variety of shoulder-fired weapons—and in 1943 the gun designers were approached with a specification demanding a lightweight weapon that used less propellant than a recoilless gun or a rocket, yet with sufficient accuracy to hit a 1m(3.28ft) square target at 750m(820yd).

Rheinmetall-Borsig decided to apply a new ballistic idea to this weapon, one that they had been developing for some time. This was the Hoch-Niederdruck-System (high-low pressure system) in which the high pressure caused by the propellant combustion was confined in a relatively heavy breech section; it was then allowed to bleed gradually into the lightweight barrel to provide a lower pressure to propel the projectile. In this way the ballistic advantages of regularity and controllable burning, which accrue from high pressure, were available and the gun barrel could also be exceptionally light. In order to relieve the system of further stress, the barrel was smooth-bored and the projectiles were fin stabilised.

The carriage, as first designed, was exceptionally light; indeed, it was soon found to be too light for the job and had to be redesigned. It was an interesting concept though, with a torsion bar of laminated steel plates carried on the cradle trunnion and acting as the balancing-press to compensate for the muzzle weight. A similar torsion bar in the axle housing gave spring suspension to the wheels. The cradle was little more than a cage containing separate recoil and recuperator cylinders, much lighter than the usual design of a bored-out steel block. The improved

An 8cm PAW on display at Aberdeen Proving Ground Museum.

The 8cm PAW 600 or 8H63, High-Low Pressure gun. This is the original version with lightweight trail. The muzzle-brake is missing.

carriage was more robust and orthodox, but a large number of PAW 600 weapons were also mounted on old PAK 38 carriages as a stop-gap expedient; a PAK 40 muzzlebrake was fitted to the gun when so mounted.

In all, some 260 guns were built between December 1944 and the end of March 1945, when production stopped. Krupp was also developing a 10.5cm version at the war's end: this, the 10cm PAW 1000 (later renamed 10cm PWK 10H64), never reached the prototype stage.

Data
Calibre: 81.4mm/3.20in.
Length of gun: 2951mm/116.18in.
Length of bore: not known.
Rifling: smoothbore.
Breech mechanism: vertical sliding block, electrically fired.
Traverse: 55°.

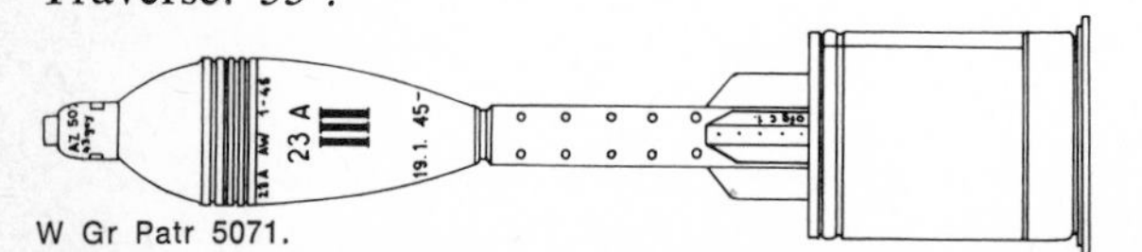

W Gr Patr 5071.

Elevation: −6° to +32°.
Weight in action: 600kg/1323lb.

Performance
Firing standard hollow charge projectile weighing 2.70kg(5.95lblb).
Muzzle velocity: 520mps/1706fps.
Maximum range: 750m/820yd.
Penetration at 750m: 0° 140mm/5.51in.

Ammunition
Fixed rounds; cartridge case length 158mm (6.22in).
8cm W Gr Patr H1 4462: fuzed AZ 5075, projectile weight 2.70kg(5.95lb), complete round weight not known.
This was a modified 8.1cm mortar bomb carrying a hollow charge liner. The end of the tail boom was attached by a spigot and shear-pin to a heavy iron plate pierced with eight venturi-like holes. The plate was crimped into the mouth of a 10.5cm le FH 18 cartridge case that carried the primer and the charge. On firing, a pressure of about 1100kg/cm²(13585lb/in² or 6.06ton/in²) was generated in the case and this then passed through

Breech end of the 8cm PAW at Aberdeen. Notice the relatively simple breech mechanism.

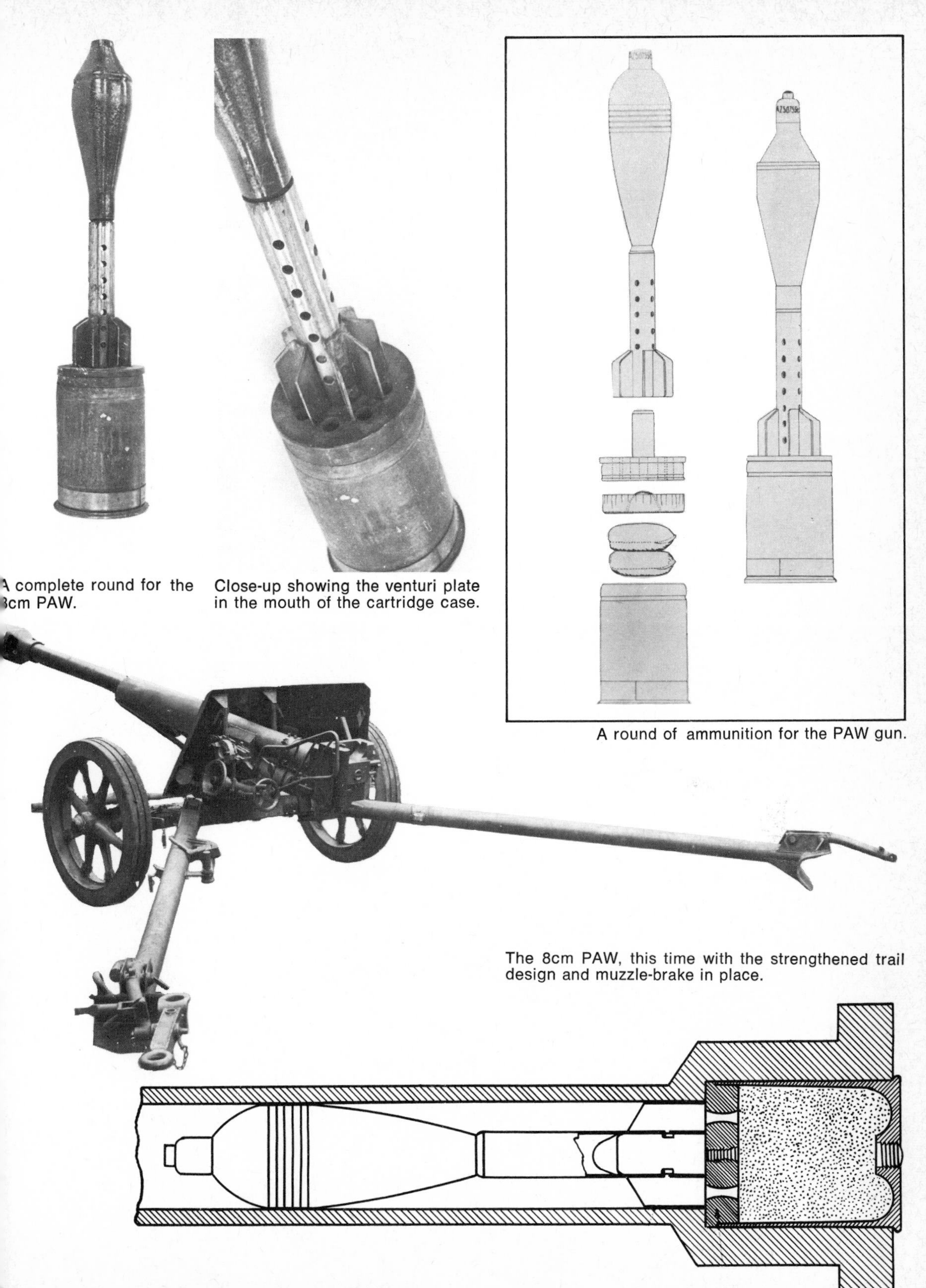

A complete round for the 8cm PAW.

Close-up showing the venturi plate in the mouth of the cartridge case.

A round of ammunition for the PAW gun.

The 8cm PAW, this time with the strengthened trail design and muzzle-brake in place.

Diagram of the ammunition used in the 8cm PAW gun.

the holes to expand in the chamber space behind the projectile. When the pressure reached about 550kg/cm²(7825lbin²or 3.49ton/in²) the shear-pin gave way and released the bomb from the plate and spigot, allowing it to be propelled from the bore. The propelling charge was 360gm(12.70oz/0.79lb) of Digl B1 P.

8cm W Gr Patr 5071: fuzed AZ 5075, projectile weight 4.46kg(9.83lb), complete round weight 8.30kg(18.30lb).

This was of similar design to the foregoing round, but the projectile was filled as an anti-personnel high explosive bomb. Three charge combinations were available, giving the following performance:

Kleine Ladung: velocity 220mps/722fps, maximum range 3400/3718yd.

Mittlere Ladung: velocity 320mps/1050fps, maximum range 5600m/6124yd.

Grosse Ladung: velocity 420mps/1378fps, max mum range 6200m/6780yd.

The case and the iron plate were separable an the propelling charge comprised two bags, on large and one small. The small bag used alon gave the Kleine Ladung, the large bag used alon was the Mittlere Ladung, and the two bag together formed the Grosse Ladung. The sma bag contained 80gm(2.82oz) of Digl B1 P and th large bag 1.31kg(2.89lb) of Digl B1 P.

Primer

The electric primer C/22 was standard.

Case Identification Number

6342/65D; the case was always a built-up stee type of 1944 manufacture.

A mock-up of the 10.5cm PAW 'high-low pressure' gun.

Krupp mock-up of the 10.5cm PAW 600, another weapon proposed on the high-low pressure system.

Another view of the 10.5cm PAW 600 mock-up. Notice the enormous muzzle brake.

8·1cm Panzerabwehrwerfer L/105

8·1cm PAW L/105

This weapon never saw service but it is included here for two reasons: firstly because it indicates the tendency towards powerful and heavy weapons in the later parts of the war, and secondly in the hope that someone—somewhere—might recognise it. More information might thus be uncovered.

The weapon was photographed in a German test ground after the war and identified as the 8.1cm PAW L/105; nothing more is known about it. No postwar reports or interrogations have thrown any light on the weapon, and the only related piece of information was discovered during examination of microfilm of Krupp's ammunition design department drawings. This revealed a single drawing of a hemispherical-based hollow charge shell weighing 3.00kg(6.62lb) and classified as *8.1cm HoL Gr L/3.1 fur PAW*. The 8cm PAW 600 was ruled out because the shell was fitted with a driving band—but by the same token could it have been for the PAW L/105 which, although of the correct calibre, was called a *werfer,* which implied a smoothbore? The PAW L/105 ordnance bore no resemblance to any service weapon. It was obviously built in two pieces, a common German practice that enabled long guns to be made on short lathes, and it appears to have been jacketed. The carriage was an amalgam of service components and specially-made parts; the wheels were those of the 10cm K 18 and the cradle and limber appear to have been taken from the 10cm s FH 18. The whole weapon had a purposeful air, but it would probably have been a cumbersome beast to handle. The gun was disconnected from the recoil system for travelling, doubtless to prevent whip in the barrel, but such a time-consuming manoeuver has no place on an anti-tank gun. On the available evidence, it seems likely that the 8.1cm PAW was a prototype that was abandoned as too unwieldy; it must, however, have had a formidable performance.

The mysterious '8.1cm PAW L/105' found after the war.

8·8cm Panzerabwehrkanone 43

8·8cm Pak 43 (Neuntoter)

In 1940 Rheinmetall-Borsig and Krupp were both given contracts to develop a new 8.8cm anti-aircraft gun to replace the Flak 37, and one of the terms of the specification was that the weapon should be capable of firing in a ground role. The Rheinmetall design was completed first and entered service as the Flak 41. This put the future of the Krupp weapon in doubt, but since the Flak 41 was giving some post-development problems it was decided to continue with the Krupp design—altering the specification to use a heavier shell and give a higher muzzle velocity. The result was called Gerät 42.

Krupp was also attempting to develop tank and anti-tank guns of 8.8cm calibre at the same time, and it was hoped that a complete family of weapons firing common ammunition would result. In course of time, however, it became apparent that the performance demanded by the new specification could not be reached and, as the Flak 41 seemed to be overcoming its troubles, the Gerät 42 project was dropped and the work was instead concentrated on the tank and anti-tank weapons (the KwK 42 and the PAK 42). The anti-tank design eventually entered service in 1943 as the PAK 43.

It was an outstanding weapon. The gun was in two sections, though this was not readily apparent since the join fell at the point where a conventional jacket might have been expected to end and the resulting appearance was of a loose barrel and jacket construction. The breech mechanism was a vertical sliding block, uncommon in Krupp designs, and was fitted with an ingenious compact semi-automatic gear; this loaded two springs during recoil, thereafter using the stored energy of one to open the breech and eject the fired case and that of the other to close the breech on reloading. The system had the advantage of lending itself to operation with very short recoil strokes, and it was closely examined by British designers after the war with the intention of using it in the breech of the then-new 20pdr tank gun. But the design relied on close cartridge case tolerances; since the British cases were made to wider tolerances than the German ones, they were liable to produce an occasional tight-fitting case that could defy extraction by spring power and so the idea was never followed through.

The Flak 43 carriage was a cruciform platform carried on two-wheel trailers (*Sonderanhänger 204*) and was closely related to anti-aircraft designs. Since the elevation required of the gun was less than that necessary in the anti-aircraft role, it was possible to discard the usual high-set pedestal and mount the gun and cradle on a low saddle revolving on roller bearings. The result was a ver low silhouette, with the top of the shield onl some 1.73m(68.11in) from the ground in the firin position. It was also possible to fire the gun fro its wheels by swinging out the two side girder and placing special firing pedestals beneath th jack feet. Two different patterns of carriage wer made—one with pneumatic-tyred wheels and on with solid-tyred spoked wheels—but in other res pects the two designs were the same. The firin gear was electric, operated from a push-butto on the layer's elevation handwheel, and safet circuits were incorporated so that the gun woul not fire if it was at an elevation and traverse a which the recoiling breech might strike the plat form outriggers.

A number of these guns were assimilated int divisional artillery regiments for use as field-cum anti-tank weapons; designated 8.8cm K 43.

Data
Calibre: 88mm/3.46in.
Length of gun: 6610mm/260.24in/21.69ft.
Length of bore: 6010mm/236.61in/19.72ft.
Rifling: 32 grooves, right-hand uniform twist, 1/2
Breech mechanism: vertical semi-automatic slidin block, electrically fired.
Traverse: 360°.
Elevation: −8° to + 40°.
Weight in action: 3700kg/8159lb.

Performance
Firing standard piercing projectile weighin 10.40kg(22.93lb).
Muzzle velocity: 1000mps/3281fps.
Penetration at 500m: 0° 207mm/8.15in, 30 182mm/7.17in.
Penetration at 1000m: 0° 190mm/7.48in, 30 167/mm/6.57in.
Penetration at 1500m: 0° 174mm/6.85in, 30 153mm/6.02in.
Penetration at 2000m: 0° 159mm/6.26in, 30 139mm/5.47in.
Firing tungsten-cored shot weighing 7.30k (16.10lb).
Muzzle velocity: 1130mps/3708fps.
Penetration at 500m: 0° 274mm/10.79in, 30 226mm/8.90in.
Penetration at 1000m: 0° 241mm/9.49in, 30 192mm/7.56in.
Penetration at 1500m: 0° 211mm/8.31in, 30 162mm/6.38in.
Penetration at 2000m: 0° 184mm/7.24in, 30 136mm/5.35in.
Firing standard high explosive shell weighin 9.40kg(20.73lb).

'he 8.8cm PAK 43 in action, with wheels removed.

The 8.8cm PAK 43 on solid tyres.

'he 8.8cm PAK 43 on pneumatic tyres.

Right rear of the 8.8cm PAK 43

luzzle velocity: 750mps/2461fps.
laximum range: 17500m/19138yd.

mmunition

'ixed rounds; cartridge case length 822mm 32.36in).

8cm Pzgr Patr 39–1: fuzed Bd Z 5127, projectile reight 10.00kg/(22.05lb), complete round weight 3.00kg(50.72lb).

'his was a conventional piercing shell with enetrating and ballistic caps, and two iron driving ands each 11.4mm(0.45in) wide. It carried the sual small bursting charge, a base fuze and a racer. The propelling charge was 6.83kg(15.06lb) f Gudol R P.

.8cm Pzgr Patr 39/43: fuzed Bd Z 5127, proectile weight 10.16kg(22.40lb), complete round reight 23.35kg(51.49lb).

'he original Pzgr 39–1 was found to be inaccurate vhen fired from worn guns, and so its use was ventually restricted to guns whose barrels had red less than 500 rounds. To replace it, a new rojectile was produced with heavier driving ands 16.5mm(0.65in) wide. In every other respect his round was the same as the Pzgr 39–1.

.8cm Pzgr Patr 40: projectile weight 7.30kg 16.10lb).

'his was a full-calibre tungsten-cored shot, similar o the Pzgr 40 shot used with the 7.5cm PAK 40. 'ew were made (since the tungsten ban came into orce before stocks could be built up) and owing o this no data on the propelling charge or the omplete round weight are available.

.8cm Sprgr Patr L/4.7: fuzed AZ 23/28, proectile weight 9.40kg(20.73lb), complete round veight 19.30kg(42.56lb).

'his was the original high explosive round, the hell of which came from the Flak 41. It was of onventional type, impact fuzed and carried two 'ES driving bands each 11.4mm(0.45in) wide. 'he propelling charge was 3.40kg(7.50lb) of Gudol R P.

Sprgr Patr 43.

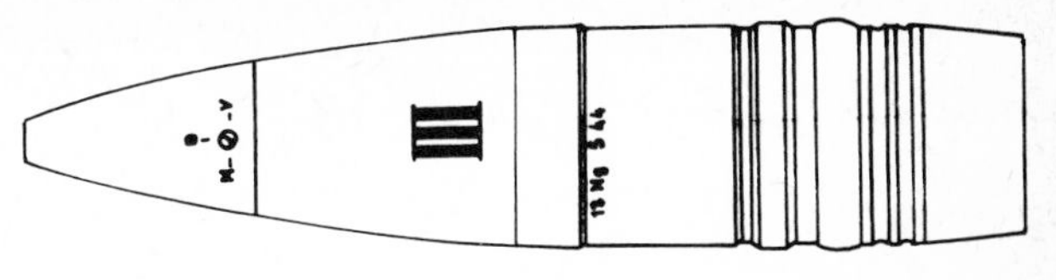

8.8cm Sprgr Patr 43: fuzed AZ 23/28, projectile weight 9.40kg(20.73lb), complete round weight 19.30kg(42.56lb).

In the same way that the Pzgr 39–1 developed instability in a worn gun, so did the original high explosive shell; it was redesigned to use two FES driving bands each 17.8mm(0.70in) wide. Apart from this feature the Sprgr 43 was the same as the Sprgr L/4.7.

8.8cm Gr Patr 39 Hl: fuzed AZ 38, projectile weight 7.65kg(16.87lb), complete round weight 16.00kg(35.28lb).

This was a hollow charge shell of the usual type. Although available to the anti-tank gun it was more commonly used by the tank guns of the family. This version had a shell with two 11.4mm (0.45in) driving bands of sintered iron. The propelling charge was 1.70kg(3.75lb) of Gudol R P.

8.8cm Gr Patr 39/43 Hl: fuzed AZ 38, projectile weight 7.65kg(16.87lb), complete round weight 16.00kg(35.28lb).

This was an improved round differing, as with the other types, only in having the 17.8mm(0.70in) FES driving bands. The remainder of the data was the same. The hollow charge projectiles achieved a muzzle velocity of 600mps(1968fps), and penetration at 1000m was quoted as 90mm (3.54in) of plate at a 30° impact angle.

Primer

The electric primer C/22 was standard.

Case Identification Number: 6388.

8·8cm Panzerabwehrkanone 43/41

8·8cm Pak 43/41 (Nierstein)

War waits not upon manufacturers, and in 1943 he situation in Russia urgently demanded more nti-tank guns. Since the barrels of the PAK 43 vere relatively easy to make, but the carriage nanufacture was lagging, a temporary expedient vas produced. The PAK 41 barrel was fitted with horizontal sliding block breech mechanism reembling that of the 7.5cm PAK 40 and the emi-automatic gear was a simplified version of hat used on the PAK 43. The carriage was a ollection of suitably modified stock components; he trail legs came from the 10.5cm le FH 18, he wheels were taken from the 15cm s FH and he saddle was a steel-plate fabrication that tied everything together. A serious fault was the absence of articulation in the suspension, which meant that the gun rested on four points of contact when firing. In spite of all this it was an effective weapon and it is on record that one knocked out six T34 tanks at a range of 3500m (3828yd). Another report stated that a T34, attacked from the rear at a range of 600m (656yd), had the engine block flung out for a distance of 5m(16.41ft) and the cupola lid landed 15m(49.22ft) away. But the PAK 43/41's weight and awkwardness were notorious, and it was nicknamed Scheuntor ('barndoor') by the troops who had to use it.

Data
Calibre: 88mm/3.46in.
Length of gun: 6610mm/260.24in/21.69ft.
Length of bore: 6010mm/236.61in/19.72ft.
Rifling: 32 grooves, right-hand uniform twist, 1/28.
Breech mechanism: horizontal semi-automatic sliding block, electrically fired.
Traverse: 56°.
Elevation: −5° to +38°.
Weight in action: 4380kg/9658lb.

Performance, Ammunition
See 8.8cm PAK 43.

An 8.8cm PAK 43/41 on display at Aberdeen Proving Ground.

Breech and sights of the 8.8cm PAK 43/41.

Rear view of the 8.8cm PAK 43/41, with spades folded ready for travelling.

Rear view of the 8.8cm PAK 43/41 in action.

12·8cm Panzerabwehrkanone 44

12·8cm PAK 44 (Durheim)

Krupp version of the 12.8cm PAK 44 in travelling mode.

This gun represented the final stage reached by anti-tank gun development during World War 2 and was probably the best anti-tank gun ever built. Its development became entwined with the concurrent development of a 12.8cm field gun required to have all-round traverse and an anti-tank capability; the same weapon eventually came to fulfil both roles, being known either as the 12.8cm PAK 44 or the 12.8cm K 44 according to its primary employment. It is fully described in the FIELD ARTILLERY section under *12.8cm K 44*, but for convenience the principal details are repeated here.

Data
Calibre: 128mm/5.04in.
Length of gun: 7023mm/276.50in/23.04ft.
Length of bore: 6625mm/260.83in/21.74ft.
Rifling: 40 grooves, right-hand increasing twist 1/27 to 1/24.75.
Breech mechanism: horizontal semi-automatic sliding block, electrically fired.
Traverse: 360°.
Elevation: −7° 51′ to +45° 27′.
Weight in action: 10160kg/22403lb/10.00ton.

Performance
Firing standard piercing shell weighing 28.30kg (62.40lb).
Muzzle velocity: 1000mps/3281fps.
Penetration at 1000m: 30° 230mm/9.06in.
Penetration at 2000m: 30° 200mm/7.87in.
Penetration at 3000m: 30° 173mm/6.81in.

Ammunition
See 12cm K 44.

Krupp PAK 44 ready for action.

Front view of the Rheinmetall PAK 44.

COASTAL
ARTILLERY

During World War 2, required to guard a coastline stretching from the Spanish border to the Arctic Circle, the Germans were forced to use every weapon they could, whether constructed, commandeered or captured. The vast majority were impressed and captured weapons: their role, a defence against invasion rather than the classic coast defence role—defence against naval attack. It is quite impossible to cover in this book every weapon that was sited with its muzzle pointed seawards; so this section is devoted to those weapons that were apparently standard models expressly designed for coast defence and intended to be used with the usual types of coast defence fire control system.

In addition to these weapons, one or two land service guns were provided with firing platforms that allowed them to be emplaced with a wide field of fire. These are discussed in the proper sections of the book. The standard railway guns could also be so sited that they were compatible with the coast defence system.

As an example of the diversity of equipment, it is instructive to examine the weapons deployed round the coast of Denmark. The immediate task was, of course, to deny entrance to the Baltic, with the secondary tasks of defending various localities against seaborne raids.

01 Four *38cm Siegfried Kanone* in single mountings at Hanstead.
02 Four *38cm Siegfried Kanone* in two twin turrets at Oxsby.
03 Four *15cm SK C/28 in Zwillingslafette* at Gradyp on Fano Island.
04 Four *10.5cm French Le Creusot guns* on Fano Island.
05 Four *15cm Bofors M1906* (probably original Danish weapons) on Fano Island.
06 Four *12.2cm Russian field guns* on the southern tip of Fano Island.
07 Four *10.5cm French guns* at Nymendegab.
08 One *15.5cm French field gun* in an armoured cupola at Nymendegab.
09 Four *12.8 German naval guns* (ex-destroyer) at Esbjerg.
10 Four *12.2cm Russian field guns* at Heune.
11 Four *12.2cm Russian field guns* at Borsinose.
12 Four *12.2cm Russian field guns* at Vrogum.
13 Four *10.5cm French guns* at Blaavanshuk.
14 Four *German 15cm K 39 field guns* on platforms at Blaavanskro.
15 Four *12.2cm Russian field guns* at West Wedsted.
16 Four *12.8cm German ex-destroyer guns* south of Esbjerg.

The four-gun 38cm batteries at Hanstead were supported by a three-gun battery at Kristiansund in Norway, and between them they were capable of covering the entire width of the Skagerrak at that point.

Although unevenly distributed, the Danish defences averaged four guns to every five miles of coastline (though this would apparently hav been increased to six guns per five miles had th weapons and men been available). In addition t the weapons detailed above, there were 14 5c anti-tank guns emplaced as anti-torpedo-bo defences and a large number of 3.7cm ant aircraft guns were so sited that they were able t engage both sea and aerial targets.

The general tenor of any nation's coa artillery is dictated by its prospective opponen the Germans were primarily concerned with th possibility of attack by capital ships of the Britis French or American navies. These ships, arme with long-range weapons firing heavy shells an heavily armoured, demanded heavy long-rang land-sited weapons that could engage the warshi before they got close enough to shell the sho installations. As a result, the trend was alwa towards heavier long range weapons.

Since control of 'proper' coast defence was i the hands of the navy, it is not surprising to fin that the majority of the weapons were of nav design and in many cases were shore-mounte with but little modification. Even such ancillarie as magazines and power plants were built in muc the same fashion ashore as they had been on th ships, although the need for such compression o space and such an accent on safety was no longe present. One notable feature was the use of loos barrel liners, normal German navy practice. Whe the gun became worn to the point of inaccurac the breech-ring was removed and the gun line was slipped out of its supporting jacket, to b replaced by a new one. This was perfectly satis factory in a shipboard installation—a turret, fo example—where a suitable hatchway was provide through which the liners passed. But the sam gun in a land emplacement, with massive con crete or earthen revetments surrounding it o three sides, was a different proposition and i some cases it was necessary to demolish part c the work to change liners. This, with the necessar rebuilding process, could take several weeks.

The mountings and defensive works we generally either turrets or casemates. The turre were often simply removed from a ship an dropped straight into a prepared concrete emplace ment, so that the supply of ammunition wa vertical from the concrete magazines surroundin the bottom of the turret shaft. More rarely th turret was specifically designed for land use: wide and flat structure with horizontal ammuni tion supply from magazines in the rear.

Casemates are technically defined as 'vaulte chambers for the mounting of guns' but th modern casemate, thanks to structural steel an reinforced concrete, is no longer vaulted. It ca instead be best described as a concrete box wit one side taken out, through which points the gun Obviously there is more to it than that, since th designer has to allow the gun sufficient elevatio and traverse to cover its desired field of fire, bu that description—accompanied by the plans and photographs of actual German defences reproduced here—will suffice.

Lighter guns were usually mounted on simple pedestals with armoured shields, with concrete defensive works offering additional protection.

3·7cm Schiffskanone C/30 in Einheitslafette C/34

3·7cm SK C/30 in Ehl C/34

The nomenclature introduces a particular feature of coast artillery—the fact that the gun and the mounting were separately accountable articles and as such were given separate terminology. (This is comparable with British practice: the Ordnance, 9.2inch Mark 10 on Carriage, Garrison, Barbette Mark 5, for example.)

The 3.7cm SK C30 was a naval pattern dual-purpose anti-aircraft/coast defence gun and was largely used as a static anti-aircraft weapon protecting larger gun installations and port areas. As an anti-aircraft weapon it had some utility, but as a coast defence weapon it would have been of scant value—except against light craft at short range.

The ordnance was a simple monobloc gun with a semi-automatic breech. It was mounted on a pedestal that carried seats for the two gunlayers: the elevation mechanism on the left and the traverse gear on the right. The term *Einheitslafette* (universal mounting) indicated its suitability for engaging surface or aerial targets, and the sights were modified versions of those used on the 3.7cm Flak weapons.

Data
Calibre: 37mm/1.46in.
Length of gun: 3076mm/121.10in/10.09ft.
Length of barrel: 2962mm/116.61in.
Rifling: 16 grooves, right-hand uniform twist.
Breech mechanism: horizontal semi-automatic sliding block, percussion fired.
Traverse: 360°.
Elevation: −10° to +80°.

Performance
Firing standard high explosive shell weighing 0.68kg(1.50lb).
Muzzle velocity: 1000mps/3281fps.
Maximum range: 6600m/7218yd.
Effective ceiling in anti-aircraft role: 2000m/6562ft.

Ammunition
Fixed, cased charge.

Projectiles
3.7cm Br Sprgr Patr 40 L/4.1 Lh 37M: fuzed 3.7cm KZ 40, projectile weight 0.68kg(1.50lb), complete round weight 1.78kg(3.92lb).
This was a high explosive incendiary shell with tracer; it could be used for shooting at surface or aerial targets.
3.7cm Sprgr Patr 40 L/4.1 Lh 37: fuzed 3.7cm KZ 40, projectile weight 0.68kg(1.50lb).
This differed from the foregoing in omitting the incendiary additive to the filling. Both these shells could be found with either two iron (FEW) or three copper driving bands. Red, yellow or white tracer units were fitted, the colour of the trace being indicated by a coloured painted band above the driving bands.

Propelling Charges
The Br Sprgr round used 350gm(12.34oz) of naval R P 38N, while the Sprgr round used 360gm (12.70oz) of naval R P 32. Unfortunately no details are known of the composition of these naval propellants.

Primer
The percussion primers C/13nA St or C/33 St were standard.

Case Identification Number
None: the case may be identified by the base-stampings *3.7CM 30ST* or *3.7CM C/30.*

7·5cm Panzerabwehrkanone 40 in Lafette Marine 39/43

7·5cm Pak 40 in LM 39/43

This was the standard 7.5cm PAK 40 anti-tank gun, together with its cradle and recoil system, lifted from its field carriage and dropped (after slight modifications) into a naval pedestal mounting. The resulting weapon was employed by the navy as a shipboard gun for light coastal craft and also as a light coast defence gun in an anti-torpedo-boat role—much in the same fashion as the British 12pdr.

The principal modifications made to the PAK 40 were the changed valving of the recoil system that reduced the length of recoil to 700mm

(27.56in), and the movement of the trunnions to a position farther forward on the cradle at the point of balance (doing away with the need for balancing gear). The recoil stroke could be reduced in this way since the mounting was securely anchored in concrete and was more resistant to the recoil force than the wheeled field carriage.

The pedestal was turntable-mounted, the turntable being secured to the emplacement by heavy anchor bolts and holdfasts. A 10mm(0.39in) thick shield was provided to protect the gun crew.

Data
Calibre: 75mm/2.95in.
Length of gun: 3700mm/145.67in/12.14ft.
Length of barrel: 2461mm/96.89in.
Rifling: 32 grooves, increasing right-hand twist.
Breech mechanism: horizontal semi-automatic sliding block, percussion fired.
Traverse: 360°.
Elevation: −10° to +40°.
Weight in action: 2680kg/5909lb.

Performance
Firing standard high explosive shell weighing 5.74kg(12.66lb).
Muzzle velocity: 550mps/1805fps.
Maximum range: 7680m/8399yd.
Firing armour-piercing shell weighing 6.70kg (14.77lb).
Muzzle velocity: 792mps/2599fps.

Ammunition
Fixed, cased charge.

Projectiles
7.5cm Sprgr Patr 34: fuzed Kl AZ 23, weight 5.74kg(12.66lb).
The standard high explosive shell. The driving band could be either bimetallic (KPS) or of soft iron (FEW). The filling was 650gm(22.92oz/1.43lb) of amatol 50/50 with a smoke box for indicating the strike.
7.5cm Pzgr Patr 39: fuzed Bd Z 5103, weight 6.70kg(14.77lb).
An armour-piercing shell with penetrating and ballistic caps. A small cavity contained a bursting charge of 16gm(0.56oz) of RDX/wax. The fuze carried a tracer in its base.

Propelling Charges
Charge used with high explosive shell: 780gm (27.51oz/1.72lb) Gudol B1 P.
Charge used with armour-piercing shell: 2.75kg (6.06lb) of Dgl R P.

Primer
The percussion primer C/12nA was standard.
Case Identification Number
6340.

8·8cm Schiffskanone C/35 in Unterseebootslafette C/35

8·8cm SK C/35 in Ubts L C/35 (Krokos)

This was an entirely naval design of gun, unrelated to the many 8.8cm Flak and PAK weapons mentioned elsewhere. Only small numbers of these were installed in casemate mountings, and it is believed that the design's employment in the coast defence role was not a common practice.

The gun was of multi-section construction, in a similar fashion to the 8.8cm Flak 36, and had a vertical sliding breechblock with semi-automatic gear. The mounting was a low pedestal with shield, provided with duplicate sets of gears so that laying could be done from either or both sides. An unusual feature (a reminder of the gun's U-boat origin) lay in the provision of chest pads upon which the layers could lean. One faced forward and one faced the gun and, when the situation demanded it, the normal traversing gear could be disengaged—whereafter the weapon could be traversed by the layer facing the gun using his chest pad to push the gun about its pivot.

Data
Calibre: 88mm/3.46in.
Length of gun: 3990mm/157.1in.
Length of barrel: 3735mm/146.8in.
Rifling: 32 grooves, right-hand increasing twist
Breech mechanism: vertical semi-automatic sliding block, percussion fired.
Traverse: 360°.
Elevation: −4° to +30°.

Performance
Firing standard high explosive shell.
Muzzle velocity: 700mps/2297fps.
Maximum range: 12350m/13506 yd.
Firing star shell.
Muzzle velocity: 600mps/1969fps.

Ammunition
Fixed rounds, cased charge.

Projectiles
8.8cm Sprgr Patr C/35 L/4.5 KZ: fused EK Zd C/28, weight of complete round 13.65kg(30.10lb
The standard high explosive round. The shell ha two bimetallic (KPS) or two soft-iron (FEW driving bands and two deep cannelures for th

ttachment of the cartridge case. Like all naval esigns, the shell used block filling inserted rough a screwed-in baseplate.

8cm Pzgr Patr C/35: fuzed Bd Z 5127, weight f complete round 13.90kg(30.65lb).

his, an armour-piercing projectile, was fitted with allistic and penetrating caps. A small explosive harge was inserted in the base, initiated by the ase fuze. Two soft-iron (FEW) driving bands ere used.

8cm Leuchtgeschoss: fuzed Lg Zdr S/33, weight f complete round 11.20kg(24.70lb).

his was a star shell fitted with a naval pattern rass time fuze of the powder-burning type.

Propelling Charges

For the high explosive shell: 1.91kg/4.21lb of naval R P40N.

For the armour piercing shell: 1.79kg/3.95lb of naval R P 40.

For the star shell: 575gm/20.28oz/1.27lb of naval R P C/12.

Primer

The percussion primer C/12nA St was standard.

Case Identification number

None: the case could be identified by the base-stamping 8.8—*35*St or C/*95*.

0·5cm Schiffskanone C/32 in 8·8cm Marine pivot afette C/30D

0·5cm SK C/32 in 8·8cm MPL C/30D

his had originally been a shipboard anti-aircraft/ urface dual purpose gun introduced in 1932 for aval service. It was later adapted to a modified .8cm pedestal mounting to economise on deck rea, a version that was also used in a number f coast defence installations.

The gun used an electrically-driven power ammer mounted above the breech, which was vertical sliding block with semi-automatic gear. he mounting was a simple pivot secured to its mplacement by twelve heavy bolts. It was pro- ided with power control from the fire-control room and the associated mechanical fuze-setter was also remote-controlled.

Data

Calibre: 105mm/4.13in.

Length of gun: 4740mm/186.61in/15.55ft.

Length of bore: not known.

Rifling: not known.

Breech mechanism: vertical semi-automatic sliding block, percussion fired.

Traverse: 360°.

Elevation: −3° to +79°.

.5cm SK C/32 showing the sights and automatic fuze-setter.

Weight in action: 15231kg/33584lb/14.99ton.

Performance
Firing the standard high explosive shell weighing 15.06kg(33.21lb).
Muzzle velocity: 785mps/2576fps.
Maximum range: 15350m/16787yd.
Firing star shell weighing 14.70kg(32.41lb).
Muzzle velocity: 650mps/2133fps.
Maximum range: 9500m/10389yd.

Ammunition
Fixed rounds, cased charge.
10.5cm Sprgr Patr C/32 L/4.4 KZ: fuzed EK Zdr C/28, weight of complete round 23.30kg(51.38lb) This was the standard high explosive shell, fitted with two copper driving bands. The propelling charge was 3.97kg(8.75lb) of naval R P C/38 powder. The cartridge case was attached to the base of the shell by two cannelures. A reduced-charge version was also available for practice firing. The shell was unpainted from the shoulder to the tip (the remainder was painted yellow) and the propelling charge was 1.12kg(2.47lb) of R P C/38. The packages were labelled Kleine Gefechtsladung (small fighting charge), whereas the full-charge packages were labelled Gefechtsladung.
10.5cm Pzgr Patr C/32: fuzed BdZ f 10cm Pzgr, complete round weight 23.30kg(51.38lb).
This was a normal armour-piercing shell with penetrating and ballistic caps, a small explosive charge, a base fuze and a tracer unit. Two alternative projectiles existed, one with a single copper driving band and one with two sintered iron (FES) bands. The propelling charge was 4.50kg (9.92lb) of R P C/38.
10.5cm Lt Ges C/32 L/4.1: fuzed Zeit Z S/60nA, complete round weight 21.25kg(46.86lb).
This, a time-fuzed base ejection parachute sta shell, was of standard blunt-nosed naval patter Two alternative shells existed: the prewar patter with one thick and three thin copper drivin bands, and the wartime model with two FE bands. The propelling charge was 3.33kg(7.34lt of Leuchtgeschoss Pulver C/40.

Primer
The percussion primer C/12nA St was standar
Case Identification Number: C/32.

Details of the 10.5cm SK C/32 in a 8.8cm MPL mounting

10·5cm Schiffskanone L/60 in Einheitslafette

10·5cm SK L/60 in Ehl (Fichtennadel)

This was a Rheinmetall-Borsig design of dual purpose anti-aircraft/coast defence, introduced in 1937–8. It was a close relation to the contemporary 10.5cm Flak 38 gun from the same maker.

The gun was built up from multiple sections. A vertical sliding breechblock with semi-automatic gear was used and an electrically-driven power rammer was fitted. This was of the usual German roller pattern in which two diabolo-shaped rubber rollers, mounted in the breech-ring, moved inwards as the gun ran out after recoil. They were spinning rapidly, and as the fresh round was placed between them they gripped and propelled it into the chamber. The block then closed automatically and the gun fired. At the end of the recoil stroke a cam caused the rollers to separate, thus allowing the empty case to b ejected between them. This was an efficient an reliable system used on a number of Germa anti-aircraft guns, and also copied by the Amer cans on their 90mm M2 gun.

The gun was mounted on a pedestal incorpora ting an arrangement whereby the pivot could b displaced in order to level the gun trunnions i the emplacement floor was out of true. A machin fuze-setter was carried on the mounting and cor trol was by 'follow-the-pointer' dials operate from the fire control room.

Data
Calibre: 105mm/4.13in.
Length of gun: 6840mm/269.29in/22.44ft.
Length of bore: not known.

10.5cm SK L/60 in a beach defence position on the Belgian coast.

Rifling: 36 grooves, right-hand uniform twist, 1/30.
Breech mechanism: vertical semi-automatic sliding block, percussion fired
Traverse: 360°.
Elevation: −10° to +80°.
Rate of fire: 15rpm.
Weight in action: 11750kg/25909lb/11.57ton.

Performance
Firing the standard high explosive shell weighing 15.10kg(33.30lb).
Muzzle velocity: 900mps/2953fps.
Maximum range: 17500m/1938yd.
Practical ceiling: 12500m/41013ft.

Ammunition
Fixed rounds, cased charge.
So far as can be ascertained the ammunition fired from this gun consisted of the projectiles used by the 10.5cm C/32 gun, fitted to the cartridge case of the 10.5cm Flak 38.

15cm Schiffskanone C/28 in Kusten Marine Pivot Lafette C/36

15cm SK C/28 in Kust MPL C/36 (Begonie)

This is the first of what might be termed the 'true' coast defence equipments since, although the ordnance was of naval origin, the mounting was a purpose-designed coast defence central-pivot.

The gun was of orthodox monobloc construction with a vertical sliding breechblock. The mounting was an enlarged pedestal pattern and had an enveloping shield, in which a loose section moved with the gun's elevation and depression. All movements were manually controlled, and the gun was hand-loaded. Laying was by 'follow-the-pointer' dials on the mounting, which received data transmitted from the control room.

Data
Calibre: 149mm/5.87in.
Length of gun: 8291mm/326.42in/27.20ft.
Length of bore: 7815mm/307.68in/25.64ft.
Rifling: 44 grooves, right-hand increasing twist, 1/50 to 1/30.
Breech mechanism: vertical semi-automatic sliding block electrically fired.
Traverse: 360°.
Elevation: −5° to +35°.

15cm SK C/28.

Front view of the 15cm SK C/28.

Performance
Firing standard high explosive shell weighing 45.50kg(100.33lb).
Muzzle velocity: 785mps/2576fps.
Maximum range: 23500m/25700yd.

Ammunition
Separate loading, cased charge.

Projectiles
15cm Sprgr L/4.6 KZ m Haube: fuzed KZ C/27, weight 45.50kg(100.33lb).
This was a shell with a ballistic cap, the nose fuze beneath the cap, and a wooden actuating rod running from the fuze to a plug at the tip of the cap. Two copper driving bands were fitted, and a lead ring was let into the shell behind the rear driving band—acting as a decoppering device by scrubbing away any copper deposited in the barrel by the driving bands.
15cm Sprgr L/4.5 Bd Z m Hb: fuzed Bd Z C/38, weight 44.80kg(98.78lb).
This was a piercing-capped type of shell with a base fuze, but not of such construction and low explosive capacity as the Pzgr pattern. It was more the equivalent of the British 'Common Pointed' type. The ballistic cap had a black arrow pointing to the base to indicate the presence of a base fuze, and the lead decoppering ring was used.
15cm Pzgr L/3.8 m Hb: fuzed Bd Z C/38, weight 45.30kg(99.89lb).
This, an armour-piercing shell of conventional construction, was intended to attack more heavily armoured ships.

Propelling Charges
This was 14.10kg(31.09lb) of Dgl R P in an artificial silk bag, contained in a separate-loading cartridge case.

Primer
The electric primer C/22 was used.
Case Identification Number: C/28.

5cm Schiffskanone C/28 in Kusten Dreiheitslafette .M-43

5cm SK/28 in Kust Dhl LM-43

'his gun was the same as that of the previous ntry, mounted in a more elaborate armoured ·arbette mounting. Its performance and other ata were essentially the same (except that the total veight would have been somewhat higher owing to he armour), though it has not proved possible o determine an exact figure. What is of interest n this weapon is that figures are available that vell illustrate the complexity inherent in manu-acture of large artillery equipments. Study of hese figures throws new light on the problems hat face armies when they choose to demand new gun as soon as possible.

'ASK	Weight of material required (kg)	Manufacturing time in hours
Conversion of naval gun to suit land mounting	2400	500
'ront armour ...	34000	1200
Mounting base ...	6050	300
Pivots and racers ...	11650	800
Turntable	14100	3000
Armoured turret ...	87600	1200
Training gear ...	2950	2100
Ammunition supply, hoists, etc. ...	3500	5500
Sighting system ...	200	600
Electrical control. gear, lighting, etc.	5550	800

While much of this work could be done concurrently, it is nonetheless obvious that the provision of just one coast artillery gun was a long job. The table, moreover, takes no account of the actual assembly and testing of the mechanical arrangements, something that was always done in the gunbuilding shop, after which it was taken to pieces to be shipped to its selected site and there reassembled.

15cm Schiffskanone C/28M

5cm SK C/28M

This, although the same gun as the previous two ntries, was fitted to a mobile mounting of very dvanced design; in action it rested on a platform tabilised by six outriggers and for transport it vas carried on two four-wheel bogies.

The platform was of box-section and carried he gun mounting, a pivot with roller and ball-aces. Two beams extended to connect with the ransport bogies and four outriggers were hinged o the patform folding upwards for travelling. 'acks were fitted at the outer ends of the out-iggers and their weight was balanced by torsion ·ars that assisted raising and lowering operations. The bogies were identical; fitted with independent uspension on all wheels and Ackermann steering, he equipment could be towed from either end, he wheels of the rearmost bogie being locked in he fore-and-aft position. Air brakes were fitted to .ll the wheels.

Twin loading trays were provided to aid rapidity of fire; one was in use while the other was being replenished.

Postwar examination reports spoke highly of this Rheinmetall-Borsig design: 'It has balance and proportion and appears to be the outcome of a judicious consideration of all the problems involved in the design of such a weapon' said one. The only fault that could be found was a practical one—the difficulty of manoeuvering the bogies by hand when assembling them to the mounting. Each weighed three tons and, as all four wheels were connected for steering, they tended to progress in a series of sweeping curves.

Data
As for 15cm SK C/28 with the following exceptions.
Elevations: −7° 30′ to +47° 30′.
Weight in action: 19761kg/43573lb/19.45ton.

Performance, Ammunition
See 15cm SK C/28.

15cm Schiffskanone in Zwillingslafette

Although sometimes called a turret mounting, his is better described as of barbette type—since there was no overhead cover for the crew. The twin guns could be elevated independently or together and alternative hand or power control was available for all operations, except the manual-operated loading process. This was little more than the original two-gun shipboard mounting dropped into a concrete emplacement.

The mounting was at the top of a vertical turret-type shaft, through which ran hoists supplying ammunition from the underground magazine. The gunlayers sat on the front of the mounting, protected by small cupolas; fans were fitted t keep them supplied with fresh air and to clea away gun fumes. The armour thickness wa approximately 150mm(5.91in) at the front an 50mm(1.97in) etsewhere.

Details of this weapon's dimensions, perform ance and ammunition are exactly the same as th previous entry.

15cm Torpedobootskanone C/36

15cm Tbts K C/36 (Anemone)

This, as the name implies, began life as a torpedo-boat gun; numbers were taken into use for coast defence. The 15cm C/36 was usually mounted on its original ship's turret-like shielded central pivot and set in a casemate.

The gun was a simple monobloc barrel in a jacket, with sliding block breech. Operation was accomplished entirely by hand and data was transmitted to the pointer dials from the fire control room.

Data
Calibre: 149mm/5.87in.
Length of gun: 7013mm/276.10in/23.01ft.
Length of bore: 6772mm/266.61in/22.22ft.
Rifling: 44 grooves, right-hand increasing twist 1/40 to 1/30.
Breech mechanism: horizontal sliding block electrically fired.
Traverse: governed by the casemate—usually 120°
Elevation: −4° to +40°.

Performance
With standard high explosive shell weighin 45.50kg(100.33lb).
Muzzle velocity: 835mps/2740fps.
Maximum range: 19525m/21353yd.

Ammunition, Projectiles, Propelling Charges
See 15cm SK C/28.

A 15cm Tbts K, unshielded and in a casemate.

15cm Tbts K going into action.

NOTE

After the war a specimen of the 15cm Tbts K C/36 was found in a test establishment; it had been modified to use bag-charge ammunition. Although still in the experimental stages, it was an interesting example of an attempt to convert a sliding block mechanism into a bag-charge gun. One such attempt has already been discussed in the case of 15cm s FH 18/43, in which a steel obturating ring was used, but the Tbts K reverted to a variation of the De Bange method by boring a hole through the block and inserting an axial bolt with a mushroom head having a very pronounced conical seat. A similar seat was cut in the breechblock, and between the two faces was fitted an obturating pad of synthetic Buna rubber. When the breechblock was closed, the face of the vent bolt completely covered the rear of the chamber; when the gun was fired the pressure pushed the mushroom head back, which in turn placed intensified pressure on the Buna pad—thereafter squeezed forward to form a tight seal around the chamber mouth.

The designers admitted that they had not perfected the system and that their greatest problem had been the production of a pad material that would resist the high pressure and temperature involved for more than just a few rounds.

No details of the bag charge used with this weapon are known; presumably, since the gun was still in the experimental stages, the charges were never finalised.

15cm Schiffskanone L/40

15cm SK L/40

This was an elderly Krupp equipment that had been a fortress and coast defence gun since the days of World War 1.

The barrel was a built-up design recoiling in a ring cradle. The recoil system was mounted alongside the cradle—a hydraulic buffer on one side and a spring recuperator on the other—and was unusual in that the piston rods were attached to the mounting and the cylinders recoiled with the gun. The reverse is usually the case.

The mounting was a central-pivot pattern with a large shield completely enveloping the breech. The shield's armour was 105mm(4.13in) thick on the front face, 55mm(2.17in) at the sides and 25mm(0.98in) on the roof. The entire mounting was usually enclosed in a concrete casemate.

Data

Calibre: 149mm/5.87in.
Length of gun: 6010mm/236.61in/19.72ft.
Length of bore: 5585mm/219.88in/18.32ft.
Rifling: 44 grooves.
Breech mechanism: horizontal sliding block, percussion fired.
Traverse: To 360°, dictated by the design of casemate.
Elevation: −10° to +30°.

Performance

Firing standard high explosive shell weighing 45.50kg(100.33lb).
Muzzle velocity: 805mps/2641fps.
Maximum range: 20000m/21872yd.

A 15cm SK L/40, shielded and in a casemate mounting.

The ammunition for this gun was most unusual in that the gun fired both fixed and separate-loading cased ammunition interchangeably. This was to be avoided, since the gas-wash at the mouth of the separate-loading case invariably caused erosion of the inner surface of the gun chamber. When the fixed round was loaded, the case spanned the eroded area and, on firing, was expanded (be it ever so slightly) into it; this rendered extraction difficult or even—in some cases—impossible. Just how this hazard was avoided in this weapon is now far from clear, though it may well be that they never did sufficient firing for erosion to be a problem.

Another remarkable feature was that the fixed round of ammunition weighed about 75kg (165.4lb), well above the weight that one man could comfortably handle. The question thus arises of whether fixed ammunition of such dimensions is a viable proposition, since it rather defeats all the concept's objects and virtues if two men are needed to lift it.

Fixed Rounds

15cm Sprgr Patr L/40.

This projectile was fitted with an elderly brass detonating fuze of unknown nomenclature and had a single copper driving band. It weighed 45.50kg(100.33lb). The case was crimped into a recess behind the driving band and contained 10.40kg(22.93lb) of naval Str P DM/9.

Separate-Loading Projectiles

15cm Sprgr L/40: (KZ f 15cm L/40), weight 45.50kg(100.33lb).

This was almost identical to the projectile used in the fixed round, differing only in having two copper driving bands (instead of one) and no crimping groove for the case.

15cm Lt Ges L/40: fuzed Lt Ges Zdr S/33, weight

ot known.
'his star shell was fitted with a combustion-attern time fuze dating from World War 1. The hell was of the normal base ejection pattern.

eparate-Loading Propelling Charges
'or the high explosive shell the cartridge case 'as longer than that used in the separate-loading ound but carried the same 10.40kg(22.93lb) harge. The star shell charge (Leuchtgeschoss Ladung) used the same type of cartridge case as the high explosive shell, and consisted of 7.10kg (15.66lb) of Leuchtgeschoss Pulver 40.

Primer
The percussion primer C/12nA was standard for all rounds, although the C/13nA small-gauge primer has been reported on old-model cases.

Case Identification Number
C/95 stamped into the case-base.

5cm Unterseeboots und Torpedoboots Kanone L/45

5cm UbtsuTbts K L/45

)ne of the more modern weapons found in the ;ermans' coast defences, this also started as a aval shipboard weapon before large numbers vere installed in seaward defences. A dual-purpose nti-aircraft surface gun, it was provided with uitable sights and fire control equipment to allow : to change rapidly from one role to the other.

The gun was mounted in a ring cradle with pring recuperators and hydraulic buffers above nd below the cradle respectively. The cradle was runnioned to a small top-carriage assembly that evolved on a roller-race on top of a pedestal nchored to the emplacement. Two gunlayers vere used, one for elevation and one for line, oth seated on the left of the gun. An enveloping hield was fitted.

)ata
:alibre: 150mm/5.91in.
.ength of gun: 6620mm/260.63in/21.72ft.
.ength of bore: 6240mm/245.67in/20.47ft.
Rifling: 48 grooves.
Breech mechanism: horizontal sliding block, percussion fired.
'raverse: To 360°, depending upon the emplacement.
:levation: −4° to +45°.

'erformance
'iring standard high explosive shell weighing ·5.30kg(99.89lb).
'ull charge: velocity 680mps/2231fps, maximum ange 16000m/17498yd.
'iring star shell weighing 40.35kg(88.97lb).
'ull charge: velocity 500mps/1641fps, maximum ange 10600/11592yd.

Ammunition
Separate loading, cased charge.

'rojectiles
5cm Sprgr L/4.1 KZ: fuzed EK Zdr C/28 or)opp Z S/60, weight 45.30kg(99.89lb).
This was the standard high explosive shell and vas of conventional design with two copper driving bands.
15cm Sprgr L/4.1 m Bd Z: fuzed Bd Z C/36, weight 45.30kg(99.89lb).
This is a 'common pointed' shell—pointed and base fuzed but with a relatively large explosive filling and little penetrating power against armour. It was mainly intended for use against light craft and against the unarmoured upperworks of heavier ships.
15cm Hbgr 16: fuzed Hbgr Z 17/23 or Dopp Z 16K, weight 57.40kg(126.57lb).
This was an elderly design of ballistic-capped high explosive shell. The fuzes were also elderly types, specially designed for use beneath the ballistic caps and provided with extended actuating rods. The use of a time fuze under a ballistic cap is to be deprecated, since the cap has to be completely removed to set the fuze—a process that does nothing to improve the rate of fire. On the other hand it must be admitted that time fuze fire with coast artillery was an uncommon pastime.
15cm Lt Ges L/3.5: fuzed Zeit Z S/60nA, weight 35.60kg(78.50lb).
This was a standard parachute star shell of the nose ejection pattern. A prewar design, it was fitted with a single copper driving band. Its maximum range was 7500m(8202yd).
15cm Lt Ges L/4.3: fuzed Zeit Z S/60nA, weight 40.35kg(88.97lb).
This was an improved star shell, longer and heavier and of the base ejection type. Two soft-iron (FEW) driving bands were fitted. This shell ranged to 10600m(11592yd).

Propelling Charges
For high explosive shells the charge was 8.10kg (17.86lb) of R P 12.
For the star shells, 7.50kg(16.54lb) of naval Tri R P was used.

Primer
The percussion primer C/12nA was standard.

Case Identification Number
The case bore the base-stamp C/95, the same as that of the L/40 coast defence gun.

17cm Schiffskanone L/40

17cm SK L/40

This was another elderly weapon retained for coastal use, although a number of barrels were also taken for railway gun mounting (see 17cm K[E]), and dated back to the turn of the century. The gun was of built-up construction and was mounted in a ring cradle, beneath which was a hydrospring recoil system. This in turn was trunnioned into a top-carriage revolving on a pedestal. A curved front shield of 100mm(3.94in) plate was usually fitted but the remaining protection was usually given by the emplacement, which was generally of the casemate type.

Although completely of manual operation, the guns were generally fitted with the newest and most efficient fire control systems in which data were transmitted from the remote fire control room to pointer indicators on the mounting. Though old, the gun was no older than many similar designs in British or American service and when opportunity arose it gave a good account of itself.

Data
Calibre: 173mm/6.81in.
Length of gun: 6900mm/271.65in/22.64ft.
Length of bore: 4992mm/196.54in/16.38ft.
Rifling: right-hand increasing twist, 1/45 to 1/30.
Breech mechanism: horizontal sliding block, percussion fired.
Traverse: to 360°, depending upon the emplacement.
Elevation: −5° to +45°.

Performance
Firing standard high explosive shell weighing 62.80kg(138.47lb).
Maximum charge: velocity 875mps/2871fps, maximum range 27200m/29746yd.

Ammunition
Separate loading, cased charge.

Projectiles
17cm Sprgr L/4.7 KZ m Hb: fuzed EK Zdr Sprgr or Dopp Z S/90, weight 62.80kg(138.47lb
This was a normal high explosive shell with ballistic cap and a fuze beneath. The filling wa 6.40kg(14.11lb) of TNT in a cardboard container and the shell had two copper driving bands.
17cm Pzgr m Bd Z: fuzed Bd Z C/38, weight nc known.
This, an armour piercing shell, was fitted wit ballistic and penetrating caps and the usual sma explosive filling. It was also fitted with two coppe driving bands.
17cm Lt Ges L/3.4: fuzed Zeit Z S/60nA, weigh 58.50kg(128.99lb).
This was the usual short-nosed naval pattern o base ejection parachute star shell, fitted with tw copper driving bands.

Propelling Charges
Various alternative charges were provided a different times, all of which produced the sam ballistics.
High explosive shell, 1: 22.60kg/49.83lb R P C/1
High explosive shell, 2: 20.50kg/45.20lb R P C/1 of different dimensions.
High explosive shell, 3: 23.60kg/52.04lb R P C/3
High explosive shell, 4: 25.30kg/55.79lb R P 38 B
Star shell: 13.40kg/29.55lb of R P C/12.

Primer
The percussion primer C/12nA was standard.

A 17 cm SK L/40 in a shielded centre-pivot mounting.

20·3cm Schiffskanone C/34

20·3cm SK C/34

Another ex-naval design, this weapon was normally turret-mounted on a central pivot. There is little of note in its design, being an orthodox weapon fitted in a ring cradle. Full power operation was provided to control elevation, traverse and the loading cycle, and data was transmitted from the fire control room to the usual type of Magslip follow-the-pointer dials.

Data
Calibre: 203mm/7.99in.
Length of gun: 12150mm/478.35in/39.86ft.
Length of bore: 11587mm/456.18in/38.02ft.
Rifling: 64 grooves, right-hand increasing twist, 1/50 to 1/30.
Brech mechanism: horizontal sliding block, percussion fired.
Traverse: to 360°, depending upon the emplacement.
Elevation: −5° to +40°.

Performance
Firing standard high explosive shell weighing 122.00kg(269.01lb).
Full charge: velocity 925mps/3035fps, maximum range 37000m/40,463yd/22.99mile.

Ammunition
Separate-loading, case charge.

Projectiles
20.3cm Sprgr L/4.7 m Hb: fuzed KZ C/27 or Dopp Z 28K, weight 122.00kg(269.01lb).
This was the standard high explosive shell, fitted with a ballistic cap over the fuze. Three copper driving bands were fitted and the base was prepared for a tracer unit (but plugged).
20.3cm Sprgr L/4.7 m Bd Z m Hb: fuzed Bd Z C/38, weight 124.00kg(273.42lb).
This was a similar shell to the previous model but had a longer ballistic cap and a base fuze
20.3cm Pz Sprgr L/4.5 m Bd Z m Hb: fuzed Bd Z C/38, weight 123.00kg(271.22lb).
Similar to the previous models, this shell was slightly shorter and was designed as a piercing shell. A lead ring was fitted behind the two copper driving bands to act as a decoppering agent
20.3cm Sprgr Ub L/4.6 KZ M Hb: fuzed KZ C/27, weight 39.20kg(86.44lb).
This was similar to the standard shell but was slightly shorter, much lighter, and had a special filling designed to give a prominent cloud of white smoke on bursting. This was a practice or training shell.
20.3cm Pz Sprgr L/4.4 m Hb: fuzed Bd Z C/28, weight 123.00kg(271.22lb).
Very similar to the other piercing shells in construction, this (a naval design) was otherwise slightly shorter. It also had a pronounced 'waistline' at the base of the ballistic cap and three copper driving bands.

Propelling Charges
Two charges, full and reduced, were provided. The reduced charge was contained in the cartridge case, which was closed by a brass cup, and the additional section (to make up the full charge) was issued in a cylindrical cloth bag that was loaded ahead of the case.

A 20.3cm SK C/34 in a shielded barbette mounting.

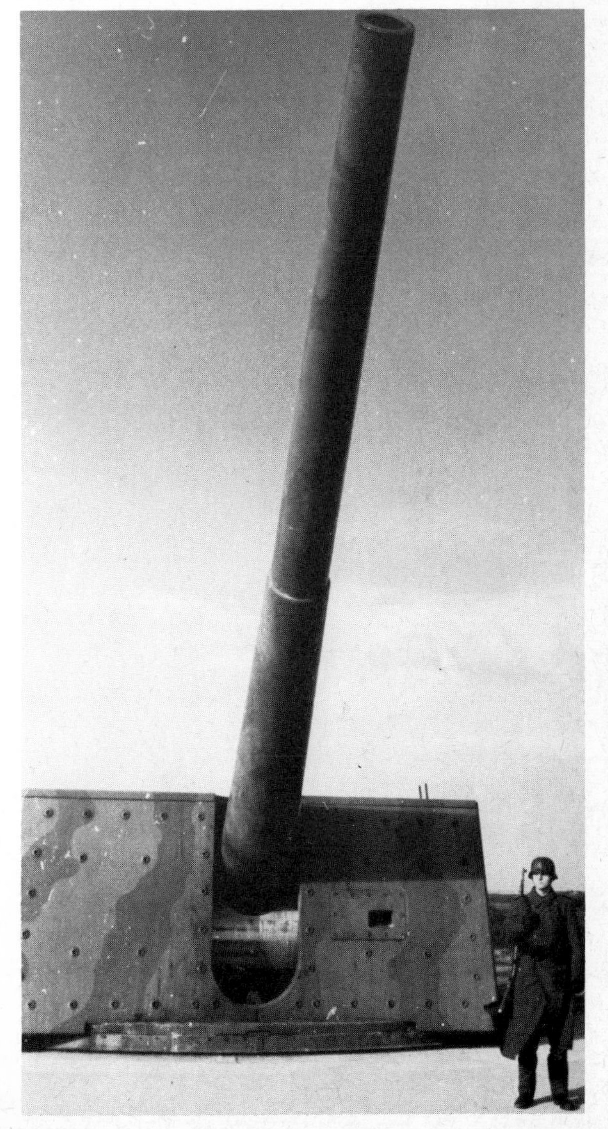

Reduced charge: 30.50kg/67.25lb R P 38.
Full charge: 20.70kg/45.64lb R P 38 Bu added to the reduced charge.

Primer
The percussion primer C/12nA was standard.
Case Identification Number
None: the case could be identified by the base-stamp W KARTH 34.

NOTE
An unconfirmed postwar statement averred tha a low-pressure experimental model of this gu had been built and successfully fired. Little furthe information has ever come to light, except tha another report stated that with a charge weigh of 46.50kg(102.53lb) it attained a muzzle velocit of 918mps(3012fps) with the Pzgr L/4.4 shell.

24cm Schiffskanone L/40 in Dreiheitslafette C/98

24cm SK L/40 in Drh L C/98

This weapon was an orthodox design of gun mounted on a barbette carriage—a central pivot mounting sunk into a pit so that the gun working platform was slightly below ground level and acted as a shield for the ammunition handlers in the pit. It was installed with either a frontal shield or a full turret, as the location demanded. Elevation was controlled from the gun's working platform but traverse was controlled from the pit, acting on dial indications.

Data
Calibre: 238mm/9.37in.
Length of gun: 9550mm/375.98in/31.33ft.
Length of bore: 8900mm/350.39in/29.20ft.
Rifling: right-hand increasing twist, 1/50 to 1/30.
Breech mechanism: horizontal sliding block, percussion fired.
Traverse: to 360°, depending on the emplacement
Elevation: −5° to +45°.

Performance
Firing standard high explosive shell weighing 148.50kg(327.44lb).
Full charge: velocity 810mps/2658fps; maximum range 26750m/29254yd.

Ammunition
Separate-loading, cased charge.

Projectiles
24cm Sprgr L/4.2 m Bd Z u KZ m Hb: fuze EK Zdr f Sprgr or Dopp Z 16 plus Bd Z f Sprgr weight 148.50kg(327.44lb).
This was the standard high explosive projectile supplied with both base and nose fuzes. It wa fitted with two copper driving bands and th filling was 16.33kg(36.01lb) of TNT in pre-presse blocks. A different model of this shell was fuze with either a KZ C/27 or a Dopp Z S/90 nos fuse and a Bd Z C/28 base fuze.
24cm Pz Sprgr L/4.1 m Bd Z: fuzed Bd Z f Sprg K, weight 150.50kg(331.85lb).
A piercing shell, this was slightly shorter tha the high explosive shell and had penetrating an ballistic caps and a base fuze.

Propelling Charges
A two-part charge was used. The reduced charg was carried in the cartridge case and the ful charge increment was supplied in a separate bag
Reduced charge: 37.50kg/82.69lb R P C/32.
Full charge increment: 6.90kg/15.21lb R P C/3

Primer
The percussion primer C/12nA was used.

The 24cm SK L/40 in Dreiheitslafette C/98

A barbette-mounted 24 cm SK L/40.

24cm Schiffskanone L/35

24cm SK L/35

This was a very elderly equipment dating from c.1910 in its coast artillery role. A Krupp design, it retained a unique pattern of breechblock in the form of a half-cylinder with the curved face to the rear. There are sound theoretical reasons for this, of course, but it must have made removal and assembly more than usually difficult. The mounting was of the central pivot type with a box-like steel structure supporting the gun and working platforms, all revolving on a rather small diameter racer-ring.

Data
Calibre: 238mm/9.37in.
Length of gun: 8400mm/330.71in/27.56ft.
Length of bore: 7800mm/307.09in/25.59ft.
Rifling: not known.
Breech mechanism: horizontal sliding block, percussion fired.
Traverse: to 360°, depending upon the emplacement.
Elevation: −5° to +45°.

Performance
Firing standard high explosive shell weighing 148.50kg(327.44lb).
Full charge: velocity 675mps/2215fps, maximum range 20200m/22091yd.

Ammunition
Separate-loading, cased charge.

Projectiles
See 24cm SK L/40.

Propelling Charges
A single charge was contained in a brass cartridge case and consisted of 31.00kg(68.36lb) of R P C/32.

Primer
The percussion primer C/12nA was used.

Case Identification Number
None: the base-stamp KART F TH BR K (ie: for Theodor-Bruno-Kanone) was used.

28cm Schiffskanone L/40

28cm SK L/40

This Krupp design, dating from 1901 and first introduced for the 'Deutschland' class of pre-dreadnoughts, was extensively used in coast defences during both wars. The method of mounting ran the gamut of every conceivable design from modified railgun mounts, through barbettes, pedestals (some in pits and some at ground level) and shielded cupolas, to full turret installations. Power operation was usually provided regardless of the type of mounting. The gun, taken for coast use in 1914, formed the starting point for a series of 28cm designs that differed in little except their barrel lengths.

Data
Calibre: 283mm/11.14in.
Length of gun: 11200mm/440.94in/17.36ft.
Length of bore: not known.
Rifling: 80 grooves, right-hand increasing twist, 1/50 to 1/30.

Above: A 28cm SK L/40 in a barbette mounting, unshielded and with an unusual amount of camouflage for a coasta defence gun.
Below: A 28cm SK L/40 being prepared for action.

reech mechanism: horizontal sliding block, percussion fired.
raverse: to 360°, depending on the emplacement.
levation: −5° to +45°.

erformance
iring standard high explosive shell weighing 40.00kg(529.20lb).
'ull charge: velocity 820mps/2690fps, maximum ange 29500m/32261yd.

mmunition
eparate-loading, cased charge.

rojectiles
8cm Sprgr L/4. 1 KZ u Bd Z m Hb: fuzed KZ C/27 (or Dopp Z S/90) and Bd Z C/38, weight 240.00kg(529.20lb).
A ballistic-capped shell with nose and base fuzes, this was filled with 18.70kg(41.23lb) of TNT in pre-pressed blocks.

Propelling Charges
A single charge-bag was contained in a brass case. The charge consisted of 67.00kg(147.74lb) of R P C/32 or 64.00kg(141.12lb) of R P C/12.

Primer
The percussion primer C/12nA was used.

Case Identification Number
None: the base-stamp 28CM KARTH C/95 was used.

28cm Küsten Haubitze

28cm Kust H

This elderly Krupp design was closely related to the 28cm Haubitze L/12, the heavy field weapon, from which it differed principally in using a cased charge instead of a bagged one.

The weapon dated back to the turn of the century when the use of howitzers for coast defence was in its heyday, the object being to drop shells on to the less heavily armoured decks of ships and to obtain results in that way (rather than battering against the massively armoured sides). With the arrival of higher-velocity guns and better piercing shells this system was gradually abandoned, but several countries retained them in their defences until World War 2—particularly the USA. This model was, however, the only coast howitzer still used by the German defences.

Like the howitzer L/12 it was emplaced on a turntable, in the coast role anchored into the concrete emplacement rather than a laboriously dug-in transportable platform. The installations were usually deep pits concealed from the shore but it is doubtful if many were in active use.

Data
Calibre: 283mm/11.14in.
Length of gun: 3396mm/133.70in/11.14ft.
Breech mechanism: horizontal sliding block, percussion fired.
Traverse: to 360°, depending on the emplacement.
Elevation: 0 to + 70°.
Weight in action: 37000kg/81585lb/36.42ton.

Performance
Firing standard high explosive shell weighing 350.00kg(771.75lb).
Charge 6: velocity 379mps/1243fps, maximum range 11400m/12467yd.

Ammunition
Separate-loading, cased charge.

Projectiles
28cm Sprgr L/3.5 m Bd Z: fuzed Bd Z f Sprgr 28cm H, weight 350.00kg(771.75lb).
This was a pointed steel piercing shell of very dated appearance, with a short nose and single driving band close to the base.

Propelling Charges
No details are known of the six charges available.

28cm Schiffskanone L/45

28cm SK L/45

This was similar to the L/40 weapon in all respects except that the barrel was 5 calibres longer. The gun was introduced in 1907 for the 'Nassau' class dreadnoughts and the battle cruiser SMS 'Von der Tann'; the shore mountings were of the same assorted types.

Data
Calibre: 283mm/11.14in.
Length of gun: 12735mm/501.38in/41.78ft.
Length of bore: not known.
Rifling: right-hand increasing twist, 1/50 to 1/30.
Breech mechanism: horizontal sliding block, percussion fired.
Traverse: to 360°, depending on the emplacement.
Elevation: −5° to +45°.

Performance
Firing standard high explosive shell weighing 284.00kg(626.22lb).

Full charge: velocity 875mps/2871fps, maximum range 36100m/39479yd/22.43mile.

Ammunition
Separate-loading, cased charge.

Projectiles
28cm Sprgr L/4.4 m Bd Z u KZ m Hb: fuzed EK Zdr f Sprgr (or Dopp Z 16) and Bd Z f Sprgr, weight 284.00kg(626.22lb).
This was the original standard high explosive shell, a ballistic-capped pattern of World War 1 design and using old pattern fuzes.
28cm Sprgr L/4.4 m Bd Z u KZ m Hb: fuzed KZ C/27 (or Dopp Z S/90) and Bd Z C/38 weight 284.00kg(626.22lb).
This was the same as the previous model bu was fitted with modern pattern fuzes.

Propelling Charges
A single bag was contained in the cartridge case consisting of 106.00kg(233.73lb) of R P C/12.

Primer
The percussion primer C/12nA was used.

Case Identification Number
None: the case bore the base-stamp L/45/50.

28cm Schiffskanone L/50

28cm SK L/50

The third of the Krupp series of 28cm naval barrels to be used as coast guns, this again differed from its predecessors principally by its length—another increase of 5 calibres. The only other change lay in the recoil system that, instead of being entirely below the ring cradle, was equally divided with two hydraulic buffer cylinders above the cradle and two hydropneumatic recuperators below. The mountings were generally fully-shielded barbettes. The original 28cm L/50 was introduced in 1909 for the battlecruisers 'Moltke', 'Goeben' and 'Seydlitz'.

Data
Calibre: 283mm/11.14in.
Length of gun: 14150mm/557.09in/46.42ft.
Length of bore: 13304mm/523.78in/43.65ft.
Rifling: right-hand increasing twist, 1/50 to 1/30.
Breech mechanism: horizontal sliding block, percussion fired.
Traverse: to 360°, depending on the emplacemen
Elevation: −4° to +45°.

Performance
Firing standard high explosive shell weighin 284.00kg(626.22lb).
Full charge: velocity 905mps/2969fps, maximun range 39100m/42760yd/24.30mile.
Reduced charge: velocity 786mps/2579fps, maximum range 30200m/33027yd.

Ammunition
Separate-loading, cased charge.

Projectiles
28cm Sprgr L/4.4 m KZ u Bd Z m Hb.
This is the projectile used with the L/45 gu
28cm Sprgr L/3.6 m Bd Z m Hb: fuzed Bd Z C/36, weight 302.00kg(665.91lb).
A piercing shell, this was fitted with ballistic an

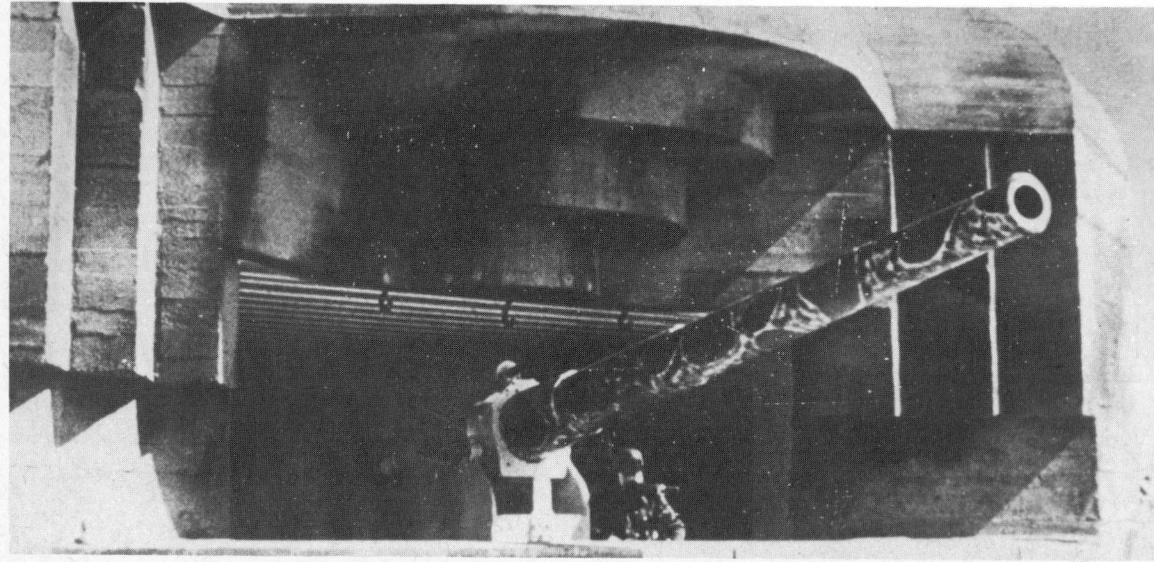
A casemate-mounted 28cm SK L/50.

enetrating caps and a base fuze.

8cm Pzgr L/3.2 m Bd Z m Hb: fuzed Bd Z C/38, weight 302.00(665.91lb).

This was an armour-piercing shell with penetrating and ballistic caps and a base fuze.

Owing to the extra weight of these last two projectiles, their performance differed from the standard as follows:

Full charge: velocity 890mps/2920fps, maximum range 31000m/33902yd.

Reduced charge: velocity 770mps/2526fps, maximum range 25000m/27340yd.

Propelling Charges

This consisted of a reduced charge in the cartridge case and a full-charge in a separate bag.

Reduced charge (Hauptkart): 70.00kg/154.35lb R P C/12.

Full charge increment (Vorkart): 36.00kg/79.38lb R P C/12.

Primer

The percussion primer C/12nA was standard.

Case Identification Number

None: the case used the base-stamp L/45/90.

30·5cm Schiffskanone L/50

30·5cm SK L/50

After reviewing the collection of somewhat elderly equipments in the 24cm and 28cm class, it is a relief to turn to this weapon—which although using an ex-World War 1 shipboard gun, was a Krupp design and a highly efficient and modern weapon that could justly be considered one of the best coast artillery equipments ever built. The Germans claimed that the 30.5cm SK was particularly accurate at long range and that it was capable of high rates of elevation, traverse and firing owing to the highly mechanised installation.

Some of these guns were built under contract by Skoda and showed very small differences owing to manufacturing processes; there was, however, one major difference, for the Krupp guns used the usual sliding block breech whereas the Skoda models used an interrupted-screw breech mechanism (although it still used a cased charge). Both types had the same ballistic performance.

The mounting was invariably a turret within a casemate of then-modern reinforced-concrete construction. The turret rested on the top half of a massive ballrace and was also partially supported by a system of leaf springs mounted on a supporting wall around the racer. The recoil shock drove the turret down on the springs to rest on the support wall and thus relieved the ballrace of any hammering. The turret itself was two-storied; the upper compartment contained the gun, its controls and its loading gear, while the lower floor housed the ammunition-hoist motors and gear, the elevation and traverse motors, and an air compressor. Beneath the turret level (at the rear) was an underground magazine, from which ammunition was delivered on trolleys to the handling room by way of flash-proof doors. From the handling room the ammunition was sent up hoists to a gallery at the level of the lower turret compartment. Arriving at this level it passed through more flash-proof doors on to a trolley which was then pushed around the gallery to another set of flash doors leading into the turret. There the projectiles and the propellant were transferred to the final hoist and delivered to the gun-house level. It will be appreciated that the insistence on flash-proof doors indicated the naval parentage of the design.

Twin-gun turrets were also provided (in smaller numbers than the single-gun type); they were of essentially the same pattern.

The detachment required to operate the single gun numbered 54 men, 27 of whom were solely concerned with moving ammunition about.

Data

Calibre: 305mm/12.01in.

Length of gun: 15250mm/600.39in/50.03ft.

Length of bore: 14185mm/558.46in/46.54ft.

Rifling: 88 grooves.

Breech mechanism: horizontal sliding block, percussion fired.

Traverse: to 360° depending on the emplacement

Elevation: −4° to +45°.

Weight, without armour: 177000kg/390285lb/174.23ton.

Performance

Firing standard high explosive projectile weighing 250.00kg(551.25lb).

Normal charge: velocity 1050mps/3445fps, range figures not available.

Super charge: velocity 1120mps/3675fps, maximum range 51000m/55774yd/31.69mile.

Firing armour piercing shell weighing 405.00kg (893.03lb).

Normal charge: velocity 820mps/2690fps, range figures not available.

Super charge: velocity 855mps/2805fps, maximum range 32500m/35542yd/20.12mile.

Ammunition

Separate loading, cased charge.

Projectiles

30.5cm Sprgr L/3.6 m Bd Z u KZ m Hb: fuzed

KZ C/37 (or Dopp Z 45K) and Bd Z C/38, weight 250.00kg(551.25lb).
This was the standard high explosive shell for long-range firing, fitted with a ballistic cap and nose and base fuzes.
30.5cm L/3.4 m Bd Z m Hb: fuzed Bd Z C/38, weight 250.00kg(551.25lb).
This, a semi-armour-piercing shell designed for the attack of lighter vessels, was fitted with penetrating and ballistic caps and a base fuze.
30.5cm Pzgr L/3.4 m Bd Z: fuzed Bd Z C/38, weight 405.00kg(893.03lb).
This was an armour-piercing shell designed for the attack of armoured capital ships. It was fitted with penetrating and ballistic caps and a base fuze.
30.5cm Minengeschoss L/4.8.
This was an experimental high-capacity thin-walled shell weighing 275.00kg(606.38lb) and carrying 103.00kg(227.12lb) of explosive. It was apparently intended as a long-range bombardment shell, but development was not completed before the war ended.
30.5cm/20cm Sprgr L/4.6 TS.
Another experimental shell under development at the end of the war, this was in the form of a parallel-walled finned bomb with over-size fins and a discarding sabot at the mid-point of the body. No details of performance are known.

Propelling Charges
The propelling charge was divided into two sections to give normal and super charges. The normal portion was in the cartridge case and the 'super' increment was in a separate bag.
Normal charge: 127.00kg/280.04lb R P C/12.
Super charge: 20.00kg/44.10lb R P C/12.

Primer
The percussion primer C/12nA was used.

38cm Schiffskanone C/34

38cm SK C/34 (Siegfried)

The gun used in this equipment was originally developed by Krupp in 1934 for the battleships 'Bismark' and 'Tirpitz'. When it was adapted for coast defence the chamber length was increased and a special long range shell, the 'Siegfried Granate', was developed.

The mounting was very similar in layout to that described for the 30.5cm gun: a double-compartment turret within a modern casemate, with an attendant underground magazine. Full power assistance was provided for elevation, ramming and hoisting.

Probably the best-known installation of 38cm SK C/34 guns was the 4 of *Batterie Todt,* on Cap Griz Nez, which were used during the war to shell Dover and the south-west coast of England —and which duelled with their British equivalents, the 15in guns of Wanstone Battery at Dover. The 15in guns, however, had the final say in the matter and, in 1944 assisted by air observation, obtained a direct hit on one of the 38cm weapons.

Data
Calibre: 380mm/14.96in.
Length of gun: 19630mm/772.83in/64.40ft.
Length of bore: 18405mm/724.61in/60.38ft.
Rifling: 90 grooves, right-hand increasing twist. 1/36 to 1/30.
Breech mechanism: horizontal sliding block, percussion fired.
Traverse: to 360°, determined by the emplacement.
Elevation: −4° to +60°.

Performance
Firing standard high explosive shell weighing 800.00kg(1764.00lb).
Full charge: velocity 820mps/2690fps, maximum range 42000m/45931yd/26.10mile.
Firing special long-range shell weighing 475.00kg (1047.38lb).
Full charge: 1050mps/3445fps, maximum range 55700m/60914yd/34.61mile.
Reduced charge: 920mps/3012fps, maximum range 40000m/43744yd/24.85mile.

Ammunition
Separate-loading, cased charge.

Projectiles
38cm Sprgr L/4.6 m KZ m Hb: fuzed KZ C/27, weight 800.00kg(1764.00lb).

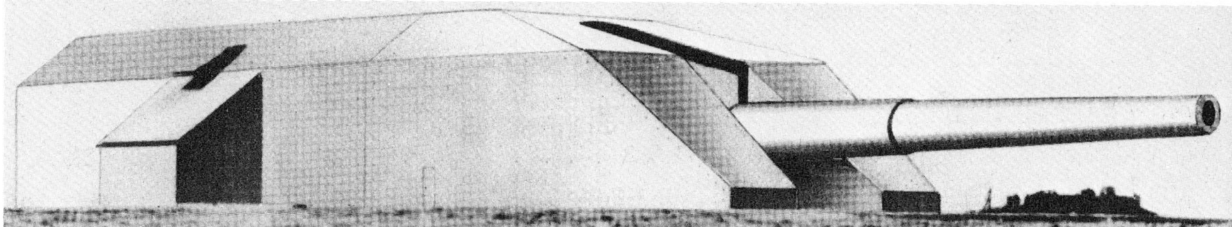
A 38cm SK C/34 in a turret.

This, the standard high explosive shell, was fitted with a nose fuze under the ballistic cap.

38cm Sprgr L/4.4 m Bd Z m Hb: fuzed Bd Z C/38, weight 800.00kg(1764.00lb).

A semi-armour-piercing shell for the attack of lightly armoured vessels, this was fitted with penetrating and ballistic caps and a base fuze.

38cm Pz Sprgr L/4.4 m Bd Z m Hb: fuzed Bd Z C/38, weight 800.00kg(1764.00lb).

This was a full armour-piercing shell fitted with penetrating and ballistic caps, a base fuze, three copper driving bands and a lead de-coppering ring. This was capable of dealing with the heaviest ships afloat.

38cm 'Siegfried Granate' L/4.5 m Bd Z u KZ m Hb: fuzed Hbgr Z40K (or Dopp Z 45K) and Bd Z 40K, weight 495.00kg(1091.48lb).

This was the special lightweight long-range bombardment shell; of army design, it was fitted with special fuzes beneath a ballistic cap and also carried a base fuze. The bursting charge was 69.00kg(152.15lb) of TNT.

Propelling Charges

Two charges were provided, one for the standard 800kg shell and a special charge for the 495kg Siegfried Granate. The standard charge was divided into two sections; the main section was packed in the cartridge case and the subsidiary portion was packed separately.

Hauptkart f 38cm K: 110.00kg/242.55lb R P C/38

Vorkart f 38cm K: 101.00kg/222.71lb R P C/38.

These charges were divided for convenience in handling and were not normally fired separately (not Hauptkart only) as a fighting charge, although this could be done to provide a practice charge.

The special 'Siegfried Ladung' also came in two portions, but this could be fired as either a reduced or a full charge;

Hauptkart 'Siegfried Ladung': 133.00kg/293.27lb Gudol R P.

Vorkart 'Siegfried Ladung': 123.00kg/271.22lb Gudol R P.

It will be noted that an army propellant was used.

Primer

The percussion primer C/12nA was standard.

Case Identification Number

It is believed that 6597 was allotted but that it was never applied; the cases were distinguished by the base-stamp 38CM—34.

A 38cm SK C/34 (Siegfried) in a shielded casemate mounting on the French coast.

40·6cm Schiffskanone C/34 in Schussgerät C/39

40·6cm SK C/34 in SG C/39 (Adolf)

This was also a Krupp 1934 design, originally intended for battleships of the never-built H-Klasse. No modification was done to prepare the guns for coast defence work; indeed, since some guns had breechblocks opening to the right and some to the left, it is apparent that 'handed' pairs of naval guns destined for twin-turret installations had been split up for land service.

The mounting, like those of the 30.5cm and 38cm weapons, was a massive turret revolving on a ballrace and was usually protected by a casemate. The turret was, in this application, a single level gun-house on a pedestal, with the rear of the mounting supported on bogies travelling on a rail track. Four underground magazines, two for cartridges and two for shells, delivered their ammunition by hoists to the rear of the emplacement, from whence it was conveyed to the rear of the turret on trolleys and hoisted to the ramming tables. It is of interest to note that—although power assistance was provided for elevation, traverse and ammunition hoisting—ramming was done by hand, though towards the end of the war some installations added power-ramming.

Data
Calibre: 406mm/16.00in.
Length of gun: 20300mm/799.21in/66.60ft.
Length of bore: not known.
Rifling: not known.
Breech mechanism: horizontal sliding block, per cussion fired.
Traverse: to 360°, determined by the emplacemen
Elevation: 0 to +60°.

Performance
Firing standard high explosive shell weighin 1030kg(2271lb).
Full charge: velocity 810mps/2658fps, maximun range 42800m/46806yd/26.59mile.
Firing the long-range shell weighing 610k (1345lb).
Reduced charge: 970mps/3180fps, maximun range 46700m/51071yd/29.02mile.
Full charge: 1050mps/3448fps, maximum rang 56000m/61241yd/34.80mile.

Ammunition
Separate-loading, cased charge.

The 40.6cm SK C/34 (Adolf) in a shielded casemate.

A further view of the 'Adolf' barbette in the Krupp factory.

A side view of the two-gun barbette for the 40.6cm 'Adolf' assembled in the Krupp factory for final adjustment before despatch to its firing site.

Wooden mock-up shells for the 40.6cm SK 'Adolf' showing the ammunition hoist arrangement in the factory mock-up.

Projectiles

40.6cm Sprgr L/4.8 m KZ m Hb: fuzed KZ C/27, weight 1030kg(2271lb).

This, the standard high explosive shell, was fitted with a ballistic cap over the nose fuze. Three copper driving bands were fitted.

40.6cm Sprgr L/4.6 m Bd Z m Hb: fuzed Bd Z C/38, weight 1030kg(2271lb).

A semi-armour-piercing shell, similar to the high explosive type in outline but fitted with penetrating and ballistic caps and a base fuze.

40.6cm Pz Sprgr L/4.4 m Bd Z m Hb: fuzed Bd Z C/38, weight 1030kg(2271lb).

This was an armour-piercing shell with penetrating and ballistic caps and a base fuze.

40.6cm 'Adolf Granate' L/4.2 m Bd Z u KZ m Hb: fuzed Hbgr Z 40K (or Dopp Z S/90K) and Bd Z 40K, weight 610kg(1345lb).

This, an army development for coast gun use, was a special lightweight long-range high explosive shell with a ballistic cap. It was fitted with three copper driving bands at the base and a copper centering band at the shoulder. The filling was 78.00kg(171.99lb) of TNT.

Propelling Charges

Two charges were provided, one for use with the standard 1030kg shells and one for use with the Adolf Granate. The standard charge was supplied in two parts, for convenience in handling, and consisted of the following:

Hauptkart f 40.6cm: 149.00kg/328.55lb R P 40 Bu
Vorkart f 40.6cm: 152.00kg/335.16lb R P 40 Bu

The Hauptkart fitted into the cartridge case, while the Vorkart was in a cloth bag and was loaded ahead of the Hauptkart. The 'Adolf Ladung' also consisted of two portions that could be fired as a reduced or full charge.

Hauptkart 'Adolf Ladung': 160.00kg/352.80lb Gudol R P.
Vorkart 'Adolf Ladung': 203.80kg/449.38lb Gudol R P.

Primer

The percussion primer C/12nA was used.

Case Identification Number

None: the case bore the base-stamp 40.6 W34 ST.

A casemate battery in course of construction.

A Krupp photograph of a twin-turret 40.6cm SK installation, assembled in the factory for testing.

RECOILLESS ARTILLERY

The recoilless gun development undertaken in the Third Reich encompassed a wide variety of weapons, most of which have no place in this book: enormous weapons slung beneath aircraft for attacking battleships, one-shot devices for downward firing into bomber formations, and multi-barrel assemblies for fighter aircraft—all were built and all used the recoilless principle. For the sake of space, and owing to the fact that few can be rightly classed as artillery, attention must be diverted to the true artillery pieces.

As a background for those readers not acquainted with these weapons, a précis of the development of these guns will prove instructive. When a gun is fired, in accordance with Newton's third law of motion, the action of the shell moving forward is balanced by the reaction of the gun moving backward (or recoiling). The difference in velocity and distance of the two movements is attributable to the difference in mass.

Although the prospect of a recoilless gun had attracted one or two experimenters in the nineteenth century it was not until the arrival of the aeroplane that there was a real incentive to develop one. During World War 1 it was hoped that large guns could be mounted on aircraft to attack airships and ground targets, but 25–30mm was the largest practical calibre—above which the recoil began to break up the aircraft's fragile structure. Commander Cleland Davis of the US Navy solved the problem by producing a gun that was actually two barrels joined back-to-back to a common chamber. The front barrel was loaded with the projectile while the rear barrel accommodated a 'countershot'—an equal mass composed of grease and fine lead shot. A cartridge was placed between the two and, when fired, it propelled both projectiles from their respective rifled barrels at equal velocities. Since the reaction of each barrel was identical and acting in opposite directions, each cancelled the other and the result was a recoilless gun. Needless to say such a device had its disadvantages, the principal of which was the emergence of the countershot from the rear of the gun at high speed—but making it of grease and fine shot ensured that it soon disintegrated under centrifugal force. The Davis aircraft gun was used in limited numbers by the British Royal Naval Air Service, but as a ground gun the problem of the countershot was insuperable.

At some time in the 1930s Rheinmetall looked again at Davis' ideas and patents (and those of other inventors who had tried to improve upon them) and began to develop some heavy countershot weapons for aircraft use in which the cartridge cases were ejected rearward to serve as the countershots. Although perfected, such guns were not used during the war, but the work led to some further thinking on the general question of recoillessness; if a gun could be made recoilless by discharging a countershot of the same mass as the main projectile at the same velocity, then equal results could obviously be obtained by using a countershot of half the weight projected at twice the velocity—or a quarter of the weight at four times the velocity, or any other fraction and multiple the designer cared to select. If this calculation is carried to its limits, the point is eventually reached where a very light stream of gas particles can be discharged at very high velocity and still achieve recoilless results. It was from this premise that Rheinmetall worked first to develop more aircraft guns and then to produce a field artillery weapon. The first successful application of the principle by the company is attributed to Dr Heinrich Kleine and most of the German work in this field was done by Rheinmetall-Borsig, although Krupp in Germany, Skoda in Czechoslovakia and Böhler in Austria also undertook some development at various times.

The work on field weapons began in 1937 and the results were first revealed in the airborne attack on Crete in 1941. This was due to the fact that they had been primarily developed as lightweight weapons suited to use by airborne troops to provide such units with heavy shell-power in a gun capable of being dropped in pieces by parachute. The guns were later issued to mountain troops, were extensively used in the Carpathian mountains, and appeared to a lesser degree in parts of the Italian campaign. Towards the end of the war Leichtgeschütze were less in evidence. Production ceased in 1944 because of a shortage of ammunition and because there was little possibility of production capacity being allotted to replenish stocks. The weapons' worst fault was their appetite for propellant, a commodity by then in short supply; indeed, by the last months of 1944 it was, to all intents and purposes, a rationed item.

To explain this defect a reversion must now be made to the mechanism, and a study undertaken of how the German guns worked. One can attain recoillessness by simply putting a shell into a gun, leaving the breechblock open and lighting the propellant in the chamber: provided enough propellant is used, the desired result will be obtained. This is, of course, a wasteful idea and, moreover, unconfined propellant is difficult to ignite satisfacorily; an unrestricted aperture at the rear also demands a large quantity of gas to fill it. So the Rheinmetall 'light guns' used cartridge cases in which the bases were cut out and replaced by thick discs of frangible plastic. These were held in the chambers by breechblocks that were pierced by convergent-divergent Laval nozzles, extended at the rear by jet pipes. When the propellant was ignited the pressure built up rapidly inside the case, ensuring complete ignition of all the charge, and then—as the shell began to take the rifling at a pressure of about two tons per square inch—the disc shattered and allowed part of the propellant gas to pass into the nozzle and exhaust to the rear of the gun.

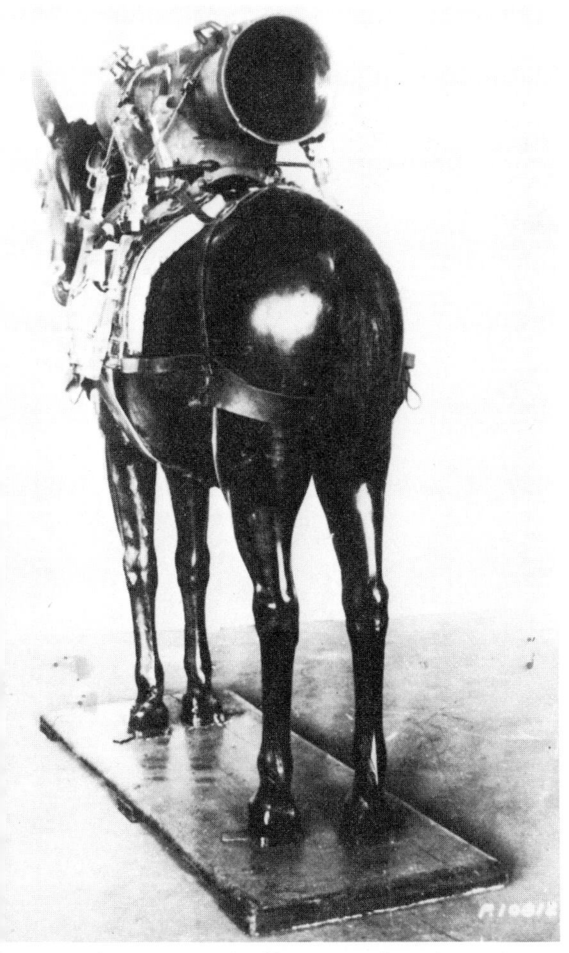

n unusual suggestion by Krupp—pack mule carriage r a recoilless gun.

This is a simplified view; there are many small forces to be considered (such as the friction between the shell and the bore, and the slight imbalance which occurs on the disc breaking before the shell is properly seated in the rifling) but these are relatively easily overcome by adjusting the nozzle dimensions, although perfect recoillessness is rarely achieved.

If the shot is to be propelled at a worthwhile velocity and a balancing stream of gas is to be exhausted, the charge has to be increased to provide sufficient powder to satisfy both these demands; a factor of three was generally quoted by German designers as more or less true at 305mps(1000fps) velocity, gradually decreasing at higher velocities. In other words, it took three times as much propellant to push the shell from a recoilless gun as it did to achieve the same velocity from a conventional weapon.

One feature of German recoilless gun design stands out when compared with the contemporary work done in Britain and the USA: the Germans used conventional ammunition—that issued for conventional weapons of the same calibre. No attempt was made to take advantage of the peculiar ballistics—the low pressure and relatively low acceleration—found in recoilless guns to produce unconventional ammunition, something that was principally undertaken in Britain. This is quite inexplicable, especially when one considers the accent on ammunition improvement in every other sphere of the OKW's artillery activity.

Perhaps the last word on these weapons lies with a German officer who, in the course of discussions after the war, was asked about their employment: 'They were a good deal more popular with the designers,' he said, 'than they ever were with the users.'

·5cm Leicht Geschütz 40

·5cm LG 40 (Olmutz)

'his, the first of its kind to be introduced, was riginally known as the L G 1 but was later renamed in accordance with the usual 'year of rigin' terminology system. It was built in four arts, each capable of parachute descent without ie need for special packing; the ordnance split ito barrel and breech assembly, while a simple op carriage and a wheeled tripod assembly formed ie rest of the equipment. Although Rheinmetall ere responsible for the basic research, both they nd Krupp were given development contracts nd both produced prototypes. The Krupp model sed a very simple side-swinging breech mecanism and was mounted on two motorcycle heels, while the Rheinmetall type used a orizontal sliding breechblock and two small ircraft-type wheels. The latter was the one ccepted for service. Extensive use was made of light alloy in the mounting to save weight; and, to prevent the back blast from ricocheting on to the detachment, the elevation and traverse gears were interconnected so that the normal 360° traverse was restricted to 30° each way as soon as the elevation reached 20°.

The firing mechanism was placed in a streamlined housing in the centre of the jet venturi, so that a normal type of primer in the centre of the plastic case base could be used.

The danger area at the rear of the gun extended to 100m(109yd) for practice firing or 50m(55yd) for combat firing; this, however, referred only to the actual jet blast, and stones and débris were disturbed some considerable distance beyond this. Firing instructions also emphasised the danger to the detachment members' ears from the blast, and recommended them to plug their ears tightly

Loading a prototype Krupp recoilless 7.5cm gun.

A prototype of the Krupp recoilless 7.5cm gun being demonstrated at the manufacturer's works. Note the four-round ammunition carrier mounted on the barrel.

The 7.5cm Krupp Prototype LG 1, with a side-swingin breech and a guard to protect the gunlayer.

with clay or mud before opening fire.

A total of 450 of these guns were made, 170 by Rheinmetall-Borsig at Düsseldorf.

Data
Calibre: 75mm/2.95in.
Length of gun: 750mm/29.53in.
Length of bore: 458mm/18.03in.
Rifling: 28 grooves, uniform right-hand twist, 1/52.
Breech mechanism: horizontal sliding block, percussion fired.
Traverse: 360° below 20° elevation, 60° above 20° elevation.
Elevation: −15° to +42°.
Weight in action: 145kg/320lb.

Performance
Firing standard high explosive shell weighing 5.83kg(12.86lb).

The 7.5cm LG 40—the Rheinmetall design which was accepted for service.

'ull charge: velocity 350mps/1148fps, maximum ange 6800m/7434yd.

mmunition

eparate-loading, cased charge.

rojectiles

.5cm Gr 34 A1, 7.5cm Gr 38 H1/B.

'hese were the shells fired by the 7.5cm Geb 36.

5cm Pzgr rot.

This was the shell fired by the 7.5cm F K 16 nA.

Propelling Charge

The charge consisted of a silk-cloth bag containing 1.21kg(2.68lb) of Digl Str P with a gunpowder igniter stitched to the bottom; this was carried in a cartridge case with an 85mm(3.35in) aperture in the base that was closed by a plastic disc. A percussion primer C/43 was screwed into the centre. The case-mouth was closed by a cardboard cup.

·5cm Ruckstossfreikanone 43

·5cm RFK 43 (Nürnberg)

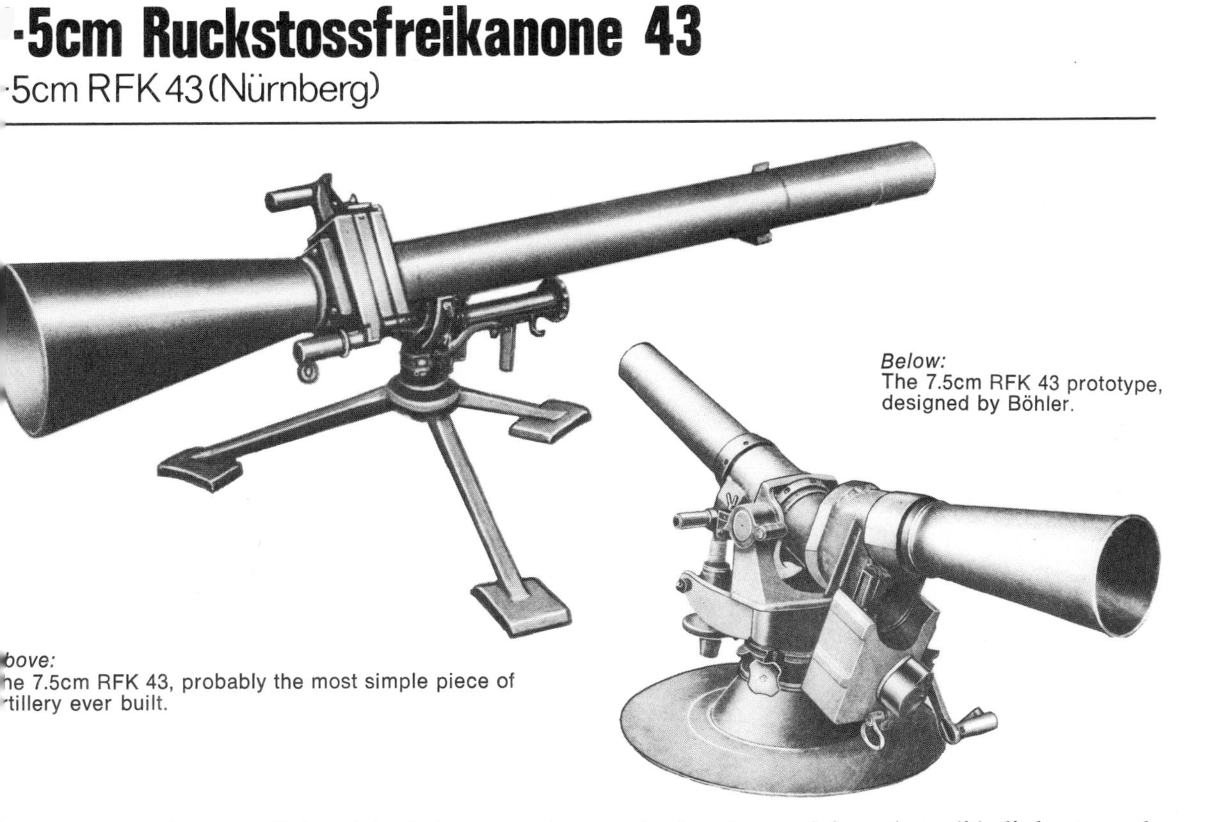

bove:
he 7.5cm RFK 43, probably the most simple piece of 'tillery ever built.

Below:
The 7.5cm RFK 43 prototype, designed by Böhler.

'his was intended as a lightweight infantry antiank weapon. Development contracts were given Böhler, Krupp and Rheinmetall-Borsig; the rupp and the Rheinmetall versions were adopted or service, though it is not thought that many vere made. The original idea of mounting the ring mechanism in the centre of the venturi see 10.5cm L G 40) had been discarded by the ime these designs were prepared, and the firing nechanism was fitted to the side of the chamber. 'he Böhler design used a solid breechblock that nclosed the end of the chamber, sliding vertically, vith the venturi taking gas from the top of the hamber and pointing slightly upwards—probably n an attempt to divert some of the blast away rom both the detachment and the ground. This ppears to have been a sound idea until the enturi eroded and began to pass too much gas, fter which time the rear end received a downward thrust on firing that did little towards helping the accuracy of the gun. It was probably this feature that led to its rejection.

The Krupp design used the simple side-swinging breech and venturi that had been offered with their LG 1 prototype. This could be quickly detached for carriage so that the complete weapon split into three pieces: barrel, breech and mounting. The mounting was a simple baseplate with a free pivot supporting the trunnions; no elevating or traversing gear was fitted—the layer simply pushed the gun about. In an attempt to make simplicity complete, a cartridge case of cardboard was originally tried, but this was taking things too far and a plastic base case (similar to that for the L G 40), was finally adopted.

The Rheinmetall weapon was a departure from the firm's normal sliding-block breech and, in fact, reverted to the shotgun breech design used in the 7.5cm IG 18. When the rather complicated breech linkage was operated, the venturi stayed put and the barrel pivoted about the trunnions to raise the breech above the fixed breechblock. The gun was simply pivoted on its three-legged mount, similar to Krupp's design, and was pushed about by the layer to effect the aim.

Data (Rheinmetall-Borsig version).
Calibre: 75mm/2.95in.
Length of gun: 1211mm/46.68in.
Length of bore: 692mm/27.24in.
Rifling: 24 grooves, right-hand uniform twist, 1/25.5.
Breech mechanism: shotgun pattern, percussion fired.
Traverse: 360°.
Elevation: −3° to +45°.
Weight in action: 43.13kg/95.10lb.

Performance
Firing standard hollow charge shell weighin 4.00kg(8.81lb).
Standard charge: velocity 170mps/558fps, max mum range 2000m/2187yd.

Ammunition
Fixed round, cased charge.

Projectiles
7.5cm Hl Gr Patr 43.
No data is available for this round.

8cm Ruckstossfreiwerfer 43

8cm RFW 43

This weapon, of unknown parentage, was apparently under development at the end of the war but—although granted official service nomenclature—it never reached the hands of troops and only one incomplete specimen survived the war. It was a weapon of the utmost simplicity consisting of a barrel, a removable interrupted-thread breech plug carrying the venturi, and a baseplate and trunnion assembly similar to that of the RFK 43. The loading procedure was simple: the venturi was seized and rotated one-sixth of a turn and removed, the round inserted, and t venturi replaced. A percussion firing mechanis also of spartan simplicity, was fitted to the si of the chamber. As a final garnish, the barrel w smoothbored—hence the nomenclature 'werfe The whole weapon was 2000mm(78.74in) long, t barrel length was 146.5mm(57.68in), and t weight was 90.00kg(198.45lb). No details beyo these have ever come to light on the weapo particularly in respect of its ammunition or pe formance.

10·5cm Leicht Geschütz 40

10·5cm LG 40 (Olpe)

This was a Krupp design originally known as the L G 2/Kp to distinguish it from the contemporary development—the L G 2/Rh—being done by Rheinmetall-Borsig.

A defect in the original 75mm L G design that became apparent after some use, as outlined above, was that the rapid erosion by the gas blast through the venturi of the firing mechanism housing; the mechanism itself became clogged with fouling. To cure this, a new type of cartridge case was developed in which the primer was inserted at the side of the case and where a 'bandolier' igniter surrounded the bottom of the propellant charge to ensure even ignition. This, of course, demanded precise breech location of the cartridge so that the primer cap lay under the firing pin, and this was done by making a wedge-shaped surround for the primer housing which engaged in a matching recess in the chamber wall. The firing mechanism was mounted on top of the breech-ring.

A second defect revealed itself in action: after about 300 rounds had been fired, the mountings began to disintegrate. This was partly due erosion of the jets, leading to out-of-balanc forces, but principally owing to the torque im parted to the gun structure as the projecti engaged in the rifling. So the recoilless princip was extended in a radial direction by weldin curved vanes inside the jet nozzle that we curved in the opposite direction to the riflin these then instigated an opposite torque in the j and thus balanced the turning moment acting o the carriage.

The LG 40 was more or less an enlarged versio of the Krupp 7.5cm model, with the same sid swinging breech and large pneumatic-tyred wheel A short box trail was fitted, simply as a suppor and a shield also appeared. The whole equipme could be dismantled into five parachute load each in a container: barrel, breech, carriage bod axle and trail, and wheels. Each container hel in addition to the gun parts, four rounds ammunition plus a rifle and small-arms ammun tion for the detachment. The L G 40 could als be dropped in the assembled condition, packe

The 10.5cm LG 40 firing.

ıe 10.5cm LG 40 in the firing position.

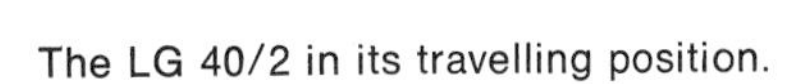

The LG 40/2 in its travelling position.

ı a special shock-absorbing crate.

The original version had the mounting made f aluminium/magnesium alloy, but when this ıaterial became scarce a new pattern in welded eel was issued. Guns with the light alloy mount-ıgs were then known as L G 40–1 and those ith the steel mounting as L G 40–2.

ata

alibre: 105mm/4.13in.
ength of gun: 1902mm/74.88in.
ength of bore: 1380mm/54.33in.
ifling: 32 grooves, right-hand increasing twist, /17.25 to 1/11.75.
reech mechanism: side opening, percussion fired
raverse: 80°.
levation: −15° to +40° 30′.
Veight in action: 388kg/856lb.

erformance

iring standard high explosive shell weighing 4.80kg(32.63lb).
tandard charge: velocity 335mps/1099fps, maxi-ıum range 7950m/8695yd.

Ammunition

Separate-loading, cased charge.

Projectiles

10.5cm F H Gr 41: fuzed AZ 23v(0.15) or Dopp Z S/60, weight 14.80kg(32.63lb).
In spite of the changed number, examinations of specimens and drawings reveal this shell to be the same as the 10.5cm F H Gr 38 used with the le F H 18 howitzer. A bimetallic (KPS) driving band was fitted and the filling was 1.38kg (3.04lb) of poured TNT.
10.5cm Gr 39 H1/B: fuzed AZ 38, weight 12.25kg (27.01lb).
This was also the shell used with the le F H 18. When fired from the L G 40, owing to its lesser weight, it developed a muzzle velocity of 373mps (1224fps) and a maximum engagement range of 1500m(1640yd) was stipulated.

Propelling Charges

This was a single charge consisting of 3.09kg (6.81lb) of Gudol R P with a bandolier igniter of NZ Man P wrapped around the lower end of the sticks.

Primer

The percussion primer C/13nA St was standard.

10·5cm Leicht Geschütz 42

10·5cm LG 42 (Olten)

This was Rheinmetall-Borsig's 10.5cm model, originally known as the L G 2/Rh. Although constructed to the same general specification, it was completely different and seems to have been made in greater numbers than its Krupp competitor—since many more L G 42 guns were found postwar than L G 40.

The breech was a horizontal sliding block with venturi and jet, and with the firing mechanism on top of the breech-ring. Torque vanes were fitted in the jet nozzle. The mounting was a light tubular tripod attached to an axle with drop arms and small wheels, a shield was fitted, and in the interest of stability the elevating gear was arranged to prevent elevations of more than 20° if the jet pointed outside the angle formed by the rear tripod legs.

The L G 42 could be broken into four loads for parachute landing (the Krupp gun broke into five) and also came in two versions—the L G 42–1 and L G 42–2—one of which (42–1) employed light alloy in certain of the carriage components.

Data
Calibre: 105mm/4.13in.
Length of gun: 1836mm/72.28in.
Length of bore: 1374mm/54.09in.
Rifling: 32 grooves, right-hand uniform twist, 1/17.8.
Breech mechanism: horizontal sliding block, percussion fired.
Traverse: 360° at elevations less than 20°, 71° 1[illegible] at elevations above 20°.
Elevation: 15° to +42° 30'.
Weight, L G 42–1: 540kg/1191lb.
Weight, L G 42–2: 552kg/1217lb.

Performance
Firing standard high explosive shell weighi[illegible] 14.80kg(32.63lb).
Kleine Ladung: velocity 195mps/640fps, maximu[illegible] range 3400m/3718yd.
Grosse Ladung: velocity 335mps/1099fps, max[illegible] mum range 7950m/8695yd.

Ammunition
Separate-loading, cased charge.

Projectiles
10.5cm F H Gr 38 and variants, 10.5cm Gr [illegible] rot H1/B, 10.5cm Gr 39 rot H1/C, 10.5cm F [illegible] Gr 38 Nb, 10.5cm F H Gr Br.
These are the projectiles used with the 10.5c[illegible] le F H 18, to which reference should be ma[illegible] for details.

Propelling Charges
By the time that this weapon was developed, [illegible] considerable volume of data had been accumulat[illegible] concerning recoilless firing and it had been di[illegible] covered that it was possible to develop adjustab[illegible] charges for this type of gun. Provided that t[illegible]

Right:
10.5cm LG 42 on its tripod mounting.

Below:
Front view of the 10.5cm LG 42/1.

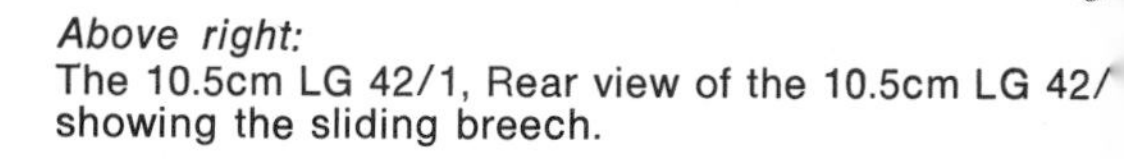

Above right:
The 10.5cm LG 42/1, Rear view of the 10.5cm LG 42/ showing the sliding breech.

ıture, the granulation and the weight of propellant ere carefully selected, the recoilless action was pre-rved. Consequently this was the first recoilless eapon to offer adjustable charges. (The British mm, developed shortly afterwards, was the cond—it had three charges.)

The charge consisted of three bags: the Kleine adung, the Grosse Ladung, and an adjusting arge. The last was in the region of 100gm .53oz) of Gudol R P and was used to adjust e particular propellant batch to give the cessary recoilless characteristics with the desired ballistic performance. At temperatures over 30°C the adjusting charge was discarded, since the increased performance owing to the high temperature rendered it superfluous. At temperatures below 30°C it was left in the case with whatever charge bag was being used. The Kleine Ladung consisted of 1.40kg(3.09lb) of Digl R P while the Grosse Ladung was 2.90kg(6.39lb) of Gudol R P in two different granulations.

Primer

The percussion primer C/13nA was standard.

0·5cm Leicht Geschütz 43

)·5cm LG 43

his Rheinmetall-Borsig equipment was an im-oved version of the L G 42, but few were anufactured. The gun resembled the L G 42 ıt was in fact slightly different in dimensions ıd totally different in rifling. The carriage was e principal visible change, a more-or-less con-ntional split-trail design with a third leg at the ont. Torsion bar suspension sprung the ıeumatic-tyred wheels and a light shield was ted. The usual Rheinmetall restriction on eleva-ɔn and traverse was used, no more than 13° evation being possible when the blast pipe ɔinted outside the trail legs.

The equipment could be quickly stripped into ght parachute loads, using the elevating and aversing hand wheels as keys to release the rious connecting pins. When in action the L G rested on the tripod, wheels clear of the ground.

Data

Calibre: 105mm/4.13in.
Length of gun: 1845mm/72.64in.
Length of bore: 1377mm/54.21in.
Rifling: 32 grooves, right-hand increasing twist, 1/18 to 1/16.
Breech mechanism: horizontal sliding block, percussion fired.
Traverse: 360° below 13° elevation, 120° above 13°.
Elevation: −25° to +40°.
Weight in action: 524kg/1155lb.

Performance, Ammunition

No definite figures are available, but reports indicate that the performance was approximately the same as the L G 42. The ammunition was the same.

Left:
The 10.5cm LG 43 with tubular trail and a more robust carriage than its predecessor.
Below
Front view of the 10.5cm LG 43.

15cm Leicht Geschütz 292

15cm LG 292

This weapon was also a Rheinmetall development, intended for use by airborne troops as a heavy weapon. Production of recoilless guns stopped in 1944 and thus only prototypes of this gun were ever made. It was also known as the 15cm L G 42 and, from what accounts remain, was a enlarged version of the 10.5cm L G 42. It wa said to have fired the standard 38.00kg(83.79l 15cm shell at a velocity of 300mps(984fps) to range of 6000m(6562yd).

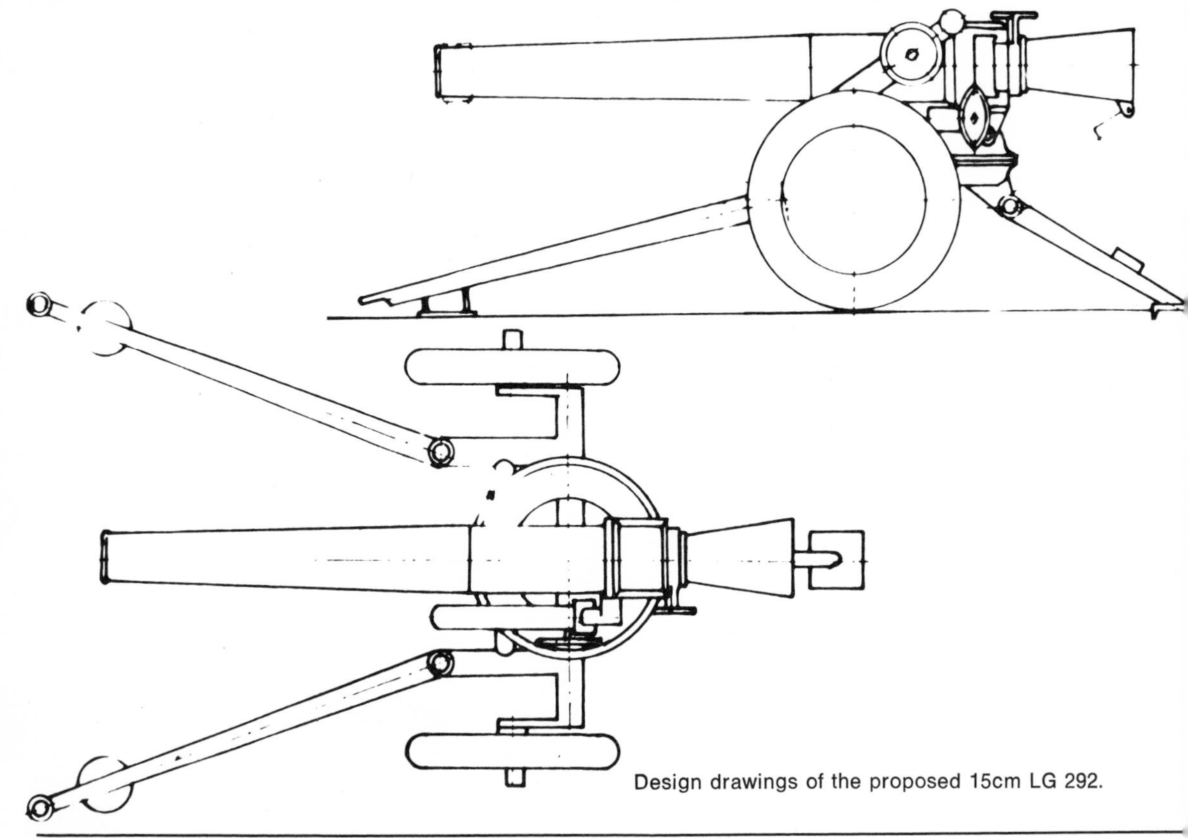

Design drawings of the proposed 15cm LG 292.

Miscellaneous Projects

Among the wide variety of recoilless developments that were given varying amounts of attention during the war, one or two are worth mentioning. (It must be borne in mind that whenever a new weapon showed promise there was always a rush to get on the bandwagon, and numerous hares were started in different directions. We can only afford space to deal with the fatter ones.)

Krupp had two interesting projects on hand: the 10.5cm L G 2 Glatt and the 15cm L G 3 Glatt, both smoothbore weapons firing over-long fin-stabilised hollow charge shells. Some postwar statements asserted that they were to fire Röchling shells but, since their muzzle velocities were 240mps(787fps) and 260mps(853fps) respectively, no further heed need be paid to that story. Another development of theirs was the 10.5c L G 2–550 P, intended for turret mounting in tracked vehicle.

The Hanomag company was involved in a pr ject to develop a 28cm recoilless gun for coa defence; the design had been completed and pr liminary tests indicated that it would have been workable weapon, but whether a recoilless g could have delivered an armour-piercing shell sufficient striking velocity at long range—t prime requirement of a coast defence gun— open to doubt. This weapon was being develop for the German Navy, who were also sponsori 8.8cm and 15cm guns for both coast defence a for mounting in light vessels (enabling the latt to carry heavy guns with minimal deckblow

APPENDICES

ONE: AMMUNITION

Cartridges

Artillery cartridges are generally classified by the gun's method of obturation—the method of sealing the breech against the unwanted escape of propellant gas—into two groups, *cased* or *bagged-charge* rounds. Cased charges have the propellant contained in a metallic cartridge case, the expansion of which gives the necessary seal. Bagged charges are contained in cloth bags and the sealing of the breech is done by a resilient pad contained in the breech mechanism. Cased charges can be further divided into three groups.

The fixed round. In this the projectile is firmly attached to the mouth of the cartridge case and the whole round is manipulated and loaded as a single item.

The separate-loading round. In this, as the term implies, the shell is loaded into the breech and rammed home; the cartridge is then loaded separately.

The semi-fixed round. This is a compromise between the other two in which the shell and case are fitted together for loading but can be separated for packaging or in order to have the propelling charge adjusted by the gunner before firing.

That, then, is the general classification—but in considering German artillery cartridges some modifications are necessary. The semi-fixed round can be forgotten, since it was never used in Germany, and the bagged charge can be all but forgotten since only one standard German weapon (21cm K 39) used it (although, had the war continued, the system would have been introduced more widely in order to conserve cartridge-case

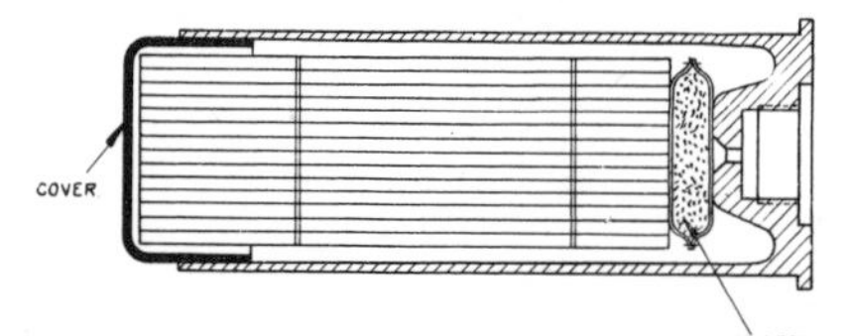

A typical cased cartridge, with the igniter above the primer and a sheet propellant cover at the mouth.

metal). With this exception the standard ammuni tion of the German artillery was the cased cart ridge, either fixed or separate loading, the latte being generally used above a calibre of 10.5cm.

In the development of substitute cartridge case Germany had no peer. The standard materia throughout the world has always been *cartridg brass,* an alloy of 70% copper and 30% zinc, bu during World War 1 the shortage of copper bega

Cartridge cases for the 10.5cm le FH 18: Left, drawn brass; centre, wrapped steel; right, built-up steel.

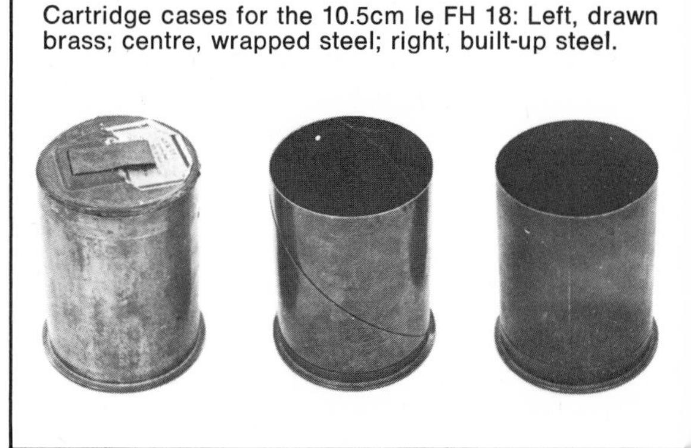

to be felt and some experiments with substitut materials were made. These were revived in th 1930s and many designs of steel case wer developed, which are dealt with in full detail i Appendix 2. One of the hardest tasks lies in matin the various cases with the original weapon and, t assist in this, Appendix 2 also gives full identifi cation data for all known German cartridge cases

The cartridge case performs several function besides sealing the breech; it contains the propellin charge (protecting it from rain, sun, dust and othe ill effects), it carries the ignition system, and b forming a rigid strut between the breechblock an the projectile it can assist in ramming and locatin the shell correctly in the breech chamber. Th most important of these is, of course, the functio of carrying the propelling charge which, of material commonly spoken of as 'smokeles powder', was in the German service usually in th form of sticks (rather like macaroni) or in smal grains (resembling the same macaroni chopped into short lengths). For guns with fixed-weight propelling charges, such as anti-aircraft or anti-tank guns, this propellant was weighed out, bundled (if in sticks) or bagged (if granular) and then placed in the case. A cap, also of propellant material but formed into a sheet and moulded, covered the ends of the bundle of sticks in order to prevent them shifting during transit and loading. To ensure ready and thorough ignition of the charge, small *igniters*—bags of gunpowder—were placed at the base of the charge where they would be ignited by the primer in the base of the case.

Separate-loading charges were much the same, but with a cover over the end of millboard, thin sheet tin or formed-sheet propellant. An igniter was again fitted; in some designs this was at the front end of the charge, the central portion of the charge being of large diameter tubular propellant so that the primer's flash could pass up and fire the front igniter.

With howitzers it was desirable to be able to adjust the charge in order to vary the trajectory; in these cases a basic charge was secured in the case and additional sections or *increments* were placed in the case alongside the base portion. In the very large guns the base portion of the charge often completely filled the case, and the incremental sections were bagged and loaded ahead of the cased section to replace some of the Teilkarten in a large charge. Thus, a howitzer might have seven charges: charges 1 to 6 being combinations of Teilkarten, but charge 7 would be a separate one-piece charge replacing all the Teilkarten (and would be known as Sonderkartusche 7).

Guns were often provided with adjustable charges and these were generally referred to as *Kleine* (small), *Mittlere* (medium) or *Grosse* (large) charges, which were built up from various combinations. Thus the 15cm Kanone 18 had the following charges:

Kleine Ladung, made up of Sonderkartusche 1 which (in this case) was a special 'small charge' and not a combination of all the various Vorkarten or Teilkarten.

Mittlere Ladung made up of Hauptkartusche and Vorkartusche 2.

Grosse Ladung made up of Hauptkartusche and Vorkarten 2 and 3.

The object was to provide the gunners with various charges which enabled them—within limits—to select a trajectory suited to the task in hand and also to fire only sufficient propellant to get the shell to the target, thus economising in propellant and saving wear on the gun barrel.

The propellant itself was one of four types:

Diglycolpulver (Digl). A double-base propellant (ie a combination of two main constituents, diethyleneglycol dinitrate [DEGN] and nitrocellulose) with the addition of methyl centralite to stabilise it and potassium sulphate to reduce flash.

Gudolpulver (Gu). This was Diglycolpulver with the admixture of about 30% of gudol (nitroguanidine) to reduce flash.

Nitroglyzerinpulver (Nigl). A double-base propellant of nitroglycerine and nitrocellulose stabilised with methyl centralite, akardite or diphenylamine.

Nitrocellulosepulver (Nz). A single-base (nitrocellulose only) powder, stabilised with diphenylamine, with sodium oxalate and potassium sulphate added to reduce flash.

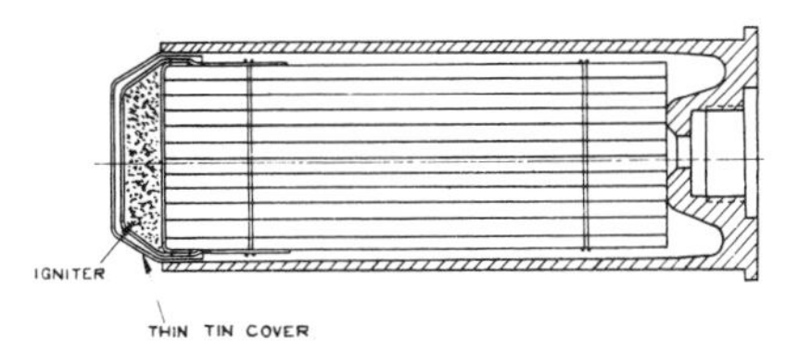

Another common design of cased cartridge which has the igniter at the front beneath a thin tinplate cover.

Of these four propellants Nitroglyzerinpulver was the most powerful, bulk for bulk, but at the same time it developed the highest flame temperature and thus caused most erosion of the gun barrel. The others, owing to the absence of nitroglycerine in their structure, were less powerful but burned at lower temperatures and were thus less erosive. The various additions to reduce flash were usually expected to increase the volume of smoke produced on firing; Gudolpulver was expected to be the coolest-burning powder but, though practically flashless, it produced most smoke.

Primers

The primer is a separate component screwed into the base of the cartridge case; and German primers were quite different from those found, for example, in British or American cartridges, the principal difference having been the apparent absence of any visible form of sensitive cap. The body of a German percussion primer was plain steel, thinned at the centre. The sensitive cap was inside, under the thin section, which thus simplified the sealing of the primer against damp. When the firing pin in the breechblock of the gun struck the primer, it was sufficiently powerful to indent the thin base and crush the sensitive material within—causing it to ignite. This in turn ignited the gunpowder in the primer magazine, and this burst open the cover and allowed the flash to enter the cartridge, igniting the main charge.

Some German primers did appear to have a cap, but these were electrically-fired types; what appeared to be a cap was simply a contact stud which, on close examination, could be seen to be insulated from the rest of the primer by a thin ebonite sleeve. When loaded into a gun, a contact pin pressed against the stud and the electrical circuit was completed through the body of the case to the gun chamber. When the firing trigger was operated, current flowed through the contact into the primer and passed through a wire into a 'fuze-head', a fine-wire filament surrounded by a sensitive compound. The flow of current rapidly brought the filament to white heat, igniting the compound which then fired the gunpowder igniter and the main charge.

The filament wires, though small and supported as well as could be designed, tended to break, particularly in weapons using power ramming (when the cartridge is accelerated and decelerated rapidly), and a notable German innovation was the *conducting composition primer* in which the filament was replaced by a sensitive compound mixer with graphite, a conductor of electricity. When the firing current entered the primer it passed through the mixture, owing to the graphite's conductivity: graphite, however, also possesses high electrical resistivity. This meant that the resistance afforded to the applied voltage led to a large current passing through the graphite, which also had the effect of rapidly raising the material's temperature. Hence the sensitive compound quickly reached the critical temperature at which it ignited.

Another possible source of failure with electric firing circuits was the liability of faulty contacts between the contact pin of the firing mechanism and the central contact stud of the primer, owing to wear and dirt. Another unique German development, intended to obviate this trouble, was the *induction-fired primer.* This was basically a standard C/22 or C/23 electric primer with the filament connected to an induction coil let into the primer base. The gun's breechblock had a similar coil let into its face. The breechblock coil acted as a primary transformer coil, being fed from a suitable electricity supply through the firing-trigger switch. When the cartridge was in place and the breech closed, the two coils were aligned, so that putting a current into the primary coil induced a current flow in the secondary coil (in the primer) and fired the charge. This system operated successfully with a gap of as much as 1mm(0.04in) between the breech face and the cartridge case and primer.

Another interesting development in cartridge design was the *self-ramming cartridge.* In cases of high-velocity guns using fixed ammunition erosive wear at the leed, the commencement of the rifling, soon began: the shell when loaded no longer fitted snugly. It instead sat in the eroded area, and when the charge exploded the shell was blown out of the case and 'ran up' through the eroded space until it struck the rifling. There it was violently checked until sufficient pressure built up to engrave the driving band and move the shell once more. This sudden acceleration, sudden check, and re-acceleration placed great strain on the shell and fuze; it also caused the chamber pressure of the gun to fluctuate wildly and dangerously. The self-ramming charge, which was developed for the 8.8cm anti-aircraft gun, consisted of a normal charge wit a cardboard tube located centrally in the propellar bundle. At the bottom of the tube was a sma bag igniter and at the top of the tube, beneat the shell, was a much larger bag igniter. Th firing flash from the small igniter passed up th tube to light the large ejector-igniter. The explosio of this was sufficient to eject the shell from th cartridge case, across the eroded section of th chamber and into the rifling at a relatively lo velocity before the flash from the igniters had tim to ignite the main propelling charge. This dela was about 0.004–0.005sec (4 or 5 milliseconds), b the end of which time the shell was seated in th rifling to await the development of full pressur from the propelling charge.

Recoilless Gun Cartridges

All of the cartridges for the German recoilless gun used frangible (*ie* disintegrating or fragile) blow out bases of plastic material, and the filling of th case with propellant followed normal practice Early designs had the centre of the plastic bas drilled and threaded to take a small primer, an the firing mechanism was contained in a stream lined housing in the centre of the venturi tube The firing pin struck the primer and this in tur fired the charge in the usual way. As the pressur built up so the base blew out and shattered, allow ing a stream of gas to pass through the bottom o the case and through the venturi. It was then vente behind the gun, counteracting the recoil thrus owing to the projectile being fired out of the barre —action and reaction, according to Newton's Laws being equal but opposite.

The lumps of plastic and the primer were als shot out at the rear, making unpleasant missiles but (owing to the flame-blast and the dirt kicke up at the rear of the gun) there was a large dange area behind all recoilless guns and it is unlikel that anyone was ever seriously hurt by a flyin primer. The rate of erosion of the firing mechanisn and its housing was more serious, but this wa eventually overcome by designing guns with th firing mechanism on top of the chamber and cart ridges with the primer in the side instead of th base. A special 'bandolier' igniter was wrappe around the lower end of the charge to promot even ignition. The case was so shaped around th primer that it formed an indexing key whic ensured that, when loaded, the primer and firin mechanism coincided.

High Explosive Shells

The high explosive (HE) shells, basic weapons o all artillery, are much the same irrespective o which nation designed them. They are simpl steel canisters containing explosive and furnishe with suitable fuzes to initiate detonation at th

A complete round of high-explosive for the 10.5cm le FH 18. The bagged propelling charge has been removed from the cartridge case.

correct time and place. Having said that, however, it is necessary to qualify such a definition and show that design of an explosive shell is not quite so simple as it first appears.

Firstly consider the body of the shell: although usually made of steel, cast iron has been used at times and—of course—there are various types of steel. The requirements are readily stated: the shell must withstand the acceleration in the bore, it must be non-porous so that the flame from the propelling charge cannot penetrate and explode the contents, and, when the contents are detonated properly by the fuze, the metal must disintegrate into the maximum number of lethal fragments. Once these operational requirements are satisfied, economic ones must be considered: the steel chosen must be readily available in peace or war, and it must be of a type amenable to shaping and cutting without the need for highly expensive or specialised machinery.

Before World War 2 the question of lethality had not been fully explored. Provided a shell broke into a fair number of impressive fragments it was considered satisfactory, but during the course of the war much fundamental research was done (and more has since been done) into determining just how big a fragment was needed to incapacitate a man. If it can be shown, for example, that a fragment weighing 0.1oz (2.8gm) is lethal, then a 10lb (4.54kg) shell can be expected to produce 1600 fragments; a shell which produces but 800 is obviously less efficient. On the other hand a shell producing 3200 0.05oz (1.4gm) fragments is not delivering lethal units and is therefore totally inefficient. This and similar arguments occupied a number of experts, and by 1945 it was generally accepted on the Allied side that a 0.04oz (1.1gm) fragment was the ideal size, giving a good combination of weight, velocity and range from the point of burst. But the size of fragment was not entirely dependent upon the shell—the explosive used also had a bearing on it. In an extreme example, a high-grade steel shell filled with gunpowder was found to split into a few large low-velocity fragments with poor range, while a cast-iron shell filled with TNT generally disintegrated into virtually non-lethal powder.

German practice was to use a steel with a yield strength of about 26ton/in^2(4095kg/cm^2) which, with their standard fillings, gave good lethal fragmentation and produced a strong body with reasonable capacity. Manufacture was usually achieved by the universal method of forging from billets, piercing with a mandrel and forcing through a die, though some shells were made from seamless steel tube. The bodies were then machined to shape, and it is noteworthy that the external shape was relatively roughly machined except for two sections, one near the shoulder and one near the driving band, which were carefully finished to close tolerances. This system permitted faster production by semi-skilled labour than the British system of finish-machining the whole surface. The shells were then tested under high pressure, to detect any porosity or forging faults, and were thereafter internally varnished to prevent the explosive filling reacting with the metallic shell-wall.

Filling with high explosive was done either by pouring in the molten explosive or by pre-pressing the explosive into shaped blocks and hand-placing the blocks into the shell cavity. The latter system demanded a large entry hole, and so many designs had either a screwed-in baseplate or the body and nose in two screwed sections. The actual explosives used were many and varied, depending on the machinery available to a factory or the economic situation at different times during the war. The explosive used in a shell was indicated by a code number painted on the outside, and a list of those found on artillery shells will be found in the section devoted to ammunition markings.

The most difficult part of explosive shells design is the development of a suitably graded *exploder system.* The basic difficulty is that if a high explosive is to be used in the violently accelerative environment of an artillery projectile, it must be relatively inert to stand all the shocks. This means that it is usually relatively insensitive too, and thus difficult to ignite by the tiny detonator carried in the fuze. To achieve satisfactory detonation it is necessary to build up a graded train of explosives, beginning with the highly sensitive (but relatively weak) fuze detonator; this initiates the fuze magazine, less sensitive and somewhat stronger, and this in turn detonates an *exploder* in the shell. This is either a bag or a pre-pressed pellet of an explosive more sensitive than the main filling, and it is suitably protected so that any knocks or jars suffered by the shell will not effect its ignition. In German designs the usual construction had a steel plate at the head of the shell carrying a central thin-steel tube, which ran axially into the main filling. The exploder was then inserted into this steel tube or 'exploder container' and the fuze was screwed into the shell, so that the magazine rested on the plate and was in contact with the exploder. This method of construction also had the advantage of sealing the head of the shell against the ingress of dirt—or the hands of inquisitive soldiers.

Armour-Piercing Projectiles

Armour-piercing (AP) shells are highly specialised and involved products. Basically they are projectiles with hardened tips designed to penetrate armour and containing small charges of high explosive, together with fuzes in the shells' bases. This sounds simple, but the development of a successful piercing shell is a long business. The nose must be hard in order to pierce the target armour, but the body must be sufficiently resilient to withstand the enormous stresses placed on it during penetration. The explosive must be sensitive enough to be detonated by the fuze, yet inert enough to prevent premature detonation by the shock of impact—since the shell must penetrate before the explosive functions. The fuze has to be set in action by the shock of impact but must delay its initiation of the explosive filling until the shell has penetrated the armour and passed into the target, so that maximum damage will be done. The attachment of the base fuze must be so good that it does not fall out of the shell body either on impact or during the penetration phase. Finally the explosive must be as powerful as possible, consistent with insensitivity, because there is little of it: most of the shell's bulk and weight is of solid steel in order to develop sufficient penetrative power.

Once velocities are increased in order to penetrate more difficult targets the designer runs into trouble. At a striking velocity of the order of 2500fps(762mps) the impact shock is so great that the tip of the shell invariably shatters and penetration fails. In order to overcome this, a metal *piercing cap* is fitted over the point. This directs the impact shock away from the tip to the shell shoulders and the shell can then cut through the cap and begin penetration, partially supported at this critical moment by the remains of the cap. Since the optimum shape for a piercing cap is not usually the best shape to promote easy flight, a thin metal *ballistic cap* is often placed over the piercing cap and the shell nose.

German practice in this field was more-or-less in line with the rest of the world, though there were one or two interesting oddities. The shell material was originally a nickel-chromium-molybdenum steel, but as this quality became scarce a silicon-manganese-chromium type took its place. This could be hardened satisfactorily (so that penetrative performance was the same) but the alloy was more brittle and tended to shatter more easily, thus failing to carry through into the target.

In 1943 a design of shell was introduced that had an alloy tip flash butt-welded to a plain carbon steel body. This economised on alloy steel and also had an interesting by-product: when striking at an angle, the tip often broke off cleanly across the weld to leave a flat-headed shot which, in some types of angled attack, could be advantageous.

The explosive used was invariably pre-pressed blocks, formed to the cavity shape and inserted from the rear. An absorbent washer or wooden block was usually inserted into the head of the cavity to act as a shock absorber, though in some cases the top explosive pellet was heavily desensitised by the addition of montan wax and doubled as a shock absorber.

Armour-piercing shot in the sense of a solid steel mass, as used by the British Army, was unknown in German service. They claimed that solid shot invariably went right through a tank and they preferred the explosive-containing shell, which would enter the tank and detonate to do more positive damage. The specialised tungsten-cored

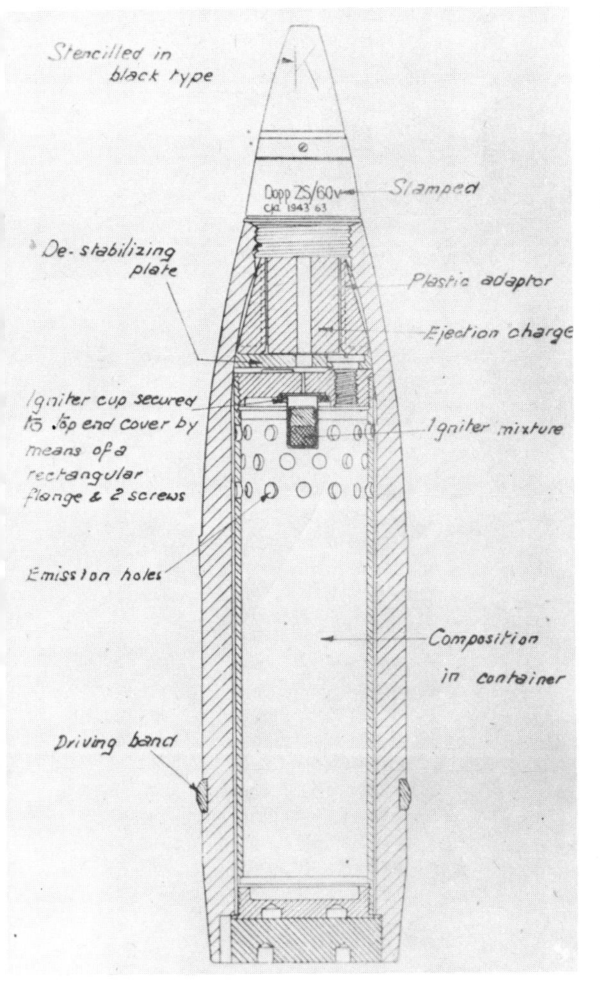

A drawing of a gas shell loaded with an arsenical smoke canister, for use with the 10.5cm le FH 18.

armour piercing projectiles are discussed in the section devoted to unorthodox projectiles.

Carrier Shells

Carrier shells are those in which the body itself is no more than a vehicle which goes to the target area and there releases the payload to take effect. The most common example is the smoke shell, but others in this class include incendiary, gas, illuminating star, flare, propaganda and shrapnel designs.

There are four basic ways of getting the payload out of the shell: by bursting the shell, by ejecting the contents through the base, by ejecting them through the nose, or by emitting them from the shell over a period of time. (The last system was not used by the Germans.)

Bursting shell. This type is practically identical to the high explosive shell. A small charge of explosive is held in a central container and the payload substance fills the rest of the cavity. When the explosive is initiated it breaks open the shell and distributes the contents. This method is commonly used with smoke shells in which the smoke agent is white phosphorus, titanium tetrachloride or an oleum/pumice mixture, the latter being the most common German filling. The same general construction is used for gas shells. One advantage of this type of shell is that it is ballistically much the same as the high explosive shell for the same weapon, so that the two patterns can be interchanged without need of extensive corrections to the gunsights. Another advantage is that the shell only requires a simple impact fuze.

Base ejection shell. In this class the shell body is tubular and closed at the base with a pinned or screwed-in baseplate. A time fuze is fitted to the nose and beneath this is a small gunpowder bursting/ejecting charge. The principal German employment of this system was for the coloured-smoke indicating shells, in which the body was filled by a metal container holding the smoke composition. At the top, near the gunpowder charge, a pyrotechnic delay filling led to the smoke mixture, and at the bottom a round metal plate was loosely attached to the canister by a screw at one edge.

When the time fuze functioned, it ignited the gunpowder. This exploded and generated a flash that lit the pyrotechnic delay and (ultimately) the smoke composition; it also generated the pressure that pushed the canister down, shearing off the baseplate and allowing the canister to eject into the sky. The eccentrically-mounted plate swung out of alignment with the canister, owing to the spin imparted during flight, and thus became a rough form of airbrake that slowed the canister and caused it to fall rapidly to the ground, instead of tending to follow the shell's trajectory. Once on the ground the filling continued to burn, emitting coloured smoke from the hole left by the dissipation of the pyrotechnic delay.

Nose ejection shell. The particular German application of this method was in anti-aircraft defence, where a most effective incendiary shrapnel shell was developed. The system was broadly similar to base ejection, but the shell's base was solid and the head weakened. The gunpowder ejection charge was at the base with a flash tube running down to it from the fuze. Around the flash tube were numbers of light metal platforms carrying small incendiary pellets of thin steel containing barium nitrate and magnesium, together with a detonator. When the fuze functioned, the ejection charge blew all the pellets through the nose of the shell and the spin ensured their distribution. The shells went into service with the 8.8cm anti-aircraft gun in 1944 and over a million were made. They were moderately effective (one unit claimed 25 aircraft had been downed and 25 had been set on fire for the expenditure of 8100 rounds), but large numbers of the pellets were ineffective owing to striking side-on and thus failing to initiate their detonators. A later design, more aerodynamically efficient, was in the development stage when the war ended.

Unorthodox Projectiles

Tungsten-cored armour piercing shot (Panzergranate 40 or Pzgr 40)
The use of tungsten as an anti-tank projectile stemmed from the defect mentioned in discussing steel armour piercing shells, where the shot shattered on striking the target at velocities in the region of 2500fps (762mps). The addition of a piercing cap merely raised the shatter velocity by a few hundred feet per second and did not remove it entirely, so that where higher striking velocities were visualised —with taper-bore guns, for example—a harder shatter-proof substance was needed. Tungsten carbide was the usual material so utilised, though experiments were made in Germany with uranium carbide. The first application of tungsten material was in the projectile for the Schweres Panzerbüchse 41(sPzB41) taper-bore anti-tank gun, where the use of a tungsten core lent itself to the construction of a collapsing body. This particular application will be examined in a later section.

Once the advantages of tungsten were appreciated, and the velocity of anti-tank gun projectiles was gradually driven higher by the necessity to penetrate thicker and harder targets, it was explored as a component in more conventional shot. Tungsten could not be used simply as a substitute for steel to make a full-calibre projectile; in the first place it was expensive and scarce, and (more important) its density was such that a full-calibre projectile weighed almost twice as much as a conventional one of steel. It was hence impossible to obtain a worthwhile muzzle velocity. The technique adopted was to make a core of tungsten, which was then mounted in a full-calibre body made of steel, light alloy or plastic. Since the body was merely a holding device it could be made quite light and the overall weight of such a composite projectile was somewhat less than a steel shot, so that the standard charge could be used to attain a higher muzzle velocity. Unfortunately the ability of a projectile to retain velocity during flight is largely dependent upon its cross-sectional density—a relationship of weight and diameter— and owing to the built-up lightweight section the composite shot had poor carrying power. As a result, although their penetrative power at short range was impressive, they tended to be less effective than common steel shot at ranges beyond about 1000 metres.

A later German development that tried to improve this situation, while economising in material and manufacturing time, was the *arrowhead shot.* This was no more than a sheathed tungsten core with a pair of full-calibre bearing surfaces and a thin metal ballistic cap; in other words, it was a tungsten core in a heavily relieved body. Its physical appearance raised questions about the airflow over such an angular shape at high velocities, but it did not appear to suffer from this and its performance (especially penetrative ability) was rather better than the earlier type. The sectional density value, however, was no improvement. The design was extensively copied in postwar years by the Soviets.

Taper and squeeze-bore projectiles (Panzergranate 41 or Pzgr 41)
As has been outlined, the original taper-bore weapon was an anti-tank gun and its projectile was a tungsten-cored shot. In order to allow for the diminution in bore size it was necessary to provide the sheathed core with skirt-type driving and centering bands, leading to a projectile which at first glance resembled the Pzgr 40 arrowhead shot. The skirts of the taper-bore shot were, however, swept to the rear and were of a thinner and more malleable metal, so that when propelled down the bore they were gradually collapsed in symmetrical fashion. Later developments for larger calibre anti-tank weapons were on similar lines. Another identifying feature of the Pzgr 41 was the presence of holes in the front centering band that allowed the air between the bands to be expelled during the squeeze.

A tungsten-cored shot for the 2.8cm sPzB 41, sectioned.

High-explosive shells, using steel shell bodies fitted with collapsible skirts, were also developed for the anti-tank guns, but when work began on larger calibres the flange system was abandoned in favour of an easier-to-manufacture system using a rear driving flange and three soft-metal compressible studs; these replaced the front centering band. The studs sat in wide recesses in the shell-wall that allowed the soft metal to be displaced into them as the ‘squeeze’ took place, while the rear flange was formed with a hemispherical section anchored in the shell wall and acting as a hinge during the squeeze. This *bolt centering device* was developed very successfully by Dr Banck of Rheinmetall-Borsig.

The tungsten-cored shot for the 7.5cm PAK 41.

Dr. Banck's collapsing bolt shell, using a sintered metal skirt at the rear. This is a 105/88mm example for use in a cone-bore anti-aircraft gun.

Discarding sabot projectiles (Treibspiegelgeschosse)
An enormous range of sabot shells was developed in Germany with the intention of either increasing the range of field guns or reducing the time of flight of anti-aircraft shells. Very little work was done in the anti-tank field, for in 1943 the supply of tungsten for ammunition was stopped and without tungsten there was little point in developing high-velocity projectiles. A small number of developments were tried using a normal armour piercing shell as a subprojectile, but these were of little practical value and few entered service.

A notable feature of German development was that advantage was taken of the sabot feature to develop the best ballistic shape for the shell. The normal full-calibre shell was not always the best possible shape, since a large proportion of the body wall was always parallel in order to obtain a stable bearing in the gun barrel: when support and alignment were being done by the attached sabots, the shell shape could be designed for optimum flight performance, which added to the advantages already gained by sabot design.

German sabot projectiles can be broadly classed in four groups:

1. Semi-sabot, which subdivides into three classes.
a. Shells that were of full calibre at the base but had a discarding centering device at the shoulder.
b. Shells that were of full calibre at the shoulder but had a discarding centering device at the base.
c. Shells that were entirely sub-calibre, with a discarding sabot at the rear and a non-discarding centering device at the shoulder.

These were all attempts to reach the ideal projectile shape. The third class had the shoulder units aerodynamically shaped, to give the least possible drag, but they were retained on the shell to eliminate the tendency of the discards to generate instability as they left.

It might be as well to consider at this point the basic ways in which the sabots were discarded. Any one of three forces was used to get rid of the sabot at the muzzle; *air drag* that slowed the angular sabot and allowed the streamlined projectile to go on, *centrifugal force* that flung the sabot sections outwards with enough force to shear various locking pins or wires that had previously held them to the shell, and *propellant gas pressure* that could be used to dicard the base-end sabot.

It will be understood from these systems that unless the discarding action is clean and symmetrical, it is quite possible for a portion of the discard to strike the subprojectile and deflect it slightly—leading to instability and inaccuracy.

2. Pot sabots
The pot sabot was extensively tried in the hope of achieving a symmetrical discard. As the name implies, the pot sabot resembled a pot in which sat the subprojectile. Released by gas pressure (and forced off by that and air drag), the pot's withdrawal was axial and, hopefully, so symmetrical that it did not disturb the subprojectile.

3. Cage sabots
These were less common, consisting of a ba section connected to the shoulder section and ea relying on the other for correct discard. In o version the shoulder ring was broken into segmen on acceleration and was flung out by centrifug force after leaving the muzzle, thus releasing t base section to be discarded by air drag.

Examples of various sabot principles tried by German designers.

base and shoulder ring

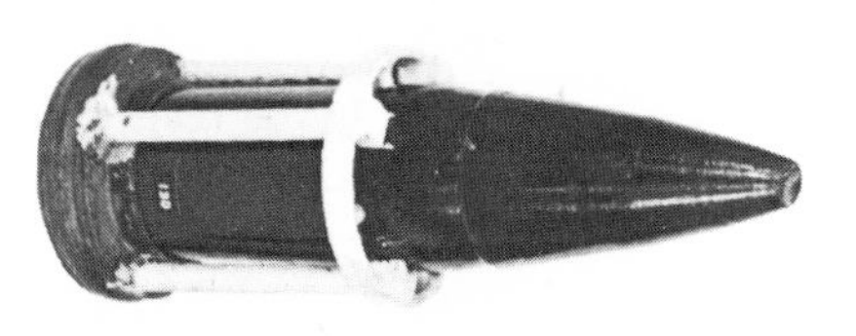

cage

base ring and aerodynamic supports

base and shoulder rings made of wood-filled phenol resin

4. Separate ring sabots
These were the most common and a number e tered service with various weapons. In this ty the shoulder and base sabots were entirely ind pendent. The shoulder unit was usually discard by centrifugal force and the base unit by gas pre sure or air drag. A wide variety of types w produced in this group and in most cases the su projectile exhibited a much-improved ballist shape.

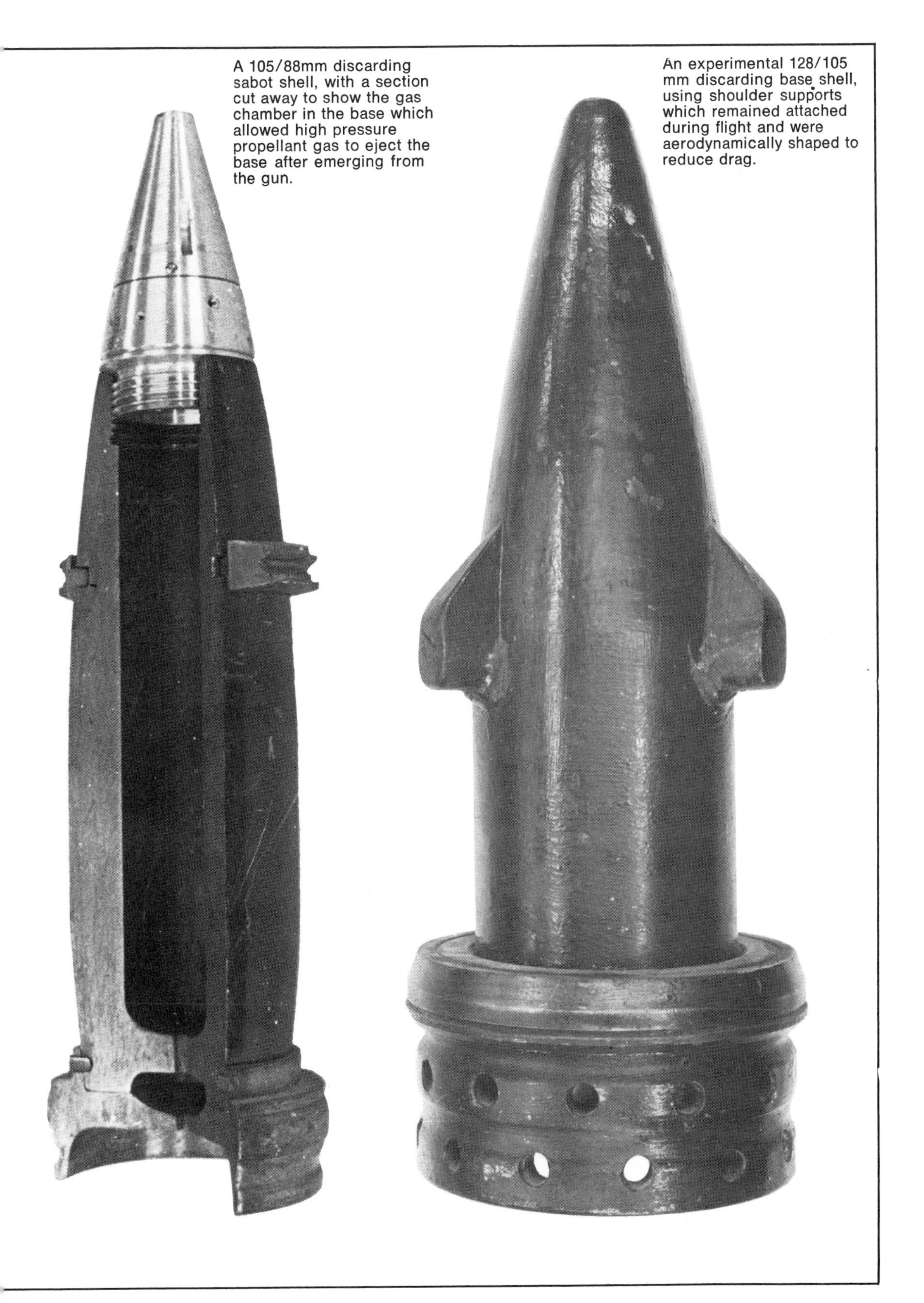

A 105/88mm discarding sabot shell, with a section cut away to show the gas chamber in the base which allowed high pressure propellant gas to eject the base after emerging from the gun.

An experimental 128/105 mm discarding base shell, using shoulder supports which remained attached during flight and were aerodynamically shaped to reduce drag.

Fin-stabilised shells (Klappleitwerke Geschosse)
The development of fin-stabilised shells in Germany, already briefly outlined, was in pursuit of three objects: to attain higher velocities by removing the resistance of the rifling, to allow longer and higher-capacity projectiles to be more easily stabilised, and to be able to fire unspun projectiles from rifled guns. The first important fin-stabilised projectile developed in Germany, however, fitted into none of these categories. This was the *Röchling anti-concrete shell* (Rö-Geschoss), development of which had been begun well before the war—as a private venture—by Röchling Eisen- und Stahlwerk of Düsseldorf.

The development of anti-concrete projectiles, as a distinct class of shell, was a phenomenon of continental Europe. With massive concrete fortifications on every border and memories of the fate of the Belgian forts in 1914, the attack of concrete was considered a special case and several *Beton-Granaten* were provided for various weapons. These were much the same as armour piercing shells but had plain conical heads covered by ballistic caps and were made of steel of about 45ton/in^2 yield strength.

Röchling felt that these projectiles, designed as they were on a formula (Petry's) dating from before World War 1, were inefficient and that penetrative performances could be improved by providing a shell of greatly increased sectional density. Since the projectile for this task had to be of large size—21cm was the preferred calibre—any thoughts of tungsten were immediately ruled out and the Röchling shell eventually evolved into a long sub-calibre projectile with a discarding band at the shoulder and a pot sabot at the rear. Wrapped around the tail, inside the pot sabot, were four flexible fins which sprang out as the pot sabot was drawn off by air pressure. Fired from a conventional gun the Röchling shell left the bore spinning, but the amount of spin was insufficient to stabilise such a long body and the fins took over the job as the velocity dropped during flight.

The penetration of the Röchling shell was awesome. It was not used in 1940, but after the occupation of France and Belgium a number of trials were made against French and Belgian defensive works; one record speaks of a shell passing through 3m of earth cover, 36m of concrete, a layer of broken stone, a gun casemate and into the floor beneath. It then passed through the floor and 5m into the earth beneath before coming to rest. This, of course, was an inert test projectile, since the live article was fuzed to detonate when the retardation owing to penetration had stopped, that is, when the projectile entered a space in the work.

The achievement of this performance demanded exacting specifications and manufacture. The shell had to be made from chrome-vanadium steel, and the design of the fins was a long series of trials and disappointments before success was achieved.

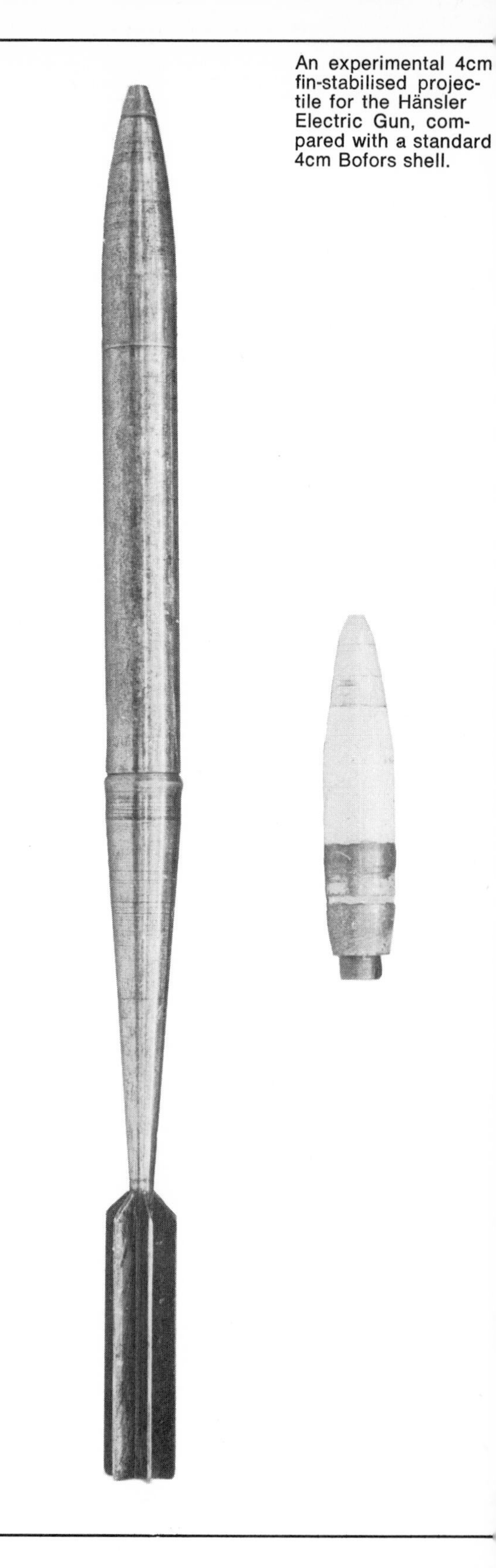

An experimental 4cm fin-stabilised projectile for the Hänsler Electric Gun, compared with a standard 4cm Bofors shell.

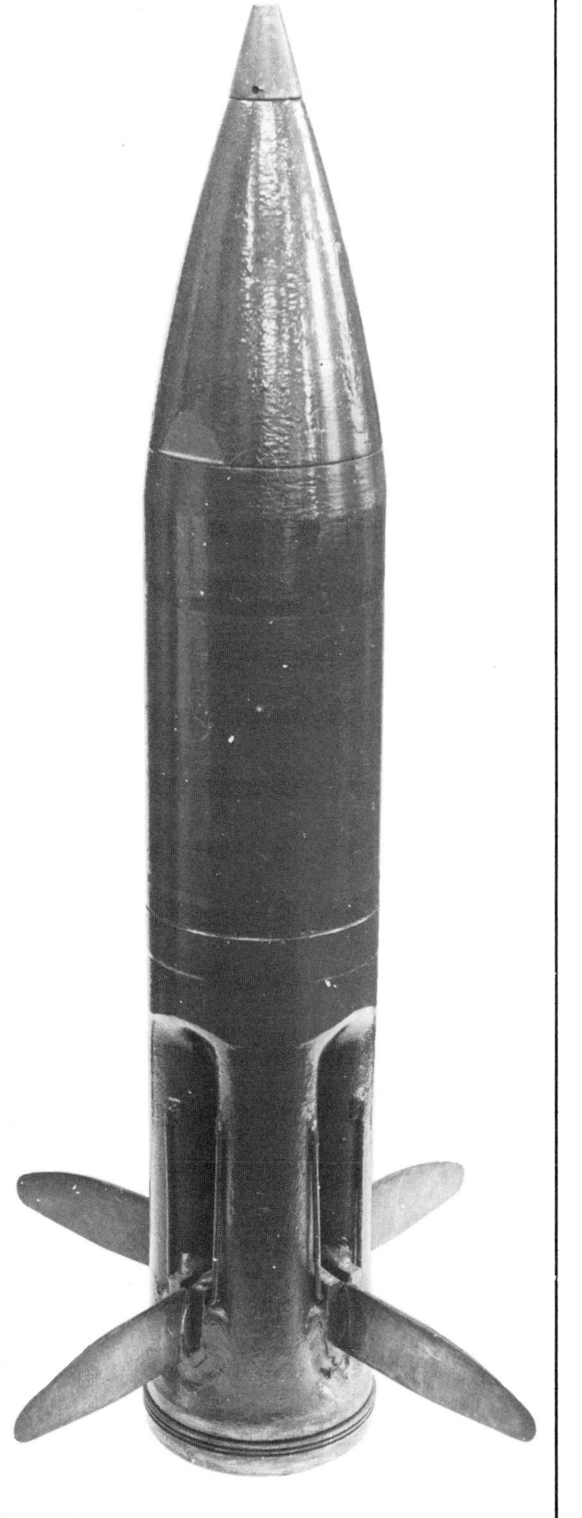
15cm Gr. Hohladung mit Klappleitwerk. A hollow charge shell with spring-out fins and a free-rolling sealing band.

And after all that, when some 8000 had been made and stockpiled, the shells were hardly used. A few were fired against the fortress of Brest-Litovsk in the 1941 invasion of Russia but use of the Rö-Geschoss was thereafter stopped by Hitler, who was so impressed by its performance that he was afraid of a specimen falling into enemy hands—from which the design could be copied and then used against Germany. From then, Röchling shells could only be used with his express permission and so, since this was rarely requested and even more rarely granted, the shell was more or less forgotten.

The success of the Rö-Geschoss stimulated interest in fin-stabilisation and the Peenemünde research station began extensive studies, using wind tunnels to determine the optimum shape of body and, more especially, of fins. In the course of these studies some considerable discoveries were made that greatly influenced future design, one of the most fundamental of which was that the accepted practice—*eg* on mortar bombs—of using a tail boom to carry fins of the same calibre as the projectile was quite unacceptable when the projectile travelled at supersonic speeds. It was found necessary in this case to provide super-calibre fins that stood well proud of the projectile silhouette, into the airstream. This discovery led to the development of sub-calibre projectiles with full-calibre fins and a variety of full-calibre projectiles with fins arranged to be expanded into the airstream after ejection from the gun muzzle.

Towards higher velocities

In the high-velocity long-range class the *Peenemünder Pfeilgeschoss* (Peenemünde arrow shell or PPG) was the principal design, a dart-like subprojectile with full-calibre fins and a central three-piece discarding sabot. The first pattern used a telescopic tail unit that was pushed out by propellant gas pressure to increase the length of the projectile after ejection from the barrel, but one trial firing was enough to show that the mechanical difficulties were enormous. Then Oberingenieur Gessner of Peenemünde proposed the *Treibzapfelgeschoss* (shaft-propelled shell) in which a form of pusher piston behind the shell forced it up the bore and then fell clear at the muzzle. This was tried and found wanting, since placing all the propulsive force on the tail of the shell led to enormous set-back stresses through the shell body and the dead weight of the pusher piston unit lowered the velocity.

After several other ideas had been tried and discarded, Gessner proposed the *Treibringgeschoss* (driving-ring shell), which turned out to be the correct solution. He placed a three-piece sabot around the waist of the shell to act not only as a centering device but also as the thrust mechanism that transferred the propelling gas thrust to the projectile. This meant that only the front half of the sabot was under compression during acceleration, while the rear section was under an expansive

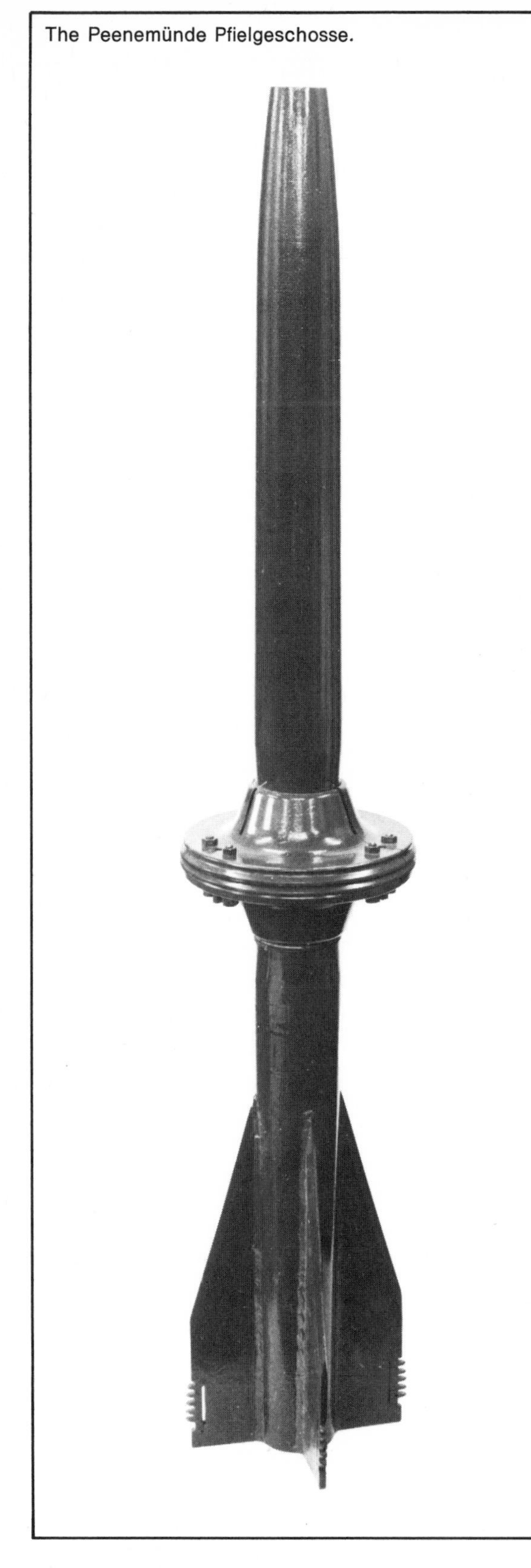
The Peenemünde Pfielgeschosse.

stress (but this was considerably diminished by g pressure on the projectile base). The fins we fitted at their extremities with soft iron tips whi were a tight fit in the gun barrel. This shell w developed for a 31cm smoothbore version of t 28cm Kanone 5(E) railway gun and saw son service, small numbers being fired at the US 3 Army in the later days of the war.

The Treibringgeschoss was also taken up Fliegeroberstabsingenieur Bleissner of GL Flak the anti-aircraft design section of the Luftwaf and a 10.5cm version was designed for use as anti-aircraft projectile; it was thereby hoped reduce by some 25% the time of flight to 10,00 altitude. Development was begun at Bochum Verein under Dr Köster and successful trials we undertaken, but the war ended before producti for service could be planned. One of the difficult facing the developers was the demand for hig grade steel with which to make the PPG sh bodies.

Among other advantages of the 10.5cm PPG w the virtual disappearance of barrel wear owing the adoption of the smoothbore barrel, but a di advantage lay in the construction of the shell fro high-quality steel since, even with the reduc stress that was due to the driving ring design, t high velocities attained still placed a heavy stra on the shell body during acceleration.

Towards longer and higher-capacity shells

The second group—fin stabilisation in order allow the use of unusually long shells—was only the development stage as the war ended. The pr jectiles were called *Minengeschosse,* referring their high capacity for explosive, but this ter was very misleading since almost any shell wi above-average capacity was called a 'Minenge choss': the term did not specifically relate to fi stabilised types. The interesting feature of the projectiles was that they were intended to be fir from conventionally-rifled guns and so, to allo this to happen and still have the shell unspun, 'sealing band' was fitted. This resembled a drivi band in appearance and shape but was mount on roller- or ball-bearings so that, when forced in the gun rifling to seal the propellant gases, rotated with the rifling and did not rotate the she With the frictional and accelerative forces at wo it was inevitable in practice that some spin w transferred to the projectile, but the designe claimed that this could initially be kept belo 30% of the normal rate and that (once the fi opened) this residual spin would be further reduc by the air resistance to the rotating blades.

The vanes developed for these projectiles to three forms. The first was a group of flexible blad coiled and concealed in the hollow tail of the pr jectile and mounted on a telescopic shaft, so th after emerging from the muzzle the shaft extend to the rear and the fins sprang open. The shaft w

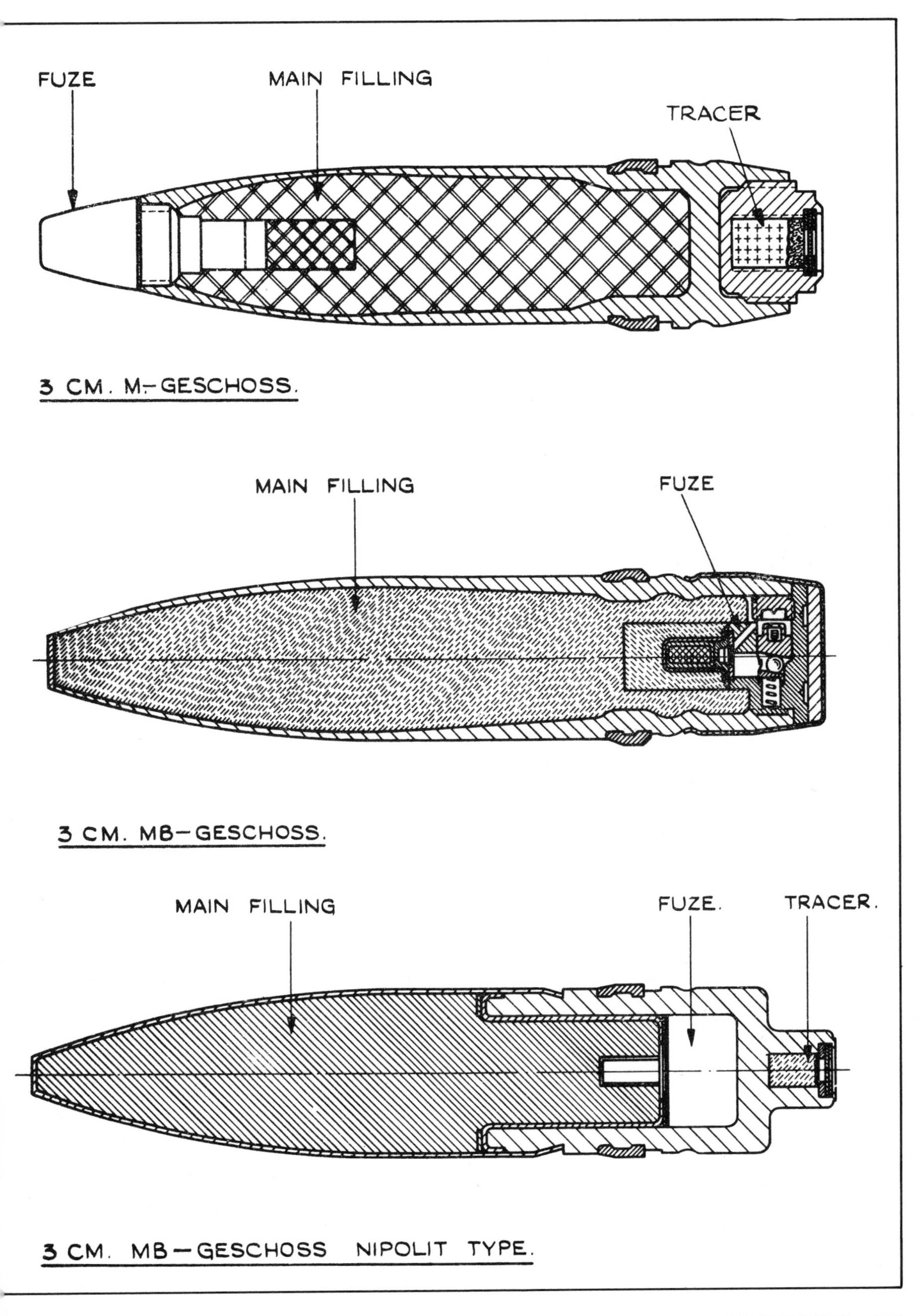
FUZE
MAIN FILLING
TRACER
3 CM. M-GESCHOSS.
MAIN FILLING
FUZE
3 CM. MB-GESCHOSS.
MAIN FILLING
FUZE.
TRACER.
3 CM. MB-GESCHOSS NIPOLIT TYPE.

extended by allowing a portion of propelling gas to enter an inner chamber through a restricted port. This built up a reserve of pressure in the chamber of about 20ton/in² that tended to push the shaft out, but so long as the projectile was in the gun bore (where the same propellant pressure existed all around the projectile base) the equality of pressure prevented any movement. Once clear of the muzzle, the 20ton/in² pressure trapped within the shell could not escape quickly enough from the restricted vent, its pressure against the shaft was only resisted by atmospheric pressure (14.7lb/in²), and so the tail shaft was extended.

The second pattern of vanes might be called the 'umbrella' type from the fin action. The fins, mounted on an extension shaft with a powerful spring, were so hinged that they could open at the rear like an umbrella's ribs. A thin wire held the closed fins against the spring pressure during loading, but this was sheared by acceleration forces and allowed the spring to force the fins open after leaving the muzzle.

The last and best system was the 'jack-knife fin' in which four fins, hinged at the rear, were carried in an extension of the shell body. They were quite loosely mounted and, on leaving the muzzle, the residual spin was sufficient to throw them open, whereupon they were locked by simple spring-catches. This system had the advantages of mechanical simplicity and reliability, and also the virtue that air resistance tended to keep the fins firmly open.

Unspun projectiles and rifled guns

The third class of projectile, which used fin-stabilisation because of a need to fire a non-spinning projectile from a rifled gun, applied only to hollow charge anti-tank projectiles. It is widely known that the hollow charge shell relies on focusing the energy of a shaped and lined explosive charge in order to penetrate armour, and after initial enthusiasm for the principle had died down it was found that spinning the projectile tended to dissipate the energy of the explosive jet. It was this that led to intensive development of fin-stabilised rocket launchers of various sorts, intended to deliver hollow charge warheads—*eg* the American bazooka or Ofenrohr, its German equivalent.

The advantage of the hollow charge shell in providing low-velocity howitzers and guns with a useful anti-tank capability was too great to relinquish without some effort being made to overcome the spin problem, and several of the shells that were built on the lines of the 'Minengeschoss' mentioned above were also developed as hollow-charge weapons. So far as external appearance goes, there was no difference; it was merely the internal arrangement of the shell that varied. The idea was quite successful but development had not been carried to its conclusion when the war ended. In later years the principle was further explored by many countries and has since been widely adopted.

Rocket assisted shells (Raketengranate or Raketengeschosse)

A considerable amount of research was done Germany on this aspect of improvements in p formance, since the rocket as a weapon was accepted fact and a large amount of techni

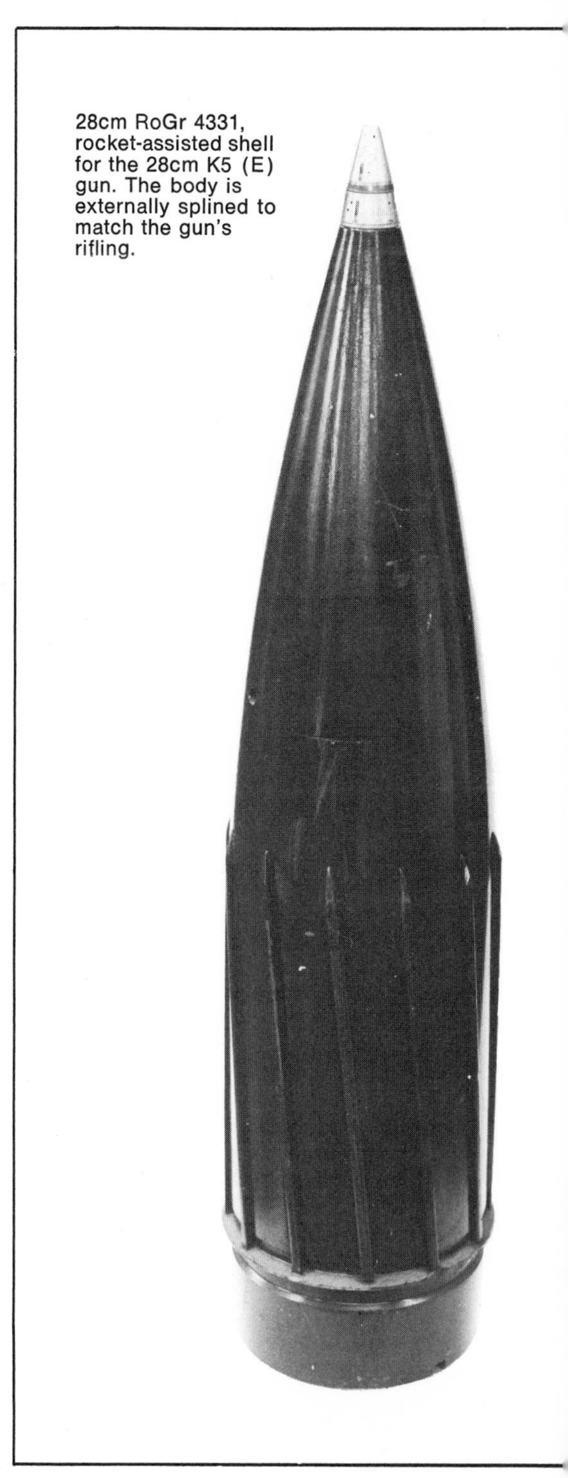

28cm RoGr 4331, rocket-assisted shell for the 28cm K5 (E) gun. The body is externally splined to match the gun's rifling.

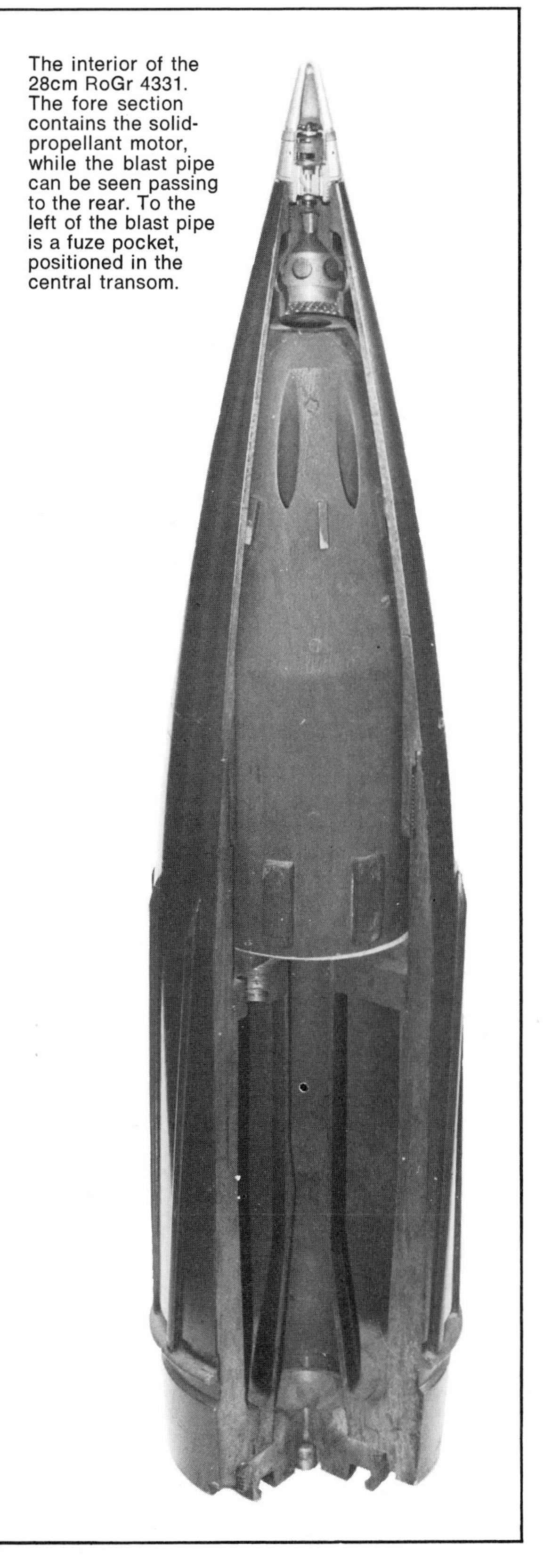
The interior of the 28cm RoGr 4331. The fore section contains the solid-propellant motor, while the blast pipe can be seen passing to the rear. To the left of the blast pipe is a fuze pocket, positioned in the central transom.

knowledge was available. There were three basic classes of projectile:

1. Those with the propellant at the rear and the high explosive payload in the nose.

2. Those with the propellant chamber in the nose, the payload at the rear, and the rocket efflux arranged around the body of the shell.

3. Those with the propellant chamber in the nose, the payload at the rear, and the rocket efflux directed down through the payload compartment by an axial blast-pipe.

The first type flew well enough but tended to drive the explosive section well into the ground before detonation occurred, masking the effect on the target. The second class was developed to cure this defect, which it did but produced an even more serious one—severe inaccuracy owing to the rocket blast disturbing the airflow over the shell body. The third type was developed to solve this problem and was considered to be the best design.

The first rocket projectile issued to service was a 15cm shell used with the s FH 18 in the Russian campaign of 1941, but it was very much an experimental model and the involved firing instructions and warnings that went with it did nothing to imbue the users with confidence in the new weapon. However, it taught the designers lessons that were taken into account when the 28cm Ro. Granate 4331 was designed and issued. Other designs were also produced in limited numbers, notably a 12.8cm shell for anti-aircraft use.

The principal drawback to these projectiles was the inaccuracy owing to off-line thrust at ignition time, and thus the 28cm shell had a range dispersion zone about the target of some 4% of range. This, at a maximum range of 85km, meant that 50% of the shells would fall within 3.4km of the target, the rest falling up to 13.6km away.

The Tromsdorff athodyd (ramjet) shell has been briefly discussed and there is little that can usefully be added. Its development was at a very early stage when the war ended, and although a few had been fired in 15cm calibre none had carried a payload. Two basic types of shell were under development; the *ring* type, in which the incoming air flowed around an annular space surrounding the shell body proper, and the *tube* type in which the airflow was down an axial pipe running through the shell from front to rear, both appeared before the war's end. Three calibres were then under investigation (15cm, 21cm and 28cm) and theoretical figures had been deduced for their probable performances:

15cm athodyd shell: muzzle velocity 1000mps (3280fps), range 180km (112miles).

21cm athodyd shell: muzzle velocity 1000mps (3280fps), range 200km (124miles).

28cm athodyd shell: muzzle velocity 1250mps (4100fps), range 400km (248miles).

It was hoped that the 28cm design would manage to accommodate a 13kg (28.67lb) payload of high explosive.

Fuzes

The standard fuzes used with German artillery shells fell into three groups: nose percussion, base percussion and time. Most of them were simple and effective mechanisms based on well-tried mechanical devices. The *Aufschlagzünder* (AZ, or nose percussion fuzes) all used the Krupp-patented system in which a number of eccentrically-mounted blocks were surrounded by a leaf spring that kept the striker and the detonator apart until the centrifugal force generated by the spinning shell caused the blocks to swing outwards. Most percussion fuzes were fitted with adjusting screws whose operation selected either direct-action or delay, thus allowing the shell to penetrate light cover before detonating. The delay was achieved by a centrifugally-governed leaf shutter beneath the main detonator. If direct action (or non-delay) was selected, the shutter slid out under the influence of the centrifugal force and left a direct path for the flash from the detonator to pass into the fuze magazine. If 'delay' was selected, the shutter was locked in place and the flash was diverted into a channel filled with a pyrotechnic delay powder, which took a short time to burn through (times in the order of 0.15sec were usual) before igniting the fuze magazine. Some fuzes incorporated two or even three delay units, each giving different times but a refinement that is — while perhaps theoretically justified—of doubtful utility in practice.

Nose fuzes are divided into two types: those that are actuated by striking the target and having a striker or needle driven into the detonator (*direct action*), and those that are actuated by the deceleration of the shell on landing at the target, when an inertia pellet in the fuze runs down and drives a needle into a detonator. The second class is known as *graze action,* since the mere graze of the shell on the ground is sufficient to actuate the fuze without demanding an outright head-on impact. Most German nose fuzes incorporated both types of action as a form of insurance.

Bodenzünder (base fuzes), by virtue of their location in the shell, were of necessity graze action types. Owing to the need for the deceleration to be sensed by the pellet, and the physical movement required, a very small delay was inherent in all graze fuzes.

Zeitzünder (time fuzes) were almost invariably mechanical. Combustion-time fuzes, those relying on the burning of a train of pyrotechnic composition, were exceptionally rare and those few that were used were introduced at the war's end owing to the shortage of mechanical fuzes.

The mechanical fuzes used were of two types: spring-driven by the Krupp-Thiel mechanism or centrifugally driven by the Junghans mechanism. The Germans distinguished the mechanisms by adding Fg (Fliegewicht—flying weight) to the names of the centrifugally-driven models. Thus the Zeitzünder S/60 (60sec time fuze) was a Krupp mechanism, while Zeitzünder S/60Fg had a centrifugal drive. Most field weapons used combination time and percussion fuzes that were of mechanical actuation with the addition of a simple percussion mechanism. These were known as *Doppelzünder* (Dopp Z). Numbers on time fuzes indicated the running times of the timing mechanisms at their maximum settings, but one or two corruptions appeared; the Dopp Z S/90/45, for example, had a 45sec mechanism regeared to run for 90sec to suit it to use in long-range guns. Perhaps the strangest feature of German time fuzes, to British eyes, is the complete absence of time markings on the fuzes themselves. All German time fuzes were set by setting machines, either hand-operated or mechanically linked (in the case of anti-aircraft guns) to the predictor. These setters were highly accurate and it was felt that there was no point in putting numbers on the fuzes—in the first place they could not be seen when the fuze was in the setter, and in the second the graduations would never be so accurate as the setting machine. Checking the machine by reading the fuze setting was hence pointless. Whatever other virtues the system had, it certainly speeded up production by eliminating a time-consuming engraving process and it is noteworthy that British and American designs developed after the war also omitted the visible time-scale.

Proximity fuzes, which use electronic sensors to detect the targets and to detonate the fuzes at the correct lethal distances, were never used in German artillery. There were some forty-five such developments being undertaken by the end of the war, but the vast majority were intended for guided missiles where the launch conditions were much more gentle than the violent accelerations of an artillery shell. The missile configuration also gave the designers more space with which to experiment. One of the few gun developments was Kühglockchen, an electrostatic fuze under development by Rheinmetall-Borsig for possible anti-aircraft use, but it did not even reach the prototype stage before the war ended.

The following table lists the standard German artillery fuzes and their salient characteristics.

Aufschlagzünder/Nose Percussion Fuzes

AZ 1: Aufschlagzünder 1. A direct-action and graze fuze for low-velocity guns, of 49.5mm (1.95in) gauge and with an optional 0.15sec delay. The fuze was 105mm (4.14in) long.

AZ 1/1: Aufschlagzünder 1/1. This was a modification of the AZ 1 in respect of the delay unit assembly. Both models were usually painted dark grey, although later production was often of rust-proofed steel.

Kl AZ 1: Kleine Aufschlagzünder 1. This was mechanically the same as the AZ 1 but had a shorter (91mm/3.60in) body.

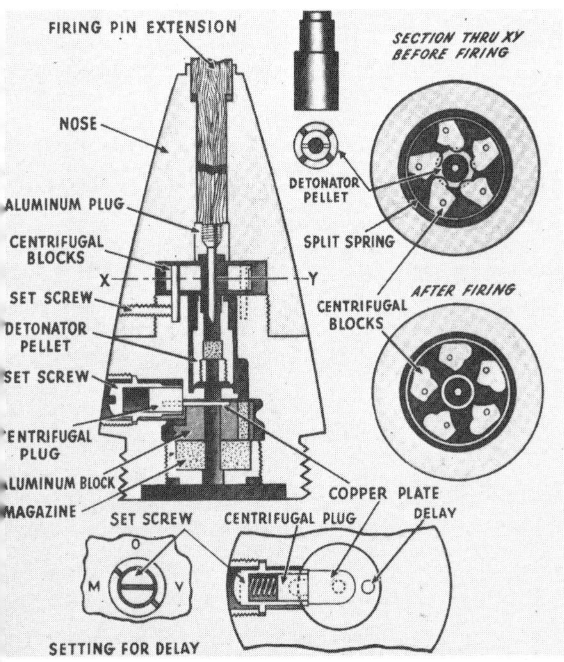

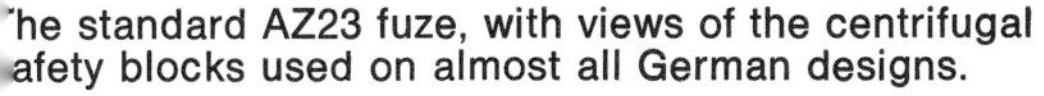
'he standard AZ23 fuze, with views of the centrifugal afety blocks used on almost all German designs.

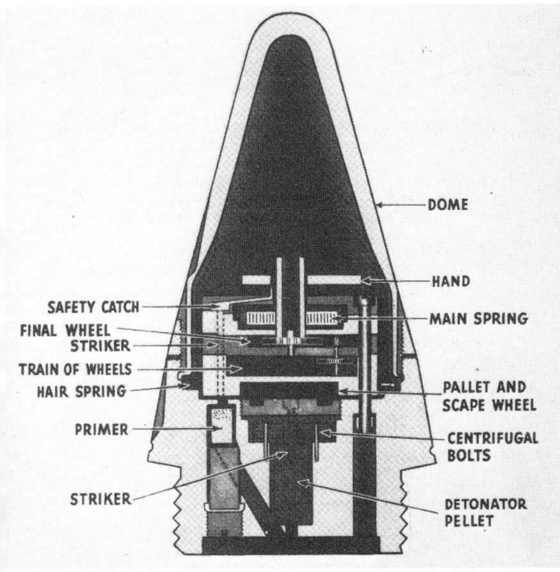

ectioned view of Dopp Z S/60s mechanical time nd percussion fuze.

4Z 2: Aufschlagzünder 2. This, much the same s the AZ 1, was of composite sheet-steel and lastic construction. The fuze was of rust-proofed inish and had a red ring at the tip.

Hbgr Z 17/23: Haubegranate Zünder 17/23. This vas a shortened form of the AZ 23 used beneath ballistic caps. The fuze ended in a cup that accepted the long wooden striker rod.

AZ 23v (0.15): Aufschlagzünder 23 mit Verzögerung 0.15 Sekunde. This fuze formed the basis for a large range of subvarieties. It was basically a 49.5mm(1.95in) gauge direct-action and graze fuze with an optional delay of 0.15sec. The tip was closed by a light foil disc covering the wooden striker rod, and bore safety was ensured by five interlocking blocks interposed between the detonator and the striker. The fuze was 111mm(4.37in) long and the body was ogival. Early models were of aluminium but those of later production were of steel, painted deep olive green. There was no difference between the AZ 23 and the AZ 23v (0.15), as the latter term replaced the former as the range of subvarieties proliferated.

AZ 23v (0.15) Pr: Aufschlagzünder 23 mit Verzögerung 0.15 Sekunde und Presstofhülse. This was a wartime design using a phenolic resin plastic body within a thin steel casing. The designation reads 'nose percussion fuze model 23 with an 0.15sec delay and a plastic body'.

AZ 23v (0.25): Aufschlagzünder 23 mit Verzögerung 0.25 Sekunde. This was similar to the '(0.15)' pattern but had a slightly longer delay. These fuzes were issued during the early part of the war, but the delay was found to be excessive and they were replaced by the standard AZ 23v (0.15).

AZ 23 umg (0.8): Aufschlagzünder 23 umgeändertes Modell mit Verzögerung 0.8 Sekunde. This was totally different in appearance from the standard AZ 23 and used a different mechanism to set the delay. The fuze was of rust-proofed steel, 79mm(3.12in) long of which the head was no more than 31mm(1.22in). To set the delay a collar surrounding the nose was turned, although the internal direct-action and graze mechanism was the same as that of the AZ 23v (0.15) pattern.

AZ 23 umg (0.15): Aufschlagzünder 23 umgeändertes Modell mit Verzögerung 0.15 Sekunde. This was essentially the same as the last, but with a delay of 0.15sec as opposed to 0.8sec. The term umgeändertes Modell in the designation means 'altered model'.

AZ 23 umg m 2 V: Aufschlagzünder 23 umgeändertes Modell mit 2 Verzögerungen. This was a similar fuze to the two preceding types but was fitted with two delay units (0.2sec and 0.8sec).

AZ 23/28v (0.1): Aufschlagzünder 23/28 mit Verzögerung 0.1 Sekunde. This fuze was similar to the AZ 23v (0.15) but was fitted with a stronger spring between the needle and the detonator so that it could withstand firing at high-velocity.

AZ 23/28 Zn: Aufschlagzünder 23/23 Zink. This was the same as the AZ 23/28v (0.1) but was made from zinc alloy: the tip was marked yellow.

AZ 23/40: Aufschlagzünder 23/40. This was again similar to the AZ 23/28 but was manufactured in a different way, with a screwed-in tip and forward section. It was made of light alloy.

AZ 23/42: Aufschlagzünder 23/42. This was a standard AZ 23 with the centrifugal segments and spring designed to open at a lower spin rate. The fuze was used with the 10.5cm Geb H smoke shell.
AZ 23 Geb: Aufschlagzünder 23 für Gebirgsgeschütze. This was the standard AZ 23 mechanism in a shorter (91mm/3.57in) body of light alloy, and was intended for use in mountain guns. The delay was 0.25sec and the fuze had a blue tip.
AZ 23 Neb: Aufschlagzünder 23 für Nebelgranaten. This used the normal AZ 23 direct-action and graze mechanism without the delay pellet. The fuze was marked around the body with a series of punched indents, thus facilitating identification at night. It was used with smoke shells.
AZ 23 Tr: Aufschlagzünder 23 für Treibspiegelgeschossen. This was an experimental fuze of the AZ 23 pattern, but it was internally strengthened to withstand high velocities and was used with discarding sabot shells.
AZ 23 St: Aufschlagzünder 23 mit Stahlgehäuse. This was a standard AZ 23v (0.15) made of rust-proofed steel over a light alloy core; the fuze was of late (c.1945) manufacture.
Kl AZ 23: Kleine Aufschlagzünder 23. This was no more than the standard AZ 23 mechanism in a smaller body — 68mm(2.69in) long by 33mm (1.30in) in maximum diameter—for use with tank and anti-tank guns whose calibre was less than 7.62cm(3.00in). The fuze had an optional delay of 0.15sec and was made of light alloy.
Kl AZ 23 Nb: Kleine Aufschlagzünder 23 für Nebelgranaten. This was a reduced-size AZ 23 Nb for use with tank and anti-tank guns.
Kl AZ 23/1: Kleine Aufschlagzünder 23/1. This was similar to the Kl AZ 23 and was of slightly different construction; it had an optional delay of 0.10sec and was painted olive green.
Kl AZ 23 umg: Kleine Aufschlagzünder 23 umgeändertes Modell. This differed from the Kl AZ 23 in shape, being more conical, and in weight (28gm/1oz less)—all of which was due to simplified manufacturing techniques.
I Gr Z 23 nA v(0.15): Infanterie-Granaten Zünder 23 neuer Art, mit Verzögerung 0.15 Sekunde. Although the basic AZ 23 mechanism was one of the best and most reliable fuzes ever designed, it seems that it did not satisfy everyone's demands and that an improved version was developed just before the war. This used an unusual mechanism; the bottom of the detonator carrier was coned and sat in a conical recess in a heavy iron ring. Once the usual centrifugal blocks had swung clear, any movement of the ring, whether forward on impact or sideways in the event of a broadside landing, would—owing to the interaction of the coned faces —drive the detonator on to the needle and fire the fuze. This is an all-ways fuze, very useful in hand grenades but of doubtful utility in shells that do not often land broadside. The improved fuze failed to replace the AZ 23.
le I Gr Z 23 nA: Leichte Infanterie-Granaten Zünder 23 neuer Art. This, a modification of th above pattern, was designed for use beneath balli stic caps. The nose was belled out to take the usua wooden extension rod, but the fuze was replace by the Hbgr Z 35 K.
I Gr Z 23 nA Zn v(0.15): Infanterie-Granate Zünder 23 neuer Art, mit Zinkhülse und Verzö gerung 0.15 Sekunde. This was of similar desig to the I Gr Z 23 nA but was of two-piece con struction of zinc alloy instead of aluminium allo The fuze had a yellow tip. The term neuer A means 'new pattern'.
S I Gr Z 23: Sichere Infanterie-Granaten Zünde 23. This was similar to the standard AZ 23 bu had a safety pin that passed through the nose an positively locked the centrifugal segments in th safe position: the pin had to be withdrawn pric to loading.
K Z C/27: Klappensicherungzünder Konstructio 27. The nomenclature C/27 identifies this fuze a of naval pattern and early specimens were usuall marked M for Marine. Later models bear the usua 'WaA' army inspection stamps. It was a short fuz for use with an extension rod under a ballisti cap, and the mechanism was similar to that of th AZ 23 but without the optional delay featur The K Z C/27 had a steel body.
EK Z C/27 f Sprgr m Haub: Empfindlich Klap pensicherungzünder C/27 für Sprenggranate mi Haube. This seems to have been the same as th previous fuze except for the brass body. All th examined specimens bore prewar dates, and it i possible that the difference in name may be n more than a change of designation.
EK Z C/28: Empfindlich Klappensicherungzünde C/28. This was a large (112mm/4.42in long aluminium fuze using the AZ 23 mechanism wit the deletion of the optional delay unit. The wor Empfindlich means 'sensitive'.
EK Z C/28 nA f Sprgr: Empfindlich Klappensi cherungzünder C/28 neuer Art für Sprenggranate This was a shorter version of the previous typ presumably introduced at a later date on accoun of the designation neuer Art (new pattern). Th fuze was 76mm(3.00in) long and was made o brass-coated steel.
KZ 28 P: Klappensicherüngzünder 28 mit Panzer kopf. This was a direct-action fuze, 110mm(4.35in long and of rust-proofed steel. The term mit Pan zerkopf translates as 'with armour cap'.
AZ 35 K: Aufschlagzünder 35 kurz . This use the basic AZ 23 mechanism contained within new steel body 125mm(4.94in) long. The fuze wa unusual in German service as it had a protrusio into the shell of 48mm(1.90in); principally use with the 17cm Kanone in Mörserlafette, it had a optional delay of 0.3sec.
Hbgr Z 35 K: Haubgranaten Zünder 35 kurz. Thi was a shortened (kurz—'short') version of the AZ 35 K for use with an extension rod under a ballisti cap. The setting mechanism was a collar aroun the nose instead of the usual slotted screw

but the mechanism was otherwise the same. The optional delay was 0.05sec.
KZ C/36: Klappensicherungzünder C/36. This was a small direct-action fuze for naval and coast artillery shells of the older blunt-nosed type. The fuze was 56mm(2.19in) long and had a gauge of 40mm(1.58in).
AZ 38: Aufschlagzünder 38. This was a small and simple direct-action fuze for use with hollow charge shells. It contained a striker over a powerful detonator, the two being separated by the usual centrifugal blocks. The fuze was 38mm(1.150in) long with a gauge of 18mm(0.69in).
AZ 38 St: Aufschlagzünder 38 mit Stahlhülse. This was a wartime production expedient: similar to the AZ 38, it had a steel body of more angular contour.
AZ 39: Aufschlagzünder 39. This was a small direct-action fuze used with 5cm tank and anti-tank guns. An unusual mechanism, it contained a sliding plate that prevented movement of the striker, being locked safe by two centrifugal bolts. A steel ball in a vertical channel ran forward during flight into a hole in the locking plate, thus adding weight so that centrifugal force could slide it free and arm the fuze. The AZ 39 was 53mm(2.10in) long and had a gauge of 28mm(1.10in).
AZ 39 Zn: Aufschlagzünder 39 Zink. This was the same as the above type but with a body of zinc-based alloy instead of aluminium.
AZ 39 Pr: Aufschlagzünder 39 Presstoff. This was the same as the AZ 39 but was of a plastic material covered by a thin steel sheet.
Hbgr Z 40 K: Haubegranate Zünder 40 kurz. This was outwardly identical to the Hbgr Z 35 K, the only difference lying in the construction of the delay mechanism.
AZ 47, AZ 48 and AZ 49: These three Aufschlagzünder were similar to the AZ 39; smaller than the original, they were all intended for use in 2cm shells. The fuzes were 32mm(1.25in) long and had gauges of 15mm(0.59in).
KZ 128: Klappensicherungzünder 128. This was identical in shape and size to the AZ 23, but had no optional delay unit and was made of rust-proofed steel. The fuze was a late war design for mountain artillery and was hence marked with a blue tip.
AZ 5045: Aufschlagzünder 5045. A very small direct-action fuze for 2cm shells.
AZ 5072: Aufschlagzünder 5072. A very small direct-action fuze for use with 2.8cm and 4.2cm taper-bore high explosive shells. The pattern was 32mm(1.25in) long and had a gauge of 15mm(0.60 in).
AZ 5075: Aufschlagzünder 5075. This was a direct-action fuze derived from a rifle grenade fuze and used with the 3.7cm Steilgranate 41 hollow charge bomb. Since the projectile was fin-stabilised, no centrifugal arming device could be used and the fuze was armed by set-back on firing.
AZ 5080: Aufschlagzünder 5080. This was similar to the AZ 5072, but was larger. It was used with the 7.5cm PAK 41 shell.
AZ 5095: Aufschlagzünder 5095. This was an improved version of the AZ 5075, having an arming device locked by a safety pin to prevent movement owing to rough handling in transit. The pin was removed before firing.
AZ f Hbgr: Aufschlagzünder für Haubegranate. This was a shortened fuze of the AZ 23 type, without the optional delay, for use beneath a ballistic cap. Manufactured of brass, it appears to have been a prewar design that was largely replaced during the war by other models.
3.7cm Kpf Z Zerl P: 3.7cm Kopfzünder Zerlegen (Pulverzug). The literal translation of the fuze's name is '3.7cm nose fuze with self-destruction activated by a powder train': used with 3.7cm Flak guns, delay was achieved by a power-burning train that ultimately destroyed the shell.
3.7cm Kpf Z Zerl Fg: 3.7cm Kopfzünder Zerlegen Fliegewicht. Similar in appearance to the previous pattern, this used a centrifugal mechanism to effect self-destruction. A striker was kept from a detonator by a centrifugal bolt assembly, but as the effect lessened with the reduction in spin towards the end of the shell's flight so a spring was able to force the bolt back, thus releasing the striker to fire the fuze.
5cm Kpf Z 2 Zerl P: 5cm Kopfzünder mit 2 Zerlegen (Pulverzug). This was similar to the 3.7cm fuze but could be set to give two times to self-destruction either by igniting the full powder train or by initiating it part-way along its length.
K Z f 5cm St: Klappensicherungzünder für 5cm, mit Stahlhülse. This, a small steel-bodied direct-action fuze, was used with 5cm tank and anti-tank guns.
K Z f 15cm Sprgr L/4.1: Klappensicherungzünder für 15cm Sprenggranate 4.1 kaliberlange. This was used with the 15cm Ubts u Tbts K, and was a steel pattern with a brass tip; it carried a simple direct-action mechanism.
K Z f 15cm Sprgr L/4.0: Klappensicherungzünder für 15cm Sprenggranate 4.0 kaliberlange. This was a short (83mm/3.25in) brass fuze of elderly design only with the Schiffskanone L/40. Direct-action only.

Bodenzünder/Base Percussion Fuzes
Bd Z C/36: Bodenzünder Kunstruction 36. This was a naval fuze 72mm(2.84in) long with a gauge of 32mm(1.26in). A simple graze mechanism was fitted with the usual centrifugal block safety device. Early production fuzes were of brass with light alloy caps, and were marked 'Bd Z C/36'. This pattern was superseded by one with a steel body and a light alloy cap, marked 'Bd Z 36'
Bd Z C/38: Bodenzünder Konstruction 38. This was another brass naval fuze, 72mm(2.85in) long with a gauge of 40mm(1.58in). The mechanism was similar to that of the C/36, the only difference being in its size and shape; a coned closing cap

was used. Early models were marked 'Bd Z C/38' while those of late production were marked 'Bd Z C/38 KV', in which KV (Kleine Verzögerung) indicated the inclusion of a short delay unit in the design.
Bd Z 40 K: Bodenzünder 40 mit Klappensicherung. This was a steel army fuze, similar to the C/38 in all but size. It was 75mm(2.94in) long with a gauge of 40mm(1.58in).
Bd Z 44: Bodenzünder 44. This army fuze was 39mm(1.53in) long, and was usually so fitted that the majority of the fuze protruded from the bottom of the shell: it was fitted with a tracer.
Bd Z 5103: Bodenzünder 5103. This was fitted with an extremely simple graze mechanism that was held in the safe position by a shear wire. A tracer was carried in the base.
Bd Z 5103:* Bodenzünder 5103*. This, similar to the previous pattern, omitted the pyrotechnic delay unit that was fitted to the 5103.
Bd Z 5103/1: Bodenzünder 5103/1. This was similar to the 5103, but was much smaller and lacked the tracer element.
Bd Z 5124: Bodenzünder 5124. This had the usual graze mechanism, but with an optional length of delay obtainable by turning a screw in its base. This locked the usual centrifugal shutter and forced the detonator flash to pass through a pyrotechnic delay unit.
Bd Z 5125: Bodenzünder 5125. This was similar to 5124 but was of different shape—entirely cylindrical and screw-threaded for all its length.
Bd Z 5127: Bodenzünder 5127. This fuze used an arming mechanism that comprised two steel balls retained by a steel collar and a shear pin. This locked the cocked striker and on impact the collar was flung forward, shearing the locking pin and allowing the balls to move out, thereby releasing the striker. This gave an unusually fast reaction time for a base fuze.
Bd Z 5130: Bodenzünder 5130. This was a simple shear-wire fuze used as an alternative in the 3.7cm Steilgranate 41.
Bd Z m V u K: Bodenzünder mit Verzögerung und Klappensicherung. This was a naval fuze using a normal graze mechanism, and the names indicates 'with delay and centrifugal safety device'. The fuze was used with the 28cm Gr Be.
Bd Z f Sprgr K: Bodenzünder für Sprenggranate mit Klappensicherung. This was similar to the previous pattern but was slightly shorter.
Bd Z f 7.5cm Pzgr: Bodenzünder für 7.5cm Panzergranate. This was a small fuze that was intended for use with armour piercing shells. It used a simple graze mechanism with a centrifugal safety, and a threaded cavity at the base accepted a tracer element.
Bd Z f 8.8cm Pzgr: Bodenzünder für 8.8cm Panzergranate. This was the same as the preceding pattern but in a larger body.
Bd Z f 10cm Pzgr: Bodenzünder für 10cm Panzergranate. This was again the same mechanism as the Bd Z f 7.5cm Pzgr, but in a still larger bod
Bd Z f 15cm Gr 19 Be: Bodenzünder für 15cm Granate 19 Beton. This fuze carried two differen lengths of optional delay selected by turning a larg screwhead in the base. This rotated the whole fuz mechanism within a casing, aligning the flas channel with either one of the two pyrotechni delay units or with a plain channel to give th fastest action.
Bd Z f 21cm Gr Be: Bodenzünder für 21cm Granate Beton. This, although resembling the 15cm pattern, was a different mechanism. A screw offse in the base selected delay or non-delay and a centrifugal locking plate was held in the saf position by a plunger that was driven forward under the pressure of the propellant gas, to fre the plate.

Zeitzünder/Time (Mechanical) Fuzes.
Zt Z S/5: Zeitzünder, 5 Sekunden. This was the standard Zt Z S/30 with the clock mechanism regeared to give a maximum running time of 5 seconds. It was used with the 28cm high explosive shells to give very accurate airbursts at shor ranges.
Zt Z S/28: Zeitzünder, 28 Sekunden. This was a modified S/30 running for 28sec and with a safety pin that passed through the body and locked the clock mechanism.
Zt Z S/30: Zeitzünder, 30 Sekunden. This was the standard German time fuze. Made of aluminium it was 112mm(4.40in) long with a gauge of 50mm (1.96in) and the dome was revolved to set the time of operation. The mechanism was a Krupp-Thiel clock and the maximum running time was 30sec.
Zt Z S/30 Zn: Zeitzünder, 30 Sekunden, Zinkhülse This was the same as the preceding type but with a body of zinc-based alloy.
Zt Z S/30 K: Zeitzünder S/30 kalt. The same as the S/30, but with a blue stripe and the letter K (for kalt, cold) on the nose to show that it was specially lubricated to operate in extreme cold.
Zt Z S/30^1*:* Zeitzünder, 30 Sekunden, minimum setting time 1sec. This differed principally from the S/30 in external shape (being more rounded) and had a minimum running time of 1sec.
Zt Z S/30^2*:* Zeitzünder 30 Sekunden, minimum running time 2sec. This differed from the previous type only in the minimum running time.
Zt Z S/30 Fg: Zeitzünder, 30 Sekunden, mit Fliegewicht. As the S/30 but with a Junghans centrifugal drive mechanism replacing the Krupp-Thiel clockwork system.
Zt Z S/30 Fg^1*:* Zeitzünder, 30 Sekunden, mit Fliegewicht, minimum running time 1sec. The same as the previous type with a restriction preventing setting for times shorter than 1sec.
Zt Z S/30 Kurz. This, although called kurz (short) was exactly the same size and appearance as the S/30 except for a patch of green paint on the nose. But the setting keyways were displaced 4° from their usual place, so that when machine-set the

ıze functioned about 100m short of the set point) distribute incendiary shrapnel effectively at the ɛt range.
't Z S/30 Fg Kurz: Fg equalling Fliegewicht. 'his was the Junghans centrifugal pattern of the /30 Kurz.
't Z S/30 CC: This was a redesigned Zt Z S/30 ith the addition of a highly-sensitive CC percus- ion mechanism to the nose unit, changing the nose hape. A red band was painted beneath the new rass nosecap. It is believed that these were an xperimental batch of 30000 fuzes for anti–aircraft se, and that the red band was intended to indicate heir unsuitability for setting in the standard fuze- etting machines.
't Z S/45: Zeitzünder, 45 Sekunden. This, of the ame contours and appearance as the S/30, used different gearing of the clock to give a maximum unning time of 45sec. Various models of this fuze ppeared towards the end of the war, some of vhich had long tapered caps to improve their allistic shape.
't Z S/60: Zeitzünder, 60 Sekunden. This was imilar to the S/30 but ran for one minute. The hape was slightly different: the tip of the nose vas belled out and then flattened, instead of being ounded. Length: 104mm(4.08in).
't Z S/60 nA: Zeitzünder, 60 Sekunden, neuer Art. This was a much shorter 'new pattern' deriv- ıtion of the S/60 with a curved head and a pointed ıose; 80mm(3.16in) long, it was used only with 3.8cm star shells.
Zt Z S/120: Zeitzünder, 120 Sekunden. This was he standard S/30 with the clock mechanism re- geared and altered. The body had the '30' barred- out and '120' placed alongside it. The fuze tip was painted blue and a safety pin was incorporated. It is believed that this fuze was introduced for use in mountain guns firing at high angles that gave long times of flight.

Brennzünder/Time (Combustion) Fuzes.
Lg Zdr S/33: Lange Zünder, 33 Sekunde. This was an elderly design of double ring fuze, 64mm(2.52in) long and made of brass. It was used only with 8.8cm and 10.5cm star shells and had a 33sec maximum burning time.
BZ S/30: Brennzünder, 30 Sekunden. This was an experimental two-ring fuze of the same contours as the mechanical S/30 patterns. Developed late in the war, it is thought that few were used.
BZ S/30 St: Brennzünder, 30 Sekunden, mit Stahl- hülse. This, the same as the preceding type, dif- fered only in the steel body.

Doppelzünder/Time (Mechanical) and Percussion Fuzes.
M Dopp Z 28 K: Marine Doppelzünder 28 mit Klappensicherung. This was a naval pattern, 111mm (4.38in) long. The lower section was made of rust- proofed steel and the nose portion of aluminium. The maximum running time was 125sec, the mini- mum 28sec.
E Dopp Z S/30 Fg[1]: Empfindlich Doppelzünder, 30 Sekunden, mit Fliegewicht, minimum running time 1sec. This fuze was similar to the Zt Z S/30 Fg[1] but with the addition of a direct-action percus- sion mechanism in the nose, which was cut flat at the tip.
E Dopp Z S/30 CC: Empfindlich Doppelzünder, 30 Sekunden, with CC percussion mechanism. This was a Krupp-Thiel clockwork fuze with the im- proved CC percussion unit in the nose. The cap was painted red and it is reported that 360,000 such fuzes were made for the extended trial of the 'direct-action' fuze theory at the end of the war. This fuze was more or less a production model of the Zt Z S/30 CC.
Dopp Z S/45 K: Doppelzünder, 45 Sekunden, mit Klappensicherung. This, of the same dimensions as the AZ 35 K, used a Krupp clock and a graze percussion element. The running time was 125sec with a minimum time of 45sec.
Dopp Z S/45-125: This was the early name for the 45 K.
Dopp Z S/60 S: Doppelzünder, 60 Sekunden, mit Schlagzünderschraube. This, of similar appearance to the Zt Z S/30, carried a spring-drive Krupp-Thiel clock running for a maximum of 60sec and a graze percussion element. This fuze was the most common of its class.
Dopp Z S/60 V: Doppelzünder, 60 Sekunden, Vereinfacht. This was a Dopp Z S/60 with the nose cut flat and with a direct-action percussion unit beneath, which on being struck released the timing unit's firing-arm to fire the detonator.
Dopp Z S/60 Fg: Doppelzünder, 60 Sekunden, mit Fliegewicht. This was the same as the S/60 V with the substitution of the Junghans centrifugal mech- anism for the Krupp-Thiel clock.
Dopp Z S/60 Geb: Doppelzünder, 60 Sekunden, für Gebirgsgeschütze. This was similar to the S/60 S but was slightly shorter and had a rounder tip—which was painted blue.
Dopp Z S/90: Doppelzünder, 90 Sekunden. This was similar to the S/30 but had a maximum run- ning time of 90sec. A safety pin was inserted through the body to lock the clock mechanism in transit.
Dopp Z S/90 St: Doppelzünder, 90 Sekunden, mit Stahlhülse. A version of the preceding fuze made of steel instead of aluminium.
Dopp Z S/90/45: This was a Dopp Z S/45 re- geared to run for 90sec.
Dopp Z S/100-200: This was similar in appearance to the S/90 K, having a deep intrusion and a flat top. This fuze was for long-range guns and the mechanism was geared to give running times between 100 and 200sec. It is believed that few of these fuzes were made, and that still fewer were actually issued.
Dopp Z S/100 K: Doppelzünder, 100 Sekunden, mit Fliegewicht. This was a later name for the Dopp Z S/100-200.

TWO: AMMUNITION MARKINGS

Like every other nation, the Germans entered the war with a rational marking system and the best intentions, but—like every other nation—such things as the proliferation of ammunition types and the introduction of new explosives soon upset the classification and turned it into a succession of exceptions and makeshifts. (It is, however, doubtful if the German system ever approached the complexity of the British one, which confounded the nomenclature still further by attempting to change systems in the middle of the war.)

Nomenclature

Gun projectiles were named in accordance with four different systems:
1. By calibre: *15cm Gr 18*—15cm Granate 18, or 15cm shell model 18.
2. By gun type: *F H Gr*—Feldhaubitze Granate, or field howitzer shell.
3. By construction: *Haubgr 16 umg*—Haubegranate 16 umgeänderte, or altered capped-shell model 16
4. By description: *8.8cm Sprgr L/4.6*—8.8cm Sprenggranate (high explosive shell), 4.6 calibres long.

In the case of fixed ammunition the abbreviation Patr (for Patrone, or cartridge) and the title of the relevant gun were often added to the nomenclature—eg 7.5cm Sprgr Patr PAK 40 or 7.5cm Sprenggranate Patrone für Panzerabwehrkanone 40 (high explosive shell for the model 40 7.5cm anti-tank gun). Of the naming systems mentioned above, 1 and 2 were the most common; 3 was used only for obsolescent designs and 4 was rarely used by the army, being more common to the navy and the Luftwaffe.

Projectiles/Basic Body Colours

The shells were painted in the following colours:
olive green, olive drab or field grey: high explosive, anti-concrete, smoke, chemical, or hollow-charge shells, and case shot.
black: armour piercing shot or shell.
silver grey: high explosive shell for 3.7cm anti-tank gun.
white and red: propaganda shell.
yellow: anti-aircraft high explosive shell.
red and blue: anti-aircraft incendiary shrapnel shell
pale green: star shell.

Projectiles/History, Contents and Operation Markings

A variety of markings were stencilled over the basic body colour, serving to give complete identification of the shell's history, contents and mode of operation. The shell can be divided into six marking zones:
1. Immediately below the fuze.
2. On the *ogive* or head.
3. On the parallel part of the body.
4. Immediately above the driving band(s).
5. Immediately below the driving band(s).
6. On the base.
Zone 1 contained the fuzing factory's location monogram and date. *Zone 2* carried the code of the explosive filling and the weight marking. *Zone 3* carried information about the shell's action, together with the date and place of filling (if it was a smoke shell). *Zone 4* contained information on the date and place of filling with explosive and details relating to the design and construction of the driving band. *Zone 5* usually gave the calibre, if this was mentioned at all. *Zone 6* usually carried a brief summary of the more important details marked on the side—generally listing such details as the driving band, the filling, the fuze, and the weight.

Weight markings were stamped in the form of Roman numerals from I to V, a shell of standard weight being marked III, those lighter by given percentages II or I and those heavier by IV or V. The remaining stencilled markings are tabulated as follows.

Mark	Colour	Position	German	English
	white	3	Ausstoss	ejector shell
B	black	1, 2 or 5	Ausstossbüchsen	shell containing ejection canisters
l	black	3	Sprengladung mit Aluminium-Griess	granular aluminium flash producer incorporated in the filling
or *Buntr*	black	3	Buntrauch	shell giving a red smoke burst
l	white	3	Blindgeschoss	inert filling
lau	black	3	Blau	blue smoke
o	black	3	Ausgebohrte Pressstahlgranate	forged steel shell with cavity bored out
r	black	3	Brandgeschoss	incendiary shell
eut	black	3	Deutgeschoss	indicator shell
u	white	3 or 4	Kupfer	copper driving band
x	red	3	Exerziergeschoss	drill
	black	3	Ferngeschoss	long-range shell
ES	white	3 or 4	Führung Sintereisen	sintered-iron driving band
EW	white	3 or 4	Führung Weicheisen	soft iron driving band
l, Hl/A Hl/B l/C	black	2	Höhladung	hollow charge shell model A, B, C
or Kt	black	3	Kartätschen	case shot
g	black		Kilogram	follows weight of shell in kilograms
h	black	3	Kammerhülse	central burster tube
PS	white	4	Kupfer Presstahl	bimetallic driving band
eucht	white	3	Leuchtgeschoss	star (illuminating) shell
M	black	1 or 2	lange Mundlochbüchse	lengthened exploder container
e	black	1	Lose Sprengstoffkorpen	high explosive shell with loose block filling
S	white	2 or 3	Leuchtsatz-sprengladung	illuminating shell
R	black	2	mit Rauchentwickler	shell contains smoke-box for observation of burst
b or *N*	white	3	Nebelgeschoss	smoke shell
	black	3	ohne Füllung	without filling (on 2cm shells only)
M	black	2	ohne Mundlochbüchse	without exploder container
R	black	3	ohne Rauchentwickler	without smoke-box
g or *P*	black	3	Perlitgusstahl	shell made of 'pearlitic' cast steel
h	black	3	Phosphor	shell contains phosphorus
11	black	3	Rauchentwickler	contains 'smoke-box type 11' (or 12 etc)
ot	black	3	Rot	red smoke
S	black	3	Reizstoff	contains irritant filling
pr Br	black	3	Spreng Brand	explosive/incendiary filling
tg	black	3	Stahlgussgeschoss	cast-steel shell
	black	4	tschechoslowakisch	shell has modified driving band to suit Czechoslovakian guns
p	red or black	3	Tropen	suitable for tropical use
	black	3	Unterrichsgeschoss	instructional projectile
b	white	3	Übungsgeschoss	practice shell filled with gunpowder
b Al	white	3	Übungsgeschoss	practice shell, filled with gunpowder and aluminium
b B	white	3	Übungsgeschoss typ B	practice shell, filled with gunpowder and a sulphur trioxide smoke-box
b T	white	3	Übungsgeschoss typ T	practice shell, filled with gunpowder and Tetrachloronaphthalene
b W	white	C	Übungsgeschoss Weiss	practice shell giving white smoke puff
b R	white	3	Übungsgeschoss rot	practice shell giving red smoke puff
p	black	3	Verpackung	dummy round for package trials
Kh	white	3	weite Kammerhülse	wide central burster-tube
B	black	1	Zwischenboden	diaphragm shell
	yellow	1		for use only with time and percussion fuzes
	white	1		for use only with percussion fuzes
	black	1		for use only with time fuzes

Mark	Colour	Position	German	English
+ + +	red	1		exploder system incorporated in main fillin
Red ring around shell		4		modified driving band
White ring around shell		3		position of centre of gravity for shell abov 28cm calibre
White ring around shell		1		shell for 7.62cm Russian weapons
White tip to armour-piercing shell				8.8cm low capacity armour-piercing shell
Yellow ring around shell		3		bimetallic driving band
White axial stripes				indicate modification to shell

Projectiles/Explosive Filling Code and Additional Abbreviations

Stencilled in Zone 2, this number indicates the explosive used; the table lists those used in artillery ammunition. The missing numbers were either unused or applied to explosives used in other types of store (*eg* grenades, aerial bombs, demolition charges, etc).

1	trinitrotoluene (TNT) blocks in a cardboard container packed with magnesium cement
1A	TNT blocks in a cardboard container in waxed paper
1b	TNT blocks in a cardboard container packed with montan wax
2	picric acid blocks in cardboard containers
3	pentaerithrytol tetranitrate (PETN) in blocks
4	TNT loose in a paper carton
5	picric acid loose in a paper carton
6	TNT/wax (95 parts TNT and 5 parts wax, written as 95/5) in blocks in a cardboard carton
7	TNT pressed
8	TNT poured
10	TNT + TNT/wax (95/5) + TNT/wax (90/10) in blocks in cardboard cartons
11	TNT + TNT/wax (90/10) + TNT/wax (85/15) + TNT/wax (80/20) in blocks
12	TNT + TNT/wax (95/5) + cyclonite/wax (90/10) in blocks
13	amatol 60/40 (ammonium nitrate 60%, TNT 40%) poured
13A	amatol 50/50
14	TNT poured
15	TNT/aluminium powder (90/10) poured
16	TNT poured, plus PETN/wax (90/10) as an exploder
17	TNT/aluminium powder (90/10) poured, plus PETN/wax (90/10) as an exploder
18	TNT/cyclonite/wax pressed in blocks
19	TNT/ammonium nitrate/aluminium powde (55/35/10) poured
21	amatol 40/60 with a core of pressed TN pellets
24	picric acid poured
27	TNT/wax plus TNT pressed in blocks
28	TNT/wax plus PETN/wax pressed in block
32	PETN/wax (90/10) in waxed paper wrap pings
33	PETN/wax (85/15) in waxed paper wrap ings
34	PETN/wax (70/30) in waxed paper wrap ings
36	PETN/wax (60/40) in blocks in waxe paper wrappings
38	PETN/wax (35/65) in blocks in waxe paper wrappings
45	PETN/wax/cyclonite (35/15/50)
66	PETN/WAX (50/50)
80	cyconite
91	cyclonite/wax (95/5) in blocks wrapped i wax paper
92	cyclonite/wax (90/10) in blocks wrapped i waxed paper
95	cyclonite/TNT (60/40) in blocks wrapped i waxed paper
101	TNT/wax (85/15)
105	TNT/cyclonite/aluminium powder (70/15/15) poured
106	TNT/cyclonite/aluminium powder (50/25/25) poured
112	amatol 20/80
113	ammonium nitrate/TNT/aluminium powde

Additional abbreviations used in the description of the explosive filling include:

Abbreviation	German	English
Fp 02	Füllpulver 1902	TNT
Fp 40/60	Füllpulver 40/60	amatol 60/40
Fp5, etc	Füllpulver 5, etc	TNT plus 5% wax
Grf 88	Granatfüllung 1888	picric acid
Np 5	Nitropenta 5	PETN plus 5% wax
H5	Hexogen	cyclonite plus 5% wax

The following numerals may also be found:

Numeral	Colour	Position	Meaning
12,2	white	Zones 1, 5 or 6	calibre of shell (12.2cm)
15,2	white	Zones 1, 5 or 6	calibre of shell (15.2cm)
15,5	white	Zones 1, 5 or 6	calibre of shell (15.5cm)
35	black	Zone 3	Feldhaubitzegranate 35 (FH Gr 35)
38	black	Zones 3, 5 or 6	FH Gr 38 (hollow charge shell)
39	black	Zones 3, 5 or 6	FH Gr 39 (hollow charge shell)

0	white	Zones 3 and 6	FH Gr 40
1	white	Zones 3 and 6	FH Gr 41

artridges/Marks Found on Metallic Cases and agged Charges

'he data given on the cartridge cases was either :amped into the metal or stencilled upon it. tamping was always on the base and gave the)llowing information: the lot number of the mpty case, the year of manufacture, the manufac-rer's code mark, and the design number of the ase or the nomenclature of the appropriate 'eapon.

The design number is the positive means of nking a case to a particular weapon, and in iew of the interest shown by collectors in this spect of markings a list of design numbers ogether with case dimensions and other identifying marks) is given in Appendix 2.

Stencilling on the case gave the following information: the designation of the weapons for which the cartridge was suited, the actual weight of the propelling charge in grams, and the nature, shape and size of the propellant. The place and trade mark of the propellant factory also appeared, along with the year of manufacture and delivery number of the batch of propellant. Stencilling also detailed the place and date of filling and the code-mark of the filling factory, and lastly the standard charge temperature or tropical notation.

The only difficult item in this is the data relating to the propellant; the propellant type abbreviations have already been noted and this was then followed by abbreviations denoting the shape:

Marking	Position	Meaning
Bl	Blatt	leaf flake
Bl P	Blattchen Pulver	rectangular flake
Kr R	Kreuz Rohr	a central tube of propellant supporting the charge
NP	Nudel Pulver	chopped cord
Pl P	Plattchenpulver	multi-perforated discs
Pol P	Polpulver	solventless propellant
RP or R	Rohrenpulver	tubular sticks
Rg P	Ringpulver	in the shape of a flat ring
Stb P	Staubpulver	dust or fine grains
St P	Sternenpulver	flat six-point stars
Str P	Streifenpulver	strip

'his descriptive abbreviation was occasionally fol-)wed by a letter G, indicating that the calorific fficiency of the propellant was the standard ratio f 690 calories per gram. Following this a figure ıdicated the percentage of potassium sulphate (or ther flash-reducing agent) present in the charge. After a dash came the dimensions of the propel-ant: a set of three figures in brackets which de-oted the length, the breadth and the thickness of ake or chopped-cord propellants, or the length, e external diameter and the internal diameter in e cases of tubular cord or ring types.

Thus Digl RP 12.5—(400 5, 5/2, 5) indicated a ıbular diglycol powder containing 12.5% flash educing salts, each 'tube' being 400mm long with n external diameter of 5.5mm and an internal diameter of 2.5mm. Nigl Bl P 10, 5 (40/40/2) indicated a nitroglycerine powder in square flakes, each 40mm × 40mm and 2mm thick, with 10.5% flash reducing salts added to the charge. Gu Str P G 2 (200/10/1) indicated Gudolpulver in strips 200mm long, 10mm wide and 1mm thick, of standard calorific value and with 2% content of flash reducing salts.

Similar markings were printed on the cloth bags in which the propellant was packed; in the case of multiple part charges the charge number was also apparent. Cases for separate-loading ammunition, which were closed with caps, had a paper label giving the same information stuck to the cap.

Some additional markings found on cartridges were these:

Marking	Position	Meaning
o B D	case or closing cup	charge without decoppering foil
m B D	case or closing cup	charge with decoppering foil
Red ring	round charge bag	special part-charge only to be used with other ring-marked parts
Umgesetzt	closing cup	re-worked cartridge; usually followed by data concerning the factory doing the re-work
R	charge bag	to be used with rocket-assisted shell only
J	closing cup	examiner's mark

Marking	Position	Meaning
F	charge bag	to be used with long-range shell only
M or *Man*	case	blank charge
für Tropen	case	for tropical use
PT + 25C	base	for tropical use
V	case	*Verbesserte*—ballistically adjusted charge

Flash Reducers

These were circular bags, containing potassium sulphate or a similar agent, that were inserted in the cartridge by the gunners when firing at night in order to chemically smother the gun flash. Th German term was *Kartusche Vorlagen,* which wa usually abbreviated to *Kart Vorl.*

Primers and Fuzes/Markings

Primers and fuzes were stamped with details of the manufacturer, the date of manufacture, and the item's designation. In the case of primers the letters St indicated manufacture from steel, the model number was always preceded by C/ (for Construction) and a lot number was included in the markings. A typical primer, for example, could bear the marks C/22, RHS, 1938 and 18; the marks on a fuze could be AZ 23Nb, aqs and 1942. The fuzes also had details of any incorporated delay placed near the delay setting device. In this the following abbreviations were used:

V	Verzögerung	delay
M	mit	with
O	ohne	without
KV	kleine Verzögerung	short delay
MV	mittelere Verzögerung	medium delay
GV	grosse Verzögerung	long delay.

The delay time was indicated by: *0,15* (*ie* 0.15sec *0,20,* etc; this was generally omitted on base fuze

Painting and stencilling were rarely found o fuzes or primers. There are, however, know exceptions to this rule: fuzes that were approve for use in extreme cold were stencilled K in blac the noses of those approved for use in mountai guns were painted blue, and the noses of those mad of zinc alloy were painted yellow.

THREE: IDENTIFICATION OF GERMAN ARTILLERY CARTRIDGE CASES

The German land forces had a considerable variety of artillery weapons in service, both of native design and of captured models. It follows that the variety of cartridge cases was also considerable, and one of the principal difficulties now apparent is the identification of a case with its parent gun. This appendix, therefore, collects all the known data into a concise and convenient form that enables such identification to be made.

During and after the war several Allied agencies were at work examining and reporting on the ammunition that was captured or found. There are frequently discrepancies between their data and the information that has been discovered since the war through other channels. This is sometimes no more than a simple misprint, sometimes because data presented as facts was merely a reasoned assumption from documentary sources. Occasionally the data was revised when better information became available—but in several cases the erroneous information has been carried over, much to the dismay of the student. It is the author's belief that the only sure sources of data are either to obtain the case and physically measure it or to have a dimensioned drawing from someone who has. Each dimension presented here is from one of these two classes; when neither has been available, the data given is noted as 'unverified'.

It has not been possible to give data for every case used in German service, for in some instances the weapons were experimental or trial projects that were abandoned before the war's end, whereupon the ammunition was broken up and the records lost. Others were used solely on the Eastern and Balkan fronts and no ammunition became available to Western agencies. In some cases the entire stocks of ammunition were destroyed before they could be examined and, of course, the wholesale destruction of records in Germany after the war often prevented designs being traced or drawings discovered. The author would be grateful to hear of any cartridge case identified as German which is not tabulated here.

Case Construction and Design

The standard cartridge cases originally in German service—in common with those of most other nations—were manufactured of solid drawn brass.

However, the prospect of a major war leading to a shortage of brass led to experiments in the use of steel as an alternative material. Indeed, a similar course had been followed in the closing stages of World War 1, so that there was a certain amount of experience on which to build. In c.1937 a solid steel case was adopted. This was very similar to the brass pattern from which it differed only in the thickness of the metal and the internal contours, a change necessitated by the difference in resilience and reaction to firing stresses between brass and steel. The cases were deep-drawn on adaptations of the standard brass-case machinery, and in order to prevent rusting they were first copper-plated and then brass-plated; the interlayer of copper was necessary to 'key' the brass to the steel. In some types only the external surface of the case was brass plated, the inner surface being left coppered. Cases of this type have the suffix *St* stamped after their design number.

Effective as this case was, it was demanding in the type of steel required to give perfect performance and also demanded specialised plant for its manufacture, being based on traditional production methods and being suited only to production by firms with deep-drawing facilities. To overcome this drawback, design began on composite cases that were capable of manufacture by less specialised engineering companies.

The first composite had a drawn brass tubular body and a brass-plated machined-steel baseplate. The two units were secured together by a large steel washer over the primer boss, which was screwed to take a locking ring. Obturation—the sealing of the propellant gases that might otherwise escape to the rear—was achieved by coating the mating surfaces with a wax composition and fitting a cardboard washer beneath the steel washer. These cases, few of which entered service, carried a two-digit suffix to the basic design number, e.g. 6342/65. A variation of this pattern, even more rare, is one that uses all-steel components, brass plated and assembled in the same fashion.

By this time the war had begun and saw the introduction, as an economy measure, of drawn steel cases that were rustproofed either by phosphating or by zinc galvanising, treatments which left the case surfaces a smooth or matt grey colour. Another variation left the steel bright, as drawn, and then coated the case with a light brown or transparent lacquer. This technique was not universal, since with some weapons in which high chamber pressures arose it could lead to difficult extraction.

The next composite case to be developed was made up of a sheet-steel body and a brass base. The steel, oil-blackened to prevent rusting, was bent round a tubular former and lap-jointed with one or more spot-welds to hold the joint. In some patterns the edges of the tube were bevelled before lapping to make a flat junction. The two portions were then assembled, as before, with a steel washer, a lock ring and a cardboard washer. These cases were identified by the suffix */65A*.

This case type—while effective—still used brass, and the next move was to entirely eliminate brass by making the base from a machined-steel plate. A short steel liner was, in addition, fitted inside the case, retained by the steel washer and a lock ring. This type may be identified by the additional letter suffix B after the suffix number in cases where other composite designs existed for the same gun. Where no other composite existed the B was sometimes omitted.

These two types were not especially successful, the weak point being the long lap joint that often split on firing. This led to chamber erosion, which meant the next case loaded had less support at that point and was therefore more liable to blow open, which in turn led to more erosion—continuing until the gun was useless. However, enough data on the designs had by then been amassed to enable a final and successful pattern to be made. This used a special spirally-wrapped steel sheet body with a solid machined base. The body section was rolled from the sheet steel in such a fashion that a tube was formed, giving about 4 turns overlap at the base and about $1\frac{1}{2}$ turns at the mouth; thus the strength of the case was distributed in a manner suited to the stress it had to withstand on firing. The overlaps were coated with a wood-tar sealing composition and the steel was oil-blackened to protect it against rust. The body was then assembled to the base with a washer and a lock ring, as before, but a distinguishing feature of most of these cases was the provision of four blind holes in the base that afforded purchase for an assembly key when tightening the lock ring. Cases of this pattern usually have the suffix letter C.

A variation of this design could be seen in cases manufactured for use in the ex-Soviet 12.2cm gun 390(r) where an additional steel sleeve was fitted to the outside of the spiral, running for a short distance up from the rim. This was presumably applied as an extra seal and must have been found necessary owing to the chamber pressure in this weapon failing to obturate with the usual design. This variety carried no special identification.

Towards the end of the war two further patterns began to be introduced, apparently designed for manufacture by firms with little or no specialised machinery. The body was a reversion to a rolled sheet with a lap joint and spot welds, but the bases were actually built from layers of sheet steel instead of being machined from the solid. A round plate forming the rim had a primer hole in the centre; and ahead of this was welded a smaller diameter plate with a primer pocket and a flash hole. The rolled body had a flange at its lower edge and was surrounded by a short reinforcing sleeve, also turned in at the foot. The whole assembly was held together by the usual steel washer but, instead of a lock ring, it was clamped by four screws passing from the inside into tapped holes in the base sheet. A variation was the use of nuts and bolts to hold everything together, the bolts' heads being countersunk into the base sheet In both designs the metal was phosphated to effect rustproofing.

Cartridge Manufacturers

As with any country mobilised for total war, the number of factories making cartridge cases was legion. Each firm had its own code-letters stamped on the cartridge case base, and some of the more common are listed here:

ad Patronen, Zündhutchen- und Metallwarenfabrik AG, Schönbeck an der Elbe
ak Munitionsfabrik Vlasim, Czechoslovakia
an C Beutenmuller GmbH, Bretten
ap Otto Eberhardt Patronenfabrik, Hirtenberg
asr Hanseatische Kettenwerk GmbH, Hamburg
ajn Union Sprengstoff- und Zündmittelwerk, Alt–Berum
auu Patronenhülsen- und Metallwarenfabrik AG, Rokucany, Czechoslovakia
aux Poltewerk, Magdeburg
auy Poltewerk, Grünberg
auz Poltewerk, Armstadt
avt Poltewerk, Magdeburg
axq Erfurter Ladenindustrie, Erfurt
axs Berndorffer Metallwarenfabrik AG, Berndorf
ay Alois Pirkl Elektronische Fabrik
ba Sundwiger Messingwerke, Iserlohn
bb A Laue und Co, Berlin
bc Kupfer- und Messingwerk Berker AG, Langenburg
bd Metallwerk Lange, Bodenbach
be Berndorffer Metallwarenfabrik AG, Berndorf
bf Deutsche Röhrenwerke, AG, Mulheim
bg Enzesfelder Metallwerke GmbH, Wien (Vienna)
bh Waffenwerk Brunn AG, Povaska Bystrica, Czechoslovakia

f Niebecker und Schumacher, Iserlohn
k Metall-, Walz- und Platierwarenfabrik Hindrichs–Aufferman AG, Wuppertal
nd Maschinenfabrik Augsburg–Nürnberg (MAN) AG, Augsburg
ne Metallwerk Odertal GmbH, Odertal
qt Eugen Muller Pyrotechnikwerk, Wien (Vienna)
yc Klönne Bruckenbau Anstalt, Dortmund
yw Stettiner Schraubenwerk Johannes Schäfer, Stettin
do Waffen- und Munitionsfabrik Theodor Bergmann AG, Velten
dp Waffen- und Munitionsfabrik Theodor Bergmann AG, Werk, Bernau, Berlin
f Westfälische Anhaltische Sprengstoff AG (WASAG), Oranienburg
g Finower Industrie, Finow
ts Märkisches Werk Wilmamann GmbH, Halver
zo Heeres Zeugamt Geschosswerkstatt, Königsberg
bg Dynamit AG, Duneberg
ma Heeres Munitionsanstalt, Zeithain
nf Rheinische Westfälische Sprengstoff AG (RWS), Nürnberg
nh Rheinische Westfälische Sprengstoff AG, Durlach
om Westfälische Metallindustrie, Lippstadt
ou Waffenwerk Brünn AG, Povaska Bystrica, Czechslovakia
ph Interessen Gemeinschaft Farbenindustrie AG (IG Farben), Frankfurt am Main
ye Pitschmann Alpenlandische Pyrotechnikfabrik, Innsbruck
za Bleiwerke, Dr C Schulke, Hamburg
ba Scharfenburg und Teubert, Breitungen
cc Lunig Pyrotechnische Fabrik, Möhringen
cd Lippold Pyrotechnische Fabrik, Wuppertal
dg Zwillingswerk J A Henckels AG, Solingen
ej Märkische Walzwerk GmbH, Strausberg
el Metallwarenfabrik H Wissner AG, Brotteröde
en Selve–Kornbiegel–Dornheim AG, Sömmerda
ey Metallwarenfabrik Treuenbrietzen, Roderhof
mp Dynamit AG, Hannover
om Huck Metallwarenfabrik, Nürnberg
a Mansfeld AG, Hettstedt
b Mansfeld AG, Karlsruhe
d Stollberger Metallwerk AG, Stollberg
ee Augsburger Waffenfabrik Ludwig Pfister, Augsburg
er Metallwarenfabrik Waldhofen, Schwerte
va Draht- und Metallwarenfabrik, Salzwedel
a Hirsch Kupfer- und Messingwerk AG, Finow
tb Eisfeld Pulver- und Pyrotechnischen Fabrik, Guntersberge
a Metallwarenfabrik Treuenbrietzen GmbH, Sebaldushof
ham Dynamit AG, Hamm
has Pulverfabrik Hasloch, Hasloch am Main
hhw Metallwerk Silberhütten GmbH, St Andreasberg
hla Metallwarenfabrik Treuenbrietzen GmbH, Selterhof
hlb Metallwarenfabrik Treuenbrietzen GmbH, Belzig
hlc Zieh- und Stanzwerk GmbH, Schleusingen
hld Metallwarenfabrik Treuenbrietzen GmbH, Belzig
hle Metallwarenfabrik Treuenbrietzen GmbH, Roderhof
hrn Presswerk GmbH, Metagethen
htg Poltewerk, Duderstadt
jry Hermann Herrhold, Obernau
k Luch & Wagner, Suhl
ka Gerhardi und Cie, Ludenscheidt, Westfalen
kam Hugo Schneider AG Eisen- und Metallwerk GmbH, Skarzysko–Kamienna, Czechoslovakia
krl Dynamit AG, Krummel bei Hamburg
kry Lignose Sprengstoffwerke, Kruppamühle
kum Eisfeld Pulver- und Pyrotechnischenfabrik Gmb H, Kunigunde
kye Interprinderile Metalurie, Brasov, Romania
kyp Römanische–Deutsche Industrie- und Handels AG, Bucharest, Romania
lge Kügelfabrik Schulte, Tente
lkm Munitionsfabrik Prag, Prahá (Prague), Czechosolovakia
ma Metallwerk Lange AG, Aue/Saar
mrb Aktiengesellschaft (vormals Skoda), Prahá (Prague), Czechosolovakia
myx Rheinmetall-Borsig AG, Sömmerda
na Westfälische Kupfer- und Messingwerke AG, Ludenscheide
nbe Hugo Schneider AG (HASAG), Tachenstochau
nrh Rheinmetall-Borsig AG, Sömmerda
nyv Rheinmetall-Borsig AG, Unterluss
oa Huck Metall-, Walz- und Presswerk, Ludenscheide
oxo Teuto Metallwerk GmbH, Osnabruck
qa Wilhelm Prym, Stollberg
r Westfälische Anhaltische Sprengstoff AG (WASAG), Rheindorf
ra Deutsches Messingwerk Eveking AG, Berlin
s Dynamit AG
skd Selve-Kornbiegel-Dornheim AG, Dornheim
t Dynamit AG, Troisdorf
ta Dürner Metallwerk GmbH, Berlin
ua Osnabrucker Kupfer- und Drahtwerk AG, Osnabruck
va Kabell- und Metallwerk Neumayer AG, Nürnberg
wa Hugo Schneider AG (HASAG), Leipzig
wb Hugo Schneider AG, Berlin
wc Hugo Schneider AG, Meuselwitz
wd Hugo Schneider AG, Taucha
we Hugo Schneider AG, Langewiesen

wf Hugo Schneider AG, Kielce, Poland
wg Hugo Schneider AG, Altenburg
wh Hugo Schneider AG, Eisenach
wj Hugo Schneider AG, Oberweissbach
wk Hugo Schneider AG, Schliesen
wn Hugo Schneider AG, Dernbach
xa Busch-Jäger-Ludenscheider Metallwerk AG Ludenscheide
y Jagdpatronen Zündhutchen- und Metallwarenfabrik AG, Budapest, Hungary

The Identification Tables

Table 1/Dimensions by Weapon Order
In this table weapons are divided into groups, as in the body of the book. Within each group they are in increasing order of calibre, and within each calibre in chronological order of development. Tank guns have been included among the anti-tank guns since, although not discussed in the body of the book, they were often of common design and/or used common cartridge cases; moreover the inclusion of such data was felt to be useful to case collectors. The more common Fremdengeräte are included, as are one or two experimental weapons which seem to have been prolific in cartridge cases.

Note/Table 1
The dimensions given are correct insofar as they represent the measurements taken from one specimen case. They may, however, differ by small amounts from those of another case of the same type owing to manufacturing tolerances, human error in measurement or expansion owing to firing. Thus a difference of, for example, 0.25mm (0.01in) in mouth diameter should be accepted and not adduced as evidence of a new variety of case.

Table 2/Design Numbers
This table lists all the known '6300' series design numbers. It will be seen that there are several gaps in the sequence; in some cases no cartridge is known and undoubtedly in others the number was never used.

Table 3/Miscellaneous Identification Marks
This table lists the various identification marks that do not conform to any set or numerical pattern. They are shown in ascending order of calibre.

TABLE 1

Weapon	case length mm/in	rim diameter mm/in	mouth diameter mm/in	primer	design number	other marks
7.5cm I G 18, 37, 42, L/13, le Geb G 18	89/3.50	86/3.39	76/2.99	C/12	6341	IJG 18
7.5cm I G 18, 37, 42, L/13, le Geb G 18, case used with HE/AT shell	87/3.43	85/3.35	75/2.95	C/12	6391St	IJG 18
7.62cm I K 290(r) and F K 296(r)[1]	385/15.16	89/3.50	76/2.99	C/12	6390St	7.62J KH290(r)
7.62cm I K 290(r) and F K 296(r)[1]	385/15.16	90/3.54	78/3.07			No30M Scovill
7.62cm I K 290(r) and F K 296(r)[1]	386/15.20	89/3.50	78/3.07			505 Schneider 19
15cm s I G 33	114/4.49	169/6.65	155/6.10	C/12	6303	
7.5cm Geb K 15	129/5.08	89/3.50	77/3.03	C/12	6335	GEB K 15
7.5cm Geb G 36[2], 43	130/5.12	92/3.62	80/3.15	C/12	6359	P150 or P94
10.5cm Geb H 40	284/11.18	125/4.92	110/4.33	C/12	6327	IFH 40
7.5cm F K 16 nA	200/7.87	92/3.62	79/3.11	C/12	6343	FK 16 nA
7.5cm le F K 18	260/10.24	92/3.62	79/3.11	C/12	6316	IFK 18
7.5cm F K 38	397/15.63	99/3.90	76/2.99	C/12	6385	FK 38
7.5cm F K 7M59, 7M85	714/28.11	98/3.86	76/2.99	C/12	6340	PAK 40
10cm le F H 14/19(p) or (t)[3]	182/7.17	115/4.53	103/4.06	M35s		10cm Vz 14/19
10.5cm le F H 16, 18, 18M, etc	158/6.22	125/4.92	111/4.37	C/12	6342	IFH
10cm le HT[4]	65/2.56	118/4.65	107/4.21	C/13	6315St	IHT
10cm K 17					6302 and 6349 reported, neither verified	
s 10cm K 35 (t)[5]	681/26.81	130/5.12	111/4.37	M39d		s 10cm K35/T/
s 10cm K 18	444/17.48	129/5.08	110/4.33	C/12	6349	s 10cm K 18
12.2cm s F H 396(r)[6]	284/11.18	138/5.43	127/5.00	C/12	6395	sFH 396(r)
12.2cm K 390(r)[7]	261/10.28	144/5.67	132/5.20	C/12	6394	12,2 K 390

Veapon	case length mm/in	rim diameter mm/in	mouth diameter mm/in	primer	design number	other marks
5cm s F H 13	114/4.49	169/6.65	155/6.10	C/12	6303	FH 13
5cm s F H 18, 36, 18/40	264/10.39	178/7.01	161/6.34	C/12	6350	sFH 18
2.8cm K 44	869/34.21	192/7.56	165/6.50	C/22	6398	PJK 44
5cm K 16	725/28.54	176/6.93	157/6.18	C/12	6304	
5cm K 18	815/32.09	178/7.01	155/6.10	C/12	6352	15K18 or W 28 St
5cm K 39	527/20.75	185/7.28	165/6.50	C/12	6318	K39
5cm SK C/28 in Mrs Lafette	815/32.09	178/7.01	155/6.10	C/12	6352	L/45
5.2cm KH 433(r)[8]	261/10.28	170/6.69	158/6.22		6389	15,2 KH 433/r/
7cm K in Mrs Lafette	726/28.58	216/8.50	191/7.52	C/12	6324	17 K Mrs L
1cm 'Lang Mörser					6305	not verified
1cm Mrs 18	401/15.79	242/9.53	222/8.74	C/12	6351	21 Mrs 18
4cm K 3	1342/52.83	292/11.50	264/10.39		6308	W–Karth d K 3
8cm Kusten Haubitze						Karth d Kust H
4cm Gerät 041	443/17.44	564/22.20	595/23.43			Karth–041
5cm K (E)	816/32.13	178/7.01	155/6.10	C/12	6352	15cm W 28
7cm K (E)						17 Kan(E) C/95
0.3cm K (E)	825/32.48	246/9.69	220/8.66	C/12		W–Karth 34 St
4cm Theodor Bruno K (E)						Karth d Th Br (E)
4cm Theodor K (E)						Karth C/95
8cm Kurz Bruno K (E)	1222/48.11	318/12.52	292/11.50	C/12		W Karth d Kz Br
8cm Lange Bruno K (E)						Karth L/45/50
8cm neue Bruno K (E)	798/31.42	358/14.09	327/12.87	C/12	6309	K5
8cm K 5 (E)	798/31.42	358/14.09	327/12.87	C/12	6309	K5
8cm Siegfried K (E)	818/32.20	472/18.58		C/12		38cm–34
0.6cm Adolf K (E)	874/34.41	510/20.08	476/18.74	C/12		40,6 W 34 St
0cm 'Gustav' K (E)	1300/51.18	960/37.80	863/33.98	C/12		
.8cm sPzB 41	187/7.36	48/1.89	30/1.18	C/13	P 345	
.7cm PAK 36	248/9.76	51/2.01	38/1.50	C/13	6331	3,7cm PAK
.2cm le PAK 41	406/15.98	59/2.32	45/1.77	C/13	6329	4,2cm PAK
.7cm PAK 36 (t)	402/15.83	64/2.52	50/1.97	M40	522	M36
.5cm PAK and KwK 184 (r)[9]	311/12.24	58/2.28	46/1.81			184
cm PAK 38 and KwK 39	419/16.50	77/3.03	51/2.01	C/12	6360	
cm KwK 38	289/11.38	77/3.03	51/2.01	C/22	6317	5cm KwK
.5cm PAK 40	714/28.11	98/3.86	76/2.99	C/12	6340	PAK 40
.5cm KwK 40 and StuK 40	493/19.41	101/3.98	80/3.15	C/22	6339	KwK 40
.5cm PAK 97/38	338/13.31	87/3.43	75/2.95			75
.5cm PAK 41	543/21.38	110/4.33	80/3.15	C/12	6344	Patrh PAK 41
.5cm KwK 38	243/9.57	92/3.62	75/2.95	C/12	6354	KwK
.5cm KwK 42 and StuK 42	638/25.12	124/4.88	76/2.99	C/12	6387	KwK 42
.62cm PAK 36 (r)	714/28.10	100/3.94	79/3.11	C/12	6340	PAK 44 Rh
cm PAW 600, 8H65	158/6.22	125/4.92	111/4.37	C/22	6342	
.8cm PAK 43, 43/41, and KwK 43	823/32.40	146/5.75	90/3.54	C/22	6388	KwK 43
10.5cm PzJg K L/100 (experimental)	1103/43.43	167/6.57	107/4.21			ZB–SK21236
12.8cm PAK 44	869/34.21	192/7.56	165/6.50	C/22	6398	12,8 PJK 44
12.8cm K 40 Pz Sfl (experimental)	825/32.48	166/6.54	141/5.55	C/22	6345	12,8K 40 PzSfl
12.8cm PAK 44 (experimental)	1180/46.46	215/8.46	136/5.35		30295	1–VIII–30295 St
.7cm Flak 18, 36	262/10.31	47/1.85	38/1.50	C/13	6348	Flak 18
cm Flak 28[10]	310/12.20	62/2.44	42/1.65	C/13		4cm 28
.7cm Flak 36(t)	403/15.87	64/2.52	49/1.93			M36 4cm
.7cm Flak Böhler (ö)[11]	235/9.25	56/2.20	48/1.89			Enz 4.7cm M35
cm Flak 41	346/13.62	68/2.68	52/2.05	C/12		5cm Fl 41 St

Weapon	case length mm/in	rim diameter mm/in	mouth diameter mm/in	primer	design number	other marks
5.5cm Flak Gerät 58	448/17.64	75/2.95	57/2.24			f Ger 58
8.8cm Flak 18, 36, 37	716/28.19	111/4.37	90/3.54	C/12	6347	8,8cm Flak 1
8.8cm Flak 41	853/33.58	123/4.84	91/3.58	C/22		8,8cm Flak 4
9.4cm Flak (e)[12]	672/26.46	135/5.31	97/3.82	9		9,4cm St (e)
10.5cm Flak 38, 39	766/30.16	138/5.43	106/4.17	C/22	6307	10,5cm 33 St
10.5cm Flak						
(experimental)	1034/40.71	136/5.35	111/4.37		30198	10,5 Patrh
12.8cm Flak 40						
12.8cm Flak						
(experimental)	960/37.80	166/6.54	130/5.12	C/22	6311	Gerät 40
15cm Flak	813/32.01	184/7.24	129/5.08			12,8 Patrh 41 S
24cm Flak						
3.7cm SK C/30	1495/58.86	227/8.94	152/5.98	C/22		not verified
8.8cm SK C/35	1842/72.52	355/13.98	243/9.57	C/22		not verified
10.5cm SK C/32	380/14.96	58/2.28	38/1.50	C/13		3,7cm 30 St
10.5cm SK L/60	388/15.28	111/4.37	89/3.50	C/12		8,8–35 St
15cm SK C/28 and Tbts	655/25.79	129/5.08	106/4.17	C/12		10,5cm 32 St
K C/36	766/30.16	138/5.43	106/4.17	C/12	6301	
15cm SK L/40	815/32.09	178/7.01	155/6.10	C/22	6352	C/28
15cm Ubts and Tbts K						
L/45	574/22.60	176/6.93	155/6.10	C/12		C/95
17cm SK L/40	574/22.60	176/6.93	155/6.10	C/12		15cm 95
20.3cm SK C/34						
24cm SK L/40						17cm C/95
24cm SK L/35	825/32.48	243/9.57	220/8.66	C/12		W–Karth 34 S
						Karth C/95
28cm SK L/40						Karth f Th B
28cm SK L/45						K
28cm SK L/50						28 Karth C/9
38cm SK C/34						Karth L/45/5
						Karth L/45/5
40.6cm SK C/34	818/32.20	472/18.58			6597	38cm–34 (no
7.5cm L G 40						verified)
10.5cm L G 40, 43	874/34.41	510/20.08	476/18.74	C/12		40,6cm W 34 S
15cm L G 292	155/6.10	125/4.92	112/4.41	C/43		
15cm L G 2–350	397/15.63	137/5.39	121/4.76	C/13		
(experimental)	437/17.20	178/7.01	168/6.61			LG240 St
10.5cm L G 2–540	206/8.11	172/6.77	161/6.34			LG2–350 P Rh
(experimental)						St
	627/24.69	137/5.39	117/4.61			LG2–540 St

Notes on Table 1

1. The 7.62cm IK 290(r) and the FK 296(r) were both captured Soviet field guns. Case 6390 was of German manufacture. The Scovill case was from the old Tsarist 3in gun, cases for which were supplied to contracts placed in the USA in 1916–17 and later converted for use in the newer guns. The Schneider case came from the same gun, having been supplied by France in 1917

2. 7.5cm Geb G 36. Cases marked 'p150' are often found with Afghan script markings, having been made for a contract in prewar days and taken over by the army during the war

3. 10.5cm le FH 14/19(p) or (t). These were Skoda designs owned in prewar times by the Polish and Czech armies. They both took the same cartridge case, and a small number were used by the German Army

4. 10cm le HT. This is, in fact, a breech-loading trench mortar that was mounted in turrets in some Siegfried Line defences. A normal fin-stabilised mortar bomb fitted inside the cartridge case

5. s 10cm K 35(t). An ex-Czech heavy field gun

6. 12.2cm s FH 396(r). This was the ex-Soviet o1938g 12.2cm howitz

7. 12.2cm K390(r). This was the ex-Soviet o1931/37g 12.2cm field gu

8. The 15.2cm KH 433(r) was the ex-Soviet o1937g 15.2cm heav field-gun-howitzer

9. The 4.5cm PAK and KwK 184(r) was the ex-Soviet tank and an tank gun o1932g

10. The 4cm Flak 28 was the standard 4cm Bofors gun; a few we officially in German service, to which further guns were added b capture. The case is identical to the British and US versions; it ca only be told apart by the primer (if fitted) and the base stamping

11. The 4.7cm Flak Böhler was an Austrian weapon tried out i small numbers after Austria had been incorporated into the Reich

12. The 9.4cm Flak (e) was the ex-British 3.7in anti-aircraft gu numbers of which were captured from time to time and which we employed on the North Sea coast

NOTE

Guns not mentioned in this list indicate that no data whatever i known of their cartridge cases.

TABLE 2

Number:	type of case	weapon
6301:	drawn brass/	10.5cm Flak prototype
6302:	drawn brass/	10cm K 17
6303:	drawn brass/	15cm s F H 13 and s I G 33
6303St:	drawn steel, brass plated/	15cm s F H 13 and s I G 33
6304:	drawn brass/	15cm K 16

Number:	type of case	weapon
6305:	drawn brass/	21cm Langer Mörser
6306:		reported as 8.8cm Flak 18 but not verified
3607:	drawn brass/	10.5cm Flak, production
6308:	wrapped steel, composite, oil-blackened/	24cm K 3
6309:	drawn brass/	28cm K 5 (E)
6311:	drawn brass/	12.8cm Flak 40
6315St:	drawn steel, lacquered/	10cm le HT
6316:	drawn brass/	7.5cm le F K 18
6316St:	steel, copper lined, brass coated/	7.5cm le F K 18
6317St:	steel, lacquered/	5cm KwK 38
6318:	brass/	15cm K 39
6324:	brass/	17cm K in Mrs Laf
6324St:	steel, brass plated/	17cm K in Mrs Laf
6324/78C:	wrapped steel, composite, oil backened/	17cm K in Mrs Laf
6327:	brass/	10.5cm Geb H 40
6327St:	steel, brass plated/	10.5cm Geb H 40
6329St:	steel, brass plated/	4.2cm PAK 41
6331:	brass/	3.7cm PAK 36
6331St:	steel, brass plated/	3.7cm PAK 36
6331/67:	drawn two-piece steel, zinc-coated/	3.7cm PAK 36
6335:	brass/	7.5cm Geb K 15
6336:	drawn steel, brass plated/	7.5cm Geb K 15
6339St:	drawn steel, phosphated/	7.5cm KwK 40 and StuK 40
6340:	brass/	7.5cm PAK 40
6340St:	drawn steel, lacquered/	7.5cm PAK 40
6341:	brass/	7.5cm I G 18, 37, 42 and Geb I G 18
6341St:	drawn steel, brass plated/	7.5cm I G 18, 37, 42 and Geb I G 18
6342:	drawn brass/	10.5cm le F H 16, 18 etc
6342St:	drawn steel, lacquered/	10.5cm le F H 16, 18 etc
6342/65:	drawn steel or phosphated, or brass plated, three-piece steel/	10.5cm le F H 16, 18 etc
6342/65B:	wrapped steel, composite, parkerised/	10.5cm le F H 16, 18 etc
6342/65C:	wrapped steel, composite, oil-blackened/	10.5cm le F H 16, 18 etc
6342/65D:	three-piece steel, butt-welded tube, phosphated/	10.5cm le F H 16, 18 etc
6342/65A:	brass base, steel tubular body brass plated, composite/	10.5cm le F H 16, 18 etc
6343:	brass/	7.5cm F K 16 nA
6344:	brass/	7.5cm PAK 41
6345St:	drawn steel, oil-blackened/	12.8cm K 40 Pz Sfl
6347:	brass/	8.8cm Flak 18, 36, 37
6347St:	drawn steel, zinc-coated/	8.8cm Flak 18, 36, 37
6348:	brass, belted/	3.7cm Flak
6349:	brass/	10cm K 18
6349/70C:	wrapped steel, oil-blackened/	10cm K 18
6350:	brass/	15cm s F H 18
6350/71:	three-piece steel, welded tube, oil-blackened or phosphated/	15cm s F H 18
6350/71C:	wrapped steel, oil-blackened/	15cm s F H 18
6351St:	drawn steel, brass plated/	21cm Mrs 18
6352:	brass/	15cm K 18 and K(E)
6352St:	drawn steel, brass plated/	15cm K 18 and K(E)
6352/75:	wrapped steel, oil-blackened/	15cm K 18 and K(E)
6352/75C:	wrapped steel, phosphated/	15cm K 18 and K(E)
6354:	brass/	7.5cm KwK 38
6354St:	drawn steel, copper or brass coated/	7.5cm KwK 38
6359:	drawn brass/	7.5cm Geb G 36
6359St:	drawn steel, brass plated/	7.5cm Geb G 36

Number:	type of case	weapon
6360St:	drawn steel, lacquered/	5cm PAK 38 and KwK 39
6385St:	drawn steel, brass plated/	7.5cm F K 38
6387St:	drawn steel, brass plated/	7.5cm KwK 42 and StuK 42
6388St:	drawn steel, brass plated/	8.8cm PAK 43 and KwK 43
6389C:	wrapped steel, oil blackened/	15.2cm KH 433(r)
6390St:	drawn steel, brass plated/	7.62cm IKH 290(r)
6391St:	drawn steel, copper or brass plated/	7.5cm I G 42
6394:	wrapped steel, reinforced, phosphated/	12.2cm K 390(r)
6395C:	wrapped steel, oil-blackened/	12.2cm s F H 396(r)
6395D:	three-piece, welded tube, phosphated, screwed base/	12.2cm s F H 396(r)
6398:	wrapped steel, oil-blackened/	12.8cm PAK 44
6597:		38cm Siegfried guns
30295:	drawn steel, lacquered/	12.8cm PzJg K and KwK

TABLE 3

Mark/	weapon
P150	/7.5cm Geb G 36
37–341 St	/3.7cm Flak (experimental)
P345	/2.8cm PzB 41
C/30St	/3.7cm SK C/30
3,7–36 St	/3.7cm PAK 36
4cm 28 St	/4cm Flak 28 (Bofors)
4,7cm M36	/4.7cm PAK 36(t)
522 St	/4.7cm PAK 36(t)
4cm VZ 36	/4.7cm PAK 36(t)
M36 4cm	/4.7cm Flak(t)
Enz 4,7cm M35	/4.7cm Flak Böhler
Patrh f Ger 58	/5.5cm Flak Gerät 58
75 DEC	/7.5cm PAK 97/38
SCOVILL MFG Co	/7.62cm F K 296(r)
SCHNEIDER 1917	/7.62cm F K 296(r)
8,8–35 St	/8.8cm SK C/35
8,8–30 St	/8.8cm Flak 18, 36 or 37, SK C/30
8,8 Flak 18	/8.8cm Flak 18, 36, 37
8,8 Flak 41 St	/8.8cm Flak 41
9,4cm St (e)	/ex-British 3.7in anti-aircraft gun
10cm VZ 14/19	/10cm le F H 14/19(t) or (p)
M14/19	/10cm le F H 14/19(t) or (p)
K35/t/	/s 10cm K 35(t)
10,5 Flak 33 St	/10.5cm Flak 38 or 39
10,5 Patrh 30198	/10.5cm Flak (experimental)
Patrh ZB–SK21236	/10.5cm PzJg K L/100 (experimental)
10,5cm 32 St	/10.5cm SK C/32
15cm 95	/15cm Ubts u Tbts K L/45
L/45	/15cm Ubts u Tbts K L/45
C/34	/20.3cm K (E)
W-Karth 34 St	/20.3cm SK C/34
Karth d Th Br K	/24cm Theodor Bruno guns
C/95	/24cm Theodor K and SK L/40
Karth d Kust H	/28cm Küsten Haubitze
W-Karth d Kz Br	/28cm Kurz Bruno and SK L/40
L/45/50	/28cm Lange Bruno, SK L/45 and SK L/50
40,6 W 34 St	/40.6cm Adolf K (E) and SK C/34
Karth 041	/54cm Gerät 041 'Karl'

FOUR: FREMDENGERÄT

Before the war began the German Army drew up a list—compiled from intelligence sources—of all known foreign equipment and allotted to each a distinctive number. These weapons were called Fremdengerät and the list, illustrated in some parts and with fullest available details of each weapon, was eventually published in a six-volume set that was periodically amended. Not every number was allocated; gaps were left for new weapons to be slotted into their correct places in the list, for it will be seen that the listing (after a rather erratic start) is in ascending order of calibre. The following list shows those weapons to which numbers are known to have been allotted; in many cases the identification of the weapon has not been exact, since the German terminology did not agree with the terminology of the parent country. Where the weapon is obscure, precise identification has in some cases been impossible. It will also be seen that the same general description often occupies two or three numbers; these are variations in the basic mark of weapon. It is not, finally, unusual to find the same number allotted to two similar weapons of different nationality; the distinguishing (nationality) suffix to the number affords positive identification.

One is forced to the conclusion that the intelligence service responsible for compiling this list had not done its homework very thoroughly. The British 15in Howitzer (731[e]) had been declared obsolete in 1920, and the US 16in Howitzer on railway mounting (755[a]) had never seen service at all—having been merely an experimental weapon. How many of the less well-known foreign weapons fell into this sort of category is hard to say; it might account for the difficulty in identifying them.

Fremdengerät / Identification List

01(n): 7.5cm Norwegian gun
02(f): 6.5cm French quick-firing gun
02/06(p): 7.5mm Polish modified French field gun Mle 97
5/8(ö): 7.65cm Austrian Modell 05/08, Skoda
17(ö): 7.65cm Austrian Feldkanone Modell Modell 1917, Skoda
17(t): 7.5cm Czech field gun vz/1928
18(ö): 7.65cm Austrian Feldkanone Modell 1918 field gun, Skoda
18/17(t): Czech 8cm field gun
28(p): 8cm Polish mortar
29(p): 10.5cm Polish field gun wz/16 (Rheinmetall)
30(t): 8cm Czech field gun
31(p): 4.6cm Polish mortar
34/35(r): 28cm Russian howitzer
35(t): 10.5cm Czech field gun
36(p): 4.6cm Polish mortar
37(t): 3.7cm Czech anti-tank gun
39(r): 7.62cm Russian fieldgun o1939g
97(p): 7.5cm Polish field gun, wz97/17
143(f): long-barrelled 3.7cm French tank gun
144(f): short-barrelled 3.7cm French tank gun
145(r): 3.7cm Russian infantry howitzer
146(r): 3.7cm Russian infantry howitzer
148(r): 4.5cm Russian anti-tank gun
148/1(r): 4.5cm Russian anti-tank gun
152(f): 3.7cm French trench howitzer
173(f): 4.7cm French tank gun
176(i): 4.5cm Italian mortar
177(i): 4.7cm Italian anti-tank gun modello 37
183a(f): 4.7cm French anti-tank gun
184(r): 4.5cm Russian anti-tank gun o1932g
184/1(r): 4.5cm Russian anti-tank gun o1937g
185(b): 4.7cm Belgian anti-tank gun
186(r): 4.5cm Russian infantry gun
201(b): 5cm Belgian mortar
202(e): 2in British mortar
203(f): 5cm French mortar
205(r): 5cm Russian mortar o1938g
208(r): 5cm Russian mortar o1940g
216(i): 6.5cm Italian mountain pack howitzer modello 1913
221(f): 6.5cm French mountain howitzer, Mle 1906, Schneider–Ducrest
222(j): 6.5cm Yugoslavian mountain howitzer
225(f): 6cm French mortar
229(j): 7.5cm Yugoslavian mortar
231(f): 7.5cm French gun Mle 1897

232(f): 7.5cm French gun Mle 1897/33
234(b): 7.5cm Belgian gun Mle TR
235(b): 7.5cm Belgian gun Mle 18
236(b): 7.5cm Belgian gun
237(i): 7.5cm Italian field gun modello 1937
238(f): 7.5cm French mountain gun Mle 1928
243(h): 7.5cm Dutch field gun M02/04
244(i): 7.5cm Italian field gun
246(n): 7.5cm Norwegian field gun M01 (Erhardt)
247(n): 7.5cm Norwegian field gun
249(j): 7.5cm Yugoslavian field gun M12, Schneider
251(f): 7.5cm French tank gun Mle 1935
258(j): 7.5cm Yugoslavian mountain gun M28, Skoda
259(i): 7.5cm Italian mountain gun modello 1934
271(e): 18pr British field gun
272(e): 18pr British field gun
273(e): 18pr British field gun
274(d): 8.1cm Danish mortar
274(r): 8.2cm Russian mortar o1941/43g
278(h): 8.14cm Dutch mortar
279(h): 8.1cm Dutch mortar
280(e): British 25pr Mk 1 (on 18pr carriage)
281(e): British 25pr Mk 2 (on 25pr carriage)
282(e): British 25pr on self-propelled mounting
285(j): 7.5cm Yugoslavian mountain gun M06, Schneider
286(h): 8.1cm Dutch mortar
286(f): 8.1cm French mortar
290/1(r): 7.62cm Russian field gun o1902/06g
299(r): 7.62cm Russian recoilless gun
300(j): 7.65 Yugoslavian field gun M05/08, Skoda
301(e): 3.7in British pack howitzer
303(j): 7.65cm Yugoslavian field gun
304(j): 7.65cm Yugoslavian field gun
305(r): 8.38cm Russian field gun (8.5cm o1943g)
309(j): 9cm Yugoslavian mortar
310(r): 7.62cm Russian field gun o1902/30g
315(j): 10cm Yugoslavian howitzer M14, Skoda
315(i): 10cm Italian howitzer modello 1914, Skoda
316(j): 10cm Yugoslavian howitzer M28, Skoda
317(j): 10cm Yugoslavian howitzer M28, Skoda
321(j): 10.5cm Yugoslavian mountain howitzer M16, Skoda
322(f): 10.5cm French howitzer
323(f): 10.5cm French howitzer
324(f): 10.5cm French howitzer
325(f): 10.5cm French howitzer
329(j): 10cm Yugoslavian mountain howitzer
331(f): 10.5cm French howitzer Mle 1935, Schneider
332(f): 10.5cm French howitzer Mle 1935, Schneider
333(b): 10.5cm Belgian field gun Mle 16, Rheinmetall
334(h): 10.5cm Dutch field gun, Bofors
335(h): 10.5cm Dutch field gun, Bofors
336(j): 10.5cm Yugoslavian field gun
338(j): 10.5cm Yugoslavian field gun Schneider
338(i): 10.5cm L/28 Italian howitzer
348(r): 10.5cm Russian field gun
349(r): 10.5cm Russian field gun
350(r): 10.5cm Russian field gun
352(r): 10.7cm Russian field gun o1910/30g
353(r): 10.7cm Russian gun o1940g
365(e): 4.5in British medium field gun
370(b): 12cm Belgian field gun Mle 32, Cockerill
375(n): 12cm Norwegian howitzer m/1909, Rheinmetall
376(n): 12cm Norwegian howitzer m/1909, Köngsberg
377(j): 12cm Yugoslavian howitzer M11, Schneider
378(r): 12cm Russian mortar o1938g
379(r): 12cm Russian mortar o1942g
385(r): 12.2cm Russian howitzer M1909/30
386(r): 12.2cm Russian howitzer o1909/30g
387(r): 12.2cm Russian howitzer o1909/30g
388(r): 12.2cm Russian howitzer o1909/30g
390/1(r): 12.2cm Russian gun o1931g
390/2(r): 12.2cm Russian gun o1931g
393(r): 12.2cm Russian coast gun
396(r): 12.2cm Russian howitzer o1938g
404(r): 15.2cm Russian howitzer o1938g
405(f): 14.5cm French gun
403(j): 15.5cm Yugoslavian gun
412(i): 15.2cm Italian howitzer
414(f): 15.5cm French howitzer
415(f): 15.5cm French howitzer
416(f): 15.5cm French gun
417(f): 15.5cm French howitzer
418(f): 15.5cm French howitzer
419(f): 15.5cm French howitzer
420(f): 15.5cm French howitzer
425(f): 15.5cm French howitzer
427(j): 15.5cm Yugoslavian howitzer
427(n): 10.5cm Norwegian gun
432(b): 15.5cm Belgian gun L/43
433/1(r): 15.2cm Russian gun-howitzer o1937g
443(r): 15.2cm Russian howitzer o1937g
445(r): 15.2cm Russian howitzer o1937g
453(f): 16.4cm French railway gun Mle 1893/96
454(f): 16.4cm French railway gun Mle 1893/96 (different mounting)
455(r): 15.2cm Russian howitzer o1937g on railway mounting
456(r): 15.2cm Russian coast gun o1904g

486(f): 19.4cm French railway gun Mle 1870/93
503(r): 20.3cm Russian howitzer o1931g
532(f): 22cm French gun
533(a): 8in US railway gun M1918
545(b): 23.4cm Belgian howitzer (British 9.2in Mk 1)
546(e): 9.2in British howitzer Mk 1 or 2
548(r): 23.4cm Russian howitzer IV (British 9.2in Mk 2)
550/1(a): 9.2in US howitzer M1917 Mk 1 (British 9.2in Mk 1)
556(f): 24cm French railway gun Mle 1884/17, St Chamond
557(f): 24cm French railway gun Mle 1884
558(f): 24cm French railway gun Mle 1893/96
559(r): 24cm Russian gun
561(a): 24cm US howitzer M1918
564(r): 24cm Russian howitzer
566(f): 24cm French gun
571(a): 10in US railway gun M1919
572(r): 25.4cm Russian coast gun o1910g
585(f): 27cm French coast howitzer
591(f): 27.4cm French railway gun
592(f): 27.4cm French railway gun Mle 1917
594(f): 27.4cm French railway gun Mle 1887/93
601(f): 28cm French howitzer Mle 1914/16, Schneider
602(f): 28cm French howitzer Mle 1914/16, Schneider
605(f): 28.5cm French railway gun Mle 1917
607(r): 28cm Russian howitzer o1915g
621(a): 12in US railway howitzer M1918
622(r): 30.5cm Russian howitzer Mk V (British 12in Mk 5)
623(r): 30.5cm Russian howitzer, Skoda
625(r): 30.5cm Russian railway howitzer
626(r): 30.5cm Russian railway howitzer
628(r): 30.5cm Russian coastgun
631(e): 12in British howitzer Mk 5
632(b): 30.5cm Belgian howitzer (British 12in Mk 2)
633(e): 12in British railway howitzer Mk 1
634(e): 12in British railway howitzer Mk 3
636(f): 30.5cm French railway gun Mle 1893/96
637(f): 30.5cm French railway gun Mle 1906/10
638(j): 30.5cm Yugoslavian howitzer M16, Skoda
639(j): 30.5cm Yugoslavian howitzer M11/30
651(f): 32cm French railway gun Mle 1870/84
652(f): 32cm French railway gun Mle 1917
673(f): 34cm French railway gun L/62
674(f): 34cm French railway gun Mle 1912 (6° rifling)
675(f): 34cm French railway gun Mle 1912 (4° rifling)
681(u): 14in US railway gun M1920
710(f): 37cm French railway howitzer Mle 1915, Filloux
711(f): 37cm French railway howitzer Mle 1915
714(f): 37cm French railway gun Mle 1875/79
731(e): 15in British howitzer
752(f): 40cm French railway howitzer Mle 1915/16
753(r): 40cm Russian coastgun
754(a): 16in US railway gun M1919 MII
755(a): 16in US railway howitzer M1920
772(r): 42cm Russian howitzer
871(f): 52cm French railway howitzer Mle 1916

FIVE: WEHRKREIS ORGANISATION

Germany was split into a number of Wehrkreise or military districts. In 1939 there were fifteen, numbered 1–13 and 17–18 and two more (numbered 20 and 21) were added after the Polish campaign, covering territory that had been German prior to 1918. The remainder of Poland was under control of the 'Government General', while Czechoslovakia was a separate district named Böhmen-Mähren (Bohemia and Moravia). Since the function of the Wehrkreise was principally one of recruiting, draft-finding and reinforcement, the Polish and Czech areas were of lesser importance.

In peacetime, each district contained the headquarters of the infantry corps carrying the same number: XI corps had its headquarters at Hannover, in Wehrkreis 11. The corps commander was nominally the Wehrkreis commander but, since mobilisation would have immediately removed him from the scene, the actual administration was delegated to the second-in-command.

The function of a Wehrkreis was to supervise the induction of recruits within its area, administer them during their service, train them, furnish drafts of replacements to the units based on the Wehrkreis, and finally to demobilise soldiers and resettle them into civilian life. To do this the army was basically divided into two, the active army (Heer) in the field and the replacement and training army (Ersatzheer) within Germany. Every unit in the field armies was affiliated to a similar unit in the Ersatzheer located in its original Wehrkreis. Not only did the Ersatz unit provide draftees but it also acted as a reporting unit to which soldiers went on discharge, or to which they reported after release from hospital in order to be returned to their active unit.

In the original system, Ersatz and active units bore similar numbers; thus 26. Infanterie–Regiment, a peace-time unit, was supported by I/26 and II/26 depot battalion; 507. Infanterie–Regiment, a wartime-raised unit, had only one replacement unit, 507 depot battalion. Artillery replacements for 19. Artillerie–Regiment were suitably provided by I/19 and II/19 artillery depot battalions. The infantry gun companies of 25. Infanterie–Division were replaced from 25 artillery training regiment, and so on.

In 1942 this relatively simple organisation was complicated by demands for garrisons in occupied territory, and it was decided to move recruit-training facilities into the occupied countries so that the troops could double as security and occupation forces while undergoing training. A number of such training divisions were formed, and the result was to reduce the Ersatzheere depot units in Germany to mere staffs, leaving them the paperwork but removing the actual training function. A further complication arose as the war increased in scope when, after costly battles, units demanded more replacements than their Ersatz units could produce. In such cases the necessary men were produced from a number of Wehrkreise, formed into drafts and then sent to wherever they were most needed, irrespective of the original Wehrkreis affiliation.

But in spite of modifications and changes made necessary by the inevitable expansion of the army, the Wehrkreis system worked well; the brief details of each area are shown below.

Wehrkreis I
Headquarters: Königsberg.
area: East Prussia. Extended in March 1939 to include Memel, in September 1939 to include the Ciechanow and Suwalki areas of Poland, and in 1942 the Bialystock area of Poland.
corps mobilised: I and XXVI infantry.
artillery depot regiments: 1 Insterburg, 11 Allenstein.

Wehrkreis 2
Headquarters: Stettin.
area: Mecklenburg and Pomerania.
corps mobilised: II Infantry, LXV Infantry, XXXVI mountain, LVII Panzer.
artillery depot regiments: 2 Motz, Stettin, 12 Schwerin, 32 Kolberg.

Wehrkreis 3
Headquarters: Berlin.
area: Brandenburg and part of Neumark.
corps mobilised: III Panzer, XXVIII Infantry, XXXIV Infantry, LII Infantry, Afrika Panzer Korps.

-tillery depot regiments: 3 Frankfurt, 23 Potsdam, ;8 Frankfurt.

'ehrkreis 4
eadquarters: Dresden.
rea: Sachsen (Saxony) and part of Thüringen Thuringia). Extended in 1939 to cover the north-·n frontier area of Bohemia.
orps mobilised: IV, XXIX and XXXXIV ıfantry.
-tillery depot regiments: 4 Dresden, 24 Chemnitz.

'ehrkreis 5
'eadquarters: Stuttgart.
-ea: Württemberg and part of Baden; extended 1940 to take in Alsace.
orps mobilised: V and XXV Infantry.
-tillery depot regiments: 5 Ulm, 25 Ludwigsburg, 5 Karlsruhe.

'ehrkreis 6
'eadquarters: Munster.
-ea: Westphalia and Rheinland. Extended in 940 to cover the Eupen-Malmedy district of elgium.
orps mobilised: VI and XXIII Infantry, XXXIII ıd LVI Panzer.
-tillery depot regiments: 6 Munster, 26 Köln.

Vehrkreis 7
Ieadquarters: München (Munich).
-ea: southern Bavaria.
orps mobilised: VII and XXVII Infantry.
rtillery depot regiments: 7 München, 27 Augs-urg, 79 (mountain).

Vehrkreis 8
Ieadquarters: Breslau.
rea: Silesia. Extended in 1938 to include the udetenland, in 1939 to include Moravia and in eptember 1939 to include part of southwest oland.
orps mobilised: VIII, XXXV and XXXVIII ıfantry, XLI Panzer.
rtillery depot regiments: 8 (location not known), 16 Breslau.

Vehrkreis 9
Ieadquarters: Kassel.
rea: part of Thüringen (Thuringia) and Hessen
orps mobilised: IX Infantry XXXIX Panzer.
rtillery depot regiments: 9 (location not known), 5 Kassel, 29 Erfurt.

Vehrkreis 10
Ieadquarters: Hamburg.
rea: Schleswig-Holstein and part of Hannover. xtended in 1940 to cover part of Denmark.
orps mobilised: X Infantry, XXXI and XLVI 'anzer.
rtillery depot regiments: 20 Hamburg, 22 Bremen, 0 Lübeck.

Wehrkreis 11
Headquarters: Hannover.
area: Braunschweïg (Brunswick), Anhalt and part of Hanover.
corps mobilised: XI, XXX and XLIII Infantry, XIV Panzer, LI Mountain.
artillery depot regiments: 13 Magdeburg, 19 Hannover, 31 Braunschweig.

Wehrkreis 12
Headquarters: Wiesbaden.
area: Eifel, part of Hessen, Saar. Extended in 1940 to include Lorraine and Luxembourg.
corps mobilised: XII and LIII Infantry, XXIV Panzer.
artillery depot regiments: 33 Darmstadt, 34 Koblenz, 263 Nancy.

Wehrkreis 13
Headquarters: Nürnberg (Nuremburg).
area: northern Bavaria. Extended in 1938 to cover part of west Bohemia.
corps mobilised: XIII Infantry.
artillery depot regiments: 10 Regensburg, 17 Nürnberg.

Wehrkreis 17
Headquarters: Wien (Vienna).
area: Austria. Extended in 1939 to include the southern areas of Bohemia and Moravia (Böhmen und Mähren).
corps mobilised: XVII and LXXXII Infantry, XL Panzer.
artillery training regiments: 96 Wien, 98 Linz.

Wehrkreis 18
Headquarters: Salzburg.
area: Styria, Carinthia, and the Tyrol. Extended in 1941 to cover the northern part of Slovenia.
corps mobilised: XVIII and XIX Mountain.
artillery depot regiments: 111 Hall, 112 Kufstein.

Wehrkreis 20
Headquarters: Danzig.
area: formed in October 1939 to cover the Danzig Freistadt (free state), the Polish Corridor and the western area of East Prussia.
corps mobilised: XX Infantry, XLVII Panzer.
artillery depot regiments: none.

Wehrkreis 21
Headquarters: Posen (Poznan).
area: formed in October 1939 to cover western Poland.
corps mobilised: XLVIII Panzer.
artillery depot regiments: none.

Luftgaue
The German airforce divided the country into Luftgaue, in similar fashion to the army's Wehrkreise. As mentioned in the section on

organisation of Flak artillery, the Luftgau controlled the numbering of anti-aircraft units. The areas covered by the Luftgaue can be approximated to Wehrkreis areas as follows:

Luftgau I/II (an amalgamation of two districts for administrative convenience) covered the areas of Wehrkreis 1, 2, 20, 21 and part of the General Government of Poland.
Luftgau III/IV covered Wehrkreise 3 and 4, together with portions of Wehrkreise 2, 7, 9 and 11.
Luftgau VI covered Wehrkreis 6 and part Wehrkreis 9.
Luftgau VII covered Wehrkreis 5 and 7, par of Wehrkreis 18, and Eastern France.
Luftgau VIII covered Wehrkreis 8 and a lar part of Poland.
Luftgau XI covered Wehrkreis 10 and parts Wehrkreise 2, 6 and 11.
Luftgau XII/XIII covered Wehrkreise 12, 13 an parts of Wehrkreis 9.
Luftgau XVII covered Wehrkreis 17, and part Wehrkreise 18, and Czechoslovakia.

SIX: GLOSSARY

: Ausstoss/base ejection
A: alter Art/old model
bg: abgeändert/altered, modified
bzug: firing mechanism
nhänger: trailer
nsetzen: to ram the shell
rtillerie bekampfung: counter-bombardment
rtillerieschlepper: tractor, prime-mover
ufprotzen: to limber up the gun
ufsatz: tangent sight
uftreffgeschwindigkeit: striking velocity
usb: ausbildung/training
usf: Ausführung/model, type
uswechsenbar Seelenrohr: interchangeable barrel liner
Z: Aufschlagzunder/percussion (nose) fuze
): belgisch/Belgian (pattern or origin)
atterie: battery (of artillery)
D: Bleidraht/decoppering additive
d G: Brand Geschoss/incendiary shell
d K: Bodenkammer/base burster (in shell)
d Z: Bodenzünder/base fuze
e: Beton/concrete (as in Gr Be—anti-concrete shell)
esonderen und Witterungsflüsse (BWE): ballistic error of the day
eildg: Beiladung/igniter
ettung: platform, base
hr Ldg: Bohr Ladung/gun destruction charge
l: Blatt/leaf-flake propellant
l P: Blattchen Pulver/rectangular flake propellant
ogenspitze: ogival head (of shell)
o Pr: Bohren presstahl/forged steel shell with bored cavity
r: Brand/incendiary
remsezylinder: recoil buffer cylinder
rlg: brennlange/burning time (of fuze)
r Schr: Brand schrapnell/anti-aircraft shrapnel shell
untr: Buntrauch/coloured smoke
Z: Brennzünder/combustion time-fuze
/: Construktion/model (naval terminology)
, Digl: Diglykolpulver/diglycol propellant powder
): danisch/Danish (pattern or origin)
eut: deuten/indicating

F: fern/long-range
f: für/for
Fallblockverschluss: vertical sliding-block breech
Fallsch: Fallschirmjäger/parachute troops
Fahrstellung: travelling position
Fallwinkel: angle of descent
Federvorholer: spring recuperator
Feldartillerie: field artillery
FES: Führungsintereisen/sintered-iron driving band
Fest: fixed (applied to gun mounting)
Fest: Festung/fortress
Feuergeschwindigkeit: rate of fire

FEW: Führungweicheisen/soft-iron driving band
FH: Feldhaubitze/field howitzer
FK: Feldkanone/field gun
Fl, Fg: Fliegewichtsantrieb/centrifugal drive (fuzes)
Flak: Flugabwehrkanone/anti-aircraft gun
Flugbahn: trajectory
Flughöhe: vertex of trajectory
Flugzeit: time of flight (of shell)
Fp 02: Füllpulver '02/TNT
Fp 5: Füllpulver 5/TNT plus 5%wax
Flussigkeitsrücklaufbremse: hydraulic recoil buffer
führungsring: driving band
futterohr: barrel liner
G: Geschütz/gun (implies low velocity)
Geb: Gebirg/mountain
Gel: Gelbkreuz/yellow cross (vesicant) gas
Gelandewinkel: angle of sight
Ger: Gerät/equipment
ger: gerillt/segmented or grooved
Gesch: Geschoss/projectile, shell
geschützrichten: to aim
gl: glatt/smoothbore
Dopp Z: Doppelzünder/time and percussion fuze
Drall: rifling
Drallwinkel: twist of rifling
Durchschlag: penetration (of a projectile)
(E): Eisenbahnlafette/railway mounting
E: empfindlich/sensitive (of fuzes)
(e): englisch/English (pattern or origin)
EC: Eisencentrung/iron driving band
Einschlagwinkel: angle of impact
Erhöhungswinkel: angle of elevation
Ex: Exerzier/exercise, drill

gleichformiger drall: uniform-twist rifling
Gr: Granate/shell
gr: grosse/large
Gr f 88: Granatfüllung 88/picric acid
Gr K Mun Grünkreuz Munition/green cross (lethal) gas shell
Gr W: Granatwerfer/mortar
Gu: Gudolpulver/picrite propelling powder
H: Haubitze/howitzer
H: Hexogen/hexogen, cyclonite, RDX explosive
H5: Hexogen 5/cyclonite plus 5% wax
H. (H): gehärtet/hardened
(h): hollandisch/Dutch (pattern or origin)
Hb: Haube/ballistic cap (for shell)
Hbgr: Haubengranate/shell with ballistic cap
Hbgr Z: Haubengranate zünder/fuze for use beneath ballistic cap
H1/: Höhlladung/hollow charge (pattern A, B, etc)
H Ma: Heeresmunitionanstalt/army ammunition depot
Hohenrichtung: elevation
HT: Haubitzeturm/turret-mounted howitzer (fortress)
Hülsen: case (especially cartridge case)
Höchstschussweite: maximum range
(i): italianisch/Italian (pattern or origin)
IG: Infanteriegeschütz/Infantry gun
(j): jugoslawisch/ Yugoslavian (pattern or origin)
JG: alternative form for IG
K: Kern/core (of bullet or shot)
K: kurz/short
K: Klappensicherung/centrifugal safety unit (of fuze)
K, Kan: Kanone/gun (implies high velocity)
Kart: Kartusch/cartridge
Karth: Kartuschenhülse/cartridge case
KE: Kalibereinheit/specific load of a given calibre of ammunition that filled a standard 15tonne (15000kg) rail wagon
Keillochverschluss: sliding-block breech mechanism
KH: Kanone-Haubitze/gun-howitzer
Kh: Kammerhülse/central burster tube (in shell)
KK: Kasematte-Kanone/casemate (fortress) gun
Kl: Klasse/class
Kl: klein/small
Klappleitwerke: folding fin assembly for shell
Klappsporn: folding trail spade
Kp: Kappe/cap
Kpf: Kopf/nose
Kpf Z: Kopfzünder/nose fuze
KPS: Kupferpresstahl/bimetallic driving band
KrR: Kreuzrohr/central tube of propellant in a propelling charge
Kt: Kartatschen/case or canister shot
KT: Kanoneturm/turret gun (fortress)
Küst: Küsten/coast (defence)
Kwg: Kampfwagengeschütz/tank gun (low velocity)
KWK: Kampfwagenkanone/tank gun (high velocity)
KZ: Kopfzünder/nose fuze
L: Ladenstreifen/cartridge closing-cup
L, Laf: Lafette/carriage, mounting
Lauf: barrel
L/: lange/length (of barrel or shell in calibr units)
Ldg: Ladung/charge (propelling)
le: leicht/light (in weight)
LG: Leichtgeschütz/light gun (implies recoilles
l, lg: lang/long
Lg Zdr: Leuchtgeschosszünder/time fuze for sta shell
L'spur: Leuchtspur/tracer
Lt Gs, Lg: Leuchtgeschoss/star (illuminating) she
Lichmesstrupp: flash-spotting troop
Liderungsring: obturator
Luftvorholer: pneumatic recuperator
M: Mündungsbremse/muzzle brake
M: Muster/pattern, model
m: mit/with
M, Man: Manöver/blank cartridge
M, Mod: Modell/pattern, type, model
M, Mrs: Mörser/howitzer
M, mdlchf: Mündlochfutter/gaine
Mannsch KW: Mannschaft Kraftwagen/personn carrier
MotZ: Motorisiert Zugkraftwagen/tractor draw
Mun: Munition/ammunition
Mündung: muzzle
Mündungsdeckel: muzzle cover
nA: neuer Art/new pattern
N, n, Nb: Nebel/smoke
Nbgr: Nebelgranate/smoke shell
Nachbrenner: hangfire
nF: neuer Fertigung/new method (of productio
Ngl: Nitroglyzerinpulver/propellant containin nitroglycerine
NP: Nudelpulver/chopped-cord propellant
Np: Nitropenta/PETN (high explosive)
Nr: Nummer/number
NZ: Nitrozellulosepulver/propellant containin nitrocellulose
NZ Man P: NZ manöverpulver/nitrocellulos propellant for blank charges
o: ohne/without
O: ohne Füllung/without filling (inert shell)
(ö): österreichisch/Austrian (pattern or origin)
O, Ob: ober/top
oM: ohne Mündlochsbüchse/without gaine co tainer
P: Panzerkopf/piercing cap
P: Pulver/powder
(p): polnische/Polish (pattern or origin)
Pg: Perlitguss/cast pearlitic steel
P, Ph, Phos: Phosphor/Phosphorus
PAK, Pak: Panzerabwehrkanone/anti-tank gun
PAW: Panzerabwehrwerfer/anti-tank gun (smoothbore)
P, Patr: Patrone/cartridge (implies fixed round)
Patrh: Patronenhülse/cartridge case
Pl P: Plattchenpulver/multiperforated disc pr pellant

ol P: Polpulver/solventless propellant
r: Presstoff/plastic (fuzes)
r: Presstahl/pressed-steel (shells)
S: Panzerstahl/armour (piercing)
T: Pulvertemperatur/propellant temperature
z: Panzer/armour
zB: Panzerbüchse/anti-tank rifle
zgr: Panzergranate/anti-tank shell
zKpfw: Panzerkampfwagen/armoured fighting vehicle
: Rauchentwickler/smoke-box (in shell)
: Rakete/rocket
): Russisch/Russian (pattern or origin)
, Rp: Röhrenpulver/tubular propellant
fk: Rückstossfreikanone/recoilless gun
fW: Rückstossfreiwerfer/recoilless gun (implies smoothbore)
gP: Ringpulver/propellant in rings
Gr: Raketen Granate/rocket assisted shell
ö Gr: Röchling Granate/fin-stabilised anti-concrete shell
ohrlange: length of barrel
ohrmantel: barrel jacket
ohrrücklauf: recoil
ohrweige: cradle
ot: used in ammunition designations to indicate presence of a red ring on the shell which in turn indicates 'modified pattern'
S: Reizstoff/irritant chemical shell filling
ücklaufbremse: recoil brake
undblickfernrohr: panoramic (dial) sight
: schwere/heavy
challmessung: sound ranging
chl, S, schr: Schlagzündschraube/percussion primer
chlagbolzen: firing pin, striker
chrapnell: shrapnel
chubkurbelverschluss: sliding-block breech
chusstafel: range or firing table
chussweite: range
chütz PzW: Schützen panzerwagen/armoured gun carrier
chutzschild: shield
d: sonder/special
eelenachse: axis of gun bore
eelenrohr: barrel liner
f, Sfl: selbstfahrlafette/self-propelled mounting
K: Schiffskanone/naval gun
ockellafette: pivot mounting
onderanhänger: special trailer (especially for artillery)
d Kfz: Sonderkraftzeug/special vehicle (especially for gun-carrying vehicles)
pl: splitter/splinter, fragment (of shell)
porn: spade (on gun trail)
pr: Sprengstoff/high explosive
prgr: Sprenggranate/high explosive shell
prengkapsel: detonator
pr Schw P: Sprengschwarzpulver/gunpowder, black powder
t, st: Stahl/steel
t: Stern/star
Steil Gr: Steilgranate/stick bomb
Stggr: Stahlgussgranate/cast-steel shell
Str: Streif/strip (propellant powder)
Strandkanone: coast gun
StuK: Sturmkanone/assault gun (long barrel)
StuG: Sturmgeschütz/assault gun (short barrel)
Steilfeuer: high angle fire
(t): tsechisch/Czech (pattern or origin)
Tbts K: Torpedobootskanone/torpedo boat gun
Th K: Theodor Kanone/ 24cm gun
Tp: Tropen/tropical
Teilkartusche: part-charge
Teilladung: part-charge
TrLdg: Treibladung/propelling charge
TS: Treibspiegel/subcalibre (discarding sabot)
TT: Tropentauglich/fit for tropical use
TU: Tropen untauglich/not fit for tropical use
Turmgeschtütz: turret gun (fortress)
u: und/and
Ub: Ubungs/practice
Ub A1: practice shell with high explosive aluminium filling
Ub B: practice shell with high explosive smoke filling
Ub R: practice shell giving red smoke
Ub S: practice shell giving black smoke
Ub T: practice shell filled with high explosive tetrachloronaphthalene mixture
Ub W: practice shell giving white smoke
Ubts K: Unterseebootskanone/submarine gun
umg: umgeändert/altered, modified
v: verbessert/improved
V: verbessert Ladung/adjusted charge
v: vereinfacht/simplified
V, Verz: Verzogerung/delay (in fuzes)
V, Vo: Velozitat (Mündungsvelocität)/velocity (muzzle velocity)
Vers: versuchs/experimental
Verschlusskurbel: breech mechanism lever
verst: verstärkert/strengthened
Visier: sight
Vorholfeder: recuperator spring
Vorl: Vörlage/flash-reducer additive
VRP: verkurztes Rohrpulver/short tubular propellant powder
W–Karth: Wickelskartuschhülse/spirally-wrapped steel cartridge case for separate-loading ammunition
W–Patrh: Wickelpatronenhülse/spirally-wrapped steel cartridge case for fixed ammunition
W: Werfer/mortar
Wiege: cradle
Z, Zdr: Zünder/fuze
Zdg: Zündung/exploder
Zdlg: Zündladung/gaine
Zd Mitt: Zündmittel/igniter
Zdschr: Zündschraube/primer
Zerl: zerlegen/self-destruction
ZgKw: Zugkraftwagen/tractor, prime mover
Zielfernrohr: telescopic sight
Zt: Zeit/time
Zub: Zubehör/accessories, fittings

Zuge: rifling grooves
Zündhütchen: percussion cap
Zündstellmaschin: fuze setter
Zusatzl: Zusatzladung/augmenting charge
Zunehmender: increasing twist of rifling
Zwillings: twin (gun mounting)

NOTE
It must be appreciated that while all the above are authorised abbreviations and terms, not all were in common use; the abbreviation PS (for armour piercing shell), for example, was never used in ammunition terminology. Some discretion must also be used when determining the application of abbreviations bearing more than one meaning.

#NDEX

INDEX OF WEAPONS
Y CALIBRE

2. ALPHABETIC INDEX